SPITTING IN THE SOUP

SPITTING IN THE SOUP

INSIDE THE DIRTY GAME OF DOPING IN SPORTS

MARK JOHNSON

Boulder, Colorado

3002 Sterling Circle, Suite 100
Boulder, Colorado 80301-2338 USA
(303) 440-0601 · Fax (303) 444-6788 · E-mail velopress@competitorgroup.com

Distributed in the United States and Canada by Ingram Publisher Services

A Cataloging-in-Publication record for this book is available from the Library of Congress.
ISBN 978-1-937715-27-4

For information on purchasing VeloPress books, please call (800) 811-4210, ext. 2138, or visit www.velopress.com.

This paper meets the requirements of ANSI/NISO Z39.48-1992 (Permanence of Paper).

Art direction by Vicki Hopewell
Cover: design by Andy Omel; concept by Mike Reisel; illustration by Jean-Francois Podevin
Text set in Gotham and Melior

16 17 18 / 10 9 8 7 6 5 4 3 2 1

For my parents, who granted me a love
for outdoors and library alike

CONTENTS

INTRODUCTION

The story of doping in sports is packaged for easy consumption. As it goes, morally degenerate athletes cheat to win. Get rid of these creeps and sport settles back into a state of pure fair play. The falls of cheaters like Lance Armstrong, Ben Johnson, and Barry Bonds are object lessons topped with gratifying dollops of schadenfreude. The very presence of such deviants in elite competition is an affront to the rest of us who don't take shortcuts, and their collapse pleases us by confirming our own moral superiority.

But this tidy primary school version of events is itself a fraud. Like viewing the Grand Canyon through a toilet-paper tube, its good-versus-evil reductionism leaves out layers of historical context and economic sedimentation—most glaringly by ignoring the fact that drug-free play is a relatively recent moral precept forced upon sports whose participants have always been chemically enhanced. While every doping athlete is responsible for his or her own decisions, the story of doping in sports is more complex than solo agents cheating their way to the podium. In fact, the imposition of quasi-religious values regarding personal and moral cleanliness is a relatively new invention that elite sports are still struggling to adopt. This book attempts to unpack some of the complexity that gets lost when a sportswriter has to meet the constraints of space and deadlines, or when a politician needs to appeal to the fearful instincts of his constituents.

Maintaining a good-versus-evil understanding of doping in sport allows us to turn our heads from our own role as members of a society that embraces performance-enhancing drugs and procedures. As I explore in this book, fans, athletes, governments, sports organizing bodies, and advertisers are all complicit in the championing of chemistry in the service of greater happiness and performance in life.

This context matters when considering doping in sports. The use of performance-enhancing drugs ultimately comes down to individual decisions, but to understand those choices, it helps to take into account contemporary society's gargantuan thirst for performance-enhancing drugs and procedures, as well as nearly 150 years of organized sports history—during two-thirds of which doping was *not* contrary to what we now call the spirit of sport.

Of course, when we dope in the course of our daily lives, we are (usually) not breaking any rules. Taking erythropoietin (EPO) to get ahead in a bike race is illegal, but popping a prescribed amphetamine like Adderall to improve focus and stamina in school or the workplace violates no regulations. Nor does taking Viagra to improve sexual performance. American society has repeatedly stated—via its embrace of direct-to-consumer drug pitches on television and its hands-off approach to a supplement industry that does over $30 billion in annual sales, as well as its massive spending on cosmetic enhancement procedures—that it likes drugs that make us better than well, and it likes lots of them, thank you very much.

Today, Americans use more prescription stimulants than during the post-Vietnam speed epidemic, and over 6 million of these users are aged 4 to 17. This industrial-scale doping of American youth in the interest of better mental focus and higher output suggests that while anti-doping missionaries might claim performance-enhancing drugs are immoral and that regulators know what is best for people, in practice, Americans take a more pragmatic stance. Their attitudes regarding performance-enhancing drugs outside of sports suggest that what is moral is not what is most chemically pure, but rather what is most productive.

While much of the daily coverage of doping in Olympic sports focuses on the drugs taken and the people who took them, the larger, more interesting, and most useful story is the context, the social values, and the historical events that shaped our contradictory responses to performance-enhancing drugs and technologies in sport and everyday life. The forces at play are as wide-ranging as the politics of national defense, the economics of sponsorship, insecurities over global empire and personal appearance, pharmaceutical marketing, and the redefinition of aging from a matter of fate to one of choice that empowered consumers can bend given the right medical technology.

Further, the wall between sports and society is permeable; the behavior of athletes affects the buying and drug-taking decisions of fans, and the political actions of fans can alter what athletes do behind closed doors. This book attempts to give a better understanding of this complicity and why it has never been in the interest of athlete, fan, or journalist to spit in the soup that feeds us all with the nourishing sustenance of money, entertainment, and—in the case of the Olympic Games—political clout.

Beginning with the ideals espoused by French aristocrat and Olympic founder Pierre de Coubertin, which were based on the chivalric romances he liked to read and his admiration for British public schools, in the 19th century, amateur sport was burdened with the idea that it could become a morally uncomplicated and uncompromised space in the midst of a fallen world. At the heart of this fantasy was the idea of amateurism—the belief that sport is the domain of the aristocratic leisure class, sealed off from the morally and genetically corrupted lower classes. When future Olympic managers came to realize the economic potential of the five rings, they eventually abandoned Coubertin's idea of preserving the spirit of sport and fair play in the amber of amateurism. Over time, the battle against professionalism in the Olympics was replaced by a war against drugs. And this new struggle to keep sports pure was itself an echo of larger social anxieties about countercultural social and moral decay during the 1960s.

The rise of anti-doping concerns in the 1960s led to the emergence of a complex anti-doping infrastructure that today attempts to impose moral and physical purity on the sporting universe. With no actual Edenic state of fair play to refer back to, anti-doping moralists have fabricated notions of a pristine pre–drug era that their missionary efforts would resurrect. And to create a sense of fear to justify the sometimes human-rights-violating intrusions of an anti-doping infrastructure, anti-doping crusaders, with the help of the media, made up tales about the mortal dangers of drugs that were often out of proportion to their actual, clinically documented lethality.

This book investigates why the media and anti-doping infrastructure are also loath to spit in the soup that nourishes their own existence. For example, the story of European cyclists dying en masse in the 1990s from EPO is a myth—a fabrication that neither the press nor anti-doping campaigners examined for truth. Admitting that no evidence existed conclusively linking EPO to a supposed rash of endurance athlete deaths would expose as fraud a story that in many respects justified the existence of anti-doping regulators and sensation-hungry reporters.

We are not writing about a conspiracy. Today's anti-doping bureaucracies were built on a hope in the unseen, a religious sense that, given enough commitment and focus, athletes could return to a promised land where victory does indeed belong to the strongest rather than the best enhanced. No one set about with a master plan to create a self-sustaining anti-doping industry or ginned up doping stories to sell magazines and newspapers. The stigmatization of doping in sports—after nearly 100 years during which the act was unremarkably accepted, even praised, as a sign of professional commitment—is a natural progression of human events. By understanding these transformations, and the hypocrisies they hide, we can gain better insight into where anti-doping is today and where it might go tomorrow.

Understanding the broader context of doping in sports is not the same as excusing the behavior of those who break today's rules against performance-enhancing drugs. If this were the case, then all history would be confined to narrow condemnatory or celebratory biography. It would also be hopelessly constrained by the precept that unless the explored topic reinforces society's current values, that history should not be broached.

And this tension between our desire for sports stars to step into the sunshine wearing either a black or a white hat—villain or saint—gets us to the name of this book, *Spitting in the Soup*. The phrase comes from the French expression *cracher dans la soupe*. The closest English version of this idiomatic saying is "to bite the hand that feeds you."

In the pro cycling peloton, a rider who threatened to expose a fellow rider who was doping would be scolded by his colleagues, "Don't spit in the soup." That is, do not expose the sport's drug-charged reality and spoil things for all of us. Especially after the shadow of social stigma began to creep over pro cycling in the 1960s, exposing cycling's tacit agreement to carry on its long-standing chemical traditions would only ruin the sport that nourished and supported the riders. Speaking frankly would also putrefy the broth that fed a sprawling supporting infrastructure—a rolling family of coaches, managers, soigneurs, mechanics, doctors, and sponsors.

But spitting in the soup also applies to the "good" ones—the anti-doping activists, the sports organizers, the journalists, and we, the fans, who find that honesty about our own participation in a drug-dependent and drug-hysterical society is itself a way of spoiling that which improves us. Spitting in the soup is not limited to athletes—it includes *our* complicity. And the history of our mutual responsibility for a performance-enhanced world is what this book explores.

CHAPTER 1

THE ORIGINS OF DOPING

The morning of August 30, 1904, dawned hot and humid in St. Louis, Missouri. The United States was hosting its first Olympic Games, and it was as if an oppressive blanket had been lowered over the Mississippi River town for a signature event, the marathon. Fourteen miles into the 24.85-mile run (the 26.2-mile standard was not established until 1908),[1] runner Charles Hicks—British-born but representing the United States—doubled over on the side of a road in what a *Brooklyn Daily Eagle* reporter called "sweltering heat and clouds of dust."[2] Along with the swampy conditions, Hicks and 31 other runners dodged a torture trail of unpaved roads and ankle-twisting rocks. Dust accumulated in powdery pools so deep it swallowed the runners' shoes. There was one water stop—a well 12 miles into the course. Farm dogs added misery. A pack of snarling canines chased a black South African competitor off course. Meanwhile, running in cutoff trousers and street shoes, the race's sole Cuban, a mail carrier named Félix Carvajal, scrounged fruit from an orchard along the way. The Cuban promptly puked up a gut full of pulp. In these conditions, turning to modern medicine was logical; refusing to offer it would have been ethically shocking.

A physician and Olympic chronicler named Charles Lucas trailed the 5-foot 6-inch, 133-pound Hicks in one of 20 race follow cars. While two of these support vehicles ended up flipped over in roadside ditches, the remaining parade kicked up so much dirt that runners had to periodically stop to hack their lungs free of crud. Press reports describe a California competitor named William Garcia found "lying unconscious by the roadside several miles from the stadium." Garcia collapsed from a dust-induced stomach hemorrhage. As for Hicks, Lucas felt his charge was not the favorite. "There were three other men in the race who were better runners than Hicks, and who should have defeated him," the doctor noted. "But they lacked proper care on the road."[3]

"Proper care" meant drugs. When Hicks hit the wall 10 miles from the finish, he begged for water. Hicks's Boston-based trainer, a football coach named Hugh C. McGrath, was in the car with Lucas. Hewing to cutting-edge fitness doctrines of the day, McGrath and Lucas denied the dehydrated Hicks's pleas for water. Instead, they furthered his torture by sponging his mouth with distilled water. Three miles farther along, with other runners dropping out with cramps and heat exhaustion, Lucas had to turn to more sophisticated medicines. With Hicks's pace reduced to a crawl, Lucas recalled that he "was forced to administer one-sixtieth grain of sulphate of strychnine, by the mouth, besides the white of one egg."

Though we know it as a rat killer, strychnine was a common endurance sports drug at the turn of the 20th century. "Strychnine is a grand tonic," novelist H. G. Wells exulted in his 1897 book *The Invisible Man*. In Wells's opinion, the drug was a performance-enhancing wonder that took "flabbiness out of a man." Strychnine affects the central nervous system, and when taken in small doses, it allows neurons to fire even when neurotransmitter levels are low due to fatigue. The result is a feeling of agitated energy. Indeed, swallow 100 milligrams of strychnine and your muscles will begin twitching uncontrollably. You will shiver with restless unease before respiratory arrest sets in. Although Lucas had another common chemical performance enhancer, brandy, in the car with him, he kept Hicks on the strychnine with 10 miles to go, thinking it best if Hicks abstained from other stimulants as "long as possible."

At the 20-mile mark, Hicks began to turn gray. Shock and heat exhaustion were shutting down his system. With his progress reduced to a walk-march on climbs, Lucas administered Hicks another "one-sixtieth grain strychnine," two more eggs, and a mouthful of brandy. Stopping to warm a pan of water on the car radiator, Lucas and McGrath gave Hicks a sponge bath. The roadside cleanse, raw eggs, strychnine, and brandy had their effect. "He appeared to revive and jogged along once more," Lucas reported.

In first place with 2 miles to go, Hicks began to hallucinate. He insisted the finish line was 20 miles away and begged for something to eat. After refilling their exhausted liquor canteen with booze from another support car, McGrath and Lucas gave their delirious runner brandy but no food. Two hills loomed between Hicks and Olympic glory. Reinforced with more brandy on top of the strychnine already coursing through his system, Hicks rallied, fought his way over the two summits, and took marathon gold.

At the finish, however, another athlete temporarily stole Hicks's glory. Fred Lorz of New York City had arrived first, entering the stadium to thunderous applause, and had apparently taken the win. When it was later revealed that Lorz had hitched a car ride to the finish, Lucas excoriated the disqualified New Yorker, writing that he had nearly robbed Hicks, a newly crowned hero who was only "kept in mechanical action by the use of drugs, that he might bring to America the Marathon honors, which American athletes had failed to win both at Athens and at Paris."

The position of the authorities was clear: Getting a ride in a mechanical conveyance was cheating. But taking an assist from chemical stimulants was commitment, a heroic glorification of country. After marathon failures at the first two modern Olympics in 1896 and 1900, the Yanks had turned to modern chemistry and delivered victory. Hicks's doctor publicly celebrated the win as a show of American courage and vision—a Yankee unification of chemical science and personal moxie in the interest of ultimate performance. In his post-race report, Lucas applauded drugs in sports: "The Marathon race, from a medical standpoint, demonstrated that drugs are of much benefit to athletes along the road, and that warm sponging is much better than cold sponging for an athlete in action."

After the race, a team of doctors examined Hicks and the 17 other marathon finishers to compare their before and after physical condition. In his 1998 book on the Olympics and the American experience, *Making the American Team*, historian Mark Dyreson explains that these medical experts were motivated by national pride—"a desire to convince the nation that a scientific understanding of athletic technology could guarantee the progress of American civilization." As we will see, the founder of the modern Olympics, Baron Pierre de Coubertin, linked the creation of his Games to the revitalization of French national character. In the third iteration of the Olympics, American doctors also hitched athletic excellence to national pride, attributing their boys' success to a Yankee capacity to wed brave medical technology to bold national character. An athlete's healthy body "is the safest guardian of morality and civilization" wrote James Edward Sullivan, chief of the Department of Physical Culture for the St. Louis World's Fair, which ran in conjunction with the 1904 Olympics.[4] For forward-looking, scientifically minded Americans, combining modern chemistry with natural physical ability was a point of pride and distinction—evidence of the New World common man's superiority. Alongside a World's Fair that awarded seven gold medals for the best presentations on sports science, associating the application of pharmaceutical science to American athleticism with moral corruption would have thoroughly puzzled an attendee of the 1904 Olympics.

FOR ROUGHLY the first 100 years of professional sports, mixing drugs and human endeavor did not spark moral panic and social outrage. When an elite athlete turned to modern chemistry to increase output, it was evidence of an honorable commitment to a trade.

Pedaling a bike for cash got its start in the 1860s and 1870s, a time when bike riding was gaining momentum along with the Industrial Revolution. Easy-to-ride "safety" bicycles with equal-sized wheels replaced dangerous penny-farthings. Mass production made bikes affordable on a factory worker's salary. Those same laborers organized cycling clubs, talented racers soon distinguished themselves, and promoters made a buck organizing races on the pine-board tracks called velodromes, as well as upon the world's growing network of graded roads. A man could suddenly earn a living racing a bike.

The emergence of these sporting professionals could not have happened a century earlier. Before the second half of the 1800s, professional sports largely did not exist. In a predominantly agrarian world, demand for mass entertainment was too scattered across disconnected towns and farms to make a viable market. In 1830, 91 percent of the United States population lived in rural areas; not enough people had piled into cities to create the concentration of fans that would allow professional sports leagues to thrive.

By 1890, however, cities seethed. Beaten-down souls who expended their life energy in ironworks and factory lines hungered for diversion from their lives of urban misery and filth. At a time when garbage rotted in 8-foot drifts in front of New York City's Lower East Side tenements, the percentage of the population living in American cities had grown to 31 percent. By 1920, that proportion exceeded 50 percent; for the first time, city dwellers outnumbered country folk. This demographic flip took place in large part thanks to immigrants arriving from eastern and southern Europe, and then cranking out babies in their new homeland. In Europe, rapidly industrializing countries like France and England saw similar rural-to-urban swings.

Until this demographic shift, sports were little more than folk games played in small villages. Before the spread of trains and telegraphs, sports lacked the standardized rules and regulations we take for granted today. Without trains to move large numbers of people between population centers, robust interscholastic competitions were logistically impossible.

And universities and secondary schools are where sports like rugby, basketball, and American football first took root. Apart from schools within walking distance of one another, teams played in isolation using homegrown rules. The sequestered play and lack of leagues meant there was little need for standardized rules shared outside a local region.[5]

By the 1850s, railroads connected most British and many European towns. Telegraph systems along these rail lines moved information at previously unfathomable speeds. For millions of years of human history, the top velocity of long-distance information was limited by the speed of a carrier pigeon, horse, or wind-propelled boat. None had the electron's capacity to travel without pause across North America or the Atlantic. The first transatlantic telegraph message was sent in 1858. Three years later, telegraph messages linked the United States coasts. Messages that took weeks by ship or Pony Express now took minutes. In terms of accelerating news and binding people with shared experiences, the reduction of the transmission time for a round-trip message from 20 days to mere minutes was earthshaking. Wire services made national and international news local, and newspapers engaged nations in pro sports comradeship. When a San Francisco father read Chicago newspaper baseball scores to his son, they became part of a virtual community of fans who never saw one another, yet shared common interests and sports dramas.

Sports promoters saw francs, pounds, dollars, and pesos in this suddenly limitless fan base. Paris got its first velodrome in 1879 and built six more between 1892 and 1897. Such facilities were often financed by municipalities pressed to provide a social and physical pressure-relief valve for the unrest building in immigrant tenements. By 1899, nearly 300 cycling ovals were scattered across France. In Russia, in 1892, the roaring success of bike race ticket sales inspired a promoter to organize that country's first soccer game during a break between races at St. Petersburg's Semyonov Hippodrome.[6]

Track racing flourished in the United States. Reporting on a sold-out six-day race at New York City's Madison Square Garden in December 1912, the *New York Times* described a near riot when police tried to eject fans who had bribed their way past door monitors. Forty-eight hours into the six days of racing, the *Times* described the infield as "one solid mass of humanity."[7] In his history of American bike racing, *Hearts of Lions*, historian Peter Nye describes 38,000 spectators showing up in Springfield, Massachusetts, for the town's annual Diamond Jubilee bike races, more than doubling the town's population of 35,000.[8]

Given so many paying and wagering fans, stars took home astronomical sums. In 1914, Australian six-day megastar Alf Goullet earned $11,500 in prizes and appearance fees for a single race series. Earning $5 a day, an assembly-line laborer in Henry Ford's auto plant would need to work 2,300 eight-hour days—six years and four months—to earn what Goullet banked in less than a week. And as cycling paydays increased, so did the interest in these new professional sportsmen. Snowballing media coverage rapidly drew more paying fans to the track.

At a time when the average annual wage for an African American was $150, black rider Marshall "Major" Taylor unleashed a lethal sprint to scoop upward of $850 for a day of racing—$24,000 in today's dollars. Taylor began making a living from cycling in 1896, a time when 600 pros were already plying their trade on velodromes across America. Managed by a Broadway theater producer named Billy Brady, Taylor captivated more than 30,000 fans per event at Madison Square Garden and Brooklyn's Manhattan Beach velodromes. In return, Brady paid Taylor half the gate. In 1901, Taylor raced in 16 European cities for $5,000, a sum 3,000 percent greater than most African Americans earned in a year. The 23-year-old killed it in Europe, winning 42 races during his tour. The highlight came when Taylor raced French world champion Edmond Jacquelin at the Parc des Princes Velodrome in Paris. Future Tour de France impresario Henri Desgrange promoted the event, and 30,000 spectators watched their French hero slug it out against the American sensation for a whopping $7,500 pot.[9]

While track racing was the fan-friendly media darling of the day, pro road racing was also growing. In France, newspaper owners sponsored races to increase circulation. The burgeoning community of sports fans (and bettors) was hungry for on- and off-field scoops on their athletic heroes. By organizing races, newspapers essentially created newsworthy events that in turn drew readers. This consumer demand allowed the papers to sell more advertisements for cars, tires, bicycles, and tonics. Inaugural road events included Bordeaux–Paris and Paris–Brest–Paris in 1891, Paris–Roubaix in 1896, and the Tour de France in 1903. Paris–Roubaix was founded as a way of publicizing track events at a new Roubaix velodrome and to increase sales of *Le Vélo*, the then-dominant French sports newspaper.[10]

In 1890, there were about 50,000 bikes in France. By 1910, there were 3 million. At the same time the bicycle industry was pumping out products, the automobile industry was also beginning to fire on multiple cylinders. With at least four French auto builders vying for business, and countless bike and bike accessory companies doing the same, there was a significant demand for advertisements to get products into French minds, creating pools of money and public demand that fueled the growth of pro cycling. It was a world of pay for play that offered dedicated and talented athletes, most drawn from the lower class, elevator rides to wealth and status.[11]

In the midst of this explosion of professional sports, athletes taking drugs to ply their trade was not the scandal it is today. Rather than report on drugs from a position of moral outrage and disgust, the press described athletes enlisting chemicals to extend human performance as an unremarkable matter of fact. Cycling did not operate under the disapproving glare of paternalistic anti-doping agencies and morally outraged fans. Nor did the press link doping with moral depravity. If anything, when newspapers wrote about doping, they did so to illustrate an athlete's exemplary commitment to his craft.[12]

With big money and enormous fan interest at stake, professional cycling needed to deliver spectacle, drama, and heroic suffering. Riders took drugs to help make that happen. On December 16, 1900, the *New York Times* described a high number of injured riders dropping out of a Madison Square Garden six-day race. Even after competitors "had been liberally dosed with stimulating drugs," the *Times* reported, the infernal pace of racing and crash-sustained injuries were too much. Rather than helping riders gain an advantage over their competitors, drugs dispensed during turn-of-the-20th-century bike races were described as aids meant to merely keep the riders upright during grueling multiday events.[13]

Indeed, in the context of sports competition that then prevailed, doping was an outrage only when it impeded performance. A report from the November 26, 1894, edition of San Francisco's *Morning Call* newspaper dramatized the immorality of go-slow doping. A story titled "Doping a Racer" described a British horse trainer named Dan Danson who was caught poisoning a racehorse to force the animal to run slower than its normal pace. Concerned that such subterfuge would scare away horse-racing fans, the anti-doping police didn't mess around. Danson was executed. The *Morning Call* described another doping-to-go-slow case involved Clipsetta, a horse that was wiping up tracks in the American South. The paper recounted Clipsetta's early demise by way of the needle: "The night before the race this fiend in human form, by some means, gained access to the stable" and injected the horse with drugs. On race day, "the splendid filly died in awful agony."[14]

While society frowned on doping to maim a horse, giving a steed stimulants to accelerate it was no big deal. In a 1901 piece titled "'Dope' an American Term" the *New York Times* described "shrewd turfmen" using drugs to "get more speed out of certain horses" than bettors and bookies thought the animals had in them. While chemically maiming a horse was unethical, the *Times* reported that few believed using stimulants to speed up a horse "was either discreditable or dishonest."[15]

With time, the term *doping* made its way from the stables into vernacular speech. "To dope" became shorthand for slowing down or speeding up an animal or person. Doping to retard performance had negative connotations. Doping to push performance carried little judgmental baggage. An October 19, 1903, *New York Times* article, "'Dope' Evil of the Turf: Jockey Club Stewards Keenly Watch for Horse Druggers," described sleuths hanging out on paddock rails looking for any sign of drug-induced slowness. "The amateur detectives are on the lookout not for the good of racing, but for the benefit of their own betting operations," the paper explained. Doping was immoral because it was bad for the gambling business. The same piece suggested doping was an American invention that ultimately made its way to the Old World. Commenting on the spread of this novel American method for rigging horse gambling to England, France, and Austria, the *Times* observed that "there has never been coined a term which has attained the popularity that the one 'dope' has achieved." The neologism *doping* "implies impropriety," the paper explained. Its use to slow down a horse in the interest of fixing a race was not seen as "legitimate and fair."

Due to whispers of these artificial efforts to slow down a horse, the track-going public was becoming convinced horse races were rigged. "Nearly every regular visitor to the tracks can point out half a dozen or more men who are known as 'needle doctors' and who are asserted to make a profession of 'doping' horses for trainers who are not familiar with the uses of drugs," the *Times* warned in the October 1903 story. However, even with spies trying to get the inside dope on the condition of horses, it was not always easy to identify which long-odds horses might have been doped to go faster and which favorites had been doped to slow down. Indeed, according to the *Oxford English Dictionary*, the phrase *to dope out*, a variation on the more modern expression *get the inside dope*, entered common usage about this time as a colloquial way of saying you had privileged information.

John Gleaves has written extensively on the history of horse doping. A professor at California State University, Fullerton, where he teaches the philosophy and sociology of sport and the history of human performance enhancement, Gleaves's research suggests that the drugs those horses were getting probably had no actual effect on their performance. "This was just hocus-pocus," Gleaves told me when I visited him at his university office not far from Disneyland. "They actually believed they were speeding horses up and slowing them down, but they were using things like mercury and rosemary and tincture of thistle—crazy stuff. And that didn't make the horse go any faster."

When not using syringes, trainers would sometimes drill holes in a horse's leg, pour in supposedly performance-crushing toxins, then hide the drug-stuffed cavity with leg wrappings. Newspaper descriptions of innocent animals being subjected to these cruel methods also soured public attitudes toward the notion of slow doping. "You are not going to get a guy to lay a dollar bet if he thinks the race is fixed," Gleaves noted. And without the thrill of money on the line, horse racing does not draw wagering fans; as Gleaves pointed out, "If you don't have gambling, horse racing is not that interesting." Left unchecked, horse doping could undermine the sport's economic calculus—taking money out of the pockets of gamblers and putting it into the wallets of track and horse owners.

Written and enforced by the powerful Jockey Club, the first American anti-doping law passed in 1897. Designed to protect the gambling industry, the law gained an enforcement mechanism when horse racing introduced its first dope tests in 1912. The checks were theoretically able to identify the presence of cocaine or opium in a horse's saliva. While there is little evidence to suggest the tests worked, the Jockey Club's message that the sport now had technology to root out drug-hobbled horses was a strong signal to track gamblers that their bets were square.[16]

Thoroughbred racing became concerned about doping's financial harm at the same time pro cycling boomed in the United States. Beneath the 1903 *Times* piece on the evils of horse doping was a report on a new cycling record set at the Parc des Princes velodrome in Paris: 52 miles, 918 yards in one hour. A column to the left held more cycling stories, but the scandal of the day involved a protest over the winner of a 100-mile race in upstate New York. Riders were upset because the victor, M. Eustes of the Brower Wheelmen, "took pace from an automobile." Getting a draft from a car was cause for moral outrage.[17]

During the period that racing authorities clamped down on go-slow doping at hippodromes, plenty of money was being wagered in velodromes at six-day bicycle races. The winner of these events was the man who could grind out the most laps over 144 hours. On December 10, 1897, four days into a six-day event at Madison Square Garden, the *New York Times* reported that race leader Charles Miller had covered 1,606 miles. According to the story, the Chicago rider's face was "drawn and haggard," his eyes "sunk deep and inflamed." He had slept only four hours since the race had started four days earlier. "His trainers are scarcely able to keep him off the track for a single hour's sleep each day," the paper marveled. While it was common knowledge that competitors turned to artificial stimulants to fuel these monumental endurance efforts over what the *Times* called "six days of agony," newspaper reporters saw no reason to lump human drug taking in the same category as horse doping.[18]

As to the question of why cyclists racing at Madison Square Garden were not given the same anti-doping scrutiny as horses across the East River in Queens at Aqueduct Racetrack, Gleaves told me the public and officials assumed human athletes were always going to attempt to win. If a cyclist wanted to throw an event, he didn't need to take drugs to soft-pedal or feign fatigue. At the dawn of pro sports, corruption had little to do with doping to go fast; instead, it was performance-slowing subterfuges that corroded fan confidence. The most famous example from team sports arose when Chicago White Sox players conspired to throw the 1919 World Series. That eight players were banned for life from baseball suggests just how seriously the sports world took performance-degrading strategies that threatened ticket sales.

The assumption was that you would only dope human athletes to improve their performance, Gleaves told me. In six-day races, both the public and promoters wanted riders to go faster and harder. If it made for more exciting bike racing, the consensus was "We want you to dope them all. We want them all to go fast," Gleaves said. There was no fear that riders were surreptitiously doping themselves to lose. "Every cyclist there is trying to win because that's how they get paid," Gleaves observed. Doped cyclists presumably went faster, and that was all good for track racing at the turn of the century, so few complained about "ethical" violations. A professional cyclist's crowning moral obligation was to seek victory with all his might. For the first century of professional sports, doping to go faster fulfilled that professional obligation and illustrated just how malleable ethical connotations were in regard to doping.

Echoing the differing attitudes toward drugs that either retarded or enhanced performance, a six-day write-up in the *New York Times* on December 12, 1903, described performance-enhancing drugs as a logical and correct aid for the riders. Some 1,600 miles into that winter's event at Madison Square Garden, the paper described a French rider reaching for a bottle containing the antiseptic carbolic acid when he was meant instead to get a hand up of performance-supplementing beer. Averting disaster, the rider's trainer, Tom Eck, grabbed the rider's hand and swept the carbolic acid to the floor, smashing it. The *Times* reports that afterward the French athlete "was profuse in his thanks to Eck."[19]

As word of this minor drama spread across the infield and made its way up to the cigar-smoke-shrouded fans, it twisted into a rumor that trainers were poisoning certain riders with drugs—horse racing's old doping problem. Although alcohol and other stimulants were perfectly acceptable for six-day riders, even the hint of the administration of output-retarding drugs was cause for scandal.

Three days earlier, a *Times* sportswriter covered the specter of riders being doped in the old victory-crippling hippodrome way. After fans were spotted handing riders champagne, a rumor flew "that some of the contestants were being drugged." That is, riders were allegedly being doped to slow them down. As the news washed all the way up to the nosebleed seats—becoming more salacious with every uninformed retelling—whispers became shouts. With some riders so exhausted they were falling off their bikes midrace, the notion took root that partisan fans were feeding riders champagne laced with poison. This was an outrageous breach of sporting standards, a go-slow chemical wrench in the gearworks of fair play. Although the hysteria seemed to be little more than the work of overheated imaginations, the paper commiserated with the athletes, pointing out that at 1:00 a.m. the zombie-like riders "seemed sadly in need of a stimulant."[20]

From the days of the first professional races in the 1870s, pro cycling was a sport for the working classes, and the competitors were the same laborers who saw alcohol and stimulants as a necessary tool for enduring the remorseless nature of their work and the hard-fisted bosses who ruled the mines and factories. Endurance sports like cycling and marathon were spiritual brethren to the labor of extracting coal or threshing wheat; going without the substances available to help grind through your days was illogical, even unprincipled. As Gleaves told me, if it involved working for money, fans and the press did not stigmatize taking drugs to improve your efforts. By and large, the public was "OK with laborers taking stimulants to do their job better, whether it's going into the coal mine, whether it's going out to the farm field, or whether it's going out to your bicycle."

At the same time that cycling was taking off as a profession, cocaine and caffeine were mixed with all manner of popular alcoholic and non-alcoholic drinks, most famously in Coca-Cola, which in the 1880s began bottling the invigorating Peruvian coca plant and West African kola nut and selling it as a patent medicine. During the same era, at least seven other companies sold variations of Vin Mariani, a mixture of Bordeaux wine with coca extract that was first concocted by a Corsican pharmacist.

In 1896, the popular American sports and outdoors magazine *Outing* ran a two-page advertisement touting the performance-enhancing qualities of Vino-Kolafra. A mixture of wine and kola nut extract, the beverage was pitched as a coach-sanctioned drug. Headlined "A New Factor in Athletics. The Banishment of Fatigue," the ad cited "the rapid pace of life and the limitations of human endurance" as obstructions between Americans and success. Explaining that the tonic is used by "athletes of our leading colleges," and illustrated with drawings of rowers, divers, hurdlers, racewalkers, and shot-putters, the advertisement quoted Yale University trainer M. C. Murphy. The drink kept his college athletes "braced, and besides giving the system an immediate lift, improves the general health." Many decades before performance-enhancing drugs would be stigmatized as potions of anti-fair-play devils, this Ivy League coach had no reason to be ashamed about recommending Vino-Kolafra. It "certainly is a remarkable drug," he stated in an effort to get more Americans—college athlete and office worker alike—marching down to the local shop to load up on the stimulant.

Research on cocaine's effects on physical output went back decades. In 1876, the august *British Medical Journal* (*BMJ*) published a study by Sir Robert Christison on the performance-enhancing effects of coca leaf. The British doctor was inspired to take up his research after reading German zoologist Eduard Pöppig's 1835 book *Travels in Chile, Peru, and on the River Amazon.* Based on five years of field studies in the Andes, Pöppig described Peruvian natives banging out 50-mile hikes fueled on nothing but coca leaves. Cocaine, Pöppig concluded, "has a really wonderful power in supporting the strength under prolonged fatigue without food."[21]

Using the traditional Peruvian spelling *cuca*, Christison's *BMJ* piece recounted the tale of a 62-year-old Peruvian miner who worked "at laborious digging five days and nights without food, or more than two hours of sleep nightly, his only support being half an ounce of cuca leaves every three hours." Another European researcher, Dr. T. I. von Tschudi, reported that when he was working in the 14,000-foot Peruvian highlands, coca leaves allowed him to "climb heights, and pursue swift-footed game, with no greater difficulty than in similar rapid exercise on the coast." In sum, von Tschudi encouraged, "the moderate use of coca not only is innocuous, but may even be conducive to health."[22]

A medical professor at the University of Edinburgh, Christison was so intrigued by these South American reports that he began his own investigations, often using his students as human cocaine rats. In one study, he had two young scholars walk 16 miles. Their only meal was breakfast at 9:00 a.m. After their 16-mile ramble, Christison denied the famished students food and instead gave them tea made from an eighth of an ounce of coca mixed with carbonate of soda and a dash of plant ash. After downing the Peruvian infusion, Christison marveled that "hunger left them entirely, all sense of fatigue soon vanished." Indeed, even after an all-day walk and no postexercise food in their bellies, the students were so revitalized by their Peruvian tea that they left to promenade Edinburgh's high street for an hour "with ease and pleasure." Coca, it seemed, removed fatigue and revived a tired person's "ability for active exertion."[23]

In a subsequent 1875 study, Christison asked 10 students to walk 20 to 30 miles without eating. At the end of their starvation hikes, the scholars drank a coca infusion. Christison reported that four subjects got moderate relief, four complete relief, and two felt no effect at all. "No disagreeable effect was produced at the time or subsequently, except that a few felt a brief nausea after their dose, owing probably to the form of the infusion in which it was taken," he concluded.[24]

Christison also tested coca on himself. He walked 15 miles without chewing coca and reported that the task left him physically ruined and "unfit for mental work." Two days later, he did the same 15-mile walk, but this time with a coca assist. Christison had plenty of good to say about the drug's enhancing powers: "I was surprised to find that all sense of weariness had entirely fled, and that I could proceed not only with ease, but even with elasticity." In two subsequent tests, Christison climbed 2.5 hours to the summit of a 3,000-foot mountain, then chewed coca leaves in preparation for his descent. Again the coca eliminated fatigue. "I went down the long descent with an ease like that which I used to enjoy in my mountainous rambles in my youth," the doctor raved. "Chewing cuca removes extreme fatigue, and prevents it," Christison concluded. "No injury whatever is sustained at the time, or subsequently in occasional trials."[25]

As if athletes needed more justification to make this wonder drug part of their training table, Christison also recounted how a coca leaf infusion helped a cyclist. He described one M. Laumaillé making a 760-mile bike ride from Paris to Vienna in 12 days. Sixty miles from Vienna, Laumaillé was a physical wreck, demolished by days of bogging through "a road of fluid mire." Although Vienna was within striking distance, the French velocipedist wanted nothing more than to flop down in the muck and sleep, but then he reached for a "small supply of the liqueur de coca, an Indian tonic." After swigging this Peruvian booster, Laumaillé reported his strength flooding back. Encouraged by this report, along with his own studies, Christison concluded his piece by expressing his hope that pharmacists would get to work to create an over-the-counter cocaine solution, and "without looking for a patent."[26]

Sixty-five years later, scientists still praised the use of performance-enhancing drugs in sports. In 1941, Springfield College professor, exercise physiologist, and sports science researcher Peter Karpovich defined the prevailing non-judgmental attitudes toward performance-enhancing drugs. In his "Ergogenic Aids in Work and Sport," Karpovich rounded up current research on the physiological effects of substances, including alcohol, cocaine, amphetamines, hormones, pure oxygen, fruit juices, and sugar. Published in the *Research Quarterly of the American Association for Health, Physical Education, and Recreation*, Karpovich's study urged readers to avoid the term "doping" when referring to performance-enhancing drugs and athletes. "At present its use is objectionable since it connotes an administration of drugs akin to opium," Karpovich cautioned. That is, a drug that made one soporific—think horses with holes in their ankles—and was worthy of opprobrium, unlike compounds that made you lively.[27] To avoid this negative association, he recommended calling performance-enhancing drugs—as powerful as cocaine and as benign as fruit juice—ergogenic aids.

As for the ethics of using drugs to improve performance, the highly influential Karpovich saw no fair play compromises if drugs did no harm. "It may be stated here that *the use of a substance or device which improves the physical performance of a man without being injurious to his health, can hardly be called unethical*," Karpovich explained.[28]

In 1956, Karpovich would write one of the first scientifically rigorous books on strength training and athletic performance. As a Russian field medic during World War I, Karpovich had been imprisoned during Joseph Stalin's dictatorship. He escaped to the United States in 1925 and became a citizen in 1935. Karpovich combined the scientist's belief in challenging received wisdom (including his own) with a doctor's obligation to do no harm. Thanks to his research that revealed weight lifting athletes were both quicker and more flexible than non–weight lifting athletes, in the 1940s, Karpovich rejected the prevailing belief that weight training made athletes slower and stiffer—an old wives' tale that, as we will see later in this book, persisted into the 1970s, when the San Diego Chargers football team incorporated anabolic steroids and weight training into their NFL preseason workouts and the 1980s, when baseball players embraced the same practices.

For Karpovich, performance-enhancing drugs were part of a holistic athletic preparation package and morally indistinguishable from proper diet, massage, sport-specific training, and rest. "All these means are available for everyone, and they may be used if so desired," he explained in 1941.[29] That said, Karpovich's Hippocratic oath ensured he was not a universal drug pusher. In cases where he could find no evidence of ergogenic benefit, he would steer athletes away from certain drugs. Writing about the amphetamines frequently distributed to World War II soldiers, Karpovich proposed that "in spite of rumors that Benzedrine has been responsible for an improvement in athletic performance, no scientific evidence has been presented as yet." Regarding hormones such as testosterone, Karpovich noted that as of 1941, research "leads to a hope that hormones might increase muscular strength and endurance in normal people." After mentioning research indicating that cocaine can increase cycling endurance, Karpovich cautioned, "Since cocaine is a dangerous, habit-forming drug, its use in athletics cannot be recommended." Likewise, he warned that the stimulant Benzedrine is a "dangerous drug and its excess may lead to insomnia, hypertonia, and circulatory collapse."[30]

Karpovich's publications and the widespread adoption of his theories of sports medicine that prevailed throughout the first century of pro sports capture the striking lack of moral hysteria in popular and scientific culture regarding drugs in sport. Performance enhancement through drugs was a matter of professional practice and scientific opinion, not individual moral degeneracy. The physiologist's counsel regarding drugs was based on their efficacy and their potential to cause physical harm, not still-dormant social constructs regarding drugs and moral ruin. Using drugs to improve performance was only a problem when those drugs were so powerful and addictive that they could harm the athlete, not because they violated a spirit of fair play or threatened society's social order. In the years following World War II, however, these neutral attitudes began a slow, halting transition—an early creep toward today's anti-doping fanaticism.

CHAPTER 2

PIERRE DE COUBERTIN AND THE FAIR-PLAY MYTH

In 1883, a French aristocrat named Pierre de Coubertin was obsessed with British boarding schools. With France suffering a crisis of confidence over a humiliating loss in the 1871 Franco-Prussian War and with the Industrial Revolution shifting power from feudal hands into those of manufacturing entrepreneurs and revolution-minded workers, the 20-year-old baron and future father of the modern Olympics saw British institutions like Eton, Marlborough, and Charterhouse as educational models that could help steady his insecure nation. That year, Baron de Coubertin made the first of many Channel crossings to study what made British public schools tick.

Born into a line of Parisian nobles with a lineage that stretched back to the 1400s, Coubertin's own education took place under Jesuit priests. Raised with the creed that faith in God grows best when combined with the cultivation of the intellectual and the physical self, Coubertin had a strong affinity for the British public school emphasis on the development of citizen-athlete-scholars. In his 20s, Coubertin dedicated himself to remaking the French school system. In particular, he wanted to emulate the British system's theory that the moral and spiritual self cannot develop apart from a strenuous physical education.

The origin of this connection between flesh and spirit comes from the schools' beginnings as training institutions for clergy. Founded by aristocratic benefactors as schools for poor lower-class boys, British schools like Eton and Charterhouse are public, but not in the American sense of a school that is open to anyone. The schools are public in that they are funded by a foundation underwritten by landed gentry who wanted to ensure the British public had a steady supply of clerics. Over time, public boarding schools transformed from their 14th-century foundation as training institutions for clerics into boarding schools for the upper classes.

For a 13-year-old member of the landed gentry being sent to boarding school, the playing field was as much a part of his education as the classroom. Rugby, rowing, and running developed what was then called "manly independence"—a combination of resolve, fear of God, courage, humility, and self-possession. And it was on British fields and rivers that the notion of amateurism flourished. The objective of sport was not to win personal glory and humiliate opponents, but rather to improve the national, physical, and moral character. The once-common British refrain "The Battle of Waterloo was won on the playing fields of Eton" describes a connection between martial and physical prowess. As Coubertin saw it, schools like Eton taught the sort of courage it took for the Duke of Wellington's troops to defeat Napoleon in his final battle in 1815.

In 1888, Coubertin published *English Education* (*L'éducation en Angleterre*), a book that provided a window into the English educational system and its athletic traditions. "Every conglomeration of men is an ensemble of vices and corruptions, and children are the seed of men," Coubertin wrote. In his view, men and their children were born inherently depraved. "The English know this; they also know that evil will be passed from one member to another unless we cut out the gangrene before it has invaded." For Coubertin, English schools, with their dedication to the preservation of aristocratic values, knew how to lop off the inbred social rot that he, like many other French noblemen, believed was corrupting the once-fierce French character.[1]

In 1871, 17 years before the book's publication, France suffered a startling military defeat in the Franco-Prussian War. Although the French provoked the war by invading Prussia (the predecessor to modern Germany), Prussian guns brought the French to their knees with mortifying efficacy. Prussia annexed much of Alsace-Lorraine. This amputation of vast tracts of French soil became a bitter reminder of France's spectacular disgrace. The loss of land, lucre, and blood also triggered intense public soul searching over why the French populace seemed to have lost the moral and physical courage to persevere and win. What was France doing wrong, noblemen like Coubertin wondered, in preparing its youth to defend the French way of life?

National turmoil continued in the spring of 1871 when Paris workers took to the streets to demand social and democratic reforms—that is, a voting voice in their personal and national destinies. The demands of the working-class clashed with the interests of both the monarchical national government and the conservative Catholic Church, two institutions that shaped Coubertin's identity. For 60 days, the Paris Commune took command of the city. Working-class revolutionaries pulled the French tricolor from Paris flagpoles and replaced it with red socialist banners. Hundreds died in pitched street battles and retaliatory executions. The Tuileries Palace, the longtime home of French monarchs, burned. Glorious France seemed to be disintegrating. It was a time of social convulsion and a clash of philosophies over the source of political power, with one side holding the ancient belief that power is handed down by God through aristocratic bloodlines, the other side rallying behind the notion that the source of authority is man (and even more radically, woman)—the politically enfranchised masses. For Coubertin, the British amateur sporting tradition held great appeal as a way for French youth to grow stronger in heart and mind, and to build a moral, political, and social bulwark against the assaults on feudal order raging in the streets of Paris.

The Industrial Revolution behind this social upheaval was also paving the way for an unprecedented era of professional sports. In a fashion alien to the public school amateur sports tradition, practicing a sport was becoming a viable way of making a living. Cycling, soccer, and rugby sporting clubs grew in the 1880s and 1890s as diversions for industrial workers. With time, these clubs and their events became more sophisticated. Cups and leagues emerged, event organizers began charging spectators for entry, and eventually club-owned stadiums sprang up in cities around Europe. Far from the moneyed world of British public schools, these professional sports were associated with the working classes who filled both stadium stands and team rosters.

It was the workers—not British aristocrats—who organized and played in soccer clubs. In 1878, railroad workers organized Manchester United in the textile city of the same name, and London munitions workers formed Arsenal Football Club in 1886. Similar worker-founded teams sprang up in industrial cities across Europe, including Barcelona, Milan, and Bilbao. At first, the teams were little more than informal clubs playing on vacant fields—they provided a sense of home and a locus of hope for displaced immigrants. Manchester United originally played matches against other teams of railroad workers. With time, promoters saw the potential in selling tickets, and the teams of workingmen gradually morphed into today's global money-printing machines.

Writing in the British magazine the *Contemporary Review* in 1898, social commentator Ernest Ensor fretted that pro sports were a morally corrupting spectacle for lower classes. "Threepence or sixpence are hoarded up all the week in order that the mind may have its brief period of excitement," Ensor lamented in a piece titled "The Football Madness." "It is the absolute necessity of some change, some interest outside the daily work which has long ceased to be interesting, that causes the huge crowds at weekly football matches." And when the workingman wagered a few coins on a match, gambling became the sauce on an already savory game. "There is the pleasure of discussing the chances, the mental exercise of speculating on the latest news or rumors, the consideration of the weather and its possible effect, the excitement of anticipation, and on rare occasions, for everybody cannot always lose, the keen joy of winning," Ensor observed.[2]

As leagues became profit-oriented, so did players. In 1894, Welsh soccer great Billy Meredith toiled in the pit mines while playing for Manchester City. The following year, he became a salaried soccer player and laid down his headlamp and pick for good. Similar transformations were taking place in rugby, long a staple sport in British schools. This monetization of sports alarmed public school traditionalists. Charging admission and paying players bonuses to jump teams were seen as grimy proletarian activities. For traditionalists like Coubertin who celebrated sports as a source of moral and physical uplift, professionalization was a social threat spearheaded by unrefined, landless working classes—a social group considered alien and inferior in both bloodline and upbringing.[3]

These class fears crystallized as the ideology of amateurism. Playing for no reason other than the chivalric notion of fair play—and, by extension, for the preservation of the aristocratic class hierarchy—was the foundation upon which Coubertin would resurrect the modern Olympics in 1896. Amateurism became a bulwark against the proletarian workers getting rich from sports and scaling the walls of power—an alarming prospect for those who believed that power and wealth were inherited, not earned through personal ambition, toil, or success in the voting booth. Building the Olympics around amateur sports at the moment the lower classes were reaching new economic heights through sports was a reaction against the Industrial Revolution's shifting of power away from the aristocracy and toward unionized lower-class workers and newly rich industrial entrepreneurs—the bourgeoisie.

Fulminating against the "warped sporting instincts" that were making rugby a competitive, money-driven spectacle in northern England, Ensor wrote in his *Contemporary Review* piece that a sport played "for the love of the game" did not exist outside British schools—the same institutions Coubertin admired. British rugby split into professional Union and amateur League associations in 1885. But even in 1883, the split between the gate-taking northern Rugby Football Union and the sport-for-sport's sake southern Football League was clear. Ensor complained that "gentlemen"—code for the landed classes—could not risk playing in money-making Union events; doing so would sink them in the "moral slough" of professionalism.

From their earliest days, cycling and running rewarded winners with cash and prizes; as a result, Ensor and like-minded public figures considered these sports morally corrupting and off limits. "Gentlemen must not run foot-races or ride bicycle races in open company," Ensor warned. Comparing pro athlete trading to American slavery, he complained that money had turned once noble sports into a matter of war, where winning came at any cost and losing meant financial ruin. When a losing team couldn't fill seats, Ensor wagged his finger at the inevitability that "it is necessary to sell the best players, so to speak, by public auction, in order to get money for present needs." He warned, "In these days a team must win its matches, or it is ruined."

With memories of Communards burning the Tuileries fresh in his mind, Coubertin was also gravely concerned about the consequences of empowered workers and enriched merchant classes. Such a change could pull political power and financial assets from noble hands. It came to the baron that a global sporting event celebrating the social-order-preserving qualities of amateurism could go far in maintaining a way of life under assault from the forces of industrialization and liberal political theories. Olympic Games critic and historian Andrew Jennings bluntly assessed what Coubertin was up to: "Concluding that sport was a positive force which could bring reconciliation between hostile classes, he resolved to create a great international festival. There was a model, moldering fifteen centuries back in the basement of history, that could be dusted down, polished up and projected as a new philosophy of fair competition and sportsmanship."[4]

Coubertin's Jesuit education, aristocratic bloodlines, close study of British school systems, alarm at the rising power of the working classes, and desire to rebuild the French character came together in the form of his Olympic project. In Paris, on June 16, 1894, Coubertin convened delegates from an existing French sports governing body called the Union des sociétés françaises de sports athlétiques. A man with a keen understanding of the power of setting, spectacle, and antiquarian trappings, Coubertin held the convention in the Sorbonne's Grand Amphithéâtre. Beneath the auditorium's soaring domed ceilings, surrounded by busts of philosopher Descartes, mathematician Pascal, and chemist Lavoisier, and with an 83-foot-long allegorical painting depicting art, literature, and science as a backdrop, delegates hashed out the principles of amateurism in contemporary society. The carefully selected setting evoked Coubertin's belief that sports should operate in the service of intellectual development, character building, and a better, more moral society. Coubertin was also partial to the location because it harkened back to the tales of medieval French and British chivalry he was fond of reading. This Sorbonne reunion was the first step toward creating a sporting event that fulfilled Coubertin's nostalgic—and explicitly religious—vision of international games as a rehabilitative force guided by revived chivalric codes of knightly conduct.

After proposing a renaissance of the ancient Olympics to the gathered delegates, Coubertin arranged for ancient Greek music to filter through the auditorium: "The First Delphic Hymn to Apollo," a musical arrangement that a French archeologist had discovered a year earlier in the ruins of the Delphi and that was rumored to have been played at the Pythian Games, an ancient Greek predecessor to the Olympics. The delegates approved Coubertin's motion to establish a modern Olympic Games. A mechanism for spreading the gospel of chivalric ideals and modern muscular Christianity through amateur sports was born. The delegates also endorsed an Olympic motto that, with time, would come to represent the enduring tension between the elite athlete's essential will to win and Coubertin's commitment to amateur modesty and self-effacing service to others: Citius, Altius, Fortius—Faster, Higher, Stronger. The first modern Olympics took place soon thereafter in 1896 in Athens.

Five months after the Sorbonne meeting, Coubertin recounted the birth of what would eventually become the International Olympic Committee (IOC) to an audience at the Parnassus Literary Society in Athens. He was rapturous: "The effect was deeply moving. In one of those mysterious glimpses that music sometimes gives us of lost worlds, for a few seconds those gathered in Paris perceived Greek antiquity in all its splendor. From that moment on, gentlemen, the Greek genius was among us, transforming a modest congress on athletic sports into a quest for moral betterment and social peace."

In the same speech, outlining his ethical reform project, Coubertin suggested that the Olympics were designed as a quasi-religious movement meant to deliver men to a state of grace. "There is no incompatibility whatsoever between Christian hopes and the cultivation of the body's abilities," he counseled. "Chivalry was a vast athletic confraternity."[5] As Baron de Coubertin saw it, the Knights of the Round Table had been evangelizing sportsmen at heart.

Coubertin told his listeners that while pro sports like cycling were growing ever more popular, money-making sports lacked the "philosophical foundation, the loftiness of the goals, the whole patriotic and religious apparatus" that he envisioned had infused the ancient Greek games. The modern games Coubertin proposed would bring religious structure to sports that, at least in 1894, were either just for fun (a Sunday afternoon spin on a safety bicycle) or for money (a six-day race for cash). Coubertin reminded his Athenian audience that during that city's ancient games, athletes underwent a purification ceremony. Today, however, "it is impossible for us to imagine a cyclist being required to go to city hall for a certificate of good conduct in order to be allowed into the velodrome, or a fencer engaging in a knightly vigil at a church, like the knights of the Middle Ages."[6] For the founder of the Olympics, the games were meant to shepherd fallen humans toward a state of grace. And by fallen, the baron meant playing for money and, by extension, striving to rise above one's appointed social class. "We know that athletics is exposed to serious dangers, that it can decline into commercialism and into the mud, and we know that we must protect it from such a fate at all costs," Coubertin warned.

In November 1896, Coubertin penned a semifictional account of the first modern Olympics for the popular American magazine *Century.* His tale warned against the perils of professionalism. When a poor Greek runner wins the marathon, moneyed fans shower him with jewelry, cash, and even a certificate for a year's worth of free meals. The impoverished peasant refuses the gifts. In Coubertin's paternalistic parable, the runner's innate respect for social order fends off the corrupting and class-disrupting influence of money. "The sense of honor, which is very strong in the Greek peasant," Coubertin wrote, "thus saved the non-professional spirit from a very great danger."[7]

Ten years later, with two Olympic games under his belt, Coubertin fretted that the Olympic wall against corrupting professionalism was eroding. He unburdened himself in a 1906 letter to Charles Simon, the secretary general of the Fédération gymnastique et sportive des patronages de France. The missive proposed that all future Olympians should affirm fealty to the following oath to compete in the spirit of sixth-century knights-errant, not industrial-era titans of commerce: "We swear that we are taking part in the Olympic Games as loyal competitors, observing the rules governing the Games and anxious to show a spirit of chivalry for the honor of our countries and for the glory of sport."[8] Starting in 1920, every Olympic athlete had to pledge to uphold this medieval vow of courage, service to the less fortunate, and religious propriety. Coubertin reminded Simon that while the Olympics had been created as "a school for moral improvement," professionalism was corrupting this institution. "The individual who was to take part in the Games had to be purified, in some sense, through professing and practicing Olympic virtues," Coubertin demanded.[9]

"Amateur sport was really about class division," John Gleaves of California State University, Fullerton, told me. Coubertin and the politically and economically connected IOC founders saw sports as a protector of social hierarchy and personal salvation. Gleaves explained that "the amateur was really about status, and it was about power. It was about excluding the working classes and the laborers." The social and economic elite, like the founders of the Olympics, knew best, and amateur sports and the Olympics grew out of the paternalistic obligation to impose this state of affairs on the wider world.

Even training was discouraged among amateurs. "The amateur athlete was the one who could just show up and play any sport" without preparation, Gleaves noted. That is why, until the ban on pros was lifted for the 1988 Seoul Olympics, the IOC prohibited coaching and training camps that lasted longer than a few weeks. Spending months or years focusing on your sport suggested a level of professional seriousness that violated Olympic amateur ideals. Part of the virtue of amateurism was that participants were not specialists, did not train, and did not even overly try to win. "You should be playing hard, but you should also appear effortless," Gleaves said of the Olympic amateur ideal.

In 1925, Coubertin wrote that the British view of a good sporting club was "a club whose members are gentlemen of the same station." He meant aristocrats. That is why Olympic regulations stated that an athlete would lose amateur status for merely stepping onto a field with professionals, even if the athlete were not being paid. It was this rule that saw Native American Jim Thorpe stripped of the gold medals he won at the 1912 Stockholm Olympics. Because Thorpe had once played baseball alongside professional players in the United States, the IOC disqualified his pentathlon and decathlon victories. While racism also fueled Thorpe's disqualification, his removal underscored the sentiment that allowing pros to play next to amateurs would be tantamount to allowing the land-tilling peasant to join the estate-owning baron at the dinner table—a fatal disruption of the social order. It was "a form of social protection, a relic of the class system," Coubertin wrote of amateurism in 1925.[10]

As he aged, Coubertin's adamantine views on amateurism softened, and he admitted it would not be such a big deal if an athlete made a few francs practicing a sport. At 62, Coubertin confessed that when he convened that first conference in Paris to revive the Olympics, he used amateurism as a lure to bring together the influential, and socially alarmed, people needed to bring his project to light, especially the public school–oriented British who ran track and field at the time. In 1925, three decades after the meeting that gave birth to the IOC, the Frenchman wrote that his keenness for amateurism had become "an enthusiasm without real conviction."[11] Although still committed to the notion that sport was "a religion with its church, dogmas, service," Coubertin admitted that basing this creed on the fulcrum of whether or not an athlete received money for playing was tantamount to dismissing the parish caretaker as "an unbeliever because he receives a salary for looking after the church." And while Coubertin's personal commitment to the purity of amateurism faded as he aged, the legacy of amateur sports as a moral purifier kept swinging about the Olympics like an antiquated censer all the way to 1988, when the IOC at last did away with the charade and allowed professional athletes into the Olympics.

While amateurism died for good at the 1988 Olympics, Coubertin's fiction of class purity and chivalric morality carries on at the heart of today's World Anti-Doping Code. We can draw a straight line between Coubertin's Olympic spiritual and moral hygiene project and the January 2015 revision of the code. The World Anti-Doping Agency (WADA) code states that worldwide anti-doping programs strive to preserve an "intrinsic value . . . often referred to as 'the spirit of sport.' It is the essence of Olympism, the pursuit of human excellence through the dedicated perfection of each person's natural talents. It is how we play true."[12]

As Danish sports historian Verner Møller sees it, Coubertin's legacy continues the unlikely endeavor of pushing a myth about intrinsic amateur and religious morality onto elite sports, a field that has only one inherent true north: to push the boundaries of human performance and win—often with the assistance of drugs. And the singular fixation of great athletes—to be better than the rest—is an ambition largely indifferent to pieties about purity and spirit. The notion that elite sports have an intrinsically moral fortifying core "is a fanciful idea that has arisen by virtue of the fact that our ears have been filled with talk about sport's positive influence," Møller explains in his 2008 book *The Doping Devil*.[13] The scholar has spent decades writing about the history of doping in sports, including a book on Danish pro cyclist Michael Rasmussen, a rider who was pulled from the 2007 Tour de France while wearing the yellow jersey for not properly reporting his whereabouts to anti-doping officials. A keen and incisive historian and social critic, Møller cites the received wisdom that sports keeps kids off the streets and out of trouble. He argues that homilies like this are driven so deeply into our psyche as received wisdom that it is difficult to objectively assess the validity of the proposition that sports equal morality. Although sports do teach discipline, patience, and commitment, these praiseworthy effects are not qualities at the core of elite sports. By-products of sporting socialization, the noble-minded, pious values Coubertin intended the Olympics to revive "have nothing to do with the essence of sport," Møller writes. "Morality is not a quality that is inherent in elite sport."[14]

Coubertin eventually admitted as much. In 1935, the father of the Olympics told a Geneva radio audience that the spirit of sport is really about going beyond what contemporary society considers normal, natural, and right. "To try to make athletics conform to a system of mandatory moderation is to chase after an illusion," Coubertin confessed. "Athletes need the 'freedom of excess.' That is why their motto is *Citius, altius, fortius*: faster, higher, stronger, the motto of anyone who dares to try to beat a record!" Sports are not inherently about creating humans who conform to a moral code drawn from fiction. As both Coubertin and Møller explain, the spirit of elite sports is to push beyond the known limits of human performance—an amoral quest.

Coubertin's Olympic idealism, bound up as it was in aristocratic paternalism, religious sentimentality, class order, and chivalric romance, turned out to be remarkably durable. More than a way of seeing who could go farther and faster, the Olympics was born as a social-reform movement, a system for better moral hygiene that would eventually accommodate anti-doping, which itself was framed as a program for protecting athletes' physical and moral well-being. A Don Quixote on a quest to return a fallen world to a state of religious and sporting pureness that never existed outside novels, Coubertin left a legacy that persists today as anti-doping missionaries strive to revive a contrived state of purity that never existed, most especially in pro sports. As we will see, over time, anti-doping interests adopted Coubertin's evangelical zeal. Clean minds and clean bodies became the centerpiece of a system of purity oaths, interrogation, surveillance, and punishment in the interest of breathing life into the Coubertinian myth of chaste fair play.

CHAPTER 3

THE FALL OF COUBERTIN'S IDEAL

When Coubertin wrote his 1896 story about the Greek marathoner who avoided "a very great danger" when he declined to accept the fiscal spoils of victory, the baron touched upon financial forces that would almost immediately begin building bridges across the moat protecting his religious sporting project from ignoble commerce. Only it wasn't so much athletes taking money that would run his chaste-minded event aground on the shoals of trade. Instead, it was unwitting Olympic organizers and savvy businessmen with products to sell.

Signs of the Olympic transition away from amateur innocence began as early as 1928, when the Amsterdam Olympic organizing committee sold advertising rights to Coca-Cola. When IOC officials arrived in Holland and saw Coke signs affixed to the walls of the Olympic stadium, they were outraged by the violation of Coubertin's rise-above-money founding values. As Olympic historians Ian Ritchie and Rob Beamish explain in their 2006 book *Fastest, Highest, Strongest*, for the IOC, the Coke decision "transformed Coubertin's sacred Games into a colossal billboard that celebrated the profane world of modern commerce."[1]

In spite of the IOC's protests about commercialization, four years later at the 1932 Los Angeles Games, the IOC was forced to wade into the muck of commerce and gain control of the licensing of Olympic symbols. In advance of the events, the Los Angeles organizing committee contracted Culver City's Paul Helms Bakery to deliver bread to 40 athlete mess halls. Helms was a bread and doughnut impresario whose delivery trucks were seen all over Los Angeles's sprawling roadways. Before the Games came to town, the baker had the foresight to register the Olympic insignia, the term "Olympic," and the motto "Citius, Altius, Fortius" in all the U.S. states plus then-territories Hawaii and the Philippines. To Helms's delight and amazement, the IOC had not registered any of its symbols, so the trademarks were his for the taking. Helms marketed his bread by packaging loaves in the colors of 19 different Olympic nations. After the close of the Olympics, he continued to advertise his bread on billboards and radio, always prominently capitalizing on the distinctive five interlocking rings and the motto "Official Olympic Supplier." (Today, Angelenos still drive past a neon Helms Olympic Bread sign above the Helms Bakery District shopping mall in Culver City.)

When U.S. Olympic Association president and recently appointed IOC member Avery Brundage got wind that a flour-coated L.A. baker had hitched his bread business to the amateur Olympic train, he was furious. As head of the USOA (predecessor to today's U.S. Olympic Committee) in 1938, Brundage paper-stormed Helms with letters demanding that he cease associating his loaves, doughnuts, and angel food cake with sacred Olympic traditions. Unfortunately for the IOC, the law was on Helms's side. Because the baker registered them first, Helms owned the rights to the Olympic symbols. He also possessed a legally binding contract with the Los Angeles Organizing Committee granting him sole rights to use the Olympic brand in his advertising.

Famously hot-headed, Brundage sued. The lawsuit dragged on for more than a decade until Helms settled in 1950 and granted many of his intellectual property rights to the rings and Olympic mottos to the IOC. Having a California baker snatch the entire stable of Olympic symbols from IOC control jolted the Olympic organizers from amateur fantasyland into commercial reality. In 1949, the IOC instructed all its national organizing committees to register the Olympic brand in their countries.[2]

Recall that in 1935, Coubertin admitted to Swiss radio listeners that it was difficult to confine sports to an artificially imposed moral code because the essence of sports is pushing human performance to unnatural plateaus, not seeking moral character. At the same time Coubertin was expressing his evolving views on amateurism from a Geneva studio, across the Swiss-German border, Adolph Hitler was preparing to host Germany's first Olympic Games.

In 1936, German pride was still injured by the nation's humiliating defeat in World War I. The unrelenting terms of 1919's Treaty of Versailles forced Germany to disarm, relinquish territories, and formally accept responsibility for causing the global conflict. In order to establish a footing for extracting financial reparations from Germany to rebuild towns and cities—retreating German soldiers laid waste to northern France—the treaty's so-called "War Guilt Clause" pinned all the blame for World War I on Germany. As the Berlin Olympics neared, Germans still burned with resentment, especially since their tax dollars had funded the reconstruction of Belgian and French industrial and mining centers during the very years the Great Depression carpet-bombed the German economy. Hitler fueled his rise to chancellor with populist, anti-immigrant, anti-Jewish rhetoric that promised to end his countrymen's collective mortification. The Olympics would allow Germany to reassert itself on the international stage as a winner, not a loser.

On the morning of August 1, 1936, Berlin's Brandenburg Gate was a joyous explosion of hanging swastikas and fluttering Olympic flags. The pageantry celebrated the arrival of a lithe, square-jawed German runner named Fritz Schilgen. The last runner in an Olympic torch relay that had begun some 2,000 miles earlier in Olympia, Greece, the 30-year-old Schilgen's entrance into Berlin marked the opening of a sporting marketing event that would show Germany was great again. As Schilgen ran past the thousands of fans lining the route into Berlin's Olympic stadium, they admired both his good looks and his torch, a sleek work of high industrial art designed by Nazi party sculptor Walter Lemcke and milled by German arms maker Krupps. The torch flame was ignited in Greece by a mirror milled by German optics company Zeiss. The Nazis had invented this 3,000-runner relay as an Olympic marketing novelty to amplify the can-do grandeur of the Third Reich; throughout the relay, the torchbearers were shadowed by a German Opel car carrying a spare torch. In the eight short years since Coca-Cola signs had horrified IOC members in Amsterdam, first corporate and now political symbolism had engulfed Coubertin's dream of self-effacing amateur endeavor. The Nazi Olympics demonstrated how spectacle and carefully managed symbol placements could market things, nations, and ideologies to a skeptical marketplace.

Two years before the Berlin games, historian, technology philosopher, and *New Yorker* writer Lewis Mumford published *Technics and Civilization*. Mumford's 1934 book explores how industrialized society created a demand for professional sports. Sport that was once an unremunerated human diversion became a product in itself: entertainment. "Mass-sport is primarily a spectacle," Mumford wrote of the transformation of sport from personal recreation to mass distraction. Industrial-era workers were so wrung by factory life that they needed to vicariously experience "difficult feats of strength or skill or heroism in order to sustain its waning life sense." And watching sports had a physiological effect on the spectator. At a football game, a properly engaged fan "pounds his neighbor's back or embraces him," depending on how his team is progressing. Being a spectator offered "relief from the passive role of taking orders and automatically filling them," Mumford wrote.[3]

Mumford also argued that we derive aesthetic pleasure from sports the way we do from art. "The spectator knows the style of his favorite contestants in the way that the painter knows the characteristic line or palette of his master," Mumford explained.[4] Fans can identify a favorite cyclist by his pedal stroke, a runner by her stride, and a soccer player by the way he kicks a ball. Mumford argued that we fill stadiums and gather around sports broadcasts because the chance-riddled exploits of sports heroes return suspense, excitement, and aesthetic pleasure to mechanized lives. At a time when the legacy of turn-of-the-20th-century scientific management guru Frederick Winslow Taylor was still working to eliminate inefficiency, randomness, and wasted time from home and factory, sport offered a place where elements of serendipity and uncertainty still enlivened our days. The bane of modern society—inefficiency brought about by uncontrolled variables—was the lifeblood of pro sports. As Mumford explained in his popular book, what industrial society took away, sports brought back. The latent monetary value in sports as spectacle grew proportionally with the industrialization and systemization of early 20th-century life. Mumford's is a critical concept, for the social utility and financial value he saw building in popular sports was about to be unlocked by the Olympics that Coubertin originally intended to preserve amateurism.

From sleep to nutrition, training to equipment, Mumford proposed that sporting excellence demands absolute dedication to craft, to the exclusion of all other aspects of a balanced life. The sports hero "represents the summit of the amateur's efforts, not at pleasure but at efficiency," he wrote. And the essence of technology is to enhance these efforts. From moving pictures to perfume, sexual performance to warfare, Mumford argued that technology delivers "a greater intensification of life." And we love to watch what's intense. Like a management consultant analyzing a factory floor, by controlling as many variables as possible, athletes, working with their trainers and doctors, compound marginal gains that in turn allow them to break the bounds of human performance—and feed the fans' desire for record-smashing spectacle. "Sport, which was originally a drama, becomes an exhibition," Mumford concluded just two years before Hitler's Olympics.[5]

To a degree unprecedented in sports history, the 1936 Games capitalized on Mumford's notions of sport as show and presented Germany's elite athletes as the acme of Nazi efficiency. The 1936 Olympics entertained by removing fans from the grimness of the seventh year of a crippling global economic depression while also selling Aryan ideology to a world that was thirsty for both scapegoats and solutions.

The 1936 Olympics were the first to be broadcast live on television and radio. Closed-circuit television viewers even saw events live. This was a miraculous collapse of time and space. Events that previously reached the world through the delayed network of newspapers and magazines, or through the visually incomplete medium of radio, now reached viewers instantly. To ensure a lasting legacy, the German Olympic Committee commissioned pioneering filmmaker Leni Riefenstahl to make a documentary about the games. Riefenstahl's 3.5-hour film, *Olympia*, used cinematic angles and techniques that were astonishingly fresh at the time, including angles of marathon runners that seem like they were shot with a GoPro, not a creaking film camera on a truck. As historians Beamish and Ritchie explain, the 1936 Olympics were "a finely crafted aesthetic" designed to celebrate white supremacy and distribute Nazi ideology to the most remote corners of the planet.[6] These Olympics both cast the template for the multibillion-dollar Olympic games we know today and profoundly challenged Coubertin's amateur ethos.

The transformation of the 1936 Olympics into a sales vehicle also forced the United States to make ethical compromises that would foreshadow later USOC efforts to shield American athletes and Olympic sponsors from doping scandals. Two hours before the 400-meter relay track event, American Olympic authorities benched the only Jewish athletes on the track and field team, relay runners Sam Stoller and Marty Glickman.

According to Glickman, head track coach Lawson Robertson explained this stunning decision by claiming the Germans had decided to put two of their strongest sprinters on their relay squad. It has long been argued that Robertson's excuse was a smokescreen, and that the real reason two Jews didn't put their feet in blocks beneath Hitler's stadium seat was that Brundage did not want to spit in the Olympic soup by embarrassing the German leader. Demonizing Jews was a fulcrum of

Hitler's rise to power. Having American Jews on a winning team would have put Brundage's host in an uncomfortable position.[7]

Brundage led the IOC from 1952 to 1972 and was a member of the America First Committee, an isolationist organization that had agitated to keep the United States out of World War II and leave European Jews to their own devices to deal with Hitler. Throughout his 20 years of IOC leadership, Brundage was adamant that political concerns should be walled off from the Olympics and that the Games should not be commercialized. In spite of Brundage's claims that he wanted the Games to remain a peaceable kingdom apart from the shilling of product or political ideology, a bitter Glickman later contended, "The decision to keep the only two Jewish athletes on the United States team out of the competition was made by American Nazis." Before his death in 1980, Glickman told *New York Times* reporter Bud Greenspan that Brundage and track coach Dean Cromwell were "sympathetic to Nazis."[8]

While Hitler demonstrated the Olympic capacity to deliver national propaganda (and get Americans to violate athletes' rights in deference to Nazi sensitivities), the story of the Adidas shoe company reveals the continuing discovery of the five rings' capacity to sell products. The shoe company's success also illustrates how inevitable it was that Coubertin's idealism and founding intentions would be swamped by the commercial potential inherent to his creation's global success; defending his commitment to a manufactured fantasy of chivalric purity became practically impossible under the weight of the Olympics' astonishing commercial potential.

Since the 1920s, German cobbler Adi Dassler had worked in a shoe business with his father and brother. In 1948, a feud split the family, and Dassler went off on his own to create a new shoe brand called Adidas. Dassler's company competed with Puma, a brand his father and brother, Rudolf Dassler, continued to run. Adi Dassler had spent years at track meets. A keen listener, his hundreds of afternoons hanging around athletes and their trainers gave him a fine understanding of athletes' shoe needs. The Adidas motto, "Function First," came to represent the upstart outfit's reputation as a company that made serious shoes for dedicated athletes. When Germany won the 1954 World Cup soccer tournament, many attributed the victory to the ingenious screw-on studs on the bottom of their Adidas shoes. When the world press attributed this national victory to a shoe brand and technical innovation, it was a signal moment in sports marketing history: Being associated with winners generated massive free publicity.

The first company to supply entire teams with shoes and give footwear to stars, Adidas took forceful steps to ensure that its brand shared the Olympic mystique that came with Coubertin's efforts to make the Games a matter of celestial high-mindedness. The forging of that link began at the 1936 Games, where Dassler arrived in Berlin toting a suitcase full of shoes and convinced black American sprinter Jesse Owens to wear a pair of Adidas spikes.

In one of the Games' most anticipated events, German long-jumper Carl "Lutz" Long uncorked a 7.87-meter flight. Observing from a perch in the 110,000-seat Olympic stadium, Hitler was delighted. With the "racially inferior" Owens up next, Hitler was sure his boy had both victory and the glorification of Aryan superiority in the bag. Owens stood silently on his mark. The clock drained 30 seconds. A minute. The crowd murmured, shifted in seats, spared glances at Hitler. After two full minutes of concentration, Owens launched. Like a rock from a slingshot, the black American let fly an 8.06-meter gold-medal leap. While Hitler fumed, a gracious Lutz wrapped Owens in a congratulatory hug. On the podium, Owens offered a crisp American military salute while Lutz extended his stiffened right arm in Nazi salutation. And as Hitler's dreams of Aryan superiority crashed, Dassler's visions of shoe domination soared. Photos of the podium ceremony streamed off presses around the world—every one showing Owens's top-of-the-podium feet clad in Adidas.

Owens won four gold medals in Berlin. Despite the fact that his skin color excluded him from many restaurants and hotels in his home country, this son of an Alabama sharecropper became an international sensation. The cause of Hitler's Olympic irritation turned Dassler shoes into an object of desire—Adidas were top shelf. After the Owens coup, athletes and coaches traveling through Germany would stop by the Dassler shoe factory to see a display containing Owens's shoes.[9]

By the 1956 Melbourne Olympics, Adidas was in a battle royal with Puma and Onitsuka, the maker of a lesser Japanese shoe called Tiger. Dassler sent his son Horst to Melbourne to ensure that his shoes got onto feet that would end up in the press. Avery Brundage had become IOC president in 1952, and in Melbourne, the American still jealously defended Coubertin's amateur ethos. In an effort to protect them from the perils of sport for financial reward, the IOC prohibited Olympic athletes from accepting free products. As a result, athletes had to buy their own equipment or get it from their national Olympic federations. However, you could drive an Adidas delivery truck through a loophole in the rule—IOC regulations allowed athletes to select "technical equipment" needed for their sport, even if it was given to them. For Adidas, there was no equipment more technical than its Function First footwear. Every day was about to become Christmas in Melbourne.

Horst gave Adidas technical equipment to any athlete who asked. To grease the asking, Horst filled a Melbourne sporting goods store with boxes of shoes that quickly became known as Melbourne spikes. He invited entire teams to drop by and pick up free gear. It was an offer few unpaid athletes could refuse. Rival Puma had quality control problems and its shoes fell apart on the Melbourne track. Meanwhile, Tiger spent an astonishing 30 billion yen on Olympic promotions but focused on long-distance running. Although the Olympics floated along on the spirit of amateurism, that raft was riding on a rapidly rising river of sponsor money.

In the 400-meter relay, the three top runners wore Adidas, including winner Bobby Morrow, a Texas farmer's son who left his team-supplied Wilson shoes behind because he preferred the German cleats. A finish photo put Morrow and Adidas on the cover of *Life* magazine. Adidas's free shoes gambit was delivering priceless brand exposure at no more expense than Horst's ticket to Australia and the shoes' production cost. In spite of the efforts of Puma and Tiger to counter Adidas's completely un-IOC-sanctioned momentum as the "Olympic" brand, athletes wearing Adidas took home 72 medals. Olympic victory became synonymous with the three Adidas stripes.

At the 1964 Summer Games in Tokyo, Adidas surreptitiously offered athletes cash bonuses for wearing its shoes. Although sponsorship payments were strictly banned by Brundage, whose nickname among athletes was "Slavery Avery," Adidas had ways of getting around the IOC's soul-saving strictures. American sprinter Henry Carr recalled transactions going down "like in the James Bond or mystery movies." An envelope-carrying Adidas rep would visit a predetermined bathroom stall. After the representative left the toilet, the athlete would slip in, pick up the envelope, and depart a wealthier amateur. "You get an envelope that had six, seven hundred or a couple of thousand dollars in fives and tens," Carr recalled. "You thought you were rich." Adidas's lavatory efforts paid handsome dividends; by the October 24 closing ceremonies, 99 athletes had medaled in Adidas shoes, far eclipsing the results turned in by Puma- and Tiger-shod contenders.[10]

Four years later, shoemakers like Adidas and Puma primed the marketing pump in advance of the 1968 Mexico City Games by showing up at the U.S. Olympic trials in Lake Tahoe and casually leaving envelopes full of cash in locker rooms. Olympians joked that the losers in Lake Tahoe were not the athletes who failed to qualify, but the schmucks who flew out of the Reno airport without a pocket full of shoe company cash.

Competition for Olympic eyeballs had become so fierce that in the run-up to the 1968 Games, Adidas was able to forge a blatantly illegal deal with the Mexican Olympic committee, giving the company exclusive rights to sell shoes in the Olympic Village. When Puma tried to ship a container of products to the Mexican capital, Mexican police kidnapped Puma representative Art Simburg as he walked through the Olympic Village. Simburg spent five days in jail without charges before the U.S. State Department freed the hapless salesman. Once he was out, the U.S. government was so concerned for Simburg's safety that it kept him under guard for the remainder of the proceedings. While the Mexico City Games were still technically run in the spirit of Coubertin's amateur ideal, events on the ground made it clear that the Olympics were making an impressive shift toward a profit-oriented value system that had little patience for quaint fiction-book principles about life and sports unburdened by fiscal striving.[11]

Olympic marketing attained astronomical reach on October 16, 1968, when American 200-meter-dash winner Tommie Smith and third-place finisher John Carlos mounted a Mexico City podium wearing black socks, black scarves, and black gloves. As the national anthem played, they raised clenched fists in solidarity with the oppressed at home and around the world. For Brundage, this assertion of human rights by two black Americans was an unforgivable violation of the Olympic oath. He immediately kicked the runners off the Olympic team. Brundage's firing trigger was primed by Smith and Carlos's earlier efforts to rally a boycott of the Games in protest of what they saw as IOC exploitation of amateur athletes while the organization itself raked in ever-increasing amounts of money. And though Smith and Carlos suffered, shoe manufacturers won. Wearing only socks in solidarity with those in the world who could not afford shoes, Smith brought a single Puma to the podium with him, where he placed it next to his feet. That single Puma shoe became an indelible element in one of the most resonant images in the history of American civil rights.

By the 1972 Munich Olympics, the notion that the Games were an amateur paradise plucked from the playing fields of *Chariots of Fire* was near farce. An American swimmer named Mark Spitz won seven gold medals. After Spitz won his second gold, Horst Dassler proposed that Adidas sponsor him. Horst was planning a new swimwear line called Arena. Getting Spitz to wear Adidas was a way for Arena—until then a small Spanish soccer ball company—to force its way onto the pool deck next to the dominant Australian swim gear maker Speedo. Although Spitz also agreed to a shoe deal, Horst still had a problem; swimmers wore sweatpants with wide leg bottoms so that they could quickly dress and undress poolside. The wide bottoms obscured the three-striped shoes on Spitz's feet. But Spitz and Horst devised a solution. After Spitz won his second gold medal, he stepped onto the podium with his Adidas shoes in hand—an unusual move for swimmers most often seen barefoot or in sandals. During the "Star Spangled Banner," Spitz dropped the shoes to his feet. Once the anthem finished, as cameras clattered and newsreels rolled, Spitz picked up his shoes and waved to the crowd.

The IOC was apoplectic. Spitz's blatant use of the Olympic podium as a product display case was too much to overlook, especially since the money changing hands for this demonstration was not going into an IOC bank account. Spitz escaped a threatened Olympic investigation due to Adidas's pull in Germany and because the IOC was unexpectedly confronted by a bigger terror. After his final event, Spitz, a Jew, was quickly spirited out of Germany due to concern he would be targeted by the Palestinian terrorists who had sneaked into the Olympic Village early in the morning of September 5 and killed 11.

After the Games, and after a speech in which Brundage equated the terrorist attacks with creeping pressure from commercialism—both forces that, in Brundage's words, threatened the IOC's efforts to keep the games "clear, pure, and honest"—Spitz retired from swimming.[12] Unleashed from the constraints of Olympic amateurism, he signed a professional sponsor deal with Arena. Three years later, at the swimming world championships in Cali, Colombia, some two-thirds of the swimmers wore Arena gear. Thanks to the star power the Olympics had granted Mark Spitz, Adidas's new swimwear line attained an industry-dominating position.[13]

According to the IOC, Olympic marketing programs put $2.63 billion in IOC bank accounts between 1992 and the 1996 Atlanta Olympics. By the 2012 London Olympics, that number had grown to $8.05 billion, with $3.85 billon of it coming from broadcasting rights. The rest came from items like ticket sales and from licensing rights associated with each Games location, such as the $65 million British Airways paid to sponsor the 2012 Games. The Olympic Partners (TOP) program licenses global rights to corporations. For instance, Coca-Cola is the Olympic Partner in the "Non-Alcoholic Beverages" category, while McDonald's pays for that honor in "Retail Food Services." One of the reasons the Olympics command such gargantuan payola is that the chivalric spirit upon which Coubertin built the games still persists, providing a flattering spotlight that corporations want to shine on themselves. No matter how tenuous the connections between Coubertin's morally restorative Games and the products and services those principles now sell, TOP is a cash cow for the IOC. TOP members pay in the neighborhood of $100 million to $200 million for the right to adorn their products and services with the five-ringed symbol of Coubertin's Olympic fantasy.[14]

Back in 1934, Mumford described how professional sports give fans aesthetic pleasure and a sense of connection with something larger than themselves. He pointed out that as sports become bigger and more professional, they strive to eliminate chance, because randomness and luck—essential elements of fair play—are antithetical to the professional obligation to win at any cost. Sports for sports' sake becomes an exhibition for commerce's sake. "Instead of 'Fair Play,'" he wrote, "the rule now becomes 'Success at Any Price.'" While the Olympics were just on the cusp of realizing their massive commercial potential in 1935, Mumford saw that for sports, with their millions of dollars invested in arenas and equipment and players, the task of maintaining their profit-generating potential would become as important as in any other business or ethical concern. "Sport is always a means," he wrote, the aim of which is to "gather a record-breaking crowd of performers and spectators" and thereby proclaim the importance of both the competition at hand and the companies that underwrite the myth of sports' essential goodness.

As Mumford presciently noted, the informal games and races that initially arose on weekend fields and country lanes as a way for Industrial Revolution–era workers to blow off steam almost immediately became professionalized. The business maintenance of sports and the specialization of its elite athletes assumed elements of the industrial era's "regimentation of life—for the sake of private profits or nationalistic exploit."[15] And in this marshaling of efficiencies in the interest of victory lay the impossibility of chemical purity for athletes.

In 1962, sports doctors from 14 European countries convened in Strasbourg and Madrid to discuss their nascent concerns about doping in sports. At this early gathering of sports medicine experts, the doctors frankly admitted that, regardless of what evidence might be discovered regarding harm caused by drugs, commercial forces would almost certainly see these revelations as a threat to their brand equity. At a subsequent 1963 meeting on doping in sports, Dr. Antonio Venerando, president of the Italian Federation of Sports Medicine, observed that as of late 1963, international sports federations had only paid attention to doping cases in exceptional instances, and then only "for the sake of publicity rather than with any intention of getting to the root of the evil." As described in a 1964 Council of Europe (CoE) report on these working meetings, he added, "In some countries doping is undertaken almost officially with a view to ensuring brilliant performances and the establishment of records which can be exploited in the field of international politics regardless of the consequences to the individual athlete."[16] (Founded in 1949, the CoE is an umbrella organization of European countries that came together in the postwar years to promote a more humane version of Europe than what its denizens witnessed during the savagery of World War II.) Already in 1963, observers like Venerando knew that getting rid of doping would be a hard sell if it interfered with sports commerce or nationalistic interests. The obligations inherent to a corporation's need to grow or a nation's desire to expand its influence were about to radically complicate society's conflicted, and radically changing, attitudes about the rightness or wrongness of drugs in sport.

CHAPTER 4

THE HOT ROMAN DAY WHEN DOPING BECAME BAD

While few within organized sports expressed concern about the use of performance-enhancing drugs until the 1960s, there was some early unease. A December 1, 1895, *New York Times* editorial, "The Use of Stimulants by Athletes: Drugs Designed for This Purpose Not Favored," took drug manufacturers to task for marketing their products to athletes. Appealing to notions of athletic purity, the piece argued that while "the alert mind of the modern drug manufacturer" had taken note of the growing popularity of sports like cycling and football, "all true athletes would disdain any such injurious and adventitious aids." The *Times* opinion writer disapproved of performance-enhancing drugs on two grounds: one, they could be injurious to health; and two, they gave athletes an advantage "true" sportsmen would frown upon. Perhaps influenced by the same aristocratic, class-preserving "trueness" Coubertin admired, the editorial concluded that innocent amateurs should stay away from the pros' methods because drugs are somehow inherently wrong: "The general effect of drug taking, and especially of the use of drugs belonging to the caffeine and cocaine class, is distinctly bad. We believe that the medical profession ought seriously to warn those with whom they come in contact professionally against the use of such things."

In 1928, 33 years after the *Times* warned readers of the undefined dangers of adventitious substances, the first whisper of anti-doping made its way into an official sporting regulation when an anti-drug statement appeared in the regulations of the International Amateur Athletics Federation (IAAF). Founded in 1912 by Sigfrid Edström, a Swedish industrialist who made his fortune in tramlines and electric motor manufacturing, the IAAF was born the same year that Edström's influence helped bring the Olympics to Stockholm. A talented runner in his youth, Edström's wealth and starched-shirted belief in amateurism helped him become an IOC member in 1920 and IOC president in 1942.

Edström clamped down on amateurs who collected race appearance fees. During its annual convention in 1928, the IAAF executive council passed strict rules outlawing athlete compensation. At the same time, the IAAF wrote what may be the sport's first anti-drug regulation. Roughly a quarter century after drugs were prohibited in horse racing, the rule defined doping as "the use of any stimulant not normally employed to increase the power of action in athletic competition above the average."[1] As vague as it was obscure, the new IAAF regulation targeted those who administered drugs, not athletes. Its passing stirred barely a ripple of press coverage, although a July 28, 1928, article on the opening of the Amsterdam Olympic Games in the *New York Times* did briefly mention the new doping ban. A sentence in the piece explained that a recent IAAF congress had debated a "proposal to suspend from amateur athletics any person involved in giving competitors 'drugs or stimulants internally by hypodermic or other methods.'"[2]

This information, however, was but one sentence buried in a long piece on an ongoing controversy over whether University of Southern California track star Charley Paddock would be allowed to compete in

Amsterdam. Paddock had angered the high priests of amateurism by insisting that his work as a sports columnist for the *Los Angeles Times* and as a Hollywood actor did not violate Olympic values. As Paddock saw it, the critical difference that preserved amateur status was that he was paid to write about sports but received no compensation for the act of playing in sports. In the eyes of the U.S. Amateur Athletic Union (AAU), the writing earnings polluted Paddock's amateur purity and threatened the social bulwark separating the working pro from the sportsman of leisure. As historians John Gleaves and Matthew Llewellyn explain in a 2013 study of this early IAAF drug rule, amateurs were expected to maintain an ideal: "The Olympic amateur played the game for the game's sake, disavowing gambling and professionalism, and competed in a composed dignified manner fitting of a 'gentleman.'" By working in sports-related roles, Paddock failed his obligation to uphold these patrician standards.[3]

The *New York Times* mentioned the new doping regulation to put a fine point on its larger exploration of amateurism, specifically the fear that professional sporting practices—and lower-class habits—were infiltrating amateur games. For Olympic organizations, the incursion of the trappings of professionalism into amateur sports—whether by making money commenting on sports or using professional sports medicine practices—was scandalous. At least on paper, the new IAAF rule seemed to come down hard on the trainers and doctors who administered performance-enhancing drugs because they were symptomatic of the professional practices that amateur governing bodies wanted to keep out of their sports. Paddock's hassles with the IAAF and AAU made a public display of efforts to wall off amateur sports from the "corrupting" influence of money and professional drug practices. As Gleaves and Llewellyn write, for those worried about protecting upper-class ease through amateur sports, the doping habits of working-class cyclists, boxers, and runners "only served to reinforce their belief that their place in the social order was well deserved."[4] Paddock's work caused alarm because it was close to his actual sport and thus threatened to puncture the wall separating doped pros from chivalric and pure amateurs.*

Thirteen years after the IAAF published its first stricture against drugs as a symptom of professionalism, the problem of how to be competitive on international sporting fields without pro-level support came to a head at the 1936 Berlin Games. After Hitler's Olympic extravaganza, the IOC fielded complaints that German teams were amateurs in name only. While they technically were not paid to train and compete, they had all the support of professional athletes, but without the obligations that came with holding an outside job. The neologism "shamateurism" came to describe a system in which government or private support allows an athlete to train full time, without having to hold a job to pay the rent and grocery bills. Critics claimed the Nazi athletes were sham amateurs.

Responding to the complaints, IOC president Henri de Baillet-Latour, a wealthy Belgian horse racing aficionado and past president of the Brussels Jockey Club, wrote an essay expressing the opinion that doping was contrary to amateurism. "Amateur sport is meant to improve the soul and the body," the IOC boss wrote. "No stone must be left unturned as long as the use of doping has not been stamped out. Doping ruins the health and very likely implies an early death." According to Gleaves and Llewellyn, this 1937 opinion is the first-ever IOC proclamation regard-

---

* While 1928 image management meant keeping pros and their ways out, in the early 2000s, damage control took the form of massive bribes to let embarrassingly doped podium placers off the hook. In 2015, it came to light that IAAF officials hid systematic athlete doping in Russia. A January 2016 World Anti-Doping Agency (WADA) independent commission report revealed that Russian runner and 2010 London Marathon winner Liliya Shobukhova paid €450,000 to IAAF officials to keep a 2011 suspicious blood test result under wraps and preserve her place in the 2012 London Olympics. The same report explained that out of 7,177 EPO tests performed on IAAF athletes between 2001 and 2009, nearly 9 percent returned atypical blood samples. Three hundred and nine of those suspicious samples came from medal winners, yet only 67 were sanctioned. While an atypical blood sample does not automatically equate to doping, 88 years after the IAAF first took steps to keep professionals' doping from tainting its amateur sheen, IAAF officials still seemed set on protecting their public image. A separate November 2015 WADA report concluded that IAAF corruption was pervasive and that drug maleficence in its Russian member federation "was an embedded and institutionalized process designed to secure winning at any cost." As a result of the scandal, IAAF sponsor Adidas severed its sponsorship relationship with the IAAF with four years remaining on its 11-year contract. See "The Independent Commission Report #1," WADA, November 9, 2015; "The Independent Commission Report #2," WADA, January 14, 2016.

ing drugs in Olympic sports. Like the 1928 IAAF note, the first-recorded IOC comment on drugs in sports was not so much a declaration against doping as against the creeping inroads of professionalism and a threat to social stratifications. It is also likely that Baillet-Latour's background in horse racing, where doping had long been a problem, inspired his special interest in human performance-enhancing drugs, since drug taking could threaten the Olympics' identity as a place where sports were practiced for the sake of goodwill among men, not financial gain.[5]

In advance of the IOC's 1938 annual meeting in Cairo, Egypt, the organization commissioned several reports on the state of doping in sports. The Belgian Medical Society for Physical Education and Sport wrote one of these papers. Titled "Rapport sur le doping" (Doping report), it matter-of-factly pointed out what everyone knew but saw little reason to condemn: "In professional sports, in cycling above all, doping is practiced on a grand scale." The report argued that in Olympic sports, doping should be condemned because "it creates a mentality contradictory to the true spirit of sports."[6] That true spirit, of course, was the class-order-preserving ethos venerated by grandees calling the shots at the British-dominated IAAF. As Coubertin reflected in 1925, "the fundamental condition" of the British sports club is one of social exclusion; "members are *gentlemen of the same station.*"[7]

The reports pointed to a level of doping that most certainly threatened to infect gentlemen with the workingman's chemicals. After reviewing these reports and acknowledging that drugs in pro sports were as common as water, on March 17, 1938, the IOC adopted its first formal statement against drugs in Olympic sports. However, in 1938, protecting sporting amateurism was beginning to seem like a small and self-indulgent problem relative to the unhinging taking place as the world's nations girded for war. With London, Dresden, and Tokyo burning, the IOC's official statement on doping gathered dust. It was not until after the defeat of Germany and Japan in 1945 that the IOC got back to business and published a new official Olympic charter in 1946. But even then, the IOC's updated delineation of its official functions and obligations treated doping as a minor subset of the organization's crowning challenge—maintaining the sanctity of amateurism.

Item six in an Olympic charter section titled "Resolutions Regarding the Amateur Status" proclaimed: "The use of drugs or artificial stimulants of any kind must be condemned most strongly, and everyone who accepts or offers dope, no matter in what form, should not be allowed to participate in amateur meetings or in the Olympic Games."[8] And that was all the IOC needed to say about doping, because the meaning was clear to everyone affiliated with the Games: If you use drugs or supply drugs to amateurs, you have crossed the threshold to professionalism and are therefore no longer welcome in the Olympic family. After all, as the 1938 Cairo report acknowledged, in vocational sports like cycling, doping was "practiced on a grand scale." The IOC's raison d'être was to tack constantly away from professionalism, not pass judgment on what professional athletes did.

The 1946 Olympic charter's single condemnation of doping was submerged among nine other entries detailing how athletes should not be paid, housed, fed, and otherwise financially supported in a way that would lead them into the moral perdition of professionalism. The 1946 charter included zero guidance on which chemical substances were unacceptable, how to go about identifying dopers, the consequences of ignoring the recommendation, or how enforcement would be organized and funded. The rule was therefore not so much a law equipped with implementation mechanisms as a signpost warning Olympic athletes to not go down the chemical road to professionalism. The IOC's commitment to building a wall between amateurs and pros was so fierce that matters of drug use kept their position in the charter as a subset of amateur protection rules all the way until 1975. That was the year the first IOC Medical Commission was created, and with it, drug use moved from the protection-focused general charter to the IOC medical code.

So what finally pushed the IOC to look at doping as an issue separate from protecting amateurism? One reason was that as pro sports grew in popularity, it became difficult to find amateur athletes who did not emulate their professional heroes' sports medicine and racing techniques. At some point, the IOC could not continue to pretend that its amateurs were not embracing professional doping habits. A 1964 report commissioned by the Council of Europe (CoE) cited an Italian survey of amateur cyclists conducted during the 1962 and 1963 race seasons. The organization reported that at the 1962 Italian amateur road championships, 14 of the top 30 finishers tested positive for drugs—46.6 percent positive among a group of non-pro riders who had been told in advance of the race that they would take part in a drug survey. Prior to that, in 1955, the Federazione Medico Sportiva Italiana tested the urine of 25 cyclists during an Italian stage race, and 20 percent were positive for amphetamines.[9]

But while the pervasiveness of doping in amateur sports was becoming too obvious for the IOC to ignore, it was a death at the 1960 Rome Olympics that forced the organization to pay sharper attention to the anti-doping rule that had been sitting quietly ignored on its books since 1938.

The 100-kilometer cycling team time trial was held on Friday, August 26, 1960, a day that saw thermometers passing the 100-degree mark along Rome's Viale dell'Oceano Pacifico. Rolling out between the Portuguese and Moroccan squads, the four-man Danish team was 33rd to start. At 9:33 a.m., the Roman sun was already punishing the softening blacktop. Falling quickly into a tempo, the Danish squad finished the first of three 32.2-kilometer laps with the fourth-best time of the day.

Then things went wrong. After passing the first time check in front of the Rome velodrome, Dane Jørgen Jørgensen dropped out; the heat was too much. Then one of the remaining three riders, Knud Enemark Jensen, began complaining of dizziness. His teammates, Vagn Bangsborg and Niels Baunsøe, rode next to the 23-year-old from Ärhus. A Danish news photographer's photo shows Bangsborg and Baunsøe riding on either side of Jensen with their hands pulling him forward by the back of his jersey. With race number 127 crinkling on Jensen's hip, the two teammates suspended the collapsing Jensen like a bicycle marionette. Their efforts were for naught. Jensen had succumbed to heatstroke. A photo in Denmark's *Ekstra Bladet* newspaper caught Jensen spilling from his bike and landing on his head.

An ambulance rushed Jensen to a medical tent. Lacking air conditioning, the dark canvas military tent was like a sauna. Interior temperatures reached an estimated 120 to 130°F. Today we know that proper treatment for the heat-stricken Jensen would have been to submerge him in an ice bath to lower his core body temperature. Instead, he got the opposite. Jensen broiled in the canvas oven for two hours. Then he died.[10]

Though Italian authorities will not release it to this day, the official autopsy reportedly attributed the first death in modern Olympic history to heatstroke, which was probably not helped by Jensen's head injury and the fact that he was severely dehydrated on a day that saw 31 other riders suffer from the same debilitating condition. The Danish riders did not carry water on their bikes; the coaches thought bottles would be too heavy. Of course, racing 62 miles in 100-degree temperatures without fluids is a recipe for physical collapse.[11]

From a physiological perspective, placing Jensen in an oven rather than an ice bath was tantamount to putting him in a coffin and nailing the lid shut when he still had a chance of survival. Properly treated heatstroke victims can be back on their feet within an hour of collapse. But left untreated, heatstroke leads to a catastrophic chain of events that includes organ failure, cardiac arrest, and cardiac stroke as the body shuts down in an effort to cope with severe physiological imbalances. As one sports medicine textbook explains, "Delay in initiating cooling makes heatstroke a potentially fatal condition."[12]

Had the press reports of the day stuck to the autopsy, Jensen's death by heat probably would have remained a somber Olympic footnote. However, the Dane's demise took on sinister overtones when the team trainer, Oluf Jørgensen, told Jensen's attending doctors that he had given his riders a vascular dilation drug called Roniacol before the race. Jørgensen had no reason to hide this fact. Although anti-doping rules were technically on the books, it was common knowledge that athletes took drugs to compete, that no one was tested, and that as long as an athlete was not openly flaunting race earnings at the Olympics, he had little to worry about concerning drug use in the Games. The chairman of the Dutch cycling federation, Piet van Dijk, reportedly said athletes were using "cartloads" of dope that year in Rome—"in royal quantities."[13]

After Jørgensen mentioned drugs, the press gathered in Rome lost interest in reporting the obvious and medically documented cause of Jensen's death—dehydration, heatstroke, a head injury, and emergency services that raised his core temperature at exactly the time when it needed to be lowered. Even though Jensen's autopsy did not mention the presence of drugs in his blood, a myth took hold that Jensen had amphetamines in his system. Drugs—not the rise in core temperature and subsequent catastrophic organ failure—became the popularly reported killer. Drugs gave Jensen's death a darkly dramatic angle that made it irresistible to the press. The Olympic scribes tailored their reports of this tragic turn of Olympic events for ominous effect.

In response to Jensen's death and the subsequent media eruption, in 1962 the IOC created a medical commission to examine doping in Olympic sports. In 1967, it assigned Prince Alexandre de Mérode, a Belgian with no medical experience, to lead the drug study group. The commission oversaw the first Olympic drug tests. They were rolled out at the 1968 Winter Games in Grenoble, France, and that year's Summer Games in Mexico City, where Swedish pentathlete Hans-Gunnar Liljenwall became the first Olympic competitor to be suspended for doping. For decades, anti-doping sentiments had remained a quiet subset of the IOC's obsession with amateurism; it was not until Jensen's death that the IOC made its first timid exhortations against doping, early protests that eventually inflated the 1946 anti-doping statement into a full-blown anti-doping industry with its own policies, procedures, and global bureaucracies, along with a tractable fleet of reporters channeling fresh winds of anti-doping moral outrage.

Short on facts but packed with speculative projections, media reports on Jensen's death became so ingrained in the public consciousness that they turned up in U.S. congressional testimony, used wrongly as evidence of the lethal effect of performance-enhancing drugs. During hearings held in 1973 on drug abuse in America, University of Oklahoma athletics physician Donald Cooper referred to Jensen's death as evidence that mixing doping and sports can kill. Jensen's death entered the congressional record when Senator Birch Bayh asked Cooper for cases in which amphetamines were "linked with serious injury or fatalities." Cooper responded, "There are reports in the literature; yes, in fact I think you will find in the 1960 Olympics there was a cyclist, a Belgian cyclist, where it happened."[14] Illustrating the secondhand nature of his testimony, Cooper got Jensen's nationality wrong. His citation of a death that had little, if anything, to do with drugs and much to do with bad trauma care illustrates the degree to which the Danish cyclist's demise took on a sinister life of its own. What was truly ominous—the lack of proper emergency care that could have saved Jensen's life—was not the story American lawmakers heard. Instead, it was the mangled parroting of a media fabrication—granted credibility by dint of the Oklahoma physician's medical training and athletic authority—that resonated with politicians, journalists, and the public. Jensen's death became one of the earliest examples in the American historical record of the dangers of doping in sport, even though it should have been evidence of the danger of practicing endurance sports in extreme heat without properly trained medical technicians on hand.

As Paul Dimeo put it in *A History of Drug Use in Sport, 1876–1976,* Jensen's reputation continued "to be sullied by those eager to use his body as proof of the health risks of doping" long after his death.[15] In his painstakingly researched account of Jensen's death and its manipulation, Verner Møller points out that because Jensen's demise "became a symbol of unethical behavior," journalists and doping researchers alike were more interested in the mythology that served their growing prohibitionary impulses than in locating facts.[16] The drug fabrication served political, economic, and social interests that heatstroke did not.

A rational assessment of Jensen's death would lead one to believe that the incident should have encouraged the IOC authorities to pass rules demanding better medical care and better monitoring of life-endangering weather conditions during competition. Instead, Jensen's death by heatstroke became the foundational event for today's anti-doping organizations. Indeed, as late as 2015, the World Anti-Doping Agency's website referred to an autopsy that revealed "traces of amphetamines" in Jensen's blood, even though no evidence exists for this claim, since the actual final autopsy report was never seen. Møller speculates that the report may stay under lock and key to this day because revealing it might be embarrassing to Italian medical authorities.

In keeping with the moral import of Coubertin's original quasi-theological project, Jensen's death helped give doping a menacing social weight greater than mere athlete health. The pan-European CoE bureaucracy was one of the first to embrace the notion that sports doping represented a social evil that, if left unchecked, would rend the fabric of society. With Jensen's death hanging in the public consciousness, in 1963, the CoE held its early anti-doping conferences in Strasbourg and Madrid. A 1964 report on the meetings described medical experts from 14 European countries (Russia and East Germany were noticeably absent) joining to discuss "the gravity of the problem and the value attached to combatting this menace by means of a joint European approach."[17] Meeting resolutions described doping as "a social evil having ramifications far beyond the realm of sport." Seeing which way the social and bureaucratic winds were blowing, the IOC agreed at its annual congress in 1964 to formally condemn drug use and instruct its national Olympic organizing bodies to let their athletes know they might be tested.

Jensen's death and these early meetings of European bureaucracies marked a change in the paradigm of drugs as substances that helped realize the optimistic vision of science at the service of human potential. Instead, doping was being redefined as an evil. Dimeo writes that these early 1960s events "set in place the modernization of anti-doping; a system that rigidly enforced moral values through scientific testing, legal restrictions, and bureaucratic procedures."[18]

Jensen's death created pressure on sports federations in places like Belgium, Holland, and Spain to take a harder look at the drug use that had always been present in bike racing, a sport that had long had an important role in those countries. The federations looked to the CoE to bring together scientific and legal experts to help them figure out how to manage a practice that after decades of being accepted as a pro trade tool was now being characterized as a threat to national moral hygiene.

In cycling, the 1964 CoE report concluded that doping had "already begun to undermine the whole structure of the sport." And since sports were understood to be both a mirror of life and preparation for it, "If doping is allowed to grow unchecked, the time will come when all the benefits accruing to the individual and to the community from the practice of sport will be lost."[19] The CoE did not provide evidence why the doping that had been an accepted part of cycling since the 1870s had suddenly become morally corrosive. Indeed, only 21 years earlier, American College of Sports Medicine founder Peter Karpovich had argued that "ergogenic aids" that improve performance without harm "can hardly be called unethical." After Jensen's death, such an opinion was out of joint with the changing spirit of the times.[20] Arguing against the position that doping is evil would soon be tantamount to defending a murder or rape; all were indefensible, a priori sins.

The CoE report dictated who held the bureaucratic capacity and paternalistic weight to build an anti-doping infrastructure. "The European community is particularly well endowed with the specialized technological, judicial, and medical savoir-faire to abolish the practice of doping and thus protect its own peoples and give a lead to the world," it concluded. The European sports doctors and administrators that the CoE had brought together in Strasbourg and Madrid were charged with an obligation to protect young athletes from doping pressures outside their control.

Historians like Dimeo and Møller have shown that just as athletes dared not spit in the doping soup that fed them, anti-doping authorities were reluctant to admit evidence that would reveal weaknesses in the nurturing fable of pure sports. By the mid-1970s, attitudes toward doping, which first celebrated the union of man and technology, and then began to worry about the potential health risks of overtaxing the human machine with stimulants, fell into two opposing camps. Dimeo describes them as "morality-driven pedagogues and scientists" on one side and athletes, drug suppliers, and innovative pharmacologists on the other.[21] The good-versus-evil frame of reference being constructed around doping was woven into the tone of the CoE report's language. "Doping is a dangerous form of moral deception," the conference attendees concluded. Because the consequences go beyond sports, "apathy on the part of those morally responsible is a crime against humanity."[22]

The CoE's approach to doping in the early 1960s set the stage for the doping battles that continue today. Rather than defining and managing drugs in sports as a health risk alongside more prevalent dangers like heatstroke, heart attacks, and head injuries, the CoE conferences helped turn a previously unremarkable practice into a moral panic that played on broader social worries. As we'll see, those anxieties had to do with the larger youth and social revolutions roiling Europe and the United States in the 1960s. The solutions that came out of those first conferences in Strasbourg and Madrid helped build the foundation for heavily bureaucratic and self-protecting anti-doping institutions that were unique to Europe, and that did not take root in the pharmaceutically laissez-faire United States until the creation of the U.S. Anti-Doping Agency in 2000.

Anti-doping policy and implementation became the domain of scientists and administrators, people who looked for solutions in rationalist, bureaucratic ways; in their view, more testing, more research, and better science would solve doping in sports. Yet these solutions were difficult to apply to a tradition with causes rooted in a century of social and economic history, not biological pathologies that could be eliminated if only science could find the right antidote. As Dimeo puts it, under the gaze of the growing pack of government-supported anti-doping organizations in Europe, "Athletes were either clean or they were guilty, they were good or evil, there was no middle ground and no scope for ethical dilemmas."[23]

According to Møller's research, Jensen's rumor-driven death-by-amphetamine story ossified into accepted fact because journalists and historians handed the story from one to the other without bothering to check primary sources. It was a house of cards that hardened into an unassailable edifice of "truth." One example of this rewriting of history to forward a preferred bureaucratic agenda can be found in the 2002 cautionary book on sports doping, *Dying to Win*. A Council of Europe publication, the book claims "Jensen collapsed and died at the Rome Olympic Games during the 175 km team time trials following his use of amphetamines and nicotine acid."[24] Apart from the fact that the time trial was 100 kilometers, not 175, author Barrie Houlihan pushes the unsubstantiated claim that not only Jensen but also two of his teammates had amphetamines in their systems.

Born of good intentions, *Dying to Win* forwarded the CoE's paternalistic agenda. Houlihan, a respected sports science professor, did not mention the 31 other cyclists who suffered heatstroke during the 1960 Rome time trial. Instead he focused on Jensen's death by a drug that was never proven to be in his system. The CoE effort to warn athletes of the dangers of drugs—dying to win—promulgated the false terms of Jensen's death tale and illustrates how both journalists and historians could write history in a way that fit a preconceived moral narrative.

Even Robert Voy, the U.S. Olympic Committee's chief medical officer during the 1988 Seoul Olympics, fell back on a manufactured version of Jensen's story. Voy is no canting acolyte, yet in his well-researched 1991 book *Drugs, Sport, and Politics*, he wrote that Jensen died "during the 175.38-km road race" while riding under the influence of "a combination of nicotynal alchol and amphetamine, sarcastically nicknamed by his competitors the 'Knud Jensen diet.'"[25] Besides confusing the road race distance with the team time trial distance, Voy's account shows that even well-intentioned physicians could easily turn to a rough assemblage of rumor to support the post-1960s received wisdom that sports doping is fatal to moral and physical health.

Austrian doctor and sports scientist Ludwig Prokop also helped foster the seedling notion that doping represented a significant moral risk to society at large. A prominent member of the European sports medicine community and a leader of early anti-doping efforts, Prokop led the University of Vienna's Institute for Sports Science for three decades and was an IOC Medical Commission member who served in 26 Olympic Games. Seeing syringes in locker rooms at the 1954 Innsbruck Winter Olympics triggered Prokop's lifelong interest in drugs in sports. Even though there was only circumstantial evidence that drugs played a role, Jensen's 1960 death compounded the Austrian's fear that performance-enhancing drugs were getting out of control. Prokop had conducted experiments with performance-enhancing drugs in 1956 and concluded that any benefit came from a placebo effect rather than the pharmaceuticals. His conclusion that drugs did not make athletes stronger or faster added to his sense that using them was a risk not balanced by any quantitative return other than potential physical harm. He felt that sports governing bodies should act.

Prokop's physician's duty to look out for the health of his patients fused with an impulse to protect athletes from their darker human and social selves and protect the Coubertinian notion of sports as character builder. As Prokop put it in the proceedings of a 1964 sports science conference in Tokyo, sports must shield athletes from drugs to "prevent sporting ideals and values from becoming falsified." Even when doping was not dangerous to the athlete's health, Prokop argued that it "must be regarded primarily as a sporting and not a medical problem." Doping, he concluded, could be regarded "as a dangerous fraud."[26] Like the conclusions of many members of the growing anti-doping establishment, Prokop's scientific judgments were clouded by a quest for social purity that was driven as much by emotion as rationality. As Møller writes, Prokop's desire to get doping out of sports "led him to make unsubstantiated claims" in the service of his cause.[27] Because of Prokop's stature in the scientific community, his statements that drugs killed Jensen became accepted as fact, even though the amphetamine claims are based on hearsay.[28] In the years following Jensen's death, this was a new phenomenon—a physician's concern for athletes' health becoming intertwined with an evangelical desire to protect sports and society from moral corruption. The fudging of the truth about Jensen's death is important in the history of doping in sports not so much because he became known as the first to die from drugs, but rather because of the way his death was unmoored from fact to serve a moral cause. In many respects, the early 1960s marks an irreversible turn of scientists, bureaucratic functionaries, historians, and journalists from proscience and prohealth researchers into moral evangelists.

Prokop wrote the official IOC report on Jensen's death. In it, he claimed amphetamines and Roniacol (pyridylcarbinol) caused the death. Prokop cited an official Italian postmortem from 1960 as the source for the report's claim that Jensen died with amphetamines in his system. However, in 1961, Italian authorities produced a report that indicated that drugs did not play a role in Jensen's death. As Møller puts it, the amphetamines in Prokop's IOC report seem to be based on a "haphazard guess" rather than any observed evidence.[29] The doctor had circumstantial evidence for the Roniacol, since the team trainer stated he administered that drug to his riders. However, the trainers did not mention amphetamines. As neither drug was illegal at the time, there would have been no punishment for telling the whole truth. It seems odd that the trainers would only reveal part of their sports medicine regime when trying to help doctors understand what happened to Jensen and his teammates—two of whom also collapsed in the heat.

Twelve years after Jensen's death, Prokop was sticking to his interpretation of Jensen's death, writing in 1972 that Jensen "broke down and died during the Olympics in Rome as a result of an overdose of amphetamine and Roniacol."[30] In 2001, however, Prokop admitted that he had never seen an autopsy linking Jensen's death to drugs. "Perhaps it was wrong of me to draw it out in the report," Prokop told Danish journalist Lars Bøgeskov, who was investigating the Jensen story. Prokop also asserted to Bøgeskov that while it might have been wrong of him to draw conclusions without evidence, in the long run, it was worth it because Jensen's "death initiated the fight against doping."[31]

Ironically, the Roniacol element of Jensen's death did support Prokop's general claim that drugs and sports can be lethal. However, with their attention diverted by nonexistent amphetamines, media and medical researchers never accurately followed up on the Roniacol angle. A vascular dilator, pyridylcarbinol was thought to improve performance by increasing blood flow to muscles. However, by expanding blood vessels, the drug also lowers blood pressure, which can accelerate dehydration and lead to the sort of dizziness, disorientation, and even organ failure that Jensen suffered in Rome. Given Jensen's overheated core temperature, a scientific argument could be made that Roniacol could have contributed to death by heatstroke. When combined with the Olympic first responders baking Jensen for the last two hours of his life, drugs may indeed have contributed to Jensen's death—only evidence does not point to the demon stimulant that spawned today's anti-doping organizations as the culprit.

In fact, an argument can be made that had he taken them before the race, amphetamines might have saved Jensen's life. Møller points out that one of Jensen's teammates, Niels Baunsøe, suffered no ill effects. If Baunsøe had used amphetamines along with Roniacol, the effect of the amphetamines could have countered the performance-degrading effects of Roniacol. While Roniacol causes vascular expansion, amphetamine sparks release of noradrenaline, a hormone that triggers vascular contraction. If it were the case that Jensen took only Roniacol while Baunsøe took that drug plus amphetamines, Møller suggests that it "seems more likely that the use of amphetamine helped or even saved Baunsøe than it is that it killed Jensen."[32] Absolute proof exists that the riders raced in extreme heat and without water. Their trainer's word provides evidence that they were all on Roniacol. The combination of these three factors can cause lethal dehydration. No evidence exists to suggest that the riders also used amphetamines. However, at the physiological level, the first three factors plus amphetamines would be less lethal than those three alone—an inconvenient possibility that undermines the simple narrative that any and all performance-enhancing drugs are bad. Growing hysteria about drugs in sports was getting in the way of a measured analysis of their actual risks and benefits—even precluding the possibility that drugs could be helpful at all. More importantly, in the interest of promoting an anti-doping agenda, the posthumous focus on amphetamines permanently turned public attention away from what was a mountain of evidence pointing to the likely cause of Jensen's death: bad emergency medical care.

As for Jensen's autopsy report, it is still inaccessible. After Jensen died, his body was spirited off to the Istituto di Medicina Legale for an autopsy by three Italian doctors. After four days, the Italians shipped his body to Copenhagen for burial—and then radio silence from Italy. The IOC sent repeated letters to Italian and Danish officials asking for the results of the autopsy, but they got nothing. It was not until seven months after Jensen's death that the IOC received official word from Italy: Jensen died of heatstroke, and there were no drugs in his system. The actual autopsy report never saw the light of day.

Today, Møller is a professor in the Faculty of Health at Aarhus University, where his research focuses on teasing out the truth from a sports doping history that is muddied with political and moral ambitions and economic incentives. From his office in Denmark, Møller told me the anti-doping campaigners who were inspired by Jensen's death are like early Amazon missionaries. Before the arrival of the Christians, Møller said, cyclists were like indigenous peoples living "with completely different notions and ideas and values." The missionaries showed up and pronounced, "We need to do something to save these people from themselves and their beliefs, and we want to christen them." Missionaries were not anthropologists interested in suspending their own prejudices in the interest of understanding foreign ways. They, like the early generations of anti-doping evangelists, were there to impose an ideology on people who never asked to be saved. In Møller's opinion, the ride-clean rhetoric some riders began to proclaim was a self-preserving feint. "Like Indians who said, 'Well, we don't want to be shot here, so we'll start saying that we are Christians,'" he thinks cyclists talked pure sports and then, once the anti-doping evangelists turned away, went "back to praying to their previous gods, or their real gods. They tried to say what the missionaries wanted to hear because they were in a disadvantaged position." Møller's research leads him to conclude that the messianic zeal of many anti-doping researchers and sports functionaries impeded their ability to get to the facts of Jensen's death, in part because those facts did not serve the needs of the growing anti-doping mission. A rider who died from heatstroke is not a useful symbolic foundation for an anti-doping campaign.

Møller's analogy of Christian missionaries imposing alien values on an isolated tribe is apt. During the first hundred or so years of cycling, society took it for granted that science at the service of higher human performance—including pharmaceutical science—was a moral good. From tuberculosis to penicillin to polio, drugs had improved human life in astonishingly positive ways. This link between science and goodness also held true for cycling, since it was the first sport truly born of a technological invention. "Man is extremely innovative," Møller told me. "Cycling is the first genuine, modern sport, in that it is related to the invention of a machine which expanded mankind's ability to travel the world by his own powers." Science was beneficial, and chemicals were part of science. "We could create a brave new world which was fantastic because of science," Møller said. And, of course, this technical virtuousness could also be applied to sports other than cycling.

The same year Jensen died, society's optimism about pharmaceutical science and faith in the motives of drug makers began to crack under the weight of a catastrophe—thalidomide. Photographs began appearing in newspapers showing babies born with severe birth defects—no limbs, no eyes, extra appendages growing from shoulders. Sold over the counter to pregnant mothers as an anti-nausea treatment, the drug developed by West German pharmaceutical company Chemie Grünenthal was causing thousands of birth defects and stillbirths in the more than 40 countries where the product had been sold since 1957. Thalidomide was eventually blamed for severe abnormalities in more than 10,000 newborns. However, it wasn't until 1961 that the chemical's full horrors would be disclosed. Until then, the public bobbed along on a bright current of faith in science and misplaced trust that pharmaceutical companies would put human safety first.

The horrors of the thalidomide disaster profoundly complicated our attitude toward the role drugs play in society. The miraculous pharmaceutical inventions that ended the nightmare of polio could also create appalling new disfigurements. And as society at large was forced to reexamine its celebratory attitudes toward drugs, inside the world of sports, bureaucracies were born that forced a similar reanalysis of the wisdom of the everyday nature of drugs for improved performance. Although thalidomide caused quantifiable death and harm that led to the establishment of stricter drug safety approval procedures, in sports, newly emerging anti-doping systems were based more on emotion than evidence.

CHAPTER 5

DOPING BECOMES A CRIME

On July 18, 1955, a French bicycle racer named Jean Malléjac collapsed on the arid slopes of Mont Ventoux. Tour de France physician Pierre Dumas recognized Malléjac's symptoms: heatstroke amplified by an amphetamine overdose. With Dumas's aid, Malléjac survived and returned for the 1956 Tour. Race organizers later dismissed Malléjac's soigneur, who reportedly administered the drugs. However, to protect the Tour de France image, they did so without mentioning why the soigneur was let go.

Doctor Dumas's firsthand experience with potentially lethal drug effects made him one of the earliest to raise doping alarms. The physician also knew drug use was a regular part of cycling and French culture. Although amphetamines became prescription-only drugs in France in 1955, they remained wildly popular and were used for weight loss, energy restoration, and as an anti-depressant. Into the late 1960s, a bottle of amphetamine "pep" pills was as common as aspirin in European and American medicine cabinets.

Popular acceptance of amphetamines, combined with the way the drug dulled sensations of fatigue and upped one's sense of willpower, made injecting or swallowing speed before competition a pre-race custom. As historian Christopher Thompson writes in *The Tour de France*, nightly rounds of team hotel rooms gave Dumas firsthand knowledge of the rich array of substances riders used to prepare and recover. Tour de France riders were as cavalier about leaving their *rendement* (productivity) supplies strewn about their rooms as a Paris apartment dweller would be about leaving diet pills on a bathroom sink.

When the press pointed out that Tour rider Roger Rivière was a "laboratory" racer whose 1958 world hour record was helped by exact medical preparations, the Frenchman took it as a compliment that supported his professional attention to detail. "It proves that I know what I want and what to do to achieve it," Rivière explained.[1]

The consequences of these sorts of drug rituals again alarmed Dumas at the 1962 Tour de France. That year, 14 riders dropped out with "food poisoning." Rider statements suggested the 14 had a negative response to something stronger than a bad plate of fish at the team hotel. In fact, it was morphine. With many riders doping on their own, without a physician's guidance or under the counsel of soigneurs trained only in the street school of pharmacology, Dumas issued an official team *communiqué* that year: clean up your paraphernalia or we'll be inspecting your rooms after each stage.[2]

The following year, Dumas organized the inaugural European Conference on Doping and the Biological Preparation of the Competitive Athlete. The January 1963 congress took place in the alpine spa town of Uriage-les-Bains, just up the hill from future Winter Olympics host town Grenoble. The anti-doping resolutions that emerged were the seeds of change that were eventually picked up by the French government and made into a federal anti-doping law.

During the summer of 1965, France and Belgium made sports doping illegal. The laws targeted the peloton's favorite pick-me-up, amphetamines. The French parliament made the punishment for using substances that could "artificially and temporarily" increase athlete output and cause potential harm a fine of 500 to 5,000 francs, a jail term of one month to a year, or a combination of a fine and jail. The fines were doubled if the drug use caused injury or death.[3] French lawmakers had two objectives: protect athletes from an exploitative sports system, and shield them from their own self-destructive impulses. Commenting on how the new law might affect cycling team managers and their riders, on June 30, 1966, French newspaper *Le Figaro* quipped, "Fear of the gendarme is excellent medicine against doping." The practice that had long been an unremarkable measure enlisted to help defeat athlete fatigue was now being officially regulated as a criminal act.

While the right-leaning *Le Figaro* suggested that criminal consequences might make athletes and trainers think twice about doping, the paper was also realistic that this new constraint was contrary to cycling tradition. "Whenever you have to make an effort that is above average, you have to take something," wrote *Le Figaro*'s sports editor Roger Flambart. "There is no other event in the world where you have to keep going in a maximum effort six hours a day for 22 days. It just cannot be done without dope."[4] *Le Figaro* saw criminal consequences as effective medicine against the newly reclassified pathology of doping but also admitted that redefining a generally accepted part of sports like cycling as a crime was no simple matter.

Even the American public was being made aware of the improbable nature of this French anti-doping project. A 1969 *Sports Illustrated* story by Bil Gilbert cited five-time Tour champion Jacques Anquetil's assertion that all his cycling colleagues doped. "Since we are constantly asked to go faster to make ever greater efforts," Anquetil explained, "we are obliged to take stimulants."[5] Under pressure from their employers, fans, and race organizers, riders like Anquetil claimed they had no agency in the question of whether or not to dope. For the French government, this was like raising an SOS flag above the factory walls; legislators felt obligated to step in and save rider-workers from exploitation.

Le Figaro's speculation that "fear of the gendarme" would deter doping ran the day after stage nine of the 1966 Tour de France. The stage saw Anquetil—a *patron* of the peloton if there ever was one—encourage his colleagues to stop riding and walk in protest of the unprecedented drug enforcement. While the French government might have thought it was protecting riders, pros like Anquetil made it clear that they did not want their government's heavy-handed sympathy. The five-time Tour champion argued that he was standing up for "the decency of the moral person and the professional bicycle racer."[6]

The rider protest was provoked when the now legally empowered representatives from the national Ministry of Youth and Sports and two French doctors knocked on French star rider Raymond Poulidor's door in Bordeaux. With the gendarmerie standing by, they rousted Poulidor from a massage table and demanded he fill sample bottles with urine. Other surprised riders faced the same fate and had to hold out their arms for needle-mark inspections. By testing for drugs, Tour organizers and the French government linked arms in an anti-drug health-and-safety crusade.[7]

The new French doping law was partly motivated by larger public health distress over drug abuse in French society as well as the exploitation of workers—the Tour's slaves of the road, hunched over their machines at an infernal pace for eight or more hours a day. Newspapers including *L'Humanité* and *Le Monde* sympathized with Anquetil and claimed that targeting cyclists for dope testing was unfairly discriminatory and a violation of their domain over their own bodies. Drug testing was also seen by many as an assault on human rights. By suddenly dropping a criminal boom on one sport, the French state was targeting a symptom, not a cause, the papers argued. These dailies also pointed out that Tour bosses were ignoring the fact that pros were self-governing grown-ups and had medicated themselves for a century without serious problems.[8]

The criminalization of doping also created a story problem for the Tour organizers. If their race was so difficult that riders had to dope to finish, was the entire endeavor a violation of human rights that should also be outlawed? Drug enforcement suddenly confronted France's most important sporting and cultural event with an existential crisis—was it a celebration or an abomination?

Anquetil, along with riders like Belgian star Freddy Maertens, defended their drug use as a matter of workers' rights and free will.[9] The suddenly nanny-like French state and Tour de France organization were hypocrites, since their "public health" campaign did not target other professions where drug taking was part of the job description. Throughout the 1960s, European office workers, factory hands, students, and housewives, rode a wave of mood-enhancing, weight-shedding amphetamines.[10] On June 30 and July 1, 1966, *Le Monde* and *L'Humanité* reminded the French people that their overall amphetamine use had multiplied five times since the drug had been removed from over-the-counter sales in 1955. That explosion was certainly not something that could be blamed on a pack of pro cyclists.[11] If drugs in cycling was really the massive health crisis the French government was making it out to be, one cyclist pointed out at the time, "European mountains would be strewn with monuments to their memory."[12] It seemed that cycling was being unfairly singled out to solve the nation's health crisis while society at large got a pass.

However, when riders protested the testing as a violation of their privacy and right to make a living, critics concerned with the connection between a growing 1960s youth counterculture movement and recreational drug use saw the peloton's tantrum as proof that cyclists were moral degenerates. Responding to the riders' stage 9 protest and chants of "No to pissing in test tubes!," Tour director Félix Lévitan hissed that the riders were "a band of drug addicts who are discrediting the sport of cycling."[13] Riders who just a few short years earlier were paragons of moral and physical courage were subsumed by a broader 1960s drug problem and recast as an indistinguishable mass of corruption.

The French government's improbable attempt to turn pro cyclists into dope-free exemplars for a drug-soaked world was bound to fail. Pre-race rituals run deep, and riders kept reaching for the standard preparations as they had for a century. On July 13, 1967, British rider Tom Simpson died on the slopes of Mount Ventoux during stage 13 of the Tour de France. Unlike Jensen at the 1960 Olympics, with Simpson, the press did not need to fabricate an amphetamine connection. Simpson, the son of a British miner, had amphetamines in his jersey pockets and his autopsy revealed amphetamines and alcohol in his bloodstream. The chemicals contributed to a heart attack due to heat exhaustion and dehydration.

While Simpson's death generated much public and press discussion of the danger of drugs in sports, neither this tragedy nor the 1965 prohibitions seemed to dampen the riders' appetite for performance enhancers. Doping continued unabated through the 1990s, when athletes adopted new and more effective drugs, most famously EPO (erythropoietin). Developed in synthetic form during the late 1980s as a treatment for patients suffering from kidney failure, EPO is a naturally occurring hormone that stimulates red-blood-cell production. Taking EPO has a similar effect on the body as living at altitude or sleeping in an oxygen tent; in all three circumstances, the body produces more red blood cells, which deliver more oxygen to muscles, thereby upping endurance. When an EPO scandal rocked the Tour de France in 1998, French legislators decided to add more teeth to their 1965 prohibition.

Three days before the start of the 1998 Tour de France, French border police found hundreds of doses of drugs in the Festina cycling team's car. The discovery sparked a series of doping revelations that nearly ended the race. Over the following three weeks, French police raided rooms and team vehicles, arrested team staff and riders, and forced cyclists to undergo searches, medical exams, and drug tests. In the ensuing cascade of drug revelations, riders protested. Four teams withdrew. Festina was loaded with French stars like Richard Virenque, Pascal Hervé, and Christophe Moreau. The admissions that began with the highly public unmasking of these cycling darlings forced the French government to reexamine its 25-year-old doping laws. As British rider David Millar observed in his autobiography *Racing Through the Dark*, Festina made it manifestly clear that anti-doping laws that had been on the books since 1965 had no effect on cycling tradition. "The enforcers of criminal and civil law had to act," Millar noted.[14]

The aggressive police drug raids that followed the Festina border-crossing incident came at the command of Marie-George Buffet, the French minister of youth and sport. The police action marked unprecedented political involvement in sports doping—a prosecutorial escalation firmly rooted in Buffet's political sensibilities. A longtime member of the French Communist Party who went on to become both the party's leader and a French presidential candidate, Buffet's defense of working-class rights was a political and personal concern. Although the French public might have been indifferent to sports doping as a form of class-based worker exploitation, she was not.

From the race's earliest days, Tour riders were variously seen as abused workers, convicts, and indefatigable machines. Between 1903 and 1926, the average winning-stage finish varied from 12 to 16 hours—the same workday as a miner in Roubaix. Knowing it made for gripping newspaper reading, Tour de France founder Henri Desgrange played up the notion of his riders as heroic laborers toiling in marathon stages. For example, even though gear-changing derailleurs had been around since the late 1800s, Desgrange banned them in the Tour until 1937. The Tour boss hectored riders, insisting that they must "leave gear changes to women and the old, you are the kings, the giants of the road, you must vanquish the obstacles with which it confronts you by your means alone, without recourse to subterfuges unworthy of you."[15]

In 1935, *L'Humanité* criticized such rider treatment as heartless abuse that only put money in the pocket of Desgrange and his advertisers. "Like an exploiter in the factory," the communist paper argued, Desgrange demanded "ever-greater productivity with less security and more fatigue."[16] Although Tour stages had been shortened to five to six hours by the mid-1980s (albeit ridden at much higher speeds than ever before), Buffet saw the exposure of Festina's impressive carload of *rendements* as the equivalent to employer-enforced doping and further evidence that the race had not kept pace with the social and political reforms that had reduced the French working shift to eight hours. For Buffet, the fact that cyclists had to dope to keep up with the infernal productivity demands of Tour owners was indefensible capitalist exploitation. After all, the Tour de France did not even share profits with the athletes who made the race a global television spectacle. Sending the French police into the riders' private sanctums was not meant to send a notice to riders alone. It also signaled race organizers and team owners that under Buffet's watch, the long employer tradition of expecting riders to turn to pharmaceuticals to do their job was over.

Buffet was also sympathetic to riders who tried to abide by French law. Christophe Bassons, a French rider for Festina who was ultimately driven out of the sport for his unwillingness to dope, described Buffet offering him support during his career. "Citizenship cannot end at the stadium gate," she assured Bassons, making a connection between his refusal to dope in the arena of sports and his obligations to act as a moral member of French society. Buffet also helped Bassons land a job when he left cycling.[17]

Tour de France historian Christopher Thompson was in France during the 1998 Tour. From his Ball State University office in Indiana, Thompson told me that French anti-doping enforcers were obsessed at that time with "the idea that you have to protect youth coming up from imitating their idols." For the French government, there was a real concern that endurance sports such as cycling were becoming so difficult that "professionals would fall into the trap that the only way they could make a living and compete is by doping—with potential threats to their health and maybe to their lives." From the French government perspective, the 1998 raids were meant to protect the riders "from themselves, from their work environment—we are going to help them help themselves because they are part of a structure that almost imposes doping," Thompson explained.

Thompson pointed out that French Communists like Buffet were also concerned about drug and alcohol use; addiction was a destructive social problem. As France industrialized in the 1800s, the bottom of a glass was one of the few places a mine or textile worker could find relief from his grim existence. This history of French class conflict, anti-drug campaigns, and debate over the role of sports in society set the stage for the French government's decision to release the cops with a vengeance on the 1998 Tour.

In the wake of what came to be known as the Festina affair, France updated its anti-doping laws. Laws enacted in 1998 required all French pro cyclists to submit to tests that gave the government a performance baseline for each rider. Future performances (and signals of doping) were measured against this physiological baseline.

Thirty-three years after *Le Figaro* wisecracked that fear of cops is a good prescription for doping, during the summer of 1998, France tested the medicine by tossing riders and team staff in prison. France also made its anti-drug laws more rigorous by legislating aggressive surveillance methods. Forcing riders to submit to tests sent a message that they could not be trusted to ride clean on their own.

At the same time, the Festina affair's spectacle of arrests and police interrogations painted a tableau of riders as unsympathetic moral deviants—so far gone, in fact, that only constant surveillance could stop their ways. Doping gained a new aura of social pestilence. As Millar wrote, after the Festina affair, "as far as the public was concerned, being a professional cyclist meant you were doped."[18] Of course, turning to drugs to prepare for the inhuman workloads of pro cycling was not new in 1998. Doping had always been the norm. What changed in 1998 was how the spectacle of police raids and jailed athletes reframed doping as a criminal enterprise. The Festina affair completed the transformation of doping from an act of valor and scientific modernity to an act of social deviance and medical abuse. No longer a proletarian hero, the dope-taking athlete was now an entitled demon.

CHAPTER 6

THE BIRTH OF THE WORLD ANTI-DOPING AGENCY

By the late 1990s, the criminalization of sports doping and corruption in the IOC helped sow the seeds of what would become an independent international anti-doping body, the World Anti-Doping Agency (WADA). Founded in 1999, the agency's charter is to harmonize anti-doping efforts across sports and nations through its World Anti-Doping Code—a set of policies and regulations constraining the substances Olympic athletes can put in their bodies. The 2015 WADA code states two objectives: to "protect the athletes' fundamental right to participate in doping-free sport" and to harmonize and coordinate anti-doping detection, deterrence, and prevention among all nations.[1] By removing the athlete's right to dope, WADA attempts to preserve the right to drug-free play.

Funded by governments and the IOC, the agency cooperates with national authorities, law enforcement, and sport organizing bodies to implement, monitor, and enforce compliance with its code. Additionally, WADA publishes an annual list of prohibited substances and maintains outreach and education programs to spread its mission.

While today's WADA is independent, it was originally born from efforts to create an anti-doping body that would be controlled by the

IOC and that would serve IOC image-management needs. However, swamped by a cresting wave of international outrage over IOC corruption and complicity with sports doping, the IOC's original intentions went awry and an independent anti-doping agency was born.

As the summer of 1998 turned to fall and with the 2000 Sydney Olympics fast approaching, IOC president Juan Antonio Samaranch was in full crisis-management mode. Along with the Festina affair, 1998 had been a Semana Santa parade of dope spectacles for the autocratic Spanish IOC boss. In January, a world championships–bound Chinese swimmer got popped while carrying human growth hormone. Beginning in March, trials of former East German coaches and doctors opened up records revealing that country's systematic doping of Olympic athletes as young as 9 years old. In August, the International Swimming Federation announced that gold-medal-winning Irish swimmer Michelle de Bruin had spiked a urine sample with whiskey—a sample that ended up being positive for androstenedione. A host of American track athletes, including multiple world record holder Mary Decker Slaney, were mired in drug suspicions. And, of course, the IOC was still trying to blow away the effluvia from 1988's Ben Johnson Olympics scandal as well as a USOC-enabled blood-doping case that barred American Nordic skier Kerry Lynch from the 1998 Calgary Winter Games. On top of all this, as the depth of the East German doping program was revealed, the IOC had to face uncomfortable questions about why zero athletes had tested positive at the 1980 Moscow Olympics, even though the medal-sweeping German Democratic Republic (GDR) athletes had been systematically drugged for the event.

With this pall of scandals already stinking up Coubertin's Olympic castle, the arrival of French police raiding hotel rooms and handcuffing stars was an Olympic fate that Samaranch desperately wanted to avoid. The last thing Samaranch and the IOC's corporate sponsors needed was the public-relations nightmare of police carting away shackled athletes from their festival of knightly sports.

Born in Barcelona in 1920 during the Spanish Civil War, Samaranch sided with Francisco Franco's fascist Falange army. After Franco became

Spain's generalissimo, Samaranch served as a sports minister. Samaranch nurtured his connections with the rich and powerful, including then–IOC president Avery Brundage, an American whose own right-wing views Samaranch encouraged during visits Brundage made to the Spaniard's seaside summer home. A self-described "100-percent Francoist" who signed his letters to Franco, "I salute you with my arm raised," Samaranch swapped his allegiance from the Spanish autocrat to the IOC after Franco's death in 1975.[2]

In 1980, Samaranch ascended to the IOC presidency. As the Olympic leader, he emphasized the "sacred unity" of the Olympic Games. This was the language of Franco, an authoritarian who ruthlessly centralized political, economic, religious, and social power under his wing in Madrid. For Samaranch, the Olympic Games offered a way to repossess the sense of religiously sanctified unity of the fascist regime that had dissolved with Franco's death in 1975.

When the French government pinned three team doctors and a soigneur with drug-trafficking charges at the 1998 Tour de France, powerful new actors entered the sporting scene in a way that was unprecedented in sports history. For Samaranch, it was almost as if the dreaded boots of Franco's Guardia Civil had threatened to turn against him, only this time in the form of the French national gendarmerie. For the IOC, these alien forces threatened to redistribute international sports-management power. News of the arrests posed a potentially serious image problem for the Olympics. As historian John Hoberman wrote in 2001, in 1998 Olympic dope testing "was widely regarded as a sham." For the IOC leadership, doping was "primarily a public relations problem that threatened lucrative television and corporate contracts." Samaranch needed a way to keep federal police forces or agents from a truly independent anti-doping organization from snooping around the Olympic Games.[3] French sports minister Marie-George Buffet's willingness to use the judicial system and police to protect athletes' health and safety threatened long-term IOC control over the management of doping in Olympic sports. As Hoberman explains, in 1998, the old IOC doping management "order was dissolving, but it remained unclear what sort of new arrangement might replace it."[4]

The Festina affair suggested to the public that the drug policies espoused by the IOC and its subordinate sports federations like the Union Cycliste International (UCI) were so weakly enforced that it took a government to expose the doping that was fueling endurance sports like cycling. Facing a communist French sports minister whose veins ran with skepticism of corporation-coddling entities, the IOC could envision its awesome power and income going up in a puff of political and judicial indifference to Olympic sponsor concerns.

The public relations nightmare worsened for the IOC in December 1998. A Swiss lawyer and IOC executive board member named Marc Hodler divulged that the 2002 Salt Lake City Winter Olympics organizing committee had paid IOC members for their votes to hold the Games in Utah. The bribery scandal exploded, eventually provoking a U.S. Department of Justice investigation. Hodler's bombshell revealed that the Olympic Games, and the IOC delegates who vote for them, are bought, not earned. With many calling for Samaranch's resignation over the raft of doping and bribery scandals, the IOC's credibility was at an all-time low. To deflect, the IOC proposed a conference.

Eager to present himself as a bold leader in a time of unrest, rebuild the IOC's reputation, and keep the management of doping under IOC control, Samaranch called for a World Conference on Doping in Sport. The congress held on February 2–4, 1999, in Lausanne, Switzerland, was intended to get the IOC ahead of aggressive state doping regulations and hoist the IOC from the muck of scandal onto the high altar of Coubertinian morality.

In planning the gathering, the IOC did all it could to preemptively contain anyone who might venture off the Olympic reservation. It drew up the agenda without input from groups outside the IOC. Olympic executives hand-selected all the conference delegates, and the meeting was structured around four working groups that would then present reports and findings to the conference chair—that chair being conveniently occupied by IOC president Samaranch. Each working group was loaded with IOC representatives and chaired by IOC vice presidents, none of whom had to travel to unfamiliar territory, since Lausanne is also home to IOC headquarters.

Although representatives from the European Union, the Council of Europe, and international government agencies were to attend the conference, the IOC barred outside organizations from dictating the conference agenda. All documents produced at the conference had to be approved by Samaranch before distribution. Likewise, the final conference declaration was to be drafted by a group the Spaniard hand picked.[5]

Samaranch and the IOC seemed to have put a lid on any independent ideas about doping control before the conference began; democratic exchange of proposals for reforms were going to be shut down before they could see the light of day. The IOC even had a ready-made name for its new anti-doping organization—Olympic Movement Anti-Doping Agency. Tied to the Olympics in name and location, the new anti-doping bureaucracy would be based within surveillance range of IOC headquarters in Lausanne, Switzerland. Even before the international delegates arrived on the shores of Lake Geneva for the conference, long-time Olympic observers had the straight dope on Samaranch's designs. A few weeks before the conference, *New York Times* readers opened their papers to find a John Hoberman piece informing them that "the real purpose of this much-heralded meeting is to enable the people who created and tolerated the doping crisis to retain virtually all of their powers. It is yet another power play by a corrupt old guard."[6]

Hoberman's opinion piece captured the swell of anticorruption disgust that would swamp Samaranch and the IOC at the conference. The IOC also found itself drowned out by an unruly and unexpectedly large pack of journalists who showed up. The IOC congress that Olympic authorities expected to be a sedate ratification of the IOC's precast vision for doping control became, in light of the Salt Lake City bribery scandal, an impromptu trial on Samaranch's tattered competency that attracted 500 reporters. Most of the scribes and talking heads got marching orders from assignment editors who smelled a bleeding lead in the prospect of a bloodied Spanish fascist swimming into a shiver of sharks who were already frenzied by Hodler's exposure of IOC corruption. As historian Jim Ferstle explained in a 2001 account of the conference, "The atmosphere clearly was one of a kingdom under siege."[7]

The conference opened with two hours of IOC fawning. IOC members deferred to Samaranch in a fashion that *Guardian* reporter Duncan Mackay described as a "Communist Party conference in the former Soviet Union."[8] But then British sports minister Tony Banks took the microphone and released the ethical hounds. Leaning over the podium, Banks growled, "In Britain we operate a rigorous anti-doping regime. We are not prepared to lower our standards to a lowest common denominator that is soft on doping in sport." That denominator was Samaranch, who sat 10 feet from Banks. Having established that the IOC was a foul and untrustworthy steward of sporting honor, Banks proposed the creation of an IOC image-management nightmare—a wholly independent drug-testing administration. "We support a totally transparent world anti-doping organization," Banks avowed, and then added the stinger—"but the IOC should not be that agency."

Barry McCaffrey, President Bill Clinton's director of the White House Office of National Drug Control Policy, was also on hand. A U.S. Army general and infantry school commander who had earned three Purple Hearts in Vietnam and led a celebrated division in the 1990s Gulf War, McCaffrey did not suffer fools. The general saw the truth in Hoberman's January *New York Times* opinion piece; in his mind, anti-doping had to be separate from the IOC. Following Banks's fusillade, McCaffrey took the podium and announced that the U.S. government believed "the legitimacy of the IOC has been damaged by alleged corruption, lack of accountability, and the failure of leadership." With Samaranch struggling to maintain a brave face while receiving an anti-doping lecture from a representative of a nation that still sold over-the-counter steroid precursors, McCaffrey did not mince words: "The IOC is rushing forward to build an institution that we cannot support—one that is more public relations ploy than policy solution."[9] McCaffrey was an intimidating presence, made more so by his role as a representative of the world's remaining superpower, and his declaration was a grenade tossed into the middle of Samaranch's carefully orchestrated attempt to keep doping control under the IOC roof.

The conference concluded on February 4 with the adoption of the "Lausanne Declaration." This agreement called for the creation and funding of an independent anti-doping authority that eventually took the name World Anti-Doping Agency. Misjudging the anger of powerful functionaries like McCaffrey and Banks, along with the press's eagerness to trumpet the public humiliation of the imperious Samaranch, the IOC unwittingly made Lausanne the locus of a global outpouring of disgust that generated the very IOC-independent anti-doping organization the IOC originally meant to preempt. The Olympic Movement Anti-Doping Agency the IOC wanted became the international World Anti-Doping Agency they didn't. The prospect of Samaranch leading the anti-doping body got booted far into Lake Geneva, along with his proposal that the doping agency's headquarters be built in the IOC's own Swiss town. Instead, WADA made its home in Montreal, Canada, symbolically out of reach of the famously drug-indifferent United States and the IOC alike.[10]

At the Lausanne conference, IOC executive board member Jacques Rogge pointed out the hypocrisy in McCaffrey's antidrug lecturing, reminding listeners that American baseball star Mark McGwire was openly taking androstenedione, a performance-enhancing drug available to anyone at American health food stores and supermarkets. "If you go on the moralizing and lecturing tone you must be sure your own house is in order," Rogge said. Funding was to come from both the IOC and governments, which meant that it would be more difficult for the IOC to use economic threats to control WADA. As a result of the Lausanne conference, doping enforcement for Olympic sports was changed from an in-house shadow show meant to cast illusions of anti-doping activism to a system where doping laws were drawn up and enforced apart from the IOC and its self-serving subagencies like the UCI and IAAF.

WADA's creation was propelled not only by disgust with IOC corruption. Geopolitical changes that came with the end of the Cold War allowed for international cooperation that would have been exceptionally difficult before the 1989 fall of the Iron Curtain. As we will see in the next chapter, as long as the Cold War raged, ideological enemies like the United States and the USSR justified their own state-enabled sports doping programs because they were in the interest of a greater good—the furthering of each nation's preferred political system and imperial objectives. During the Cold War, a quest for pure-sport romanticism didn't stand a chance against the geopolitics of communists versus capitalists. It would have been an unthinkable sign of weakness to set down weapons, including the chemical ones used on the Olympic battlefield. There was little incentive for superpowers to cooperate over an international anti-doping agency like WADA.

Everything changed with the reunification of Germany and the 1991 dissolution of the USSR. By the 1999 Lausanne conference, barriers separating antagonistic nation states had melted, allowing foes to come together over an anti-doping agreement without losing face. The World Conference on Doping in Sport represented a rare window in time when the creation of WADA was made possible by a confluence of larger political and social events. In terms of keeping doping under the IOC rug, Samaranch could not have timed it worse. But in terms of creating a globally unifying anti-doping agency, the timing could not have been better.

Hein Verbruggen attended the Lausanne conference as the president of the UCI and as an IOC delegate. UCI boss from 1991 to 2005, Verbruggen had a front-row seat for the rise of EPO and Lance Armstrong. Because he ran cycling during Armstrong's dominant 1999–2005 Tour de France years, Verbruggen is roundly accused of turning a blind eye to doping, and he still makes the unconvincing claim he did not know Armstrong was cheating. Although his management of the UCI during the Armstrong years (including accepting a $125,000 donation from the Texan) suggests questionable ethical judgment, Verbruggen has an encyclopedic knowledge of pro cycling and IOC politics. He also understands doping is not a tidy fable of right and wrong, good and evil, saved and doomed, but rather an ongoing attempt to impose a radical new morality on a traditionally drug-dependent sport. His view of the conference and why it led to the creation of an anti-doping agency that was not at all what the IOC wanted paints a clearer picture of the multiple complicities coming to bear on Olympic sports at the end of the 20th century.

Reached by Skype at his summer home in France, Verbruggen told me that going into the 1999 conference, it was clear to him that federal governments had the leverage to do something about doping in sports. The Dutchman said Marie-George Buffet showed how, with the right leadership, a government can actually effect change in athletes' habits. During his UCI tenure, Verbruggen said it became apparent that without government involvement, it would be difficult to stop performance-enhancing drug use. That said, Verbruggen believes "governments are not really interested in the doping problem." Relative to issues like health care, poverty, terrorism, infant mortality, clean water, and the economy, "there is very little interest in the world in doping in sport," he said. In his view, France's Buffet was an anomaly because she pressured the French government to enforce the anti-doping rules on its books. However, Verbruggen added, most countries are not like France, and for them, "people are much more interested in medals than anti-doping." Unless galvanized by a figure like Buffet, whose proworker beliefs made anti-doping an issue of human rights that warranted the French government's attention, Verbruggen feels politicians have little to gain from spending time or money on state-run anti-doping forces.

In a 1999 essay Verbruggen penned about the Lausanne conference, "Reflections for the World Conference on Doping in Sport," he noted that in 1999, the press expected sports governing bodies to look at doping as a facile, black-and-white issue of crime and punishment. "He who punishes rigorously, is '*doing good*,'" Verbruggen wrote of this emotionally satisfying, but intellectually dishonest simplification of the doping problem. Sticking to such a reductionist and historically ignorant interpretation of drug use prevented a "real discussion on the issue of doping. A discussion that will provide us with the answers to the future questions sport will be confronted with because of the advancing '*medicalisation*' of society and also the world of sport."[11]

While the UCI president's own complicity in Lance Armstrong's doping might lead you to dismiss his nuanced thinking as sophistry—a slick rationalization of his own refusal or reluctance to try to uproot cycling's doping cultural traditions—his call for a more contextually aware solution to the doping problem is sound. It is a response that refuses to be cowed by the braying of the you're-either-with-us-or-against-us demagogues and historically clueless pure-sport false prophets. Verbruggen's rationality also echoes a point of view Samaranch held, but which ultimately piled onto the troubles that demolished his hopes of keeping doping under IOC control.

In a 1998 interview with a Spanish newspaper reporter, Samaranch expressed his view that doping authorities should focus on drugs that are most dangerous to athletes' health. Unfortunately for the tone-deaf IOC boss, he made these comments to Spanish reporter Carlos Toro in the midst of the 1998 Festina meltdown—a moment when Buffet's roundup was churning out a composite sketch of sports doping as a black-and-white matter of criminal innocence or guilt. When the Spanish paper *El Mundo* hit the Madrid streets at dawn on July 26, 1998, Spaniards making their way to cafes and offices were greeted by the headline "Samaranch: 'The list of doping products should be drastically shortened.'" With Tour de France riders and staff still in police custody north of the border at the Tour de France, this was quite a statement.

The IOC president told Toro that enforcing anti-doping law is difficult because the act is nebulous. "Doping requires an exact definition that does not exist, and that I've been asking for years," Samaranch complained of the lack of a comprehensive list of banned substances. When Toro pushed the IOC president to define doping, Samaranch said, "Doping is any product that, first, is harmful to the health of an athlete, and second, that artificially augments his performance. If it only produces the second condition, for me that's not doping." Because it is difficult to draw a definitive line separating additive from restorative sports medicine, he argued that authorities are better off focusing on cracking down on drugs they know are harmful to athletes rather than attempting to ban everything that offended their sense of fair play. Samaranch's pragmatic, health-first approach to the problem made theoretical sense but was out of tune with the criminal hysteria whipped up by the ongoing Festina affair.[12]

Toro reminded Samaranch that in the public's opinion, there are no doping shades of gray. To fans and politicians, "there are no innocents, only those that have been found guilty and those who have not yet been found out," the journalist explained. In the dualistic view of drugs in sports, you were either hard on dopers, or you were soft. Like the emotionally satisfying but functionally disastrous American drug policy that jails addicts before treating them, neither the public nor the press had patience for the IOC leader's suggestion that sports-governing bodies deal with doping in a fashion that considered the social, commercial, and political complexities. When it came to performance-enhancing drugs, emotion ruled, not rationality.

When word got out that Samaranch was questioning the wisdom of blanket anti-doping laws and publicly wondering whether blame for doping doesn't only lie with athletes, "but rather the people around them," he provoked a storm of moral indignation. Responding to Samaranch's statements, on August 9, 1998, the *New York Times* called his commitment to the anti-doping cause "suspect." Samaranch's suggestion that performance-enhancing drugs should be allowed "unless they pose a threat to the athletes that use them," the *Times* sniffed, was "a bizarre statement."[13] Even in the United States, in the midst of a summer when the nation's sports fans were reveling in a drug-fueled home-run race between baseball sluggers Mark McGwire and Sammy Sosa, journalists had little patience for any rejection of a reductionist, emotionally pleasing condemnation of doping in sport.

Despite our need for easy scapegoats, the nature of WADA's worth shows how doping is the child of many parents and conflicting needs. From the IOC's faltering credibility, to the end of the Cold War, to

Samaranch's mistake of bringing together in one place powerful actors who could torpedo an IOC-controlled doping agency, to the French linking of doping to human rights abuses—all these elements came together in a unique moment when it was possible to create a truly independent global anti-doping bureaucracy. The formation of WADA was a milestone in the continuing transformation of sports doping from an unremarkable tradition into a threat to society's moral fiber. And with the Berlin Wall in pieces, this was an ethical crisis communist and capitalist could at least pretend they would confront together. As we will note in the following chapter, this anti-doping agreement between communist and capitalist worlds was all the more remarkable considering that the Cold War was one of the greatest accelerators of doping that the sports world has ever seen.

CHAPTER 7

DOPING AND THE COLD WAR

After World War II, doping in sports gradually transitioned from a homegrown endeavor managed by individual athletes and perhaps a soigneur into a collective science research enterprise. Energized by international Cold War tensions between communist and capitalist states, doping pivoted away from the haphazard, one-off sports survival efforts of the six-day rider or marathon runner who swallowed booze and stimulants to finish a race. As nations began to see Olympic sports as a means of achieving geopolitical ambitions, doping moved out of the kitchen and into the lab. Doping guided by old wives' tales became applied pharmacology as an element of sports science—a new field of study that demanded the collective efforts of not just one doctor or a soigneur, but experts from multidisciplinary fields of medicine, chemistry, psychology, materials science, physiology, and nutrition. And unlike earlier homespun doping practices, performance-enhancement research during the Cold War required government-level funding and organizational resources.

Whether in a university lab or a government sports development center, empirically based, labor- and capital-intensive sports science programs emerged as extensions of national defense arsenals. And within these organizations, pharmaceuticals were but one element among a host of factors studied and marshaled in the interest of higher human performance and national ambition. Motivated by Cold War objectives, governments managed and paid for these pure science and applied science programs and in doing so created the chemistry-rich high-performance sports science paradigm we take for granted today. The Cold War put sports performance-enhancement research on steroids.

This transition from homebred doping to institutionalized sports medicine took place within the context of the 50-year struggle for global supremacy that immediately followed the end of World War II in September 1945. After the defeat of Japan and the Third Reich, the Soviet Union took advantage of the postwar power vacuum and quickly expanded its presence in eastern and central Europe. Along with annexing Nazi-occupied central and eastern European nations like East Germany and Poland, the USSR attempted to gain control of the Dardanelles, a critical Turkish water route connecting western Europe's Mediterranean to eastern Europe's Black Sea. Controlling the Dardanelles would give the Soviets enormous leverage over a critical defense and trade route.

As part of these expansionist efforts at the crossroads of Europe and Asia, the Soviets also supported the Greek Communist Party in a civil war against the British- and American-backed Greek government. Still reeling from a war that had left its cities and industries in tatters, Great Britain announced in February 1947 that it could no longer bankroll the Greek fighters. Funding this proxy war was now up to the Americans. On March 12, 1947, President Harry S. Truman asked Congress for $400 million to support the fight against communist influences in Greece and Turkey. If the Soviets were not contained, the United States feared the communists would gain complete control of eastern and central Europe, and more ominously, the Middle East and its oil.

In his March 1947 request to Congress, Truman laid out his view that the world was divided into those who loved freedom and those who did not. Capitalist life "is distinguished by free institutions, representative government, free elections, guaranties of individual liberty, freedom of speech and religion, and freedom from political oppression," Truman proclaimed. The communist way "relies upon terror and oppression, a controlled press and radio, fixed elections, and the suppression of personal freedoms." Truman's binary ideology and his belief that the United States was morally obligated to support those "resisting attempted subjugation by armed minorities or by outside pressures," defined United States foreign policy into the 21st century.[1] Over time, his domino theory of communist containment demarcated not just American foreign policy, but it also accelerated the transformation of Olympic sports away from Coubertin's spiritual foundation into a nationalistic (and materialistic) pursuit.

Influenced by Truman's domino theory and feeling a sense of obligation to the United States for its efforts in defeating Hitler, after the war, western European nations allied themselves with the U.S.-led North Atlantic Treaty Organization (NATO). Beginning in Greece, the Soviet Union and United States started a half-century-long tradition of funding proxy civil wars in places as far afield as Central America, Southeast Asia, and Africa. And in the case of Vietnam, the United States directly involved itself in a decade-long struggle against a communist state. Fueled by competing allegiances to Marxist and capitalist systems, and a desire to establish economic and political bases around the planet, from the 1950s through today, the competition for land, resources, and hearts and minds played out in Nicaraguan jungles, Afghan mountains, and American and Russian space-rocket labs.

The battle also took the field in Olympic and world championship stadiums, most dramatically in East Germany. When Germany surrendered on May 7, 1945, the nation was in psychological and physical ruins. In Düsseldorf, Allied bombers left less than 10 percent of the buildings standing. Approximately 100,000 of Frankfurt's prewar population of 180,000 were either dead or refugees. A million homeless scavenged the Hamburg countryside. The February 1945 Dresden firebombing incinerated as many as 40,000 citizens. "The entire city was a sea of flame," one survivor put it. "The art and tradition and beauty of centuries had been destroyed in a single night!"[2] And those were just physical and economic tolls. Germany also lived with the obscenity of orchestrating the extermination of more than two-thirds of European Jews and millions more—a death toll estimated to be nearly 20 million people. Germany was numb—turned to stone by financial, structural, and moral collapse.

In the USSR's post–World War II scramble to seize territory and forestall the rise of another Teuton dictatorship, Germany was split into two countries. Beginning in 1949, East Germany was democratic in name only. Run by Soviet central planners, the GDR's infamous Ministry for State Security—the Stasi secret police—infiltrated every aspect of personal and public life. The omnipresent paranoia was meant to rat out potential internal agitators and turn neighbors into spies. The Stasi also monitored the coaches and administrators who managed the GDR's national athletics programs and oversaw the world's first, and biggest, institutionalized sports doping program—one that relied heavily on the administration of anabolic-androgenic steroids to young athletes. As GDR shot-putter Brigitte Berendonk recalled, the state police infiltrated every aspect of East German life. "It was an institutional scheme," she told historian Steven Ungerleider in 1998. Paranoia was constant. Even if the harmful effects of steroids injected into an unknowing teenaged athlete alarmed a doctor, Berendonk recalled that "the Stasi forced them to continue." Furthermore, "there were penalties for doctors and anyone who turned against them," Berendonk said of the consequences for challenging the state.[3]

Meanwhile, from 1945 to 1949, the United States, Britain, and France controlled the portions of Germany that became West Germany (also known as the Federal Republic of Germany, or FRG). While East Germans were busy centralizing their sporting system into a state-run, top-down enterprise, the Allies forced West Germany to do the opposite. On December 17, 1945, the Allies issued Control Council Directive Number 23, a decree that demilitarized regionalized sports in West Germany, including Berlin, a West German city-island within East German territory. As the 1936 Olympics had shown, Hitler used sporting systems for military training and public propaganda. By decentralizing sports, the Allies tried to ensure that West Germans would not retrain an insurrectional force under cover of state-run athletic organizations.

Directive Number 23 limited all sports to local clubs and stipulated that sports education must focus on "health, hygiene and recreation" while expressly avoiding "sport elements of assimilated military character."[4] Apart from some oversight by French, English, and American military commanders, West German sports were run by autonomous local clubs and without the financial or regulatory assistance of a central government coordinating bureaucracy. In contrast, in East Germany, sports were run from the top down, with government bureaucrats searching the nation for its most promising talent and sending those athletes to camps where they could live and train like pros. As historians Rob Beamish and Ian Ritchie explain, East Germany "poured human, financial and material resources into a highly rational, instrumentally oriented high-performance sport system" of a sort the world had never seen. When it started developing gold-medal athletes, the GDR sports system effectively challenged all other nations, including its unwelcome occupier, the Soviet Union, to either copy its model or get left in the Olympic dust.[5]

While postwar West Germany grew into a thriving democracy and became Europe's third-largest economy, the GDR enjoyed no such revival. Russian overseers moved East Germany's most productive factories to the USSR, leaving the GDR economy in a grinding funk and its people chronically short of food and daily necessities. With its once-mighty industrial base eviscerated by Russia, sports became one of the few ways the GDR could project a vigorous national profile—both to the capitalist world at large and to its Stalinist oppressors in Moscow—and reconstruct its battered national pride.

West Germany formed its national Olympic committee in 1948. East Germany did the same in 1951. However, the East Germans did not receive official IOC recognition until 1965. Up to that date, the IOC mandated that GDR athletes must compete alongside West Germans as a single German team. Hitler had cultivated a strong sense of superiority in the German people, especially relative to Russians, who were now their rulers. With the once-proud Teutonic empire reduced to being a puppet of occupying Russians, this humiliation at the hands of paternalistic IOC aristocrats only amplified the East German sense of *Selbstbewußtsein*—prideful self-awareness. For the GDR, building a world-dominating athletic program would prove German socialism was more productive than capitalist imperialism, reconstitute damaged German pride, and symbolically separate East Germany from the hated occupying Soviet Union.[6]

When the IOC denied East Germany a team berth in the 1948 Olympics, GDR party leader Walter Ulbricht propagandized the dismissal as a further attack on East German sovereignty. Ulbricht and GDR head of state Erich Honecker attempted to assert themselves and win back some of their bruised respect by creating the State Committee for Physical Culture and Sport (STAKO). The government-run organization was responsible for rallying East Germany's human, technical, and sporting resources in the interest of athletic success. It was a systematic, state-funded effort to produce the best athletes the world had ever known. As STAKO's charter put it, "Top athletes should be concentrated in facilities where the requirements for the systematic improvement of performance are present or can be created."[7]

Restructured in 1957 as the German Gymnastics and Sports Federation (DTSB), the organization was integrated into every East German school. Students five years old and up spent five to seven hours a week practicing sports such as gymnastics, athletics, and swimming. From teachers to doctors, physical therapists to nutritionists, the GDR's Kinder und Jugendsportschulen (Children and Youth Sports Schools, or KJS) identified East Germany's most promising child talents and funneled them into schools with full-time professional training and sports medicine support.

In 1968, the IOC ruled that East Germany could have its own team at the 1972 Munich Olympics. Manfred Ewald, a ruthless, organizationally gifted ex–Hitler Youth leader turned GDR minister of sports, ran the DTSB. With the 1972 Games taking place in West Germany, Ewald saw an opportunity to humiliate West German capitalists on their own turf while also giving the GDR a chance to assert itself against the Russian occupying state. One GDR sports promotion society gloated in 1968 that East Germany would at last be able to unfurl its flag and play its anthem in Munich, the heart of capitalist West Germany. Likening athletics to the defense of East Germany from "imperialist NATO enemies," Ewald stated that sports are "no different than any military conflict." As the GDR sports minister saw it, East German sports organizers had to carry out their battle "in the same manner as the defense of our borders—it entails detesting imperialism and its agents, including the athletes of the FRG."[8]

Fueled by national resentment, these postwar East German sports programs largely revitalized the 1930s athletic systems built under an equally indignant Hitler. For the Führer's National Socialist Party, the union of play and combat was the raison d'être for sports in the Third Reich. Sport prepared and hardened Aryan men to defend and advance the reach of a genetically pure Nazi state—sports and war fused in the interest of Nazi political ambition and ideology.

With ex-Nazi Ewald leading the effort, building the world's best sports medicine research and development program was essential to East German's national renewal project. As of 1970, drugs were an officially authorized element of a nationally synchronized sports-performance-enhancement effort called State Plan Subject 14.25.[9] In a 1977 internal report on East Germany's sports programs, the man who authorized steroid use in 1970, GDR deputy director Manfred Höppner, decreed that "anabolic steroids are applied in all Olympic sporting events, with the exception of sailing and gymnastics (female) . . . and by all national teams." The report went on to detail how four years of systematic, state-funded steroid treatments yielded performance improvements in events like shot put, discus, javelin, and running. Höppner reported that the program saw especially high performance increases "following the first administration of anabolic hormones, in particular with junior athletes."[10]

Although it was an open secret that drugs were an important element of the GDR sports program, East German leaders had to publicly deny their use because the IOC had banned steroids for the 1976 Montreal games. Drug-using athletes also contradicted government propaganda demonizing drug abuse as a symptom of capitalism. In many respects, State Plan Subject 14.25 was the sporting equivalent of the U.S. Manhattan Project. Funded by the state, the project took the nation's most gifted theoretical and applied scientists, shielded them from the world's prying eyes, and gave them the resources to refine the existing body of chemical and physiological literature into a new sports science that would fundamentally enhance the performance capacity of East German athletes. Just as the atomic bomb changed the global balance of power in 1945, the GDR athletics program forever altered how nations and sports managers conceptualized elite sports. And as Beamish and Ritchie put it, from the 1970s onward, the lushly funded East German experimental research project on human-performance enhancement redefined what it took to be the best in the world in sports. Only this time it wasn't the collectivist energy of the communist USSR or the restless inventiveness of the capitalist United States formulating a totally new and modern sports system. Rather, "the GDR set the standard toward which others moved."[11]

In the 1960s, Ewald began building the GDR High Performance Sports Commission. Its labs studied athlete responses to drugs—known euphemistically in the GDR as "supplemental means." East Germany's Research Institute for Physical Culture and Sport had a staff of 600 full-time researchers dedicated to furthering elite-level East German athletic output, and the total number of GDR sports science researchers was estimated to be 1,500. About 1,000 doctors coordinated with 4,700 coaches while 5,000 volunteers and administrators kept the infrastructure humming along. Meanwhile, 3,000 Stasi agents ensured that anyone who questioned the logic or safety of this system did not enjoy its perks for long. Historian John Hoberman describes this system as the first-ever "Communist-style mobilization of thousands of people for the purpose of producing elite athletes."[12]

The effort delivered early results at the 1964 Tokyo Olympics. East and West German athletes competed as one team, but the GDR competitors were the stars, winning more medals than their capitalist teammates. After the IOC allowed East and West Germany to field separate teams, the efficacy of the GDR state sports system became even more obvious. At the 1976 Montreal Summer Olympics, the GDR took home 40 gold medals, second to the USSR's 49 and eclipsing the United States' 34. East German women swimmers took 9 of 11 individual gold medals. After Montreal, the East German government honored a group of scientists from the University of Leipzig for their "excellent results in doping" and rewarded their success with a cash bonus.[13]

Records that came to light after the 1989 fall of the Berlin Wall indicated that beginning in 1966, some 2 million doses of anabolic steroids like the GDR-manufactured Oral-Turinabol were distributed to 2,000 elite East German athletes every year. An official directive demanded that the drugs not be delivered to athletes in identifying packaging. Under-18 athletes were told they were taking vitamins, and those older than 18 took an oath of secrecy not to divulge the nature of their steady diet of performance-enhancing "supplements."[14]

Along with his role as sports minister, Ewald led the GDR National Olympic Committee from 1973 to 1990. As an IOC insider also managing the world's most ambitious doping project, Ewald had insights into the inner workings of the IOC and its growing concerns about doping as an incursion of professional practices into the Olympic citadel of amateurism. With Ewald having boardroom access to nascent Olympic anti-doping efforts, he demanded that East German sports medicine scientists develop systems and procedures to ensure doped GDR athletes did not test positive at international events. Accordingly, the East German Central Doping Control Laboratory was built in 1977 as a central drug-testing depot.

The testing lab in Kreischa, a town near Dresden, received daily shipments of urine from athletes throughout East Germany. No GDR athlete could leave East Germany for international competition until his or her dope tests came back negative. Before the 1978 swimming world championships, East German aquatic stars Petra Thümer and Christiane Sommer spent days in Kreischa resubmitting samples that kept coming back positive for nandrolone—a performance-enhancing drug they had injected eight weeks earlier, but which lingered in the body much longer than GDR scientists had expected. Claiming an unfortunate double case of the flu, neither swimmer saw a pool lane at that year's championship event.

As an IOC-accredited facility, the Central Doping Control Laboratory also contracted its services to events and organizations outside the GDR. This setup generated revenue, dressed up the GDR as an anti-doping soldier, and gave East German scientists a heads-up on new performance-boosting drugs that some countries' athletes were getting from sources other than the GDR-owned Jenapharm chemistry labs.

In a number of cases when samples from Soviet athletes came up positive, the Kreischa lab notified USSR officials and then marked the positive as a negative. The GDR anti-doping lab became a model in how to use federal resources to tilt the odds for Olympic athletes. As we'll see later, in an effort to protect American athletes from embarrassing positives, the United States would emulate this GDR anti-anti-doping program at the 1984 Los Angeles Olympics.

GDR research into how to avoid positives from "supplemental means" led to technically sophisticated, exquisitely documented methods of micro-dosing and steroid tapering that were later adopted in sports like professional cycling. In one East German study, 241 athletes were gradually switched from anabolic steroids to the GDR-developed androgenic steroid androstenedione. East German chemists developed this synthetic hormone as a therapeutic bridge that would allow GDR athletes to maintain intense workouts and high hormone levels, but without testing positive in event drug tests. (This is the same substance that became a staple for many American baseball players and supplement users in the 1990s.)

In another case, Jenapharm developed a biologically inactive version of the naturally produced organic compound epitestosterone, a hormone that has no performance-enhancing effects, but which when artificially administered can reduce testosterone ratios to a level below a threshold used to test for drug use. The development of masking agents like epitestosterone as well as sophisticated methods for drug tapering and dosing in turn were widely adopted by edge-seeking athletes outside the GDR family.[15]

The sports medicine programs developed for the Cold War sporting arsenal were built on the shoulders of Germany's pioneering sports medicine establishment. The world's first sports medicine college was founded in 1920 in Berlin. To disseminate their research, German physicians established the world's first sports medicine journal in 1924. In addition to documenting the effect of the Jenapharm-produced anabolic steroid Oral-Turinabol on thousands of subjects throughout the 1960s and 1970s, East Germany conducted some of the earliest studies of slow- and fast-twitch muscle fibers, which pushed our understanding of the effects of interval training. These sports scientists also conducted groundbreaking biomechanical film analysis of athlete motion and were among the earliest to use hyperbaric chambers to replicate high-altitude training. Doping was just one part of an all-encompassing state-run sports medicine machine that marshaled German money and minds in the interest of rebuilding German self-esteem on Olympic and world championship playing fields.

The GDR noted that women could be particularly fertile soldiers in the ongoing reassertion of the tattered German identity. Not wanting them to "become the focus of a spectacle," Coubertin believed women had no business participating in the Olympics as athletes. Instead, "their role should be above all to crown the victors."[16] This chauvinistic legacy endured well into the Cold War era, and women's sports were discouraged in many countries, including the United States. Focusing development resources on female athletes would lead to a disproportionately high East German medal haul. East Germany could also hold up successful female athletes as examples of how the communist state liberated and celebrated women to a degree impossible in capitalist countries.

East German trainers had women take on progressively harder and longer training loads that enemies like the United States considered too tough for the female constitution. In violation of physical and social interdictions regarding female workloads, from 1960 to 1968, the average monthly training distance for a female Soviet Olympic swimmer more than doubled from 482 kilometers per month to 1,045 kilometers. In 1960, about 18.5 percent of these swimmers' time in the pool was dedicated to fast interval workouts. By 1968, speedwork constituted 59 percent of their workout. Muscle-building anabolic steroids helped these athletes recover from this enormous increase in workload and intensity.[17]

Well into the 1970s, many considered it dangerous for women to adopt stressful training workouts. This was certainly the case in the United States, where the paternalistic state of affairs was famously illustrated in 1967 when the director of the Boston Marathon physically accosted runner Kathrine Switzer four miles into the event, screaming, "Get the hell out of my race and give me those numbers!" As Switzer recalled in 2007, American coaches at the time thought running such a long distance would destroy female reproductive organs. A mix of paternalism and chauvinism drove this female exclusion from strenuous athletic events. When Switzer first suggested that she run Boston, her Syracuse University coach shushed the 19-year-old, exclaiming, "No dame ever ran the Boston Marathon!"[18]

Recognizing opportunity in the United States' systemic exclusion of "the weaker sex" from its primary American Olympic training ground, collegiate sports, GDR sports scientists researched how progressive resistance and interval training could improve female performance.

When combined with anabolic steroids to assist with recovery, detailed record keeping, and closely attentive sports medicine staff, these efforts yielded remarkable results. At the 1980 Olympics, 36.4 percent of the East German Olympic team was female, yet women brought home 49 percent of the team's medals. In a post-1976 Olympics report, GDR sports science director Höppner concluded "that women have the greatest advantage from treatments with anabolic hormones with respect to their performance in sports. . . . Especially high is the performance-supporting effect following the first administration of anabolic hormones, particularly with junior athletes."[19]

Despite the devastating health effects such systematic doping could have on youngsters, many athletes and their parents were proud and supportive of the system. As historian Hoberman explains, some GDR athletes complained not about the drugs themselves, but that their teammates were getting an unfair advantage because they were getting more powerful substances.[20] While that reaction might seem counterintuitive today, when the long-term dangers of doping are better understood, East Germans in the 1960s still carried the shame of being a war-losing, economically and spiritually eviscerated Soviet puppet state that also happened to be author of the planet's worst human holocaust. Elite-level training is by its very nature discomfiting. For many East German athletes, embracing sports science and its painful side effects was a small price to pay to regain German pride. While GDR researchers knew that one-third of their female athletes were suffering gynecological damage from heavy anabolic steroid use, these reports were not shared with athletes. It was hard to protest the delivery of still more "vitamins," as trainers called their go-to steroid Oral-Turinabol, when the pills were seen as confirmation of one's arrival at the highest level of elite German sports.

After the fall of the Berlin Wall in 1989, star German discus thrower and shot-putter Brigitte Berendonk and her husband, Werner Franke, gained access to thousands of Stasi athlete record files. While many records had been destroyed in an effort to protect the doctors and administrators who oversaw the GDR athletics programs, the preserved files detailed the systematic doping of some 10,000 athletes during the Cold War. Criminal trials that began in 1996 brought more than 400 indictments against East German coaches, doctors, and trainers. Two years before his 2002 death, German courts handed the 74-year-old sports minister Manfred Ewald a two-year suspended sentence for his role in systematically doping East German athletes, including causing bodily harm to 20 athletes due to drugs that were being administered to unknowing athletes from ages as young as nine.

Reflecting on the reality of doping in the GDR, Berendonk recalled, "Everyone was part of the scheme; it was an institutional scheme. There were penalties for doctors and anyone who turned against them. 'If I didn't do it, someone else would have done it.'" Commenting on the trials and the difficulty of testifying and exposing the dark truth of the GDR athletic system, Berendonk described it as a process of "defiling our nation, the image of our greatness and our prestige." She continued, "It is wrong to dope. Yet on the other hand, we have our coaches and our friends and they looked after us . . . so it is a dilemma—you don't want to contaminate all that they did for you." For athletes and doctors in East Germany, not spitting in the soup—polluting "the water I swim in" Berendonk called it—was the difference between a relatively comfortable life and a life of Stasi terror.[21]

In spite of the horrors that came with its unabashed drug use, the GDR system was widely emulated and continues to be today. Even after the collapse of the Eastern Bloc, the GDR system altered global sports. In a global diaspora, GDR-trained coaches and doctors spread out to the United States, New Zealand, Switzerland, France, Austria, Norway, Sweden, South Korea, and other nations. Twenty-four coaches involved with East German doping found work in the new unified Germany. In 1997, East German track and field coach Ekkart Arbeit was hired by Athletics Australia to prepare track and field talent for the 2000 Sydney Games. His contract was rescinded when Australians learned that Arbeit had spent two decades as a Stasi spy. Spread across the planet like dandelions, these coaches perpetuated the GDR's systematic, evidence-based sports medicine and performance-enhancement methods.[22]

Charlie Francis, the Canadian track coach who guided sprinter Ben Johnson to a drug-fuelled 100-meter victory at the 1988 Seoul Olympics, was one foreign coach who was awestruck by the thoroughness of the East German athlete support system. Francis described meeting renowned East German track coach Horst Hille at a 1981 coaching symposium in Venice, Italy. Hille told Francis about his team's DC-9 airplane, 21 doctors, two apartment buildings, a bus, and a fleet of cars—all to support 30 athletes. While Francis often had to put athlete travel expenses on his personal credit card and supported the entire Canadian track team with a staff of exactly one physical therapist, Hille reported that "I put in my plan and whatever I want, that's it." Even in an era when Olympic athletes were ostensibly amateurs, top runners were also handsomely paid in East Germany. "A top sprinter might make twice as much as the GDR's most successful industrial manager," Hille told Francis. A multiple gold medalist and world champion like East German sprinter Marlies Göhr "earned as much as the nation's president."[23]

GDR performance-enhancement systems were more scientifically sophisticated than anything Francis had seen in Europe or North America. For example, Francis thought he was breaking new ground when he introduced his runners to periodized training. At a time when North American training programs espoused running full throttle all the time, the thought of mixing high-intensity workouts with easy recovery runs was revolutionary. But the Canadian's training methods were still behind the curve compared to the dramatic tapering East German researchers were testing. East German track teams had their athletes running final full-speed workouts—often at world record pace—a full 10 days in advance of meets. A 10-day recuperation period was "an unheard-of gap in the West," Francis recalled. "These extended recoveries, along with the East Germans' incomparable pharmacology, massage, physiotherapy, and other support, allowed their sprinters to go at their absolute maximum on that 10th day before the meet. The work was of such high quality that a sprinter's central nervous system—first drained by the intense speed, then recharged by the 10-day taper period—would rebound like a pogo stick on the day of the competition."[24]

Francis recalled that East German research "had found the keys to the kingdom of international track: the optimal balance of work and rest to ensure that their athletes would perform at their absolute best when it counted most."[25] Historians Beamish and Ritchie suggest that this novel whole-system paradigm for performance enhancement that so astonished Francis can be traced back to a Russian agronomist named Trofim Denisovich Lysenko.

In the 1920s, Lysenko proposed that not genes alone, but rather the "internalization of external conditions" dictate an organism's heredity—its ultimate potential for growth. According to Lysenko, the latent output of an organism such as a wheat seed is determined by the interaction between the entity and its environment. Attracted to this theory that destiny is a dialogue between nature and nurture, Stalin made Lysenko head of the USSR's genetics program. Though Lysenko's theories were designed for agriculture (and failed miserably there), Beamish and Ritchie point out that his "basic assumptions may well have opened the way to a new paradigm" concerning how human performance could be altered if subjected to a carefully orchestrated set of nurturing circumstances. The same sort of massively centralized state planning meant to revolutionize Soviet farming and industry under Stalin was ported over to communist sport. Eastern Bloc nations—most dramatically East Germany—adopted sport systems whose sole purpose was to focus the collective financial, scientific, and cultural resources of the state on the nurturing and growth of athletes.

While such state-dictated communalism was anathema to capitalist nations, the system created a GDR sporting superiority that western nations were forced to confront. Until the 1950s, the conventional view of sports stuck to a theorem drawn from the first law of thermodynamics, that the total energy in an isolated organism is constant. It cannot be created, but only more fully accessed. The old model considered how to wring every last drop from an athlete's finite pool of energy—a conservation of energy model you could see at work when a turn-of-the-20th-century six-day rider would turn to stimulants to help scrape every ounce of potential energy from the bottom of his finite barrel of physical capacity. In the GDR model, the resources of large state institutions—university researchers, doctors, material scientists, nutritionists, chemists, physical therapists, physiologists—could *enhance* human performance rather than simply *exhaust* it. In the past, a track runner might focus solely on form, coordination, and economy of motion to extract more from his or her inherently finite potential speed and endurance. But the GDR's Cold War–inspired paradigm reenvisioned the athlete as an organism of nearly infinite potential whose performance limits could be expanded through the application of classified lab research, novel ergogenic drugs, and cutting-edge training methods such as the then-radical periodized training plan.[26]

Soviet and GDR sports systems became the model for all future national and professional sports programs—well-funded, systematic, obsessively measured, evidence-based sports medicine platforms that hold performance enhancement as their core defining value. As a result of western European and North American nations adopting performance-enhancement systems developed behind the Iron Curtain, today we take it for granted that an elite athlete reaches that level through the painstaking, long-term assemblage of marginal gains from a multitude of physiological and psychological inputs.

By setting this quantifiable standard, GDR sports put a bullet through the heart of Coubertin's dreams of the Olympics as a knighthood of men competing for the innate love of physical effort and guiding society from materialism toward divinity. And because pharmaceuticals were essential scientific elements of these new sports systems, the anti-doping movements that took root in the late 1960s and 1970s did not have a chance of eliminating the chemical tools essential to the central performance-enhancing raison d'être of elite sports. By establishing Olympic victory as a servant of imperial desire, first Hitler and then the GDR sporting system did much to turn drugs from a simple and relatively innocent survival tool for athletes in endurance sports into an agent of far-reaching material enhancement.

WHILE EAST GERMANY'S doping programs were designed to reassert German pride in the face of exploitative Soviet controllers and scornful NATO capitalists, in the USSR, Olympic performance-enhancing drugs programs were motivated by a more singular desire to prove the superiority of Marxist organizing political theory against the capitalist West. Following World War II, sports gave the USSR a means of continuing the war against the forces of bourgeois capitalism that Marx had described, only under the banner of Olympic sports. As one Russian explained, each Soviet Olympic victory provided "irrefutable proof of the superiority of the socialist culture over the decaying culture of the capitalist states."[27] Writing for the *New York Times* in 1978, Soviet sportswriter and recent U.S. immigrant Yevgeny Rubin noted that beginning with Soviet participation in the 1952 Helsinki Olympics, sport had become "one of the largest caliber guns of the propaganda arsenal." Visible to the entire world, "in sports everything can be measured," and that made it an ideal vehicle for a country that had to hide otherwise embarrassingly poor measures of national health like economic growth and personal freedoms. "Strong, agile, tanned, and invincible" Soviet athletes were meant to put a smiling propaganda face on a nation whose measures of human rights and economic health were decrepit. In fact, Rubin explained, that is why in the USSR, sports were overseen by the Communist Party's Department of Agitation and Propaganda.[28]

To prime the Soviet sporting machine, the Russian government dangled cash incentives for athletes and coaches. An October 1945 government decree stated: "To stimulate greater sports proficiency, the Council of People's Commissars of the USSR has permitted the All-Union Committee on Physical Culture and Sports Affairs to award monetary prizes for outstanding sports results." Bonuses of 1,000 to

3,000 rubles were available to juniors who broke national records, while world record breakers could collect upward of 25,000 rubles. On October 22, 1945, the Russian newspaper *Pravda* announced the creation of 80 sports schools where top young athletes could train without the bother of day jobs. This 1945 decree established legions of athletes who were effectively paid by the state.[29]

Female gymnasts as young as six were enrolled in sports schools where they followed relentless, meticulous training programs. The state rewarded medal winners like gymnast Olga Korbut with two-bedroom apartments, and star athletes enjoyed world travel at a time when most Russians had neither the money nor freedom to leave the country. The efforts paid off. At the 1960 Winter Olympics in Squaw Valley, California, the USSR carted off three times as many medals as the parliamentary democracy of Sweden, its fiercest winter sports competitor. That summer in Rome, the USSR clobbered the capitalists, taking 103 medals to the United States' 71. The winning trend continued in Munich in 1972, where the USSR embarrassed the Yanks by taking 50 gold medals to the United States' 33.

The Soviet sports and ranking system attempted to catch every bit of young sporting talent in its net; once identified, that physical potential was placed in camps where the youngster's life was completely dedicated to sports. Resulting victories glorified the USSR and the inevitable victory of socialism over capitalism. In 1964, Russian coach, sports scientist, and star pole vaulter Nikolai Ozolin wrote in *International Research in Sport and Physical Education* that his "government provided all the conditions for the development of sports on a mass basis: the stadiums, swimming pools, courts, and gyms." In addition to pro-level infrastructure, Ozolin explained that the USSR provided its young elite athletes with trainers, coaches, and sports medicine doctors, all free of charge.[30]

At a time when American football and baseball players stayed out of the weight room because they thought lifting would bind muscles and retard performance, the latest Soviet research had its athletes doing sport-specific weight training year-round. And the astonishing interval training Charlie Francis learned about from GDR coaches was first developed by Soviet sports scientists. Like the East Germans, Russians also included natural and synthetic supplements and drugs as part of their sports medicine programs. Capitalizing upon late 19th-century research on testosterone, in the early 1950s Soviet weight lifters injected pure testosterone into themselves to assist with training recovery.

The USSR's sophisticated physical fitness programs and Olympic medal hauls worried American leaders—they were taken as a sign of American national weakness. On a steamy July afternoon in 1955, President Dwight Eisenhower sat down for a White House lunch with baseball star Willie Mays, basketball luminary Bill Russell, and golf pro Max Elbin. Boxing champ Archie Moore was also there with commissioner of baseball George Frick. Over a 90-minute lunch with these stars and 28 other players, coaches, and sports leaders, Eisenhower and Vice President Richard Nixon discussed how to get American kids fit. Eisenhower was dismayed by a presentation showing that American youth were weak and easily fatigued compared to their European counterparts. The former Army general and war hero voiced concern that 50 percent of American World War II recruits had failed their military fitness tests. Eisenhower, a West Point varsity running back who also boxed and did gymnastics while in the military academy, felt that getting kids into sports would prepare them to pick up arms in the fight against communism. At a time when one Army general complained that too much time cruising in cars was causing recruits to have weak legs and poor "moxie," Eisenhower resolved to tighten America's form. To do so, he created the President's Council on Youth Fitness, a program that set fitness goals and rewarded American kids for passing various fitness tests.[31]

Eisenhower worried that more than flab was putting the United States behind the Soviets. In 1955, Congress authorized the addition of "In God We Trust" to all United States currency, a Cold War change intended to distinguish a nervous United States from the atheist Soviet

Union. Schoolchildren watched a 1951 U.S. Civil Defense film featuring an animated turtle named Bert. Viewable today on YouTube, the film shows how to protect yourself during an atomic bomb attack, which the narrator gravely cautions "can come at any time, no matter where you might be." The picture thrills with pre-nuclear-explosion scenes of a cyclist diving off his bike, a farmer ejecting from his tractor, and children crouching under their school desks—all techniques every American should know in order to shield their bodies from radiation. Public service efforts like these and omnipresent fallout shelter signs conditioned Americans to live with a constant fear of Soviet nuclear rain.

Nuclear dread dovetailed with alarm over the slack state of American physical fitness. The same year America added God to its currency, IOC president Avery Brundage took to the pages of the *Saturday Evening Post*—a magazine that shared his conservative disgust with communism—to tell his fellow Americans that the USSR's state-run sports program would annihilate the United States as a sporting power. "We think we are the greatest sports nation in the world," Brundage chided. "But let's not delude ourselves. We have become a race of grandstand and bleacher sitters. We think it is sport to find a good vantage point in the stands and watch professional baseball, football, boxing and horse racing."[32]

Brundage's spitting premonition of American slacker doom took *Post* readers along on his own three-week tour of the USSR's mighty sporting programs. He described a country with 4 million track and field athletes training to reach the grade of Master of Sport, the highest level in the country's sports pyramid. Training started in grade school, and kids with talent were pushed into sports-specific training tracks where they "receive the finest instruction possible," Brundage wrote. He went on to explain how "coaches and teachers are trained in institutes which deal scientifically with the mechanics and physiology of athletic competition, with biochemistry and psychology. There is a fierce drive to succeed, and, once successful, to go even higher." Unlike fat, car-driving, draft-test-failing Americans, Brundage warned, "Russia's national champions always are being admonished to do better."

Struck by the absence of chairlifts at Soviet ski hills, Brundage recounted Soviet downhill skier Konstantin Sorokin telling the perplexed American visitor that such athlete-coddling devices would never be approved in the Soviet system. Ominously, Brundage alerted his couch-bound American readers that in Sorokin's country, "sports without self-denial and self-conquest are merely amusement." To right this political and sporting wrong, Brundage urged his audience to "encourage amateur athletics and enlist our youth in a broad, revitalized program, or we are doomed to a secondary position in the world of sports."

Two years after Brundage took to the *Saturday Evening Post* to warn that Commies were kicking American's collective lazy ass, the Soviets launched humankind's first satellite, *Sputnik*. Reporting on this unexpected and scary scientific leap, the October 14, 1957, *Life* magazine quoted a Moscow citizen dismissing America as a nation of dilettantes: "Americans design better automobile tailfins but we design the best intercontinental ballistic missiles and earth satellites."[33] Four years later, the Soviet Union put the first human into space. In 1961, a year after Knud Enemark Jensen's Olympic death was falsely pinned on amphetamines and two years before Tour de France doctor Dumas organized the inaugural European Conference on Doping and the Biological Preparation of the Competitive Athlete, the U.S. populace of bleacher sitters and tailfin designers was becoming increasingly terrified by the Soviets' sporting and technological superiority.

On December 26, 1960, a month before his inauguration, president-elect John F. Kennedy used the pages of *Sports Illustrated* to send a New Year's message to the nation: Get off your duffs. In a cover essay titled "The Soft American," Kennedy took up the Brundage and Eisenhower gauntlet. He challenged his fellow citizens to get fit in the name of national pride and defense against communist threats.

The day-after-Christmas issue featured a cover photo of a decidedly active 43-year-old president and his wife, Jackie, on a boat. In the essay, Kennedy reminded readers that the Selective Service was rejecting 50 percent of American draftees for being "mentally, morally, or physically unfit." He cited a study of child fitness in the United States, Austria, Italy, and Switzerland that found that of some 7,000 children examined, 57.9 percent of the Yanks failed a flexibility and strength test, compared to only 8.7 percent of the Europeans. "In a very real and immediate sense, our growing softness, our increasing lack of physical fitness, is a menace to our security," Kennedy warned. Matching complaint with action, a month into his presidential term, Kennedy re-created the President's Council on Youth Fitness as the President's Council on Physical Fitness and put University of Oklahoma football coach Charles "Bud" Wilkinson in charge. The council distributed 240,000 copies of a national fitness program guide for the 1961–1962 school year with a Kennedy quote on the cover: "The Government cannot compel us to act, but freedom demands it." By cajoling and shaming the American populace, the executive branch made health and fitness a matter of national defense.[34]

Pressure from the Oval Office also made its way to the athletes representing the United States on global sporting stages. It was ultimately interpreted as a sanction, if not a demand, that American athletes should also use the same pharmaceuticals fueling communist Olympic success. In testimony to the U.S. Senate in July 1973, Phil Shinnick—a 1964 Olympian in Tokyo and the Rutgers University director of athletics—told the gathered senators that pressure to beat the Cold War enemy was transmitted from Washington, D.C., to coaches, trainers, and players. A terrific natural talent, Shinnick commanded respect—in 1963, while only a 19-year-old undergraduate, he set a long jump world record. Shinnick informed the Senate that in the run-up to the Tokyo Olympics, U.S. athletes had felt "political pressures to win for the country." He recalled that while employed as a coaching assistant at the 1965 World University Games in Budapest, U.S. State Department representatives shadowed the team and made comments about their obligations to their nation. "I was under constant pressure from the gentlemen at the State Department to beat the 'Commies,'" Shinnick recalled. "I could not ignore these comments since the trip was partially financed by the government." During his time on the U.S. Olympic team, Shinnick sensed anything but gold was unworthy of Americans and a gift to the communist enemy. "Implicit in this value is the assumption that the world has one winner and all the rest losers in each event," Shinnick told the committee. "This type of pressure leads toward drug abuse as clearly as the need for the coach to win to retain his job."[35]

According to Shinnick, European and Russian athletes had better medical supervision when using drugs. "There is a difference between the United States and the European countries," he said to the lawmakers who had the power to equalize this imbalance by loosening government purse strings. "There they are under more medical supervision and they are taking more drugs, I think, on a legal basis."

Shinnick was not imagining these political pressures. In 1962, Senator Hubert Humphrey had asked the U.S. Department of State to prepare a report on the Soviet sports system. Humphrey, the U.S. Senate majority whip (and future U.S. vice president under Lyndon Johnson), feared the Soviets were building up for "a major Cold War victory in 1964: a massive triumph in the Tokyo Olympics." Formerly a licensed pharmacist who had spent his 20s selling patent medicines in his father's South Dakota drugstore, Humphrey now proposed making membership in the Communist Party a felony and suggested putting ideological subversives into concentration camps. Humphrey married his understanding of the physiological and psychological power of pharmaceuticals to his dread of communists. The child of this union was a fanatical concern with the United States being humiliated in the Olympics. "Once they have crushed us in the coming Olympic battle," Humphrey warned in 1962, "the Red propaganda drums will thunder out in a worldwide tattoo, heralding the 'new Soviet men and women' as 'virile, unbeatable conquerors' in sports—or anything else."[36]

Shinnick also competed while serving as an officer in the U.S. Air Force. In his Senate testimony, he recalled pulling a muscle at the 1969 World Military Championships. Seeking advice, Shinnick spoke to a German doctor who told him that if he flew to Germany he could check into a sports hospital where rehabilitation specialists could mend him in 10 days. Lamenting the lack of a comparable elite sports medicine facility in the United States, Shinnick pointed out that for American athletes, "A lot of drug information is very contradictory." Without Soviet- or German-level sports medicine and pharmaceutical infrastructure in the United States, Shinnick told the lawmakers that American athletes were left to dope and recover on their own. That is, athletes in the United States were still using homegrown soigneur-style doping and sports medicine, while the GDR and USSR had gone pro. "We have people saying drugs don't help athletes in their athletic performance, yet athletes that I am familiar with are taking drugs and are increasing their performance from sometimes average athletes to world-class champions," Shinnick testified.[37]

In 1969, U.S. weight lifter Bill Starr told *Sports Illustrated* writer Bil Gilbert, "We are usually a long way behind the Russians in drug use." Echoing Shinnick's complaint, Starr explained that from the American athlete's perspective, the U.S. approach to doping was an ad hoc, homegrown affair that paled in comparison to the more systematic doping strategy in the Soviet Union. "They make a scientific study of it," Starr told Gilbert. "If they come up with something good, their teams all get it. Here it is a hit or miss thing."[38] Indeed, at the U.S. track and field trials for the 1976 Olympics, 23 competitors tested positive. Although none were punished, the sheer quantity of athletes being snared indicated that their self-dosing was random and lacked the professional guidance that would allow them to safely dope in training, then ease off the drugs for race-day tests. As a matter of national defense and moral righteousness in the face of the godless communists, it was time for the United States to step up.

Following his second-place finish to East German Waldemar Cierpinski in the 1976 Olympic marathon, American Frank Shorter quipped to the *New York Times* that he might win in 1980 "if I can find the right doctor." The story detailed the recent USOC formation of a committee of physicians, pharmacists, and scientists to study the effects of drugs and other sports medicine techniques on American athletes. "The success or failure of the panel could determine America's future role in international sports competition," the *Times* noted. Headed by New Jersey cardiovascular surgeon Dr. Irving Dardik, the USOC organized and financed the group to figure out how Americans could benefit from the East German level of attention to training and medicine that had embarrassed the Americans in their bicentennial year. "We want to develop methods and modalities for working with athletes that would enhance their performances and be safe," 40-year-old Dardik stated. "It's become a medical Olympics."[39]

At the 1976 Montreal Games, the USSR and East Germany won a total of 89 gold medals to the United States' 34. The same year, with American officials still smarting from this bicentennial beat-down, an East German sports doctor told the *New York Times* that his country's athletes were backed by "an entire collective of doctors, technicians and coaches—just like mission control when an astronaut is sent into space."[40] The communists were putting space-race resources into sports, and they delivered. In light of this Cold War humiliation, the USOC panel said it was ready to "look into areas considered taboo" in sports medicine. "I don't buy the concept that we shouldn't have to go that far to achieve success," Dardik argued. The doctor was not alone. In an August 1976 *New York Times* piece on the victories and masculine body shapes of East Germany's female athletes, U.S. Olympic long-jumping veteran Willye White argued that if Americans were going to win in the global sporting war, they needed to understand East German training methods: "If we're going to compete against synthetic athletes, we must become synthetic athletes," she contended.[41]

CHAPTER 8

ANABOLIC STEROIDS: SPORTS AS *SPUTNIK*

At dawn on November 20, 1943, U.S. Marines invaded a Japanese-held sliver of a South Pacific reef called Tarawa Atoll. The invasion of the remote island halfway between Hawaii and Australia was a debacle. Landing ships impaled themselves on reefs far outside their intended beach destination. Tanks intended to barrage into Japanese strongholds sank before touching land. When the marines finally made their way onto the atoll, they crawled into a four-day nightmare of machine guns, flamethrowers, grenades, mines, and rockets.

Despite their ill-launched attack, the Americans eventually took control of the island, though at a high cost—2,101 American soldiers were wounded and 6,400 American and Japanese troops were dead. Among the American grunts who survived the four-day assault was a 6-foot 4-inch, 220-pound marine named John Bosley Ziegler. Japanese bullets shredded the midwestern soldier, forcing him into months of painful physical rehabilitation. The experience inspired Ziegler to dedicate his life to medicine—specifically, to healing the handicapped and grievously injured.

After medical school and a two-year neurology residency at New Orleans' Tulane University School of Medicine, Ziegler set up his practice in Olney, Maryland. Ziegler's intellectual brilliance and good-natured eccentricity fascinated patients and friends. A friend called Ziegler "a big man with a big appetite and a keen sense of humor." Ziegler indulged a love of the Old West by donning cowboy costumes that earned him the nicknames "Tex" and "Mountain Jack."[1] Dissatisfied with the limited challenges that came with his small medical practice, Ziegler became restless. He wanted to leave a legacy as a groundbreaking medical researcher known for taking on unusual physical cases.[2]

Ziegler found an outlet for this scientific and personal ambition at Swiss drug and chemical maker Ciba, where he did side work as a consultant to their chemists. Looking for a tissue-building medicine to help rehabilitate burn and polio victims, Ciba had recently synthesized an anabolic-androgenic steroid called Dianabol. Ciba's objective was to create a drug that delivered the anabolic (muscle-building) benefits of the hormone testosterone, but without the negative androgenic (masculine-characterized) effects such as an enlarged prostate, atrophied testicles, acne, and a spaced-out feeling that can affect people using straight testosterone.

In Dianabol, Ziegler saw an opportunity to help mend patients going through the same sort of agonizing wound rehabilitation he had endured. Ziegler conducted early freelance experiments with the drug on a burn victim and a patient who had an appendectomy. While such informal drug testing might seem reckless today, the early 1950s were a time before the closely regulated drug trials that came about partly in response to the thalidomide birth-defect tragedies at the end of the decade.

A health fanatic, Ziegler lifted weights at a Silver Spring, Maryland, gym owned by weight lifting products manufacturer York Barbell. York president Bob Hoffman also published a fitness magazine, *Strength and Health*, and was a U.S. Olympic weight lifting team coach. Among the bodybuilding aficionados Ziegler met at the York gym was two-time Mr. America John Grimek. A member of the 1936 U.S. Olympic weight lifting team, Grimek's physique earned him the informal title of world's best-built man and frequently landed him on magazine covers. As

Grimek later recalled, Ziegler gained access to Nazi testosterone data while conducting Dianabol research at Ciba. After World War II, the United States and Russia had confiscated the studies from German labs with the thought that it might someday be of use for their own needs.

The Nazi research, along with earlier studies, suggested that testosterone could build muscle and strength. Eager to understand how Ciba's synthetic alternative compared, Ziegler tested Dianabol on himself and fellow York weight lifters. By providing Ziegler with Dianabol for his informal studies, Ciba was essentially running undocumented, uncontrolled clinical trials. While the practice seems alarming today, at that time, the use of a pharmaceutical company's network of physicians to test novel drug applications was quite common and unremarkable. Although Searle pharmaceuticals had marketed another anabolic steroid called Nilevar two years before Dianabol, thanks to Ziegler's personal and professional involvement with weight lifting and his patriotism, Dianabol was destined to be forever associated with sports.

In October 1954, Ziegler assisted the U.S. weight lifting team at the world championships in Vienna, Austria. While in Austria, Ziegler happened to strike up a conversation with a Soviet weight lifting coach. Over drinks, the Soviet coach told Ziegler that his athletes were getting results using testosterone as a recovery aid—such good results that they could not get enough of the stuff. Ziegler later recalled the coach telling him his lifters were "abusing the drugs heavily." Eager to bring home some of the American's training secrets, the Soviet trainer pressed Ziegler to reveal the drugs his athletes were using. Thinking the chewing gum Ziegler gave his athletes might contain a chemical elixir, the Soviet coach asked Ziegler for a sample. Knowing the active ingredient in the candy was nothing but sugar, Ziegler happily complied, providing his communist nemesis with a stick of gum that reportedly later went to a Soviet lab for analysis.[3]

Two years later, at the 1956 weight lifting world championships in Moscow, Ziegler saw the efficacy of Soviet testosterone injections firsthand when he observed Soviet lifters being catheterized to pee. As a side effect of testosterone boosting, the prostate can enlarge and impinge on the urinary tract. Without catheterization, the Russian athletes could not pass water. Impressed by the apparent ease with which the USSR's sports doctors put victory above such medical complications, Ziegler told U.S. Olympic trainers on his return to the United States that "the Eastern Bloc countries and Russians were going to use every trick to win, especially in strength sports."

Win they did. At the 1956 Summer Olympics in Melbourne, the Soviets won 98 medals to the Americans' 74. It was the first time the communist nation had surpassed the Americans in the overall medal count. After a Soviet team pulverized the United States 62 to 37 at the 1959 World Amateur Basketball championships in Chile, the *New York Times* reported that the loss had delivered "repairable but needless damage" to America's global prestige. A Santiago paper crowed, "When it comes to shooting at the moon or at a basket, the United States cannot keep up with Russia."[4] Following the tournament loss (where, incredibly, the United States sent a team of random Air Force players who had responded to a newspaper ad looking for volunteers), New Hampshire senator Henry Styles Bridges thundered that with the United States "in direct competition with Russia in all aspects and all fronts," the hapless world championship squad was like sending "a group of college students down to Cape Canaveral to take over the important job of beating the Russians in the race for space."[5]

In soccer-crazy South America, national prestige is closely linked to the performance of sports teams. Sending a schlocky hoops team was interpreted as confirmation of Yankee condescension toward nations south of the border—a particularly insulting attitude when directed at a staunchly anticommunist ally like Chile. In contrast, by sending their best players, the Russians signaled their regard for their South American hosts. Pummeled with inquiries as to why the United States had insulted Chile, and by extension all of Latin America, the U.S. embassy in Rio de Janeiro struggled for an answer. The basketball embarrassment was metastasizing into an international political scandal. The Chilean embassy went so far as to officially complain to the United States that, especially when the Soviets were involved, it was imperative that Washington "influence, either directly or indirectly, the selection of only the highest caliber teams." U.S. embassy spokesman John McKnight finally issued an apology of sorts, confessing, "This is big-league competition now—here, and everywhere else in the world—and bush leaguers have no place in the line-up."[6]

Writing that America "has more and better players per square foot than any nation in the globe," in a February 3, 1959, column, "Seeing Red," *New York Times* sportswriter Robert Daley howled that the thrashing was a "propaganda coup." Communists would use the American basketball disgrace to win hearts and minds in the Third World outposts coveted by Americans and Russians alike. "American prestige plummeted still lower in the land where we are trying to impress the citizenry with our Good Neighbor policy," Daley lamented. Ramping up his indignation, Daley warned, "Although sports is just an incidental part of the American way of life, the Soviet Union regards it as an integral and integrated part of the relentless surge toward world communism." The column then pointed in alarm to Russia's ascension in sports from track and field to hockey to basketball "and anything else they decide to concentrate on." Once they applied themselves, Russians might even do well in *tennis*, "as capitalistic a sport as can be found," Daley fumed. Conjuring up the aristocratic ghost of Pierre de Coubertin, Daley argued that in the midst of the Cold War, the "principle of sports for sports' sake is no longer operative."[7]

Daley's 1959 call to arms echoed the era's paranoid zeitgeist. The same issue of the *Times* rattled readers with four front-page stories on communist threats: the Soviet detention of a U.S. Army convoy in Germany; difficulties creating a demilitarized zone in Berlin; NASA's efforts to catch up with the Soviets in space; and the economic threat of Soviet Bloc petroleum sales in the United States. Meanwhile, days before Daley's column, a Marxist revolutionary named Fidel Castro had gained control of Cuba. That erstwhile American ally and vacation playground was suddenly a communist stronghold 90 miles from children building sand castles on Florida beaches. The Red Menace seemed *everywhere*, even in a Caribbean getaway where Americans had once escaped their cares with showers of rum, song, and sunshine. *Times* sports-page readers looking for light reading got a grave message: in the midst of the Cold War, the United States could no longer take sports as a diversionary pastime. It had to be a loaded howitzer on the front lines of international realpolitik.

The battles Ziegler had fought on a remote Pacific atoll were now playing out as proxy skirmishes on basketball courts and Olympic stadiums. The weight lifter was in tune with the high-strung spirit of the atomic times. His country's athletes had a moral and existential obligation to charge their physiology with the same chemical ammunition as their communist foes. Still legal and free of the stigma we take for granted today, steroids would take their proper place in the Cold War sporting armory. Ziegler asked Olympian and fellow York gym rat Grimek to encourage coach Hoffman to get his prospective 1960 Olympic team weight lifters on anabolic steroids.

Unsure that Dianabol was even effective, U.S. Olympic team coach Hoffman was lukewarm to Grimek's overtures. He also worried about giving his athletes a new sports medicine so close to the Rome Games, when they needed to be in undistracted peak form. "Apparently, he doesn't think it will do that much good, and may even have detrimental effects," Grimek reported back to Ziegler. "He appears doubtful." In spite of Hoffman's lack of enthusiasm about anabolic steroids for the 1960 Games, some weight lifters at the York gym began to see positive results from Ziegler's new Ciba product. Due in part to Ziegler's enthusiasm and infectious inquisitiveness about novel sports medicine, over time, many of the York lifters became steroid converts.[8]

While it's easy to make the mistake of transposing today's rigorous antidrug standards onto Ziegler's actions in the mid-1950s, doing so leads to a severe misunderstanding of his genuinely patriotic motives. Rather than dismissing Ziegler's pushing of anabolic-androgenic steroids on American athletes as moral deviance, in the mid-1950s, it was an act of medical curiosity and praiseworthy patriotism. A veteran who still felt the ache of his war wounds, Ziegler wanted to do his part to help America compete against a loaded Eastern Bloc field. It was his way of fighting the Soviet Union's intent to gobble up the Free World—liberated nations Ziegler had nearly died defending a decade earlier on a scrap of South Pacific sand.

Writer and fellow weight lifter Robert Goldman worked closely with Ziegler. Goldman recalled that Ziegler was "outraged" when he learned that the Soviet athletes had an advantage that the United States did not. "While our boys were slogging along with diets and workouts alone," Goldman wrote of Ziegler's motivations, the Soviets "were using male hormones." Ziegler's "intention was not to do harm, but to help his country out of loyalty," Goldman explained. No evidence suggests that Ziegler or the athletes and coaches around him considered steroids cheating, whether by the Soviets or the Americans. And because steroids were not a controlled substance at the time, his actions were legal. As a patriotic veteran and dedicated physician who recognized the growing importance of Olympic success during the Cold War, Ziegler believed that using his medical skills to help the York boys secure Olympic hardware was duty, not delinquency.[9]

In his 1984 book, *Death in the Locker Room*, Goldman reflects on the geopolitical forces influencing Ziegler. "Getting beaten on the playing fields, as well as in outer space and the Cold War, was a hard-to-swallow pill for American doctors who had been raised on American virtue-will-out based supremacy. The feeling of these doctors was that if they could in any way help an American athlete bring home the gold, they had somehow struck a blow for freedom." Doctors like Ziegler also assumed Eastern Bloc athletes had better drugs than the Americans. Not giving American athletes access to doping products could be seen as both unethical and unpatriotic. "The choice seemed to be give the drugs or risk an American humiliation and open the door to Communism," Goldman wrote.[10]

ZIEGLER'S EFFORTS to help wounded patients and underarmed Olympians was backed by his understanding of endocrinology. Testosterone is a male hormone. Secreted by the testicles beginning at puberty, it creates male sex characteristics like the beard, a deep voice, and sex drive. It also helps build muscles and bones—that's why boys go through dramatic physical changes when they hit puberty. Beginning in the 1880s, researchers identified testosterone's anabolic, or muscle-building, powers when they documented how castrated lab animals had smaller muscles and weaker skeletons than their intact brethren. Because steroids played such a large role in Cold War doping, it's worth taking a tour of their history.

One of the Industrial Revolution's shining examples of the mechanized age of clocks and steam engines was erected for the Paris Exposition of 1889. La Galerie des machines—the Machinery Hall—infused Paris with a modern esprit, a bright optimism that science and technology held the potential to lead humankind into a better future. Supported by 150-foot-high, 380-foot-wide arched steel girders and roofed with glass, the Machinery Hall was the world's longest open building. Filled with industrial apparatus and engines, it burst with samples of humanity's astonishing new capacity to harness and transform the natural forces that used to make it cower. The promise of science provided a hopeful context for a June 1 lecture that year at Paris's Société de biologie by a 72-year-old French physician, Charles-Édouard Brown-Séquard. His topic, bold like the times, was how to reverse aging with medicine.

Brown-Séquard announced that he had been injecting himself with juice from crushed animal testicles. The donors included a strong "and perfectly healthy dog" and "very young or adult guinea-pigs," Brown-Séquard informed his colleagues. Now, this was interesting stuff. Leaning forward in their seats, the gathered doctors and scientists hung on Brown-Séquard's every word. Unattended ashes on their cigarettes grew long.

Brown-Séquard, a highly regarded neurologist and physiologist, explained that after three weeks of injecting himself with the crushed testicle juice, as well as semen and blood from testicular veins, he felt youthful and revitalized. "A radical change took place in me," the Frenchman later reported in the British medical journal of record, the *Lancet*. "I had regained at least all the strength I possessed a good many years ago." Brown-Séquard described how injections, two in his left arm, eight in his leg, seemed to have taken 10 years off his age and diminished the indignities of being 72. Stairs he had scaled at a run just a decade earlier, he now inched up while clutching a handrail. After his injections, though, Brown-Séquard could once again take the stairs at a trot. And when he tested his arm strength, he could suddenly lift the same amount of weight as he had 26 years earlier. Measuring the distance of his urine stream, he found that the three weeks of injections had boosted his throw by "at least a quarter." And the aging human's battle against constipation was made easier by the injections; Brown-Séquard reported that he had a great "improvement with regard to the expulsion of fecal matters."

When he went off the juice, Brown-Séquard recalled that he "experienced almost a complete return to the state of weakness."[11] Testosterone, it seemed, was a drug as miraculous as Eiffel's fantastic tower that had just been completed across the Seine. Brown-Séquard's experiments were based on the widely held assumption that sexual-gland secretions were the seat of some sort of human potency and power.* His research was groundbreaking, so much so that historian John Hoberman describes Brown-Séquard as "the authentic father of our thinking about anabolic steroids and their alleged effects."[12]

In 1891, two years after Brown-Séquard's Paris lecture, more than 200 riders took on the 1,200-kilometer Paris–Brest–Paris race, which a

---

* The popular 19th-century theory that masturbation causes moral, mental, and physical deficiency was related to the notion that secretions from the "spermatic glands," to use Brown-Séquard's term, gave men strength and power. As Brown-Séquard wrote, just as castrated eunuchs "are characterized by their general debility and their lack of intellectual and physical activity," too much sex or masturbation would "produce a mental and physical debility which is in proportion to their frequency." So, he rationalized, if "spermatic anemia" caused physical and mental feebleness, then the opposite condition, "spermatic plethora," should cause a man to gain strength and power—a potential source for the old cycling tradition, upheld most famously by Irishman Sean Kelly, that riders should avoid sex the night before a race. See Brown-Séquard, "Note on the Effects Produced on Man by Subcutaneous Injections of a Liquid Obtained from the Testicles of Animals," *Lancet* 134, no. 3438 (1889): 105.

French rider won after 71 hours, 37 minutes of day-and-night racing. The growth of pro sports like cycling at the very time Brown-Séquard announced his findings on the revitalizing effect of *liquide testiculaire* led scientists to speculate on how testicular extracts might affect athletes. One of the earliest mentions came in 1894, when Austrian swimmer, cyclist, and scientist Oskar Zoth injected himself and fellow researcher Fritz Pregl with bull-testicle juice. The duo then tested their muscle strength and concluded that the extract made them stronger. Zoth closed his paper on the research by pointing to sports: "The training of athletes offers an opportunity for further research in this area for a practical assessment of our experimental results."[13]

Over time, scientists conducted research that revealed the chemical structure of the male hormones Brown-Séquard claimed made him young again. Pharmaceutical companies saw potential sales in testosterone for public health, military, and sporting use. Extracting testosterone from animals, however, was hugely inefficient. In 1927, a University of Chicago chemistry professor was able to extract a mere 20 milligrams of testosterone from 40 pounds of bull testes he collected from the Chicago stockyards. Obviously, the world's supply of bull testicles was not sufficient to fulfill the potential demand pharmaceutical companies saw in the nearly limitless number of tired, impotent, and aging people who might benefit from this new wonder drug.

Squibb pharmaceuticals began funding research on synthetic testosterone in 1926. By the mid-1930s, three drug makers were racing to synthesize mass-producible testosterone. Ciba chemist Leopold Ruzicka won the sprint and obtained the first patent for processing artificial testosterone in 1935. Along with Schering pharmaceuticals scientist Adolf Butenandt, in 1939, Ruzicka received the Nobel Prize in Chemistry for his testosterone work.

By the 1940s, the popular press was enthusiastically reporting on the new drug's anti-aging potential, drawing material from *The Male Hormone*, a 1945 bestselling book by science writer Paul De Kruif. Reviewing De Kruif's saga of the organic chemists who dared to find a medicine that could turn back time (or at least slow it down), the *New York Times* wrote that "probably no other story, except one about a cure for cancer or about the power to determine the sex of an unborn baby, would stir public imagination so widely."[14] De Kruif captured the vast demand for hormone treatment when he wrote of a silent mass of men living "on the shady side of life's afternoon" and cursed by vague ailments that, while not showing the vivid symptoms of a broken leg or failing heart, still afflicted "the former joy of living." De Kruif wrote, "This is the smoldering of the hormone hunger." As he saw it, the condition of modern man is a slide toward undefined but inevitable failure; the 1940s male hangs on, besieged by "vague worries" over "unknown but ever-threatening catastrophe." Meanwhile, "failing memory and poor power of concentration portend a mental crack-up." And this entire catastrophe of life is compounded by the sharp humiliation of "apparently failing sex function."[15]

Along with rejuvenating the collapsing heap of dysfunction that is the middle-aged body, De Kruif also saw potential for testosterone use in sports—specifically, younger sportsmen still romping on the sunny side of life's afternoon. "We know how both the St. Louis Cardinals and St. Louis Browns have won championships, super-charged by vitamins," he wrote. "It would be interesting to watch the productive power of an industry or a professional group that would try a systematic super-charge with testosterone."[16] Though it would take a decade for chemistry to catch up with De Kruif's vision, by the 1960s, American football players would indeed experiment with hormone supercharging.

After the age of 30, human testosterone production slowly declines—a biological fact that drives today's booming business selling testosterone supplements to address "low-T," the mellowing libido and slackening energy that settles in with age. Females also produce testosterone, but typically at a ratio of 1 to 8 compared to males. Females' relative lack of testosterone is why the East German sports doctors documented testosterone having a more dramatic physical effect on women than men—facial hair, deeper voices, and unusually powerful sex drives.

In the complete term for the synthetic version of testosterone, *anabolic-androgenic steroid*, *anabolic* refers to the hormone's ability to build muscle mass through a metabolic process of storing proteins and building tissue. *Androgenic* refers to the hormone's masculinizing effects; it signifies production of (*gen*) male (*andro-*) traits. *Steroid* refers to a class of organic and synthetic compounds with their own unique molecular structures. Anabolic-androgenic steroids are essentially versions of the testosterone hormone but are manufactured by a chemistry lab rather than human glands. Although steroids were first synthesized in the 1930s, so far no steroid has been invented that can deliver muscle-building anabolic effects without androgenic side effects.

Today, we know that anabolic steroid abuse can be highly destructive, even fatal. Autopsies of anabolic-steroid-using weight lifters and football players have revealed heart damage caused at least in part by heavy steroid use. Historian Steven Ungerleider's book on the East German sports system, *Faust's Gold*, revealed that female GDR athletes doped with the German anabolic steroid Oral-Turinabol, and its injectable variation, suffered a host of debilitating gynecological and mental complications. At the 2000 criminal trial of Lothar Kipke, an overseer of the GDR doping program (who simultaneously presented himself as an anti-doping crusader as a board member of FINA, swimming's IOC-sanctioned governing body), 1978 East German national swimming champion Jutta Gottschalk testified that the steroids caused intensely painful menstrual cycles. "I could climb the walls my period was so awful," Gottschalk recalled. Her son was born blind. Many other female GDR athletes were unable to bear children, and those who did conceive frequently gave birth to children with disabilities. Another swimmer, Martina Gottschalt gave birth to a son with physical deformities, including a clubfoot—second-generation side effects of the steroids administered to her as a swimmer.[17] Steroids can destroy liver cells, leading to hepatitis, and they have been linked to cancer, depression, and suicide. Men suffered from gynecomastia, or unnaturally large breasts. At the 2000 trial of GDR doping mastermind Manfred Ewald, one East German swimmer was asked how coaches explained her unnaturally deep voice. Forced to take up to 30 pills a day, plus steroid injections from the age of 11, she recalled, "They told me to swim, not sing."[18]

Back in 1958, Ziegler could not predict these harmful effects nor foresee how his drug would be abused by bodybuilders and football players. Nor could he predict that it would be systematically forced on teenagers by East German leaders seeking to push their nation out from the shadow of Soviet overseers. This lack of foresight arose in part from the indiscriminate way he tested the products coming out of Ciba's chemistry labs and the fact that Ziegler was not even sure Dianabol worked. Ziegler prescribed the drug to athletes without careful monitoring of their actual dosages and resulting performance responses. Testing without a protocol and without control groups, his attribution of muscle response to the drugs was more a collection of anecdotes than a strictly regulated clinical study.

Further complicating his measurement of Dianabol's efficacy, Ziegler was a big proponent of both hypnotism and the "maximum contraction" method of weight training. A technique resurrected from a turn-of-the-20th-century muscleman named Bernarr Macfadden, the training method involved pushing against immovable objects; it was later renamed functional isometric contraction and marketed with special equipment. Ziegler did not know if the results his athletes were getting were from this technique, from hypnotism, or from drugs—or from some combination of the three. Writing of Ziegler's work with Olympic weight lifting coach and magazine publisher Hoffman, historian John Fair noted that Ziegler "administered such a conglomeration of ergogenic aids in such an irregular manner that it was impossible to tell where the impact of one stopped and another began. Those who attribute conspiratorial designs to Ziegler, and by extension to Hoffman, must reckon with the fact that neither party was sure of what was being discovered."[19]

Although Hoffman eventually administered Dianabol to some weight lifters at the 1960 Rome Olympics, he did so with little, if any, consistency in the frequency and size of doses. While his athletes saw some improvements, Soviet lifters still crushed the U.S. team, so no one came back with a clear reading that anabolic steroids enhanced performance. During the 1960 Games, Grimek, the Mr. America Ziegler first met in his Maryland gym and supplied with Dianabol, reported back that it "didn't seem as if the 'pills' helped that much." When Grimek returned to the United States from Rome, he asked Ziegler how the Dianabol was helping the doctor's own lifting. Ziegler responded, "It's done nothing for me. The fellows claimed it did nothing for them, yet each did good or better than they've done in the past . . . in spite of LOSING."[20]

Medical uncertainty aside, the anabolic androgenic steroids soon had plenty of believers. The genie Ziegler let out of the bottle was quickly being sold, bartered, and abused by muscle builders in weight rooms around the world. By the late 1960s, lifters and other athletes were swallowing steroids in amounts far beyond what doctors recommended. Assuming that more drugs would get more results, people were taking 10 times the 5- to 10-milligram doses Ziegler and other physicians prescribed, and often "stacking" these oral doses with other injectable steroids.

In 1963, a weight lifter named Alvin Roy became a weight trainer for the San Diego Chargers NFL team. Applying Ziegler's research to the football training camp, Ciba's pink Dianabol pills appeared in bowls on the Chargers' breakfast tables to help them recover from what was then a cutting-edge NFL weight training regime. Steroids became the norm in college and pro football programs everywhere. And in local gyms, lifters could not get their hands on enough Dianabol.

Created from Ziegler's personal stew of patriotism, intellectual curiosity, and desire for professional status as a groundbreaking medical researcher, the anabolic steroid monster was out, and as much as Ziegler came to regret it, it wasn't coming back. In spite of his innocent initial motives, Ziegler was soon treating patients who were suffering from the destructive symptoms of anabolic steroid abuse. In 1967, he raged, "What is it with these simple-minded shits?" Once people got their hands on steroids, he said, "They were eating them like candy. I began seeing prostate trouble and a couple cases of atrophied testes."[21] That year, Ziegler wrote a piece in *Strength and Health* magazine condemning athlete steroid abuse.

At the 1972 Munich Olympics, U.S. track and field team member Jay Sylvester polled his male teammates about their drug use at the Games. His informal survey found that 68 percent of the American team was using anabolic steroids.[22] This self-reporting was backed up by American weight lifting team physiologist Pat O'Shea, who told the *Los Angeles Times* that every U.S. weight lifter in Munich used performance-enhancing drugs. The July 16, 1972, blurb in the paper's "Morning Briefing" section brightened Los Angeles readers' breakfasts with the news that if all the U.S. weight lifters using drugs were disqualified, "the United States would not have a team at Munich." It went on to quote Ziegler on how the drugs he first championed in the mid-1950s had spun out of control. Explaining that athletes were gulping dosages 20 times greater than what he prescribed, Ziegler fumed about why he discontinued his involvement with the U.S. Olympic team: "I lost interest in fooling with IQs of that caliber." Doping had become "as widespread among these idiots as marijuana."[23]

In 1983, the year he died, Ziegler wrote the introduction to weight lifter Bob Goldman's *Death in the Locker Room*, a book-length warning against the dangers of performance-enhancing drugs. Ziegler wrote that after getting their hands on anabolic steroids in the 1960s, athletes "turned it into one big mess." Harkening back to the early days of his medical practice in the late 1940s, when many of his patients were so wary of medicine that he had to struggle to get them to take a pill, Ziegler lamented how attitudes characterizing a "drug crazy" society had infected athletics. "Everyone is pill happy," he complained. "It started in the 1950s and by the 1960s had taken a firm hold on the public's life blood."

Months before dying of a heart attack, the man who became known as the father of American anabolic steroids lamented the loss of innocence he linked to transformation of the Olympics into a vehicle for larger national and commercial objectives. Writing of the upcoming Los Angeles Summer Games, Ziegler was defeated. "The Olympics were a time for people of all nations to join in the interplay of true brotherhood among nations," he mourned. "Now it is one cheap political ploy." Pointing to the runaway success of the performance-enhancing drugs he once championed as a possible Cold War equalizer, Ziegler concluded that the 1984 Olympics "will probably be as fixed as an illegal horse race."

CHAPTER 9

THE REDS ARE WINNING

Willye White's 1976 warning that American athletes needed to get on board with the communists' performance-enhancement program—"If we're going to compete against synthetic athletes, we must become synthetic athletes"—still rang true on the afternoon of March 3, 1983. On that day, President Ronald Reagan attended a luncheon with U.S. Olympic Committee members at the Los Angeles Biltmore Hotel. The United States had boycotted the 1980 Moscow Olympics, so the country's thin medal haul at the 1976 Olympics still left a sour taste in the mouths of dedicated Cold Warriors.

And Reagan harbored no love for Marxists. The former actor and California governor funded anticommunist rebels in Nicaragua and El Salvador and told Russian leader Mikhail Gorbachev to tear down the Berlin Wall. Even though anticommunism was a centerpiece of the Reagan presidency and saw the United States spend $5 billion fighting wars in Nicaragua and El Salvador, communist athletes continued to humiliate the United States on the playing field.[1] At the 1976 Summer Olympics, the USSR and East Germany took a collective 215 medals, more than double the United States' 94. In the first-place tally, the United

States, a country of 220 million people, took home 34 gold medals. East Germany, with a population of fewer than 17 million, flew out of Montreal with 40 golds. A communist nation with 82 percent fewer people than the United States took 118 percent more victories. At least in terms of sports, the Olympics of America's bicentennial summer revealed a nation in decline, not one celebrating 200 years of capitalist triumph.

In 1984, Reagan wanted to stop this communist victory trend, and he especially wanted to do it in his Southern California backyard. Connecting Truman Doctrine to Olympic victory, Reagan reminded the U.S. Olympic officials gathered at the Biltmore Hotel that millions of people—including impressionable children—would be watching America's first home-turf Olympics since 1932. Alluding to the 1976 Olympic debacle, Reagan leaned on the USOC heavies: "I know we won't let those kids down and won't shortchange our country by doing anything less than a first-class job." Reagan went on to mention black American Jesse Owens's victories in front of Hitler at the 1936 Berlin Olympics. Summoning his sound-stage training, Reagan recounted Owens's response when asked what it was like to hear the American national anthem play in Berlin in 1936: "It's a tremendous feeling when you stand there and watch your flag fly above all the others. I couldn't forget the country that brought me there." Underscoring his don't-let-us-down message, Reagan added, "In a free society, it all depends on us."[2] The USOC had its marching orders: Delivering medals in 1984 was more than a moral obligation; it was a matter of national defense.

Five days after his Los Angeles speech, Reagan appeared at the National Association of Evangelicals conference in Florida. He urged the attendees to resist the "aggressive impulses of an evil empire" and "speak out against those who would place the United States in a position of military and moral inferiority." Branding the Soviet Union as an evil empire became Reagan's signature, and in the same talk, he warned the Christians gathered at Orlando's Sheraton Twin Towers Hotel that with communists, "simple-minded appeasement or wishful thinking about our adversaries is folly. It means the betrayal of our past, the squandering of our freedom."[3] Defeating communism demanded resolve and creative action, not passivity. Harkening back to the Truman Doctrine, in a span of five days Reagan reminded both evangelical and Olympic leaders of their moral and patriotic obligation to take steps to turn back the tide of communism, whether it arrived in the form of a Marxist dismissal of God or as spiritually bereft communist Olympic medal hauls. For Reagan, torpor in the face of communism was not an option. As the 1984 Olympics neared, unflinching action was the only defense of freedom.

As historian Thomas Hunt explains in *Drug Games*, his 2011 book on Olympic doping, such energetic rhetoric coming from the Free World's most powerful man "made a profound impact on American sports officials."[4] After the 1984 Games, when *Sports Illustrated* reported in January 1985 that some riders on the U.S. Olympic cycling team had blood doped, U.S. Cycling Federation (USCF) president Mike Fraysse told the magazine that the USCF had been looking at blood doping for "years and years and years." Echoing the wishful-thinking-is-folly sentiment informing both Reagan and Willye White's advice, Fraysse told *Sports Illustrated*, "We weren't gonna fall behind the Russians or East Germans any more."[5]

Reagan's administration would go on to break the law by shipping arms to a terrorist state, Iran, in exchange for American hostages. Payment for these illegal arms was routed through Contra fighters in Nicaragua. For Reagan, the ends—liberating American hostages in Iran and halting Soviet communism before it crept up to the Mexican border—justified the legally gray means. The Contras were "the moral equivalent of our founding fathers," he said on March 1, 1985. "We cannot turn away from them."[6] When it came to halting the falling dominos of communist oppression, prohibitions could be pushed aside to secure the greatest good—freedom. In the 1985 *Sports Illustrated* piece on blood doping, USCF doctor Ed Burke echoed Reagan's assertiveness when he stated that, relative to the Soviets and East Germans, American performance-enhancement programs "were in the dark ages." When it came to dealing with the Russians, passivity was a losing option. "You know where we are now," Burke divulged. "Nobody says we wear white gloves." The parallels between Burke preparing his team for the 1984 Olympics and Reagan priming his nation for a battle against the communist dominos he saw falling in Central America were precise. Both blood doping and selling arms could be justified as a way of circumnavigating compliance with petty legislation that could lead to a worse evil: the ultimate loss of American freedoms to communism.

No matter how much Americans were willing to dirty their gloves to defeat communists, duplicating a sports performance-enhancement structure like East Germany's would be difficult in the United States. First, creating autocratic government agencies ran contrary to the Republican worldview, in which private enterprise, not government bureaucracies, are the default problem solvers. Second, management of United States Olympic programs was a self-mutilating hash.

In 1976, three organizations wrestled for control over amateur sports: the National Collegiate Athletic Association (NCAA), the Amateur Athletic Union (AAU), and the United States Olympic Committee (USOC). While East Germany was funneling talent into centralized, government-funded training platforms supported by elaborate sports medicine and pharmaceutical infrastructure, the U.S. organizing bodies were dismembering one another in a fight for control. Commenting on this chaos, in 1977, Olympic gold medal swimmer John Naber diplomatically told the *New York Times*, "Organization is the key to success and it would be simpler working with just one such body." Naber's coach Peter Daland was not so charitable, calling U.S. amateur sports organizations a "mess." Daland, a USC coaching legend who had guided Mark Spitz to seven victories and seven world records at the 1972 Munich Games, said, "There is no central direction for sports in this country. Our program works by happenstance while other countries are going by five-year plans and ten-year plans." He went on to explain that between pro-level training, organization, and drugs, the United States' Cold War enemies had systems that set up American athletes for almost certain failure. "We need a plan," Daland pleaded.[7]

Although Reagan did not explicitly instruct USOC officials to copy communist performance-enhancement practices, for at least eight years, the United States had been trying to get its Olympic preparation act together. Alarmed by the Americans' drubbing by communist athletes at the 1972 Munich Olympics, in 1975, President Gerald Ford created the President's Commission on Olympic Sports to study what was inhibiting U.S. athletes' gold-medal performances. Chaired by Eastman Kodak CEO Gerald Zornow, the commission spent 18 months and $1 million investigating how the United States and other countries organized their national sports programs. The group also analyzed the structure and effectiveness of 30 Olympic sports in the United States, including cycling.

Published in January 1977, the commission's final report concluded that the U.S. Olympic feeder programs needed money and organization. "There are three basic modes of sports organization employed by successful sporting nations," the report determined. "In one, government is placed in control. In another, a nongovernmental sports organization is in control. In the third, no one is in control. Only the United States uses the third method."[8]

While chaos guided U.S. Olympic efforts, athletes, coaches, citizens, and congress members knew that method one ruled in East Germany. They read about GDR government control in the papers. Following the Montreal Games, Professor Kurt Tittle, the head of the German Sports Institute in Leipzig, told the *New York Times* that every GDR gold medal was backed by "an entire collective of doctors, technicians and coaches—just like mission control when an astronaut is sent up into space."[9] Unlike the United States, which did not fund Olympic training programs with taxpayer dollars, the GDR lavished public support on its athletes and managers. Challenging the overly simplistic but morally comforting American interpretation that drugs alone made communists win, *Times* reporter Craig Whitney explained that "what the East Germans have perfected is not so much magic pills or shots as truly scientific training programs in sports from swimming to rowing to the shotput."[10] Integrated into a larger, coordinated program designed to identify, nurture, and launch athletes to world-record-breaking performance levels, the steroids East Germans and Russians used were only one brick in a larger sporting fortress.

Ford's commission recommended that the United States create a nongovernmental organizing body to oversee and coordinate all Olympic sports—if not a sporting Manhattan Project like East Germany's State Plan Subject 14.25, then at least a mission control to replace the existing disarray. The report suggested that excelling in Olympic sports is joined at the hip with national security. Alluding to the Soviet Union, the report stated that "while a nation's success in international sports competition is not indicative of the merits of its ideology—despite some countries' attempts to convince us otherwise—it surely tells us much about the vigor of that nation's sporting populace and the cohesiveness of its organization."[11] To prove that capitalist systems could also channel their creative vigor and organizational skills into wins, the report pointed to the space race. Putting a man on the moon before the Russians was a "massive victory" and "splendid example" of what the United States could do when leaders appointed an effective agency to organize the nation's human and economic potential. Without a NASA for American Olympic sports, the report confessed that "against athletes from nations for whom Olympic medals are as precious as moon rocks, U.S. competitors seem to have steadily diminishing chances of success." Although America had both a nearly bottomless quarry of raw athletic talent and the world's most potent financial resources, its "sports organizations are fragmented," the report concluded. "Not bound by common purpose or any effective coordinating system," the United States was squandering a fantastic reserve of athletic potential.[12]

To illustrate the dysfunction keeping Americans from racking up Olympic gold, the report examined the current state of the U.S. Olympic organizing committees, including the USCF. Responsible for organizing elite cycling under the umbrella of the U.S. Olympic Committee, the report painted an unsparing picture of a flawed, inward-looking organization more interested in protecting its staff and leadership than supporting Olympic-level cyclists.

The commission reported that the USCF board of directors was an insular, self-perpetuating group of insiders propped up by a nominally democratic network of local cycling clubs. The report suggested that the current Olympic system design supported bureaucracy over cycling excellence. In 1975, only 200 of the 400 U.S. clubs bothered to register with the UCSF on time, and of those eligible clubs, only 45 sent representatives to the annual meeting where the board of directors was chosen. The result of this club-level apathy was that the same board members were re-elected year after year. The permanent insider's club also created easy opportunities for fraud. The report detailed how would-be directors created bogus cycling clubs with no members and used these shams to nominate themselves. Once on the board of directors, "they represented no athletes, no coaches, no administrators—only themselves," the commission explained.[13]

The report delivered a withering account of an organizing body ill-equipped to mine the potential in a nation where, thanks in part to a petroleum crisis and rising environmental and health awareness, cycling was booming, and where Americans like George Mount, Mike Neel, and world sprint champion Sheila Young-Ochowicz were making inroads in Europe. "Overall, U.S. cycling is enjoying unprecedented popularity," the report observed. "There is little reason to suspect that the numbers of Americans who own and ride bicycles as a leisure activity will diminish and on the surface, competitive cycling ought to profit directly from this revival."[14]

Unfortunately, the USCF, like organizing bodies overseeing other Olympic sports in the United States, was incapable of mining this potential. At the time, the entire USCF staff consisted of one part-time administrator and a computer programmer paid a $75 monthly retainer to manage registrations. An outside PR firm was tasked with fund-raising and beating the bushes for sponsorships. Ford's commission did not mince words when explaining why the UCSF was impotent against European cycling powerhouses. "Apathy, inordinate demands placed on volunteer officials, lack of permanent staff, insufficient funds, and club control of the sport" were the USCF ingredients for a recipe for international sporting embarrassment.[15]

UCSF finances were a mess. According to the report, in 1975, the cycling organization brought in $174,800 and spent $194,700. Of that expenditure, $60,000 supported Olympic efforts and $25,400 went toward organizing the national championships. It was perhaps unsurprising that an Olympic body that had won zero cycling medals in Montreal (compared to the 44 percent of the total medals that went to communist nations) had not a single expense line devoted to rider development. That task was left to the local clubs, which meant junior and novice development programs were inconsistent at best, especially considering that some clubs only existed on paper. The report revealed that while lack of funds precluded the USCF from organizing a national cycling team, $21,000 went to travel and meeting expenses for the USCF board of directors. Reflecting on the use of 12 percent of the total USCF budget for self-elected board members to travel to largely unattended meetings and zero percent for building an Olympic-level squad, the report wryly concluded, "Consideration ought to be given to allocating more money to areas such as the development of a national team."[16]

The dysfunctional USCF was unlikely to identify the young American talent pushing a paper-delivery bike up the hills of the Pacific Northwest or whipping a BMX bike around a vacant lot in New England. Compared to the gene-finding machine sucking up potential athletes from schoolrooms and farmyards in the far corners of Russia and East Germany, the United States was surely missing out, especially in sports that did not draw collegiate attention.

The investigators concluded that in addition to not finding gifted athletes, the United States was not making use of the country's significant body of sports medicine research. Scientific discoveries that could be used to enhance the performance of American athletes were "often ignored because there is no effective means of putting findings to practical use." And while countries like East Germany spent "millions of dollars to coordinate their reference programs and research in human performance," the great body of sports medicine research then taking place in the United States was being scattered to the wind—as "fragmented and uncoordinated as the U.S. amateur sports system in general."[17]

Ford's million-dollar investigation documented how infighting and lack of coordination among U.S. athletic organizations undermined the Cold War battle for sporting prestige. The problem, however, had been on Ford's radar long before the final 140-page report landed on his desk in January 1977. In July 1974, one month before Richard Nixon resigned over Watergate, Vice President Ford contributed a piece to *Sports Illustrated* in which he argued that the USOC needed to be rebuilt to deliver American victories. Under a Nixon-Ford administration, though, that restructuring would be done only "with minimal federal involvement and control, and therefore at minimal cost to the taxpayer."[18] As Republicans, Ford and Nixon had to balance their party's native resistance to more taxpayer-funded government agencies with the GOP's hawkish aversion to losing face in the Cold War. "State-supported, state-manipulated athletic programs are not for us," Ford assured his readers.

A talented Division I college football player who chose law school over professional contract offers from the Detroit Lions and Green Bay Packers, Ford, like his boss, was a dedicated gridiron fan. He also shared Nixon's guiding life value, one that Nixon had picked up from his own college football coach, Wallace "Chief" Newman: winning matters. Although Nixon was only a third-stringer during his football tenure at California's Whittier College in the 1930s, the aggressive, territorial nature of the game framed his worldview. In his memoir, *RN*, Nixon recalled that Coach Newman was one of his most influential mentors. "He had no tolerance for the view that how you play the game counts more than whether you win or lose," Nixon wrote of the Native American coach. "Show me a good loser, and I'll show you a loser," Newman told the impressionable undergraduate.[19] For the college coach, defeat, even with grace, was failure. Winners are remembered. Losers are forgotten and disappear. This was an important message for a future politician who was heavily invested in Cold War ideology. "You must never be satisfied with losing," Newman confided to Nixon. "You must get angry, terribly angry, about losing."[20] Newman's belief that winning counts for everything would affect Nixon's reshaping of Eisenhower's and Kennedy's policies on the role of government and American sport.

Nixon also saw organized sports as a bulwark against social disorder. Appealing to the "silent majority" of Americans alarmed by 1960s youth uprisings against the Vietnam War and racial injustice, Nixon dismissively said he would not "be affected whatever" by a massive protest planned for Washington in November 1969. Rather than granting the howling counterculture an audience, Nixon assured his nation that he would be watching football on TV—that is, doing what conventional Americans did. As presidential historian Michael Beschloss has explained, Nixon used his love of football to distinguish himself from the long-haired antiwar protesters in the streets and presented himself as a defender of the silent majority's traditional values.[21]

Nixon and Ford freighted Olympic sports with Cold War moral cargo, and for them the highest moral obligation was to win, even if it meant trampling other prohibitions. Indeed, the administration that broke into the Democratic National Committee's offices in the Watergate Hotel and Office Building and lied to Congress about carpet-bombing neutral Cambodia saw certain rules as petty obstacles in the way of a higher ethical cause—the defeat of communism and preservation of the rights of humanity. In *Sports Illustrated,* Ford expressed the executive-office belief that "we owe it to ourselves to reassess our priorities, to broaden our base of achievement so that we again present our best in the world's arenas." The United States was ready to step up its Olympic game. It was time to toss Eisenhower's and Kennedy's fitness-for-all policies and focus on sports for the athletic elite. When it comes to sporting victories in the international arena, "I don't know of anything more beneficial in diplomacy and prestige," Ford wrote. "The broader the achievement the greater the impact. There is much to be said for Ping-Pong diplomacy."[22] Olympic losers are invisible. Winners command respect and attention.

In 1976, Georgia governor Jimmy Carter beat Ford in a close presidential election. The new president signed the Amateur Sports Act of 1978 into law without changes. As Olympic historian Thomas Hunt summarizes, the act Carter signed on November 8, 1978, was the outcome of "a Cold War perception in the late 1960s and 1970s that Soviet dominance on the Olympic fields had a detrimental impact on American prestige abroad."[23] Indeed, as early as May 1966, Vice President Hubert Humphrey had appeared on an NBC-TV special, *The Russian Sports Revolution*, and declared that the Soviets' methodical approach to preparing for Olympic sports was "a challenge to us just like Sputnik was." Unless the United States upped its Olympic preparations game, "we are going to be humiliated as a nation," Humphrey warned.[24]

With the president's pen stroke, the federal government pivoted from defense through fitness for the softening masses to defense through Olympic victories. What NASA was to America's space program, the USOC was to Olympic sport. Using the machete of an executive order to slash through the infighting between the USOC, NCAA, and AAU, the law made the U.S. Olympic Committee the authoritative coordinating corporation for amateur sports. This dictate attempted to end the often-conflicting interests and rulings of the NCAA and the AAU, an organization that had represented U.S. Olympic sports since the 1896 games but whose super-strict rules on amateurism could capriciously exclude world-class athletes from Olympic teams—as Jim Thorpe could attest after the AAU yanked his 1912 gold medals when someone mentioned he had once played baseball for $2 a day. The AAU's backward attitudes regarding female athletes also put the United States in reverse compared to the East Germans; the athletics organization fought against women in sports to the day Congress pulled the plug on its power. As for the USOC, before the Amateur Sports Act, it was little more than a glorified travel office for Olympic athletes.[25]

With Olympic authority now transferred away from the AAU and the NCAA, the USOC was empowered to identify a single national governing body (NGB) for each Olympic sport. That matter of who governs each Olympic sport in the United States had been a headache in the past, when multiple organizations had claimed to be a sport's managing authority. The consolidated organization took its onetime offering of $16 million in seed money and quickly moved its headquarters from New York City to more athlete-friendly Colorado Springs.

The USOC was designed to operate without taxpayer funding, leading the commission's executive director, Michael Harrigan, to complain that Nixon and Ford "want to clobber the Soviets but don't want to give Olympic sports a federal dime!"[26] However, the USOC did retain rights to license its name and symbols as well as IOC assets including the Olympic rings and the words "Olympic," "Olympiad," and "Citius Altius Fortius."[27] What the USOC lacked in federal cash, it theoretically would make up for by renting out its rights to Olympic brands. Any company that dared violate this policy in the process of flogging its goods would find itself fighting lawsuits backed by the limitless legal might of the federal government.

Weaving three policy threads—Republican aversion to overbearing government bureaucracy, a desire to promote American political interests abroad, and faith in private enterprise's ability to fund ambitious human endeavors—the Amateur Sports Act of 1978 set up a dynamic in which promoting sponsors and United States government objectives would have to trump the objectives of the anti-doping bureaucracies that were simultaneously taking root in the 1970s.

CHAPTER 10

SPINNING OLYMPIC GOLD: L.A. 1984

The Amateur Sports Act of 1978 set the stage for American sporting excellence to be funded by individual citizens and corporate donors. As Vice President Ford wrote in *Sports Illustrated*, the restructured game plan for American Olympic excellence would be accomplished with "minimal federal involvement and control, and therefore at minimal cost to the taxpayer."[1] In 1984, this federal emphasis on the private and corporate funding of athlete development cascaded down to the way the Los Angeles Olympic games were paid for. While Adidas was one of the first companies to show how the Olympic aura could sell products and Hitler was the first to use the Games to sell a national ideology, the 1984 Los Angeles Olympics were the first to turn the sports extravaganza into a self-supporting marketing package. Due to federal and local aversion to using tax dollars for Olympic development, the 1984 Olympics was largely dependent on corporate financial support. This created an obligation to businesses that also meant the Olympics would need to minimize public relations scandals that would surely come with the growing power of anti-doping missionaries.

The cost of upgrading civic infrastructure, building athletic facilities and housing, along with the expense of hosting and bribing the IOC members who vote on where the Olympics are held, has always been an enormous burden for aspiring Olympic cities. Writing in the publication *Revue Olympique* in 1913, Coubertin fretted that "people are worried about the increases in the amount of money needed" to host Olympic Games. Projecting into the future of the Olympic enterprise, he added, "The question is not whether they will be held, but how they will be held, and at whose expense."[2]

Although the Olympics may have been modeled after a world of idyllic amateurism, they were hosted within a market-based system that demanded payment for the land, stadiums, and commodities needed to put on an international sporting spectacle. From the beginning, Coubertin's spiritual ideals struggled with the fact that he had to execute them in an environment of hard commerce and finance. After Hitler's Games upped expectations regarding the degree of spectacle the Olympics could deliver, the financial headaches only grew for the IOC and local organizing committees.

Los Angeles voters were skeptical about picking up the tab for the 1984 Olympics because of the financial debacle that still haunted their Canadian neighbors. The 1976 Montreal Olympic Games were initially expected to cost $310 million. The official IOC post-Games report put the final cost at $1.5 billion as of 1978, a number that history would prove to be half the actual cost.[3] In its official report, the IOC tried to put a brave face on this financial slap to the province's citizens, stating that the Montreal Games "made a profound impression upon youth at a time when honest rivalry and the noble spirit of competition, as being true values of life, appear threatened by a materialistic society."[4] While it may have been a fine and lasting thing to help Canadian youth regain honest gamesmanship, Québec taxpayers were also saddled with a debt that would eat up public funds for three decades. As politicians tried to sell them on the benefits of hosting the 1984 Summer Olympics, Angelenos knew Canadians were still making interest payments on the 1976

Games. Newspaper articles in the 1980s reported that the total cost of the Montreal Olympics would be $2.4 billion by the time Québecers finally got the debt off their backs in 1991.[5] But even those projections were optimistic; Québec taxpayers did not shake the 1976 Olympic fiscal hangover until 2006, at a head-splitting cost of nearly $3 billion.[6]

As the 1984 Olympics approached, Los Angeles's citizens were wary of IOC bluster about Olympic returns in the form of honorable rivalries and morally improved youth. They may have had sunny Southern California dispositions, but they did not want to get hustled. Denver had pulled out from hosting the 1976 Winter Games when local citizens voted against spending public funds on the event. At the time, broader California antitax sentiment also undermined the IOC's normal bill-the-taxpayer operating plan. In June 1978, California voters passed Proposition 13, an initiative led by antitax agitator Howard Jarvis that strictly limited property tax increases. When L.A. mayor Tom Bradley commissioned a survey of Angelenos' opinions in 1977, 70 percent supported hosting the Games, but that backing dropped to 35 percent when pollsters asked voters how they would feel if they also had to pick up the tab. Commenting on how to pay for the proposed 1984 Games, in 1977, Los Angeles city councilman Ernani Bernardi told the *Washington Post* that he worried about hosting a "financial fiasco" like Montreal. "The only way you can guarantee this city's tax revenues is with an amendment to the city charter," Bernardi said. "No other way can we guarantee the city taxes won't go to this."[7] Accordingly, the L.A. city council proposed asking Los Angeles citizens to vote on a city charter that would ban the use of taxpayer funds for the Olympics.

Used to bullying cities into what it wanted, the IOC was having nothing of the fiscal-responsibility and voter-referendum rumblings coming out of Los Angeles. L.A. city councilman Bob Ronka was one of the primary sponsors of the city charter amendment. When Ronka tried to attend a 1978 IOC negotiating meeting in Europe, the IOC barred him. Ronka flew home and fumed to the *Los Angeles Times* that the IOC was made up of "aristocrats" who thought they could run roughshod over the California bumpkins. Meanwhile, Anton Calleia, the L.A. mayor's liaison to the IOC, was panicking about the ballot measure, telling the press that the city could not go to the IOC in good faith "and put in a bid with a referendum hanging over our heads. We'd be the laughingstock of the world."[8]

In May 1978, the IOC tried to call L.A.'s bluff. The Associated Press reported that because of the city's unbending demands, the IOC was making noises about moving the 1984 Games to Mexico City, Munich, or—unbelievably—Montreal. "I should make it clear that while there is only one applicant it does not necessarily mean it will get the Games," IOC president Lord Killanin threatened from Athens, where the IOC was considering the Los Angeles bid.[9] After weeks of negotiations, in July 1978, Bradley announced that the city council was withdrawing its bid. But the city did not have to follow through with this brinksmanship. When Lord Killanin got wind that Los Angeles was about to drop out, the IOC returned to the negotiating table in earnest. When the only remaining alternative to Los Angeles, Tehran, pulled its bid due to the Iranian revolution, the IOC had no card left to play. It was going to be Los Angeles or nothing in 1984; power rested in Southern California, not Switzerland.

Ronka's charter amendment went on the November 1978 ballot. With antitax sentiment still running strong after Proposition 13 had won by a landslide in June of the same year, Los Angeles' no-funding charter also easily passed. Los Angeles voters had upended decades of IOC tradition. Where cities were once responsible for all Olympic hosting costs and risks, it was now illegal to use California taxpayer money to fund the Olympics. With taxpayer funds off the table, the California rubes held power over the Swiss aristocrats. The final agreement Killanin and Bradley signed at the White House in late 1978 immunized Los Angeles from any financial liability for the Games. For an organization used to dealing with groveling supplicants and extracting expensive IOC benefits, this was an astonishing turn of events.

With the Olympic brand still tarnished by the Israeli athlete slaughter in Munich, gross cost overruns in Montreal, and a boycott of the 1980

Moscow Olympics, the IOC was anxious to avoid more public-relations disasters. Because Los Angeles' citizens had ruled that the IOC could not put management of the L.A. Games into the hands of public officials (who were paid by taxpayers), the IOC had to allow the 1984 Games to be turned over to a private corporation run by travel company entrepreneur Peter Ueberroth. The newly formed company was called the Los Angeles Olympic Organizing Committee (LAOOC).

With the IOC desperate to get the Games settled in Los Angeles, Ueberroth had enormous leverage over both the IOC and the U.S. Olympic Committee. He extracted a risk-sharing deal from the USOC that gave 40 percent of any surplus income from the Games to the LAOOC, which would in turn use the money to fund Southern California youth sports programs.*

Ueberroth, who would become the commissioner of Major League Baseball in 1984, also played hardball with balky sponsors. Companies who won a coveted Olympic sponsorship berth at an auction had to pay a minimum $4 million in-kind donation to LAOOC. When Kodak only coughed up $2 million of this donation, Ueberroth told Kodak's competitor Fuji that it had 72 hours to get a replacement offer on the table. The Japanese film manufacturer jumped at the opportunity. Ueberroth scratched the original $4 million Kodak contract and replaced it with a new $7 million deal with Fuji.[10]

Ueberroth also cut a $225 million TV deal with ABC, a bounty larger than the TV contracts for all previous Olympics combined. In total, the television contracts yielded $286.9 million, or $187 million more than TV revenue from the 1980 Games. The IOC had long struggled with how to manage television profits. The 1936 Olympics were the first to broadcast the events through closed-circuit TV piped into German viewing halls. As televisions entered more and more homes around the world

---

* The LA84 Foundation has granted over $220 million in funds to Southern California youth sports programs since 1985. In a sense, the legacy of the 1984 Olympics' financial success helps replace support for fitness for the masses that ended with the passing of the Amateur Sports Act of 1978.

through the 1950s, the IOC was so concerned that television money would compromise Coubertin's founding principles that it did not formulate an official television policy until 1958. That year, Brundage added Rule 49 to the Olympic Charter, a regulation that allowed each Game's local organizing committee to negotiate the terms of television rights, but gave final approval of the terms and say over how the revenue would be distributed to the IOC. Writing in 1966, Brundage warned that while TV revenue could be useful to the Olympic movement, "it can also be a great danger if Olympic ideals are not maintained."[11] Rule 49 gave the IOC TV money, but burdened local organizing committees with the hard work of negotiating with broadcasters. Local committees also had to shoulder the logistical challenges and legal risks that came with creating a television product and managing contract disputes.

Traditionally, the IOC collected all television revenue and then redistributed it in a fashion that the IOC thought would reinforce Coubertin's ideals. Ueberroth ended this practice in 1984. When it came time to decide how to manage and spend nearly $300 million in TV revenue, Ueberroth pretty much ignored the IOC's demands and used the funds in a fashion that fulfilled his obligation to Los Angeles' citizens. In an account of Ueberroth's Olympic legacy, historians Robert Barney, Stephen Wenn, and Scott Martyn explained that although the IOC was horrified to find itself in the position of "junior partner" in sponsor and TV negotiations, in the long run, Ueberroth's negotiating skills immensely enriched the Olympic coffers.[12]

Seeking funds to kick-start the development of the L.A. Games, Ueberroth used shrewd financial techniques when negotiating with TV networks. Before submitting a bid, any network interested in broadcasting the Games had to provide a $500,000 refundable deposit. Once actual negotiations began, the five competing companies—NBC, CBS, ESPN, ABC, and television production giant Norman Lear's Tandem Productions—had to ante up another $250,000.[13] Besides ensuring bidders were serious, the $750,000 up-front money gave the LAOOC working capital that compounded in interest-bearing accounts. With interest rates averaging over 20 percent through the late 1970s and early 1980s, these refundable TV deposits brought in $1,000 a day in interest alone. "We've yet to spend a penny," Ueberroth told a *Sports Illustrated* reporter in 1982. "With these current interest rates, our income is exceeding our expenses by a half-million dollars every three months."[14]

When Olympic headquarters learned that Ueberroth was striking deals without its input and that the cash was going directly to the LAOOC, IOC director Monique Berlioux demanded that the LAOOC transfer one-third of the TV deposit money to a Swiss IOC account. Berlioux was known for the imperious requirement lists sent out in advance of her Olympic business travels that demanded Evian water, elaborate flower arrangements, no early or late meetings, and dining only at the finest establishments. Indifferent to her status, Ueberroth ignored Berlioux and kept the money in the United States.

The IOC was also horrified to learn that Norman Lear's Tandem Productions was negotiating for TV rights. "Only an existing nationwide network should be considered," Berlioux scolded. Tandem was known for producing sitcom hits like *All in the Family*, *Maude*, and *Sanford and Son*, not international sports events. "The games are not a lever for anybody to set up a 'fourth network' in the USA," Berlioux warned. Ueberroth again ignored the IOC complaints, and Lear's company kept its spot at the bidding table. "I am afraid," IOC president Lord Killanin moaned in May 1979, that the unilateral dealings were "quite unacceptable to the International Olympic Committee."[15]

Ueberroth also increased prices that western Europe paid to broadcast the Olympics. The European Broadcasting Union (EBU), a consortium of European broadcasters, paid $5.95 million for rights to the 1980 Moscow Games. At that time, the EBU's purchasing power was restricted because the public ownership of most European networks limited its revenue, as did its lack of advertising. In the 1970s and early 1980s, few competing private networks existed in Europe to push Olympic rights bidding to the sorts of numbers the jostling American networks were prepared to pay. However, the EBU was the IOC's only way to get its sporting festival to the European public, and the EBU used its monopoly leverage to keep costs down. Also in 1980, Juan Antonio Samaranch replaced Lord Killanin as IOC president. A staunch defender of the EBU's position as exclusive distributor of the Olympics in Europe, Samaranch resisted Ueberroth's efforts to extract demand-based TV rights from Europe's 100 million television sets.

At a 1979 negotiating meeting at New York's Park Lane Hotel, Ueberroth told Berlioux and EBU representatives that the fee to broadcast the 1984 games in western Europe was $100 million. Considering that the EBU had paid just shy of $6 million four years earlier, a dumbfounded EBU representative dismissed the offer as "utterly out of consideration." The EBU countered at $8.33 million, and negotiations fitfully dragged along. A few months after the New York meeting, an independent Italian TV network offered the LAOOC $10 million for rights to Italy alone. A crack had opened in the European TV rights fortress. While Samaranch refused to let Ueberroth move forward with the deal, the proposition showed how out of whack the EBU's $8.33 million offer was for coverage in 32 European nations. Still fearful that the Europeans would get blacked out if market forces pushed the EBU into a $100 million corner (at $1 per television, the price was lower than the $1.69 per household that American networks paid), the IOC boss stated at the IOC's 84th Session meeting that it "was essential that everyone be able to see the Games through television."[16]

Protected by its monopoly market position and Samaranch's favoritism, EBU Olympic fees stayed relatively low, even as television reached near total saturation in European households. In late 1981, the LAOOC and EBU finally agreed to a $19.8 million fee, far lower than Ueberroth's $100 million starting offer but more than triple what Moscow had paid. When the IOC demanded $6.6 million of this EBU sum, Ueberroth told Samaranch to get lost. Referring to the IOC's blocking of the $10 million Italian offer, Ueberroth told Samaranch, "Because the IOC wishes to protect EBU, the LAOOC will be prohibited from receiving maximum amounts." Ignoring the IOC's $6.6 million demand, LAOOC kept $15.8

million of the EBU payment. If the IOC wanted more than the $4 million the LAOOC would wire into its bank account, Ueberroth told Samaranch he would have to "get it directly from EBU."[17]

American TV executives were not dummies, and they knew the $1.69 per TV household they paid was much more than the $0.14 per household the EBU shelled out for the same feed. Gradually, Samaranch came around to Ueberroth's way of seeing things. Eight years after Los Angeles, the EBU paid $75 million for Olympic TV rights to the 1992 Barcelona Games. By 2000, the arrival of private networks in Europe broke the EBU blockade and eased Samaranch's fear that his sports product would not be visible in Europe's farthest corners. Media mogul Rupert Murdoch's $2 billion offer for the Summer and Winter Games from 2000 to 2008 put European pricing on par with the United States. Long after he became commissioner of baseball, Ueberroth's Olympic TV pricing legacy continued to deliver exponentially increasing revenues into IOC coffers.[18]

Los Angeles also fundamentally altered how the Olympics made money from corporate sponsors. In Montreal, the Games pocketed $5 million from deals with 600 corporate sponsors. Ueberroth felt that going after fewer sponsors would be more lucrative than cutting hundreds of smaller deals. Trading quantity for exclusivity, in 1984, 35 corporate partners, 64 product and service suppliers, and 65 licensees brought $157.2 million in cash, products, and services to the Los Angeles Games—all of which again went immediately into the LAOOC's high-interest bank accounts.[19]

With the law putting Los Angeles taxpayer funds out of reach, and with no backup city ready to host the games, Ueberroth had the leverage to put on a Spartan Olympics that was quite unusual for the IOC. Upon accepting the LAOOC job, Ueberroth had studied the financial statements from previous Olympic Games. It was immediately apparent that construction costs were an albatross around the event's financial neck. So while the IOC typically demands shiny new buildings for its events, Los Angeles saved millions by housing athletes and staff in college dorms at USC, UCLA, and UC Santa Barbara. The 1984 Games only needed to build sports facilities for cycling, swimming, and shooting, and Ueberroth got those paid for by naming them after corporate sponsors 7-Eleven, McDonald's, and Fuji. Athletic events took place in the Los Angles Coliseum, a structure built in 1922 that had been used 52 years earlier when Los Angeles hosted the 1932 Summer Olympics.

While IOC grandees may have fumed at having to sit in a 62-year-old structure, the aristocrats from Switzerland had no way to resist. And Ueberroth's parsimony worked. In inflation-adjusted numbers, Los Angeles' $93 million in building costs were less than 6 percent of the $1.7 billion the Soviet Union spent to build facilities for the 1980 Olympics. By the 1984 closing ceremony, the LAOOC had turned a $232.5 million profit. *Time* magazine named Ueberroth Man of the Year for his management prowess.[20]

Ueberroth also capitalized on the enormous untapped value in the Olympic rings. The Los Angeles Games saw a massive increase in sponsor revenue, funds that went to both the IOC and the LAOOC. In his book *Drug Games*, historian Thomas Hunt notes that IOC boss Samaranch "was both more commercially astute than his predecessor and more assertive as a leader."[21] Open to disconnecting the Olympics from its idealized Coubertinian mooring, Samaranch liked what he saw in Ueberroth's management of costs and his savvy extraction of television and corporate sponsor dollars. Ueberroth provided a template for how the Games—usually a financial train wreck—could be run as a money-making business. John Hoberman writes that Samaranch was so inspired by the American's vision that the Spaniard subsequently "presided over an almost total commercialization of the Olympic Games that has converted the 'Movement' into an advertising vehicle for the multinational corporate sponsors and American television networks."[22]

These media outlets and corporate sponsors became the foundation of enormous power, a force that helped Samaranch lever open the door to professional athletes in 1996. The appearance of names like Magic Johnson and Wayne Gretzky made the Olympics even more valuable to corporate partners, and sponsorship rates increased accordingly.

Despite American IOC president Brundage's early warning that a flood of sponsor dollars might be "a great danger if Olympic ideals are not maintained," the 1984 Olympics were a watershed moment when the influence of parsimonious American taxpayers and a strong-willed American businessman forever displaced Coubertin's romantic "religion of the muscles" with an abiding faith in commerce as the new guiding Olympic principle.[23]

EVEN AS THE 1984 OLYMPICS transformed Coubertin's international celebration of amateurism into a jamboree of corporate products and services, the issue of drugs became more than a matter of amateur athletes embracing professional practices. When the IOC found unimaginable veins of television and product-marketing gold in the hills of Southern California, the discovery created new pressures to manage doping scandals. Whereas in the past, doping had been a problem of tarnished amateur integrity, the financial success of the 1984 Games made doped athletes a matter of soiled corporate brand equity.

In advance of the 1984 Games, the IOC Medical Commission, then led by the Belgian prince Alexandre de Mérode, set up a drug-testing lab in Los Angeles. Overseen by UCLA scientist Don Catlin, the IOC approved the lab in November 1983. A few weeks later, the USOC approached Catlin about testing U.S. athletes in advance of the Games.

At the time, Dr. Robert Voy was director of sports medicine and science and chief medical officer for the U.S. Olympic Committee. In his 1991 book with Kirk Deeter, *Drugs, Sport, and Politics*, Voy wrote that putting the IOC in charge of testing in Los Angeles was "like having the fox guard the henhouse."[24] Aside from his initial efforts to protect European television from market forces, Samaranch was an economic pragmatist, especially when compared to Brundage's single-minded amateur severity. Samaranch also worked relentlessly to unify the Olympic network, which was under considerable strain from the boycott of the Moscow Games in 1980, the year he became president. Traveling to hundreds of countries and meeting with countless IOC connections in his first three years on the job, Samaranch, as IOC member Dick Pound put it, brought a "breadth of ambition and understanding of politics" to the IOC that the insular organization had lacked.[25] As a more commercially savvy and assertive president than his precursors, the Spaniard was not one to let amateur romanticism about chemical or financial purity get in the way of the Games' enormous money-producing potential. Focused on moving the IOC forward, Samaranch also showed, in Thomas Hunt's words, "a reluctance to engage with divisive issues."[26] John Hoberman puts it more bluntly: "For Juan Antonio Samaranch and his closest associates, doping was primarily a public relations problem that threatened lucrative television and corporate contracts that are now worth billions of dollars."[27] With the IOC and LAOOC cognizant of the importance of sponsor dollars to execute their Olympic mission, there was a lot of incentive to ensure that drug scandals remained behind closed doors. Catlin's Los Angeles lab was a convenient way to screen out doped athletes before they could cause negative publicity. More than a lab to ensure a level sporting playing field, the lab was an insurance policy.

The USOC's concerns about doping were not idle speculation. The American Olympic organizing committee knew Americans doped. At the 1983 Pan American Games in Caracas, Venezuela, 15 athletes, including one American, tested positive. When the U.S. athletes saw their teammate booted for doping, they realized the drug testing in Caracas was for real. Twelve U.S. track and field team members dropped out before they even put a spike on the track.[28]

At the time, USOC vice president and U.S. track and field team chief of mission Evie Dennis argued the athletes' "individual decision to withdraw would not be taken as an implication of guilt." However, U.S. javelin thrower Curt Ransford—one of the few Americans who remained in Venezuela—said he "knew there was going to come a day when no one could hide from the testing." When Dennis arrived in Venezuela a week before the events, she learned that the Pan Am Games' drug-testing lab had new Hewlett-Packard gas chromatograph–mass spectrometer machines able to detect steroids taken months before the day of a test. Three decades after Ziegler introduced them to American Olympians, steroids were a standard element of the elite track athlete sports medicine program. Alarmed about the arrival of these new HP machines, Dennis called track and field headquarters in the United States to let them know that the team could be at risk. The American athletes still showed up, but, as Dennis later recalled, "They had to get here and see Cubans and Canadians disqualified. They asked me what the USOC was going to do so they could keep up with the Russians and others. I said we were going to do nothing, because we don't condone these drugs."[29]

As historians Jan and Terry Todd explain, before the Los Angeles Olympics, the 1983 Pan American Games were "by far, the largest drug scandal in the history of doping control."[30] Caracas offered a teachable moment; the snared athletes taught the USOC that it needed to set up a drug-testing lab *before* the Los Angeles Olympics to avoid the same PR disaster that went down in Venezuela.

In fact, the positives at the Pan American Games were nothing new. Some track and field athletes had already been caught doping at the world championships in Helsinki, Finland. Yet even though the new highly sensitive HP machines were used in Helsinki, no athlete officially tested positive—that is, no positives were reported to the public. Instead, the positives were buried from view and surreptitiously conveyed to USOC officials. The USOC in turn told the doping American athletes that if the same testing procedures were used in Caracas, they would get caught. According to Voy, the USOC used these pre-event positives to help American athletes avoid embarrassing themselves and their national team. In Voy's words, cover-ups happened "not only to protect the images of the violating athletes, but also to protect the sport organizations in charge of maintaining a level of fair play."[31]

The 1984 Olympics were not the first to view drug testing as a threat to the Games' economic viability. In 1971, IOC president Brundage expressed his belief that draconian anti-doping policies and enforcement were harmful to the IOC's economic stability. As part of the lead up to the 1972 Munich Olympics, IOC director Berlioux told Brundage that the IOC would bear the cost of two Medical Commission conferences dealing in part with doping. Brundage was not keen on the idea, and responded, "There is no use wasting a lot of money on these superfluous meetings if we can avoid it." Brundage underscored his reluctance to take a firm stand on doping by pushing for international sports federations to bear the technical and financial responsibility for enforcing anti-doping rules. An anti-doping brochure drafted in part by the IOC Medical Commission and distributed in advance of the 1972 Games put the "technical responsibility" for doping control on international federations. The IOC's obligations were limited to "moral responsibility" for the controls and their overall Olympic organization.[32] In addition to saving the IOC the cost of doping enforcement, pushing the responsibility for anti-doping onto the sports federations shielded the IOC from potential legal costs should an athlete or nation file a lawsuit due to a positive dope test.

A decade later, drug enforcement threatened the Los Angeles Olympics' financial health. "Drugs and doctors are not only controlling the Games of the XXIIIrd Olympiad," Ueberroth wrote to Samaranch in 1983, "they are beginning to gain control of the whole Olympic movement." Corporate sponsors paid handsome sums to wrap themselves in the Olympic ideology of hope, youth, and vitality. Hunt writes that "the IOC, in Ueberroth's view, should spend less time exposing doping and more time protecting the reputation of its athletes."[33] And despite the tension over how the L.A. financial windfall was to be distributed, Ueberroth had a sympathetic ear in Samaranch.

As head of the IOC in 1980, Samaranch focused on making the Olympics more economically productive. The Francisco Franco disciple had little tolerance for dissent, which made Samaranch a natural bedfellow for Ueberroth, a driven CEO who was also used to getting his way. As leader of the LAOOC, Ueberroth built a centralized business organization and gave himself ultimate decision-making authority. Ueberroth knew that the limited time and resources available to put on the 1984

Games required crisp efficiency, not messy democracy.[34] For Ueberroth and Samaranch, allowing dope-testing doctors powers that could smudge the Olympic rings made zero business sense.

Of the 86 U.S. athletes who tested positive in pre-1984 Olympic drug tests, only two were denied spots on the Olympic team—and even those two were not sanctioned.[35] The way to preserve the integrity of the sponsors who made the Games possible was to protect them from the stigma of drug use. Regardless of what the athletes needed to put in their bodies to ply their trade—and had done so for more than a century—the robust health of the Olympics depended on capping salacious doping scandals.

To manage that balance, Ueberroth and the LAOOC walked a fine line between suppressing drug scandals and avoiding them through testing neglect. On April 27, 1983, the LAOOC announced it would ignore an IOC mandate that athletes be tested for caffeine and testosterone at the 1984 Games. In what seems like a gambit to minimize drug stories and protect athlete and sponsor reputations, the Los Angeles organizers argued that unless the IOC could guarantee that its testing methods for these two substances were scientifically valid, athletes would not be examined. According to press reports, LAOOC medical director Tony Daly said that the IOC's tests for caffeine and testosterone were "arbitrary and scientifically unproven."[36] Later that year, the *Los Angeles Times* reported that the cost of these tests may have been another factor pushing the LAOOC to get rid of them.[37] Only when the IOC Medical Commission assured the LAOOC in November 1983 that the drug controls were "scientifically perfect and not assailable as incorrect" did Ueberroth's team back down and allow testosterone and caffeine testing.[38] The integrity of the 1984 Games was as much a factor of financial solvency as it was a matter of athlete purity.

Despite USOC and LAOOC efforts to keep the cloud of drug use from darkening the Olympic skies, some Americans tested positive in 1984. As the Olympics approached their August 12 closing ceremony, multiple positive samples crossed the Games' anti-doping lab test bench. Lab scientist Don Catlin reported nine drug positives to the IOC, but heard nothing back. "Those positives never saw the light of day," Catlin later recalled.[39]

With many of the television-friendly track and field events taking place at the end of the schedule, Catlin's workload was enormous, and the lab was coming up with a lot of positives. So many samples were going to the lab during the last week that many remained to be tested the day after the closing ceremony. And then Los Angeles Olympic medical director Tony Daly walked in and told Catlin to shut down the lab, even if he had not finished testing all the samples. Catlin refused, telling Daly he was under contract to test all the delivered samples in his lab.

Ignoring the LAOOC order to halt testing, Catlin and his team carried on and eventually found 20 positives. The IOC's official report on the 1984 Games lists 11. Even in the historical record, the IOC and the LAOOC cleansed the Los Angeles Olympics for smoother public and corporate consumption. The Dubin Inquiry, the damning Canadian government report on doping that came out of the Ben Johnson scandal in 1988, would later reveal that 20 athletes who won medals in Los Angeles did so while taking performance-enhancing drugs prescribed by Los Angeles doctor Robert Kerr. Those athletes still have their 1984 medals.[40]

When testing a urine or blood sample, lab technicians do not know who the sample belongs to. A number identifies each vial, not a name. This system is designed to maintain athlete anonymity and protect athlete and drug tester alike from bias. Only when a sample comes up positive is it cross-referenced to a separate database that matches sample numbers to donor names. In the case of Catlin's positive tests, the IOC needed to go to medical commissioner Mérode, who possessed the sheet of paper listing the names corresponding to each sample number. After Catlin gave Mérode his list of positives, the Belgian prince informed Catlin that the list had gone missing from his room at the luxurious Biltmore Hotel. The IOC could not identify who the positive tests belonged to, so all were considered innocent.

While the circumstances leading to the loss of the paper that would identify the positive athletes are murky, IOC member and World Anti-

Doping Agency head Dick Pound had little doubt what happened. In his book *Inside the Olympics*, Pound wrote, "It was the L.A. organizing committee that had removed the evidence before it could be acted upon by the IOC."[41] In his book on Ben Johnson and Carl Lewis at the 1988 Seoul Olympics, journalist Richard Moore points to evidence suggesting LAOOC medical director Dr. Anthony Daly had the documents destroyed to protect the L.A. Games' image, an act that would please both Samaranch and Ueberroth and further Daly's personal goal of replacing Mérode as the IOC's medical head.[42]

In 1994, Mérode blamed the missing documents on LAOOC penny-pinching—and American efficiency. The IOC medical director said that when he returned to his room at the Biltmore, workers had cleared it out in the process of converting his working office back into a hotel suite. First, Mérode said, he was told that the medical commission documents were at the LAOOC offices, but then Daly informed him they had been sent back to IOC headquarters in Switzerland. According to Mérode, when he told Daly he would return to Lausanne to inspect the records, the Los Angeles medical officer confessed that the LAOOC had shredded the documents. "The U.S. mentality was the Games were finished. They didn't want to pay," Mérode told reporters. "The U.S. attitude is not the same as the European one. They have their efficiency. Everything is done very quickly. They like to save money." Mérode did not explain whether saving money applied to getting him out of an expensive hotel room quickly or eliminating a doping scandal that could damage sponsor relations. Responding to the accusation, Daly told the *Los Angeles Times* that he did not know about any destroyed test results and said a cover-up "would be shocking." And if there were anyone to blame, Daly said, "It would not be possible for [the LAOOC] to do anything. We report the results to the IOC."[43]

Arnold Beckett was a member of the IOC's Los Angeles anti-doping committee. An authority on the then-new gas chromatography–mass spectrometry drug testing, Beckett told the press in 1996 that he believed the LAOOC destroyed Mérode's list of names because "it would have done quite a lot of damage if five or six" positives had been linked to medal winners, which "undoubtedly it would have done." Beckett added, "Some of the federations and [the] IOC are happy to show that they are doing something in getting some positives, but they don't want too many because that would damage the image of the Games."[44] In 1999, Beckett told the BBC investigative journalism program *Panorama* that covering up positives in Los Angeles in 1984 (and at the 1998 Atlanta Games) was for Olympic image management. "Is all this part of a pattern of trying to prevent too many positives?" Beckett asked, rhetorically. "In other words, we want to show at the Olympic Games that we are doing our due work in trying to prevent drug misuse in sport. But please don't get too many positives, which will tend to damage the image of sport. That is the emphasis."[45]

In the same BBC program, IOC medical commissioner Mérode said that in advance of the 1984 Olympics, U.S. officials pressed the IOC to not hold dope testing at all. Mérode recalled LAOOC members telling him, "We don't need it, and the Americans everywhere, even a majority in the United States said, 'It doesn't exist here. We don't know what is it, doping, you know.' And I say ha, ha, ha. We will see. And we have the Olympic Charter, you have to follow that. If you don't organize the control, you will not have the Games at all."

Mérode added that Los Angeles organizers were against dope tests "because they were afraid to have a bad image in the world, because there are too many doping cases." Elite sports' long and previously unremarkable tradition of using drugs to increase human performance was bumping up against a new anti-doping morality that itself challenged the remarkable financial success of the 1984 Olympics. As historian Robert Barney writes, "The financial health of both the IOC and its most flamboyant offspring, the USOC, is fundamentally embedded in the competitive zeal of U.S. television networks and corporate business giants bent on linking their endeavors with the world's most illustrious sports spectacle—the Olympic Games."[46]

CHAPTER 11

THE SPORTS ACT DELIVERS: GOLD IN '84

In its 1977 report on the state of American Olympic programs, Gerald Ford's Commission on Olympic Sports singled out the United States Cycling Federation (USCF) as a sanctioning body that handicapped American athletes by not providing coaches or organizing a formal national team. Without a "national effort to develop a pool of expert coaches," the commission concluded, American riders lining up at the Olympic Games were hopelessly unprepared to take on their Soviet and European competitors.[1] Published three years in advance of the 1980 Moscow Olympics, the report advised the USCF to hire coaches with European racing experience. America in the 1970s was exploding with kids flogging Schwinn Stingrays around the neighborhood, yet only a tiny percentage of these hill-bombing, ramp-jumping daredevils ever pinned on a race number. While America's cycling demographic potential was huge, the president's advisers saw opportunity wasted.

Two years later, things were hardly better. In 1979, the *Washington Post* stated that, with the Olympics around the corner, the United States was still unprepared to compete with riders like the East Germans. Timed to coincide with summer rides around the neighborhood, the June 23 piece, "Lack of Facilities Hurts U.S. Olympic Cyclists," informed readers that one of the world's most popular sports is a "competitive orphan" in the United States.[2]

Sixty-seven years had passed since an American cyclist's cleats had touched an Olympic podium. At Stockholm in 1912, Carl Schutte's 10-hour, 52-minute finish in the 198-mile individual time trial earned bronze. (In their official report on that race, Olympic officials alluded to the inherent professionalism that made cycling inappropriate for the amateur Olympics, arguing that "cycling thrives best by itself" and therefore "ought not to be included in future Olympic games.")[3] The *Washington Post* explained that this nearly seven-decade dry spell had a number of causes, including the paucity of U.S. velodromes, no school support for bike racing, and the lack of a professional American racing circuit to make cycling a viable career choice. And while other nations boasted well-stocked coaching staffs, the *Post* pointed out that the USCF had only hired its first coach 18 months earlier—a Polish junior champion named Eddie Borysewicz.

The USCF had brought in Borysewicz, known as Eddie B., in response to the Presidential Commission on Olympic Sports' recommendation that the USCF hire a coach and expose Americans to European-level racing and training methods. Born in 1939, Borysewicz won two Polish national junior cycling champion titles before complications from misdiagnosed tuberculosis forced him to give up racing. Subsequent work as a Polish national coach, plus university training in physical education, took him to North America for the 1976 Montréal Olympics. In America, Borysewicz developed connections with the USCF. When President Carter signed the Amateur Sports Act of 1978, the USCF got the message that it was time to end the communist humiliations. Eddie B. got the call.

As UCSF coach, Borysewicz guided the 1984 U.S. Olympic team to nine medals, four of them gold. He nurtured Nevada teenager Greg

LeMond onto a path that ended with three Tour de France victories—America's first. No figure has been more influential in making the United States a global force in pro cycling than Eddie B.

Along with his unassailable role in building Europe-ready cyclists in America, Borysewicz's reputation was set by a February 14, 1985, article in *Rolling Stone* magazine: "Olympic Cheating: The Inside Story of Illicit Doping and the U.S. Cycling Team." Adding a sensational spin to news already reported weeks earlier by *Sports Illustrated* and the *Los Angeles Times*, the piece detailed how nine of Borysewicz's riders used blood doping to prepare for the 1984 Olympics. *Rolling Stone* journalist Richard Ben Cramer described riders being surreptitiously infused with blood at a Los Angeles Ramada Inn, then gave the scene a film noir patina: "All left the hotel room with a heavy burden of secrecy. Blood doping is cheating." The piece forever tarnished the reputation of one of the most positive forces in U.S. cycling history.

Thirty years later, Borysewicz's memory of the chain of events leading to blood boosting is still clear. And the sequence is lengthy, stretching to a night in the early 1970s when, between races, he stopped in Valenciennes, France, to have dinner at the home of 1958 Vuelta a España winner and 1962 road world champion Jean Stablinski, a French pro born to Polish immigrant parents. In the middle of dinner, a knock on the front door startled the Polish friends. The unexpected guest was a whippet-thin Frenchman with the mischievous grin and sharp-edged features of a man who lived for the moment. French cycling demigod and indefatigable bon vivant Jacques Anquetil was in the house.

An object of unending media attention for his pitched Tour de France battles against fellow Frenchman and "eternal second" Raymond Poulidor, Anquetil wore the yellow jersey in every stage of the 1961 Tour—the second of his five Tour victories from 1957 to 1964. The first rider to win all three Grand Tours, Anquetil's larger-than-life aura was made even bigger by his fabled capacity to transit from an all-night party to race sign in. Anquetil was old school.

In Anquetil's view, a full race schedule was a professional obligation. He competed largely without interruption from February to October. Riding in the early 1960s, when anti-doping missionaries were making their first tentative efforts to evangelize sports with their religion of chemical purity, Anquetil told the press that as a professional, he had every right to dope to get the job done—just as pros had upheld their responsibility from the earliest days of cycling. On French television, Anquetil once told a politician it would be idiocy to attempt a 350-mile race like Bordeaux–Paris on bread and water alone. A guardian of cycling tradition, and a staunch defender of his right to work as a cyclist and mind his own health as an individual, the French superstar dismissed drug testing as a violation of his human rights.*

The Valenciennes dinner was now a party. Revealing the lifelong curiosity about the science and tradition of cycling training that served him as a coach, Borysewicz asked Anquetil how he maintained his infernal racing schedule. At that time, the Vuelta a España took place in April, and riders had a only a few days between the Spanish three-week race and the start of the Giro d'Italia, another three-week grind. And the time between was often spent traveling, not recovering. By the Tour de France in July, a rider like Anquetil would already have two back-to-back Grand Tours and six weeks of northern European spring classics in his legs. Indeed, among his classics successes, Anquetil notched victories at Liège–Bastogne–Liège, Bordeaux–Paris, and Gent–Wevelgem. Anquetil would bank 22,000 miles and 235 race days in a typical year.[4] "That's a big program," Borysewicz told me, still in awe. "This guy is so tough."

---

* Anquetil typically raced 235 days a year. A physician once told him that to do his job without drugs, he would need to trim his season to 50 days. In 1967 a newspaper reader asked Anquetil why riders did not boycott the Tour to force organizers to reduce it to a drug-free length. On July 25, Anquetil responded in *L'Humanité* that if just anyone could complete the event, "it would no longer be the Tour." As historian Christopher Thompson explains, fiendish extremity is what gives the race its cultural intrigue and financial weight, but maintaining the Tour's essential awfulness "led racers to resort to illicit and risky chemical means to reduce their suffering and allow them to earn a living." For more on this paradox and Anquetil's beliefs on doping, see Christopher S. Thompson, *The Tour de France* (Berkeley: University of California Press, 2008), 238.

Borysewicz recalled telling Anquetil that Polish riders took iron and vitamin supplements to help with recovery. Did Anquetil's doc give him something extra? "Yes," Anquetil replied. Twice a year he got a fresh transfusion of his own blood. "Because after the Giro, I can't recover for the Tour de France, so I need my blood," Borysewicz remembered the Frenchman saying. With Anquetil's oxygen-carrying red-blood-cell count depleted by a torrid racing schedule, the twice-yearly blood replenishments allowed him to recover at a rate that would otherwise have been impossible on pro cycling's sparse diet of rest days. At the time, reintroducing one's own blood was certainly not prohibited for pros like Anquetil—nor even for Olympic amateurs.*

Along with his five Tour de France victories, Anquetil had won the Giro twice and the Vuelta once. Stablinski bagged the 1966 Amstel Gold Race. Sitting at a table with men who counted nine Grand Tours, four classics, and a world championship victory between them, Borysewicz considered Anquetil's recovery method and thought, "Yeah, OK. Smart." He filed this novel bit of training information in his memory bank.

Fast-forward to 1983, and Borysewicz was now head coach of the USCF. One day he received a memo from Ed Burke, the USCF's Olympic cycling physiologist. Burke was investigating training methods employed by the dominant Eastern Bloc amateur teams. Eight months before the Soviet Union and its satellite countries would announce a boycott of the L.A. Games, Burke's memo addressed to the Olympic cycling team coaching staff and USCF management read:

---

* This is how the IOC Medical Commission defined doping products in 1968: "If nonalimentary drugs which excite normal effort either by their composition or by their dosages are used, even therapeutically, they will be considered doping products." Tom Simpson's 1967 death was the focusing event that caused the IOC to form a Medical Commission and update its doping rules that year. Amphetamines were of course specifically listed as banned products, along with central nervous system stimulants like strychnine and analgesic narcotics such as morphine. Before 1968, the rule on the books since 1938 simply said that the use of "drugs or artificial stimulants of any kind must be condemned most strongly" and that anyone who used them should not be allowed to participate in amateur events. A rider's own blood does not fit either of these descriptions. For a discussion of these rules in relation to blood doping from the 1960s to the 1980s, see John Gleaves, "Manufactured Dope: How the 1984 US Olympic Cycling Team Rewrote the Rules on Drugs in Sports," *International Journal of the History of Sport*, (2014): 1–19.

> In preparation for the Olympic Games, I am reviewing all avenues of preparation for our team, in addition to bikes, wheels, clothing, sports psychologist, etc. One significant and controversial area of improving athletic performance is the area of blood boosting. Is it doping or illegal; my personal opinion and interpretation is no. This is one more area our cyclist [sic] will be behind the world of cycling if we do not keep up with sports medicine research.
>
> I would like to take the opportunity to investigate its use with the team, but first we all must discuss this controversial topic. Please give me your opinion on this. I will do nothing further until I hear from you.[5]

Blood boosting was controversial because some at the UCSF felt the practice violated the spirit of antidrug laws. On the other hand, putting your own blood back into your system involved no drugs and therefore broke no rules. A decision on whether to go ahead was especially urgent in light of the pressure being handed down from the highest levels of government to do what it took to beat the communists at their own European games.

For Borysewicz, Burke's memo triggered memories of his dinner in France. "It clicked—Anquetil was doing the same thing," Borysewicz told me. He quizzed Burke: "Is this legal?" The USCF physiologist responded, yes, maybe. Borysewicz next telephoned the UCI's general secretary in Switzerland. Was blood doping against UCI rules? "Call me tomorrow," the UCI official responded.

The next day, Borysewicz dialed Switzerland again. "Eddie, it's legal," the UCI official told him.

Borysewicz's recollection corresponds with what others have found concerning UCI blood-doping rules at the time. California State University, Fullerton, historian John Gleaves conducted extensive research on the 1984 U.S. Olympic cycling team, and he told me that at the time Borysewicz claims to have phoned the UCI, the cycling governing body had no rules banning blood doping. In fact, as Gleaves wrote in a paper on the 1984 scandal, while the death of Tom Simpson in 1967 precipitated an amphetamine prohibition in 1968 and media coverage of unnaturally swollen athletes led to a steroid ban at the 1976 Montreal Olympics, "from 1976 until 1985, the question of blood transfusion does not appear in the minutes of any IOC annual session."[6] If the UCI considered Anquetil's technique illegal, that prohibition was not documented, perhaps because a headline-grabbing event focusing on blood doping had yet to occur. Additionally, until 1985, the IOC was reluctant to ban drugs it could not test for.[7]

As some athletes saw it, the USOC acquiesced through silence. One of the riders who received a transfusion, team pursuit silver medalist Pat McDonough, asked for the team to check with the USOC before going forward with the blood doping. "We were at a team meeting with Eddie B.," McDonough recalled, and the riders said, "We'll do it if you get a letter from USOC that says we can do it." With Amateur Sports Act pressure in the air, team physician Thomas Dickson said that when he asked the USOC "point blank" about the legality of blood doping, it did not respond. "Zero answers," Dickson recalled. The USOC provided "absolutely no direction," he added. For the riders, coaches, and doctors, no response meant go. In retrospect, the physician said, "I watched this, so I'm not blameless." However, Dickson noted, USOC silence on the matter is why the team doped, "because at the time, it was not illegal."[8]

While the USOC apparently did not get back to the team about its 1984 request for blood-doping guidance, Burke had corresponded with the Olympic Committee in 1983 regarding the topic. In response to one of Burke's queries, USOC medical director Kenneth (Casey) Clarke wrote to USOC executive director Colonel Don Miller on December 28, 1983, and explained that blood doping is "fairly widely practiced in Europe, especially among cyclists and Nordic skiiers." Miller also informed the USOC head that, medically speaking, blood packing "can now be considered ethical." However, he added that "no organization, the IOC especially, has ever clarified the ethical value" of the practice as a sports therapy.[9] At least in 1983, for the USOC, blood doping was a medically acceptable practice.

With UCI and USOC blessings (or silence) in hand and firsthand knowledge that blood boosting worked for Anquetil, one of the greatest cyclists to ever walk the Earth, Borysewicz told Burke to go ahead with the project. Burke held a meeting with the riders where he laid out the process. Borysewicz informed his team that blood boosting would level the playing field against hardened Europeans who were likely already using the technique. "Let's get even because many European riders do this," Borysewicz recalled telling his squad.

Whether to undergo the transfusion, however, would be each rider's personal choice. "No pushing. I am not the coach who tell you have to do it," Borysewicz recalled in his still heavily accented English. Borysewicz had two motives for leaving the decision to the riders. First, he was afraid that if he knew who was blood boosting, the knowledge might cloud his final decisions on which riders to select for the Olympic team. Second, he claimed he wanted nothing to do with medical decisions. The USCF had doctors to deal with riders' medical issues, and Borysewicz told me that the choice to blood dope was a matter for the riders and their doctors, not him.

After the news broke that some riders on the 1984 road and track teams blood doped, USCF president Mike Fraysse scrambled, telling *Sports Illustrated* that the governing body had "been looking into this stuff for years and years and years." Indeed, Fraysse was one of the USCF executives whom Burke's blood-boosting memo was addressed to. Alluding to the spirit of the beat-the-communists Olympic directive handed down through presidents Nixon, Ford, and Carter, and recently reiterated by Reagan in his pre-Games luncheon directive to not "short-change our country," Fraysse made it clear that he was on board with the desires of the American people and the highest level of the government: "We weren't going to fall behind the Russians or East Germans any more."[10]

Along with the USOC's silent approval, the lack of UCI rules specific to analogous blood use gave Fraysse, Burke, and Borysewicz a loophole. The Cold War–motivated Amateur Sports Act of 1978 and the corporate-funded structure of the 1984 Games gave them economic, governmental, and patriotic directives to pedal through it.

USCF board member Les Earnest had another take. Given this policy void, he told *Sports Illustrated*, "these guys moved into it and filled it in a stupid way."[11] Because the USCF decision to boost red-blood-cell counts was made at the last minute, the riders had not withdrawn their own blood ahead of time. Lacking their own supply, some infused blood from non–family members and became ill. It was a potentially very dangerous procedure, especially compared with transfusing your own blood.[12] Dr. Herman Falsetti conducted the transfusions.* A University of Iowa heart doctor with a Laguna Beach second home and a California medical license, Falsetti told the *Los Angeles Times* that the decision to boost came so close to the Games that extracting the riders' own blood would have weakened them during the Olympic trials.[13]

Looking back today, Earnest told me that the corporate Olympic funding structure ordained by the 1978 Amateur Sports Act put the interest of sponsors above health or ethical concerns. The anticommunist motives, while present, were secondary to pro–corporate sponsor intentions that were quietly working in the background to muffle any ethical reservations that the medical staff, USOC, or IOC might have about the procedure. However, Earnest is not sure sporting nationalism filtered down to the point that it influenced the riders' personal decisions to blood dope. "They just wanted to get ahead," he recalls

* In 1996 Dickson told Pennsylvania's *Morning Call* newspaper that after the 1984 Games, he had a blood bank analyze Falsetti's procedure, and it "came up with the statistic that x numbers of athletes would get sick because the proper characteristics weren't matched in the transfusions." Gary R. Blockus, "Blood in Their Veins, Medals in Their Closet," *Morning Call* (Allentown, PA), June 2, 1996.

of the athletes. "They were motivated the same way as the Russians, except with the Russians it was a more systematic approach. That is, the coaches were all trained in how to do this stuff."[14] As Dickson remembered, "When you're on the Olympic level and there's something you can do that's not illegal and it can enhance your performance, you do it."[15]

Clarke, Dickson, and Falsetti's neutral attitudes toward blood doping reflected the temperament of the medical community at large. Medical journals and textbooks from the time do not equate autologous blood transfusions—putting your own blood back into yourself—with ethical malignancy. Instead, the sports medicine establishment discussed blood boosting as a way for athletes to get the performance-enhancing benefits of high-altitude training, but without moving to the mountains. *Sports Medicine*, an authoritative British textbook published in 1976, mentions blood transfusions as a potential performance enhancer. The textbook authors placed their blood-boosting discussion in a section on "General Medical Aspects of Sport," not in the chapter on doping, an editorial decision that set the ethical framework through which doctors, nurses, and sports trainers viewed the technique. The editorial decision to include blood boosting alongside mundane preventive medicine topics such as inoculations, routine medical exams, and skin problems indicates that in 1976 the process was seen as an unremarkable tool in the sports doctor's bag—one he or she might offer in addition to sending an athlete to the Alps to train.

Sports Medicine was republished as *Sport and Medicine* in 1983, the same year Burke was canvassing U.S. cycling coaches for their opinions on blood boosting. The updated textbook continued to frame autologous blood transfusions in general health terms. It also covered technical challenges such as safe blood storage that come into play when reintroducing blood in the heat of competition. The authors conclude that, "while this method is theoretically attractive, its practice must be extremely difficult to regulate safely and efficiently under all the stresses of athletic competition."[16] In 1983, the sports medicine community focused on the technical, rather than moral, complications of blood doping.[17*]

As Burke's American cycling charges entered the final critical months of their preparations for the 1984 Olympics, a new issue of the medical journal, the *Physician and Sportsmedicine*, landed on his desk. Just in time for the Olympic year, the issue featured five articles on drugs in sports. One of them, "The Ergogenic Effect of Blood Doping," was written by York University professor Norman Gledhill and reported on his studies measuring whether blood doping affected athletic performance. The paper gave a clear yes.[18]

Gledhill conducted three tests and found that blood doping led to a 5 percent improvement in VO_2max among runners. That is, adding red blood cells allowed the tested runners to carry more oxygen—and more oxygen delivered to muscles equals more energy. The same test also found that blood-doped runners could run 35 percent longer than when

---

* Outside Olympic sports, but still within the domain of a sports physician's knowledge, in 1987, the American press suggested that blood doping was a patriotic act that could help preserve U.S. freedoms. A United Press International piece described blood-boosting research being conducted by the U.S. Army Research Institute of Environmental Medicine in Natick, Massachusetts. The March 20 article explained how military tests using autologous blood reinfusion had improved athletic performance in military test subjects. The tests were designed to discover whether blood boosting could help Special Forces perform in severe conditions such as at 14,000 feet elevation or in extreme heat and humidity. "It doesn't take a lot of imagination to come up with a military scenario where it would be very useful," the piece quoted army researcher Michael Sawka on blood doping. (Think Afghanistan, an extremely mountainous country of great interest to Americans and Russians in the 1980s, whose highest peaks reach 25,000 feet.) "We're probably the largest research institute in the world looking solely at human performance," Sawka added. "You wouldn't want to give this to a lot of troops, but you might consider it for a Special Forces or commando team on a particular assignment." He also told the UPI, "The military can go anywhere on the face of the Earth—any altitude, arctic and tropical regions—and they have to be able to perform."

Sawka also coauthored a 1986 Department of Defense report titled "Elite Special Forces: Physiological Description and Ergogenic Influence of Blood Infusion." Working with researchers at the army's environmental medicine lab, he concluded that for highly fit Special Forces soldiers, "Blood reinfusion will acutely increase their maximal aerobic power for a minimum of 10 days after infusion." The report detailed how 12 elite soldiers were tested at the army lab in Massachusetts and at the Boston University School of Medicine. Soldiers who had 600 milliliters of their own blood reinfused saw an 11 percent increase in their oxygen uptake after three days and an 8 percent increase after 10 days. More oxygen uptake means higher human performance. Soldiers infused with saline rather than blood experienced no such enhancement. United Press International, "Army Studies Blood Doping," March 20, 1987; Stephen R. Muza, Michael N. Sawka, Andrew J. Young, Richard C. Dennis, Richard R. Gonzalez, James W. Martin, Kent B. Pandolf, and C. R. Valeri, "Elite Special Forces: Physiological Description and Ergogenic Influence of Blood Infusion" (Natick, MA: Army Research Institute of Environmental Medicine, 1986).

running with their body's normal level of blood. With less than a year until the 1984 Games, the day's mail had delivered peer-reviewed evidence to Burke's office that Anquetil's old European blood-boosting trick worked. The *Physician and Sportsmedicine* gave the USCF medical staff quantified evidence that higher energy output and greater endurance comes with autologous blood infusions—music to a sports physiologist's ears.

For a sports scientist under pressure to deliver results against systematically doped athletes from Eastern Bloc countries, Gledhill's conclusion that "blood doping undoubtedly improved performance in endurance events," intrigued Burke. Like the *Sports Medicine* textbook, the article even detailed how to safely store blood between administrations and explained that regulations approving or disapproving the practice in sports were unclear at best.

From the UCI to the IOC to medical journals, signs kept pointing in the direction that the legality of blood doping was a matter of personal interpretation. As historian John Gleaves writes of the *Physician and Sportsmedicine* story, "For anyone looking for a good reason to use blood transfusions, this article certainly provided it."[19]

Burke shared the fresh research with his riders. Going into the Olympic qualifying trials period, a track rider named Danny Van Haute had been turning in lackluster times. Equipped with the *Physician and Sportsmedicine* article, Van Haute approached his father-in-law, a physician, for help in trying out the technique. Van Haute withdrew blood and had his father-in-law reinfuse it before the Olympic trials in Colorado Springs. Van Haute was transformed. With new blood cells carrying more oxygen to his muscles, Van Haute placed fourth. As fellow U.S. track rider Dave Grylls told *Rolling Stone*, "I don't know if it was the blood or what, but at the trials he was really flying. You could see it—and he didn't look like shit any time before."[20] Seeing the results inspired other riders on the team to ask Burke for the same performance boost.

Public response to the blood-doping scandal reflected the polarized attitudes of the time. Writing in *Sports Illustrated*'s "19th Hole" letters section, a sports fan from North Carolina argued that blood doping to stay on par with the Soviets was unworthy of Americans; it reduced America to "immoral and artificial ways of winning." In her February 4, 1985, missive, the reader added, "To me, winning is nothing if I can't do it on natural ability."[21] Other *SI* readers pointed out that the rules against certain performance-enhancing procedures were arbitrary. A pair of bike riders from Kansas offered their view that "many artificial means of enhancing performance are accepted by cyclists, including aerodynamic helmets and wheels, vitamin injections, and some carbo loading. Where does it stop? Will all athletes be asked to quit the intense training programs that they presently follow simply because one athlete may gain an advantage over another?"[22]

The issue of what separates moral and immoral performance-enhancing procedures had come up previously in IOC discussions in advance of the 1968 Mexico City Games. The Russians had built high-altitude training camps to acclimatize their athletes to Mexico City's 7,382-foot altitude. Was this a violation of Olympic amateur values? A *Sports Illustrated* reader and hematologist from Arizona pointed out that if the U.S. Olympic Committee was truly committed to "pure sport," it ought to question placing the Olympic training center in Colorado Springs. "What would the guardians of 'natural' sports like to do?" the reader taunted. "Require everyone competing to train at the same altitude? Maybe the USOC should be accused of blood boosting for establishing a training center at 6,000 feet."[23]

As for the riders on the 1984 Olympic team, the consensus seemed to be that while the nationalistic pressures that precipitated the Amateur Sports Act of 1978 might have weighed on USOC officials, it did not percolate down to their level. Whether or not to blood dope seemed to depend on individual rider choice, not a shared obligation to defend American honor on a battlefield with the communists (who ended up boycotting the Games, anyhow). One of the riders who blood doped, silver medalist Brent Emery, saw the procedure as another brick in the road to the race. "Cycling preparation is very, very involved on a lot of levels," Emery said in 1985. "And we have not done anything illegal."[24]

Alexi Grewal won the Olympic road race in 1984. A woodworker by trade today, Grewal told me that neither Borysewicz nor anyone else at the USCF compelled him to dope for the 1984 Games. Grewal also said that whatever pressure the U.S. government's executive and legislative branches were putting on the USOC to beat the communists never filtered down to his level. However, he also said that in 1984, he and his fellow road teammates were fully aware that riders from communist countries "were on the medical program and we were not." And while Grewal might not have personally felt the nationalist pressures weighing down on the USOC, the press immediately celebrated his win as victory over the communists. After the road events, International Amateur Cycling Federation president Valeriy Sisiov, a Russian, gave out the medals. On Monday, July 30, a UPI story crowed, "They must have been blushing Sunday in the Kremlin when a top Soviet official had to drape gold medals around the necks of Connie Carpenter and Alexi Grewal, who gave the U.S. its first-ever cycling titles."[25]

Grewal recalled that the East German and Soviet riders' drugs were one component of a state-sponsored training program that was far more sophisticated than anything imaginable by the Americans with their single coach and part-time doctors. Pinning the Eastern Bloc's dominance on drugs alone was simplistic and played to the antidrug hysteria that was gaining speed in both sport and society during the Reagan years. Grewal said he was struck by the discipline and organization of the Russian and East German training programs as early as 1981, when Borysewicz took his young American charges to Europe to race in events like Poland's Peace Race. "We recognized that they were better, more disciplined, and under more pressure," Grewal told me. "The easterners were some tough, tough guys—and very well prepared," Grewal recalled. "And really, I think, in the overall scope, better athletes than any of us."

Grewal did not resent the Eastern Bloc riders' pro-level infrastructure and pharmaceutical support. In fact, he recalls that on a human level, the East Germans were kind, and their professionalism inspired him to push his own training to a higher level. Grewal also credited

Borysewicz for creating opportunities for the Americans to race against these eye-opening riders. "Eddie B. was a great coach in the sense that he knew how to make us better, which was to take us to the big races," Grewal said. And at these early European races, after Grewal and teammates like Thurlow Rogers and Davis Phinney got their asses handed to them, Borysewicz did not make excuses. Instead, Grewal recalls, Eddie B. simply told his riders, "They had two legs just like you." Grewal says that by pointing out that the difference between a winning rider and a loser is dedication and attitude, not mountains of state-sponsored sports medicine, Borysewicz "built a lot of confidence in us."

While Grewal was not one of the nine riders who blood boosted in Los Angeles, he says his most vivid recollection of blood doping comes not from cycling, but from a college basketball player he grew up with who told him how his team doctor extracted and stored blood for the players, and then reinjected it before important games. "That was college basketball," Grewal said with a certain awe that Borysewicz and the 1984 cycling team caught so much grief for a practice that American universities were already using with their young athletes, and on a much larger scale.*

Thurlow Rogers placed fourth in the 1984 road race. In a *Los Angeles Times* interview that ran on January 26, 1985, five days after the *Sports Illustrated* article and two weeks before the sensationalizing *Rolling Stone* piece, Rogers pointed out that the legal boundaries of performance enhancement were both blurry and relative. "What about technology?" he asked in the *LA Times* interview. "In our sport, there are so many new bikes. You try to build a faster bike. When it's technology, it's great, everybody loves it. But when you do something a little kinky, it's no good."[26]

---

* Weeks before the 1984 Olympics, Grewal tested positive for ephedrine while leading Colorado's Coors Classic stage race. Suspended from racing for a month, Grewal was going to miss the Olympics until the USCF lifted the ban due to a testing technicality. Ephedrine is common in over-the-counter medicines and herbal teas. Grewal claimed the substance either came from an herbal supplement or from a legal asthma inhaler. "Drug Suspension of Cyclist Is Lifted," *New York Times*, July 24, 1984.

In January 1985, another member of the 1984 team, track rider Dave Grylls, told *New York Times* writer Michael Goodwin that USCF staffers had encouraged him to blood dope. "There was pressure to do it from the coaching staff," he told the paper. "I felt from the first day it was wrong, that it was illegal or whatever. It was the gray zone, but too far to the black end of the gray zone. Since it all had to be done on the sly, I think it was kind of sleazy," he said.[27]

Inga Thompson was also on the 1984 Olympic road squad that raced in, and won, the first-ever women's Olympic road race. Although Thompson does not recall any sense that the blood doping was linked to an obligation to defend America's national interests, she says that when the news broke after the 1984 Olympics that medical commissioner Mérode could not locate the doping test records that fingered medal-winning athletes, she realized that some athletes are truly protected by the USOC and IOC to shield Olympic sponsors and national prestige. She added that while the USCF "never made it explicit" that *team player* was a euphemism for *willing doping participant*, she feels that "it was all the innuendo of, 'who works with us and who doesn't.' But I was never actually approached to take the drugs."

What about the preparations for the 1980 Games in Moscow, an opportunity to unleash America's astonishing new talent Greg LeMond and embarrass the communists in their own front yard? The youngest cyclist ever selected for a U.S. Olympic team, LeMond was 18 when Borysewicz chose him for Moscow. Amongst the national team riders in the late 1970s, LeMond told me, Soviet doping "wasn't a focus, it wasn't the talk." Although LeMond did not get to compete in the 1980 Olympics due to the American boycott, he said he never felt Cold War political pressures reaching down to his level as an implicit or explicit instruction to dope. The Russians, however, "absolutely were on doping programs," he recalled.

Because the Olympics still clung to its amateur requirement in 1984 and LeMond had turned professional, LeMond did not race in Los Angeles. Observing what happened with blood doping in 1984, he said that there is always pressure on Olympic coaches to do whatever it takes—even dope their riders—if it will get them a win. "If you win a medal, you get your funding," LeMond said of the Olympic financing and incentive structure. The emphasis on winning creates an inducement for coaches to embrace the same doping practices that their competitors are using. Medals mean job security for coaches. "They don't care about the athletes," LeMond said, adding that the same system of reward and punishment affects the pro peloton's team directors. "If they've got an athlete, juice him to the gills so he can keep his job and sponsors," LeMond observed.

The Cold War created the context that precipitated the Amateur Sports Act of 1978 and a focus on elite athletes who could promote nationalist interests by beating political enemies at the Olympics. The act also created a nested set of pressure cookers. The anti-Soviet legacy of Nixon, Ford, Carter, and Reagan set governmental expectations that the USOC needed to deliver on in the interest of national pride and defense. This in turn created a need to find performance-enhancing procedures that would give U.S. athletes a playing field level with that of their chemically enhanced Eastern Bloc competitors. At the next level were the Olympic sponsors who applied pressure on the USOC and individual sport committees to minimize doping scandals. Then came team staff like Burke and Borysewicz who reached to the most recent sports medicine and technology in pursuit of wins that would preserve their job security. And at the center of this nest of pressure cookers were the athletes.

LeMond explained that American athletes were subject to geopolitical pressures, even though there might not have been someone explicitly telling them that they needed to dope to beat the communists. "Even at the amateur level and the Olympic level, those rumors are affecting the coaches more than the riders," LeMond said of the word on the street about systematic communist doping. And in turn, "The coaches have a huge influence on the athletes."

The Los Angeles blood-doping episode profoundly affected anti-doping practices after 1984. Like Knud Enemark Jensen's death at the

1960 Rome Olympics and Tom Simpson's demise at the 1967 Tour, the 1984 Olympic blood-doping story became a focusing event that directed performance-enhancing drug policies in a direction that was more severe and that looked to scientific solutions to stop problems that were fundamentally human and organizational in nature.

The medical community went sour on blood doping after U.S. National Institutes of Health doctor Harvey G. Klein condemned the practice in a 1985 issue of the *New England Journal of Medicine*, writing "There can be no medical justification for exposing a normal person to the serious and unnecessary risks of homologous blood transfusion." Klein's concerns had as much to do with public health as that of elite athletes.[28] In 1985, HIV/AIDS had been in the news for four years. Aside from the fact that it was killing a lot of people, HIV/AIDS was still not well understood by the scientific community. In the public's mind, the cyclists' blood doping was linked with this mysterious, scary, misunderstood, and lethal blood-related killer. Klein was concerned that if blood doping were adopted by the performance-seeking public in the same way that steroids were, "recreational use of blood transfusions would inevitably result in serious injury to many normal, healthy people."[29]

By the end of the 1980s, the days of ethical neutrality that had marked opinions on blood doping in the 1970s and early 1980s were over. As sports historian and sociologist Ivan Waddington puts it, a new anti-blood-boosting orthodoxy took root, and doctors stopped acting only as neutral medical technicians. Instead, they became moral cops who told "athletes in unambiguous terms that the use of blood doping was cheating and that this technique should not be used."[30]

The IOC also moved quickly. At its annual session in June 1985, the IOC Medical Commission banned blood doping. It also altered the definition of doping to encompass banned procedures, in addition to substances. As John Gleaves explains, the blood-doping incident galvanized the IOC Medical Commission and turned it into a body that began to express itself as an active force "intent on eradicating doping of any kind in sport."[31]

This was a dramatic change. A new, aggressive Medical Commission was emerging that would prohibit drugs even before it could test for them. And by replacing the term *drugs* with *substances*, the Medical Commission gained leeway to go after a plethora of items that were not pharmaceutical compounds. At least in rhetorical terms, the anti-doping missionaries were becoming more uncompromising.

Of course, in practice things were different. One member of the IOC Medical Commission, Italy's Dr. Francesco Conconi, had designed an autologous blood transfusion program for the 1984 Italian Olympic team. With the invention of EPO, he turned to a new and thriving business administering that more efficient form of blood boosting to a wide-ranging field of Olympians and professional cyclists—all while serving in anti-doping roles with both the IOC and the UCI.[32] While the anti-doping talk got tougher, the doping practices themselves only became more advanced.

CHAPTER 12

DR. FERRARI WAS RIGHT

On April 20, 1994, three cyclists from the Italian Gewiss-Ballan team made a mockery of the pro peloton with 30 miles remaining in the 127-mile Belgian classic La Flèche Wallonne. Entering the center of Huy, a city of 14th-century churches and cobbled squares straddling a languid loop in the Meuse River, the field jolted onto the precipitous Chemin des Chapelles, also known as the Mur de Huy. As the road headed up, Moreno Argentin, Giorgio Furlan, and Evgeni Berzin flicked their shifters into gears that only they possessed. By the top of the 1.3-kilometer climb, the trio had a 14-second gap on the field. The peloton never saw them again. After a 30-mile final loop through the rolling Ardennes countryside, the Gewiss-Ballan trio started their final climb to the finish atop the Mur de Huy. There was no need for them to send a fleeting prayer for victory toward one of the ascent's six roadside chapels; Argentin won with Furlan and Berzin taking second and third. The trio's nearest competitor, 1991 and 1992 road world champion Gianni Bugno, rolled in 1:14 later. Two and a half minutes drained from the clock before 1993 world champion Lance Armstrong finished.

Even before the Gewiss-Ballan threesome crossed the finish line, fans and riders were suspicious. Pull up the race on YouTube and you'll see why. It is a show of effortless, inhuman domination. When the teammates attack, they float away with a fluid animation a universe apart from the bobbing and heaving field gasping behind. That spring day in Belgium broadcast the awesome, performance-enhancing potential of EPO.

Following the race, a French sportswriter named Jean-Michel Rouet spoke to the Gewiss-Ballan team's Italian doctor, Michele Ferrari. The physician was rumored to be a keen proponent of the relatively new blood-boosting anemia treatment drug, recombinant human erythropoietin, or EPO, and his riders' unbelievable victory made Rouet eager to pin down the Italian. Reporting on their encounter in the April 22, 1994, issue of the French sports daily *L'Équipe*, Rouet raised the widely accepted rumor that EPO had caused a rash of Dutch cyclists to die in their sleep. Referring to events that many accepted but none stopped to challenge, Rouet all but accused Ferrari of trying to kill athletes. "A dozen Dutch riders died a few years ago," the journalist asserted. When Ferrari demurred, Rouet pressed on. "In any case, it is dangerous!" he said.

Ferrari would have none of it. "EPO is not dangerous," he retorted. "Its abuse is." Ferrari then added, "It is also dangerous to drink ten liters of orange juice."[1]

Ferrari was a protégé of Italian blood-doping pioneer Francesco Conconi—a man whose groundbreaking research into autologous blood boosting helped Francesco Moser shatter the hour record in 1984. For most reading this exchange, Ferrari's response to Rouet's interrogation immediately became evidence of the doctor's cavalier attitude toward anti-doping laws. When growing moralism about drug use in sport was superimposed upon Ferrari's statement of fact—EPO isn't dangerous, its abuse is—the Italian's willingness to challenge hardened anti-doping orthodoxies also became a sign of moral treachery. Sure, orange juice was benign, but just pick up a newspaper or cycling magazine and you'd see—EPO was a killer set loose among the peloton.

Ferrari became a poster boy for the mortal dangers of EPO and its distributors. While the Dutch riders Rouet referred to were never conclusively linked to death by EPO, the fabrication served a larger anti-doping moral agenda and the missionary effort to impose purity on sport. After the IOC expanded its definition of performance-enhancing substances and took a more aggressive approach to doping in response to the 1984 Olympic blood-boosting scandal, the characterization of sports doping as a plague gained speed. As historian Paul Dimeo explains, through the 1980s, "the construction of doping as an evil, a plague, a cancer or a temptation" was kept alive by the myth that sports were inherently good and drugs were a corrupting temptation that had to be beat out of the athletic garden of Eden. By daring to speak the truth about a drug—that under a doctor's supervision, it is safe—Ferrari fell short of the newly emboldened anti-doping evangelists.[2] Pointing out that Ferrari was correct would have been to spit in the soup of anti-doping outrage that was becoming a nurturing broth for journalists and anti-doping administrators alike.

Three years before Lance Armstrong finished La Flèche Wallonne over two minutes down on the Ferrari-charged trio, on May 19, 1991, the *New York Times* startled readers with news of a killer stalking the roadways and velodromes of Europe. "A genetically engineered drug that was created for people suffering from kidney failure has become the latest substance to be abused by athletes seeking enhanced stamina and performance," *Times* journalist Lawrence Fisher reported. "The consequences, in some cases, may be deadly." Ominously titled "Stamina-Building Drug Linked to Athletes' Deaths," the piece connected the death of 18 European pro cyclists over a four-year period to EPO. Although the *Times* headline gripped readers by their lapels and yanked them into the dirty world of European pro cycling, the story's claim that the drug was responsible for 18 cyclist deaths was based on speculation. EPO can theoretically cause stroke, hypertension, and myocardial infarction when used by dehydrated athletes, especially when taken without a doctor's supervision. Evidence also suggests that the hormone may have an anti-inflammatory and tissue-repairing effect that can aid with recovery.[3] What was not provable in 1991, or today, is that the drug killed a rash of cyclists.[4]

The number of red blood cells, or erythrocytes, in our body is controlled by a feedback loop between an oxygen sensor in our kidneys and our bone marrow—the factory that produces blood cells. Erythrocytes don't have a nucleus and can't repair themselves. After about 120 days of service, they are shot, and the spleen shuffles these red blood cells out of circulation at a rate of 2 to 3 million erythrocytes per second. Like a manager calling down to the production line when a new order for widgets comes across his desk, when the kidneys sense that our red-blood-cell count is getting low (our hematocrit level), EPO signals the bone marrow to crank up blood cell production. Stem cells start a chain of sequential divisions that eventually results in fresh new erythrocytes eager to cart oxygen to our muscles for four months. A hormone, erythropoietin, works as the middleman in this process; it binds with blood-cell receptors and triggers the creation of erythrocytes.

Like a second temporary factory manager who suddenly appears on the floor with a megaphone and starts barking out orders for more product, when a doctor injects synthetic EPO into your body, the artificial hormone tricks the stem cells in the bone marrow into creating more red blood cells. It can be a life-saving event when natural erythropoietin levels wane due to pathologies like bone marrow cancer or kidney failure.[5]

This process also works in healthy people, only instead of fooling an ailing body into boosting its flagging red-blood-cell count back up to normal, injecting EPO into a healthy human causes the bone marrow to produce more red blood cells than are normally needed. The resulting surplus of these oxygen-carrying cells can increase endurance by as much as 10 percent. The ideal adult hematocrit percentage varies between individuals and genders, but it is generally in the 40 to 54 percent range at sea level, and about 5 percent higher than that for people who live at altitude. When athletes figured out that exogenous EPO could juice their red-blood-cell count, they got the same performance-enhancing benefit as living at altitude or sleeping in a hypoxic chamber. Describing the effect of EPO on his performance, cyclist Tyler Hamilton said in his 2012 book, *The Secret Race,* "That holy place at the edge of your limits gets edged out—and not just a little."[6]

Although endurance athletes probably began experimenting with this new synthetic hormone during the drug's clinical trials in 1986, its use as a potential performance enhancer was first recognized in the early 1950s. Beginning in 1953, a University of Chicago biochemist named Eugene Goldwasser set about understanding how the human body created and regulated red blood cells. Solving this problem had tremendous life-saving potential. Inventing a way to artificially replace the body's EPO would be a boon for millions of patients affected by kidney failure. After three decades of research, Goldwasser isolated the erythropoietin gene, thereby opening the door to its synthesis.

In his autobiography, *A Bloody Long Journey*, Goldwasser recalls that not long after he began his 1953 investigations, a man with racehorses to sell came looking for equine EPO. Horses that ran faster and longer commanded premium prices, and the horseman wanted to inject his stock with EPO to increase their performance in claiming races—events where horses are sold based on their placings. As Goldwasser recalls, "He had done his homework and knew that for short races, increasing red cells was no help . . . but in longer races, having a bigger erythron [red-blood-cell count] was an advantage."[7]

Buckets of horse blood soon began showing up on Goldwasser's doorstep. Although Goldwasser never extracted enough pure EPO from the blood to test its sporting efficacy, he, like the racing entrepreneur, saw the performance-enhancing potential in the blood-regulating hormone in the early 1950s.[8] When Goldwasser's lab finally isolated the EPO gene in the early 1980s, an infant biotech startup called Applied Molecular Genetics approached him, and Goldwasser began sharing his three decades of knowledge with the company that would later rename itself Amgen. The company was funded by Montgomery Securities, an investment bank founded by Lance Armstrong's U.S. Postal Service team backer Thomas Weisel.[9]

Amgen finally cloned EPO in November 1983, opening the door to industrial scale production of a synthetic version of the hormone under the name Epogen. It also licensed the patent to Johnson & Johnson, which sold its EPO as Procrit. The startup exploded into a pharmaceutical giant worth over $100 billion today. By 2006, annual EPO sales were $13 billion worldwide.[10] After Amgen went public in 1983, the company generated a stock-market windfall that seed investor and dedicated cyclist Weisel would later use to fund pro bike racing teams and pay for his own personalized coaching by Eddie Borysewicz.

The spectacular rise of Amgen and its miracle drug coincided with what appeared to be a rash of mysterious deaths among endurance athletes. Echoing claims made in other general news and cycling-specific publications, a May 1991 *New York Times* article concluded that EPO's development came too close to a glut of pro cyclist funerals to be mere coincidence. The piece described the mysterious death of Dutch pro Johannes Draaijer, who passed away in his sleep in 1990 at the age of 27. A caption beneath a photo of Draaijer read, "Mr. Draaijer's widow believes that the drug recombinant erythropoietin was involved with his death." A pull quote declared, "You just don't get 18 deaths in 4 years, mysteriously." The story left the impression that the new life-saving anemia drug played double duty as an indiscriminate athlete killer.[11]

EPO deaths made for good news stories, even if there was no autopsy evidence that EPO was actually killing cyclists. However, the *New York Times* knew the connection between EPO and the apparent boomlet in dead cyclists was speculative, and admitted so a week later. Backtracking, the *Times* ran a correction: "A picture caption last Sunday with an article about a stamina-building drug linked to athletes' deaths misstated what is known about the death of the Dutch cyclist Johannes Draaijer. An autopsy did not specify the cause, and it is not known conclusively whether he had used the drug." Despite the correction, the rumor was already set: EPO was a new drug of athlete destruction.

If you take a lot of EPO without a doctor's supervision, in theory you can kill yourself. As University of Oklahoma chief of hematology Dr. Randy Eichner explained in the *Times* piece, increasing red-blood-cell count can thicken blood. Take too much EPO and "pretty soon you have mud instead of blood; then you have trouble." The results can be blood clotting, stroke, or heart failure. The *Times* also cited Ed Burke, the USCF physiologist who oversaw the 1984 Olympic cycling team's blood boosting. "EPO can do wonders for your aerobic capacity," Burke noted, before warning, "The problem is, it can also kill you."[12]

By sensationalizing the potentially deadly effects of EPO without reporting any evidence for a correlation with actual events, the *New York Times* seemed to be taking up the role of an anti-doping missionary whose conclusions are based on faith rather than evidence. Under a hematologist's expert care, EPO is safe. The drug saves thousands of lives every year. Yet because this drama-killing statement of fact contradicted the sensationalist thrust of a story about a scary new athlete killer, that is not the story that snowballed in the press.

In a *New England Journal of Medicine* (*NEJM*) article on the therapeutic uses of EPO published on May 9, 1991, 10 days before the *Times* piece, hematologist Dr. Allan Erslev wrote that erythropoietin "appears to be almost nontoxic."[13] Born in Denmark, Erslev graduated from medical school in 1945 and then traveled to the United States to conduct postgraduate research at Yale and at New York's Sloan Kettering Institute. Testing anemic rabbits in the early 1950s, Erslev was one of the first to identify the blood-regulating effect of EPO. In his 1991 *NEJM* piece, Erslev theorized that since EPO seemed to be nontoxic, it was viable for elective surgery patients who were concerned about contracting AIDS from donated blood. At a time when the blood-borne autoimmune-deficiency disease dominated headlines, surgery patents were afraid to use anonymously donated blood from blood banks. To eliminate the perceived risk, patients stored their own blood in advance of surgery. However, this blood banking created the problem of already sick or injured patients making themselves anemic in advance of surgery. Using

America's most esteemed medical journal to broadcast his message, Erslev told the surgical community that by using EPO, patients could safely extract and store more blood than was otherwise recommended without suffering a lower hematocrit level. With EPO therapies, "the number of donations could undoubtedly be increased," he advised.[14]

Erslev also wondered whether EPO could have a role as a rehabilitative therapy for endurance athletes. In 1991—the midst of the popular press's EPO-kills-cyclists panic—Erslev asked if "athletes engaged in exhausting long-distance events such as swimming, running, bicycle racing, or cross-country skiing would benefit from a moderate rise in hematocrit and red-cell mass." Since many world-class athletes were already anemic because their training regimes increased plasma volume and thereby diluted red-cell density, Erslev seemed to posit that the use of EPO as a sports medicine recovery therapy would merit further investigation.[15]

As for EPO dangers, Erslev postulated that the combination of lower blood volume from dehydration and higher hematocrit from EPO "would increase blood viscosity and be not only detrimental to muscular action but also the cause of possible life-threatening thrombosis." In other words, an athlete would be both slower and more likely to die from a blood clot in the brain. While Erslev did not have studies to prove it, in theory, it would seem that EPO would both *decrease* muscle performance and potentially thicken blood to the point that it might kill you. In spite of these theoretical complications, Erslev reported that the studies he had run indicated that the blood-clot problem was "quite sporadic" and in some clinical tests "nonexistent."[16]

Ten days after the publication of Erslev's article, news sources were calling the sports world to EPO panic stations. On July 14, 1991, Britain's *Independent* ran a piece with a stretched-out title worthy of its endurance topic: "Cyclists Don't Die Like This; Cycle Racing Gets Tough—and Sometimes Racers Die: But on the Track, Not at Home, in Bed, in Their Prime. Not 18 of Them. So Were They Abusing a Billion-Dollar Wonder Drug?" The piece began with a vignette of Draaijer's wife, Lisa, waking up to a gurgling sound—her husband's death rattle. It then listed other cyclists who had passed away, including Dutch pro Ruud Brouwers who fell out of bed and died on May 3, 1989, and Dutch amateur Connie Meijer, dead after abandoning a criterium on August 17, 1988. Heart failure had killed 18 cyclists in all, the *Independent* claimed.[17]

The *Independent* writer rang up retired 1970s Dutch pro Henk Vogels at his home in Australia. Vogels told the journalist, "Half the people I cycled with are now dead. They often die in their early forties after 15 years of taking stuff and going all out." In the same piece, 1984 U.S. Olympic cycling team doctor Ed Burke warned UK readers that EPO abuse "raises the red-cell count to the point where it turns the blood into sludge."

A decade later, Burke died of a sudden heart attack while cycling near his Colorado Springs home, a victim of sudden cardiac failure, the number-one killer of athletes. Burke was 53. While no one blamed his death on dope, in the early 1990s, both Burke and the journalists who quoted him were quick to pin the cardiac failure of 18 cyclists on EPO. These pieces came at such a fast pace that a supposition became received wisdom: EPO is a mass killer.

Even the *Sporting News*, a magazine that usually keeps its nose pointed firmly in the direction of stick-and-ball sports, got on the EPO-kills bandwagon, writing in a 2004 piece titled "Cycling's Deadly Downward Spiral" that "death is yet the unseen rider in world-class cycling." The story cited the death of nine riders due to heart failure between January 11, 2003, and June 30, 2004, including "one in a dentist's chair." The piece also referred its readers to the death of Italian superstar cyclist Marco Pantani in 2004. Though Pantani's autopsy singled out a cocaine overdose as the cause of death, that did not stop the *Sporting News* from attaching its amplifier to the common speculation: "Some cyclists believe he died as the other eight did—of heart failure prompted by use of EPO."[18]

On January 29, 2004, the *Sydney Morning Herald* described soccer players who had mysteriously died on the pitch. Although none of the players' autopsies indicated EPO as a cause of death, the Australian paper did not let medical records get in the way of a growing fiction. It promptly made the EPO connections that coroners did not. Citing a French investigation into doping by the Cofidis cycling team, the paper wrote, "Perhaps the soccer authorities should start an inquiry into these supposed unrelated deaths."

Marathoners also got their moment in the EPO-kills glare. "Fear on the Marathon Starting Line," blared an April 22, 2001, piece in Scotland's *Sunday Herald*. It asserted that the top runners in that year's London Marathon were wondering whether their days on Earth were so numbered that they would not have time to spend their appearance fees. The reason? EPO. Spanish marathoner Sergio García had died earlier that year at the age of 39, and coaches and runners were abuzz with speculation that his death was related to EPO. "Garcia's spectre has been stalking the corridors of the London Marathon race headquarters this week," the paper whispered. The connection between García's death and EPO was hypothetical, and yet by 2001, the EPO-kills myth was so hardened that newspapers could get away with publishing gossip in the guise of reporting.[19]

Unlike the press, EPO-using athletes separated the true risks of EPO from myth. U.S. Postal Service team rider Tyler Hamilton started using the synthetic hormone in 1997. In his 2012 book *The Secret Race,* the American compared the risk of taking EPO to the damages he suffered while racing—a catalogue of smashed bones from nose to back to ribs. "Bike racing is not a healthy sport in any sense of the word," Hamilton wrote, "so when it comes to the risks of EPO, they tend to feel pretty small."[20] In light of the actual clinical facts available in the 1990s that EPO and hypertension were "not related" in healthy patients and that the drug's causation of blood clots was "quite sporadic" if not "nonexistent," Hamilton's response to the public perception of EPO danger was rational. As Erslev and the European and American drug regulators who approved Epogen and its variants indicated, under a doctor's supervision, EPO was safe. And as Hamilton pointed out, the risk of doctor-supervised EPO use was especially slight compared to the nearly 100 percent statistical chance that a rider would suffer multiple, and sometimes life-threatening, injuries while racing on Europe's narrow roads.

Spanish scholar Bernat López researched how EPO was transformed from a life-saving miracle hormone into what he calls a "drug of mass destruction."[21] Although no evidence exists to support the claim that EPO caused any of the cyclists' deaths in the early 1990s, López's research led him to conclude that the rumor had ossified into received wisdom through media repetition. The fiction served as propaganda that made it professionally and personally suicidal to challenge the morality and righteousness of the antidrug movement.

As López sees it, the story of EPO killing loads of cyclists became a "flagship myth" for anti-doping interests. It was a story manufactured and spread by the press with the intent of scaring athletes. López, a professor at the Universitat Rovira i Virgili in Catalonia, also argues that because the general public is largely indifferent to the drug-regulating policies that are the bedrock of anti-doping organizations, anti-doping missionaries played up the deadly EPO myth as a way to gain sympathy from a public that has an otherwise insatiable appetite for legal and illegal performance- and lifestyle-enhancing drugs.

When López ran a meta-analysis of 36 academic texts that referenced the EPO deaths as evidence of the danger of EPO, he discovered a scholarly train wreck. All the articles either referred to no source for their EPO-deaths claims or noted secondary resources that cited no source. As a result of this evidence-free conclusion making, academics came up with a shambolic number of EPO deaths, ranging from 5 to 20. The victims' nationalities were also wildly inconsistent. While newspapers like the *New York Times* reported that the dead riders were Dutch, the academic researchers indicated that they hailed from Spain, Holland, Belgium, and Scandinavia. The deaths also took place during variable time frames ranging from "the 1980s and early 1990s" to "between 1997 and 2000," to "1987 to 1991."[22]

López also looked at 20 academic texts that offered evidence *against* the claim that EPO killed a bunch of cyclists in the late 1980s and early

1990s. The articles commonly pointed to genetic heart defects as the most likely cause of the deaths. None of these studies cited EPO as a potential or actual cause. If the researchers behind the 20 papers came up with any one Grim Reaper haunting bike races and marathons around the world, it was the damaging effect of extreme and prolonged training. In sum, López concluded, the 20 studies he investigated "suggest that EPO is extremely unlikely to have had the effects that have been claimed in the speculation of anti-doping sports doctors, academics, and journalists."[23]

When López performed the same analysis of coverage in the popular press, he found an even bigger mess of chronology and nationality. News reports put the number of EPO "victims" anywhere from 7 to 40, from countries including Spain, Holland, Belgium, Germany, and Poland as well as generic "Europe." Moreover, the articles cited athletes dying from EPO beginning in 1970, even though EPO was not produced for clinical trials until 1986.

When López broadened the scope of his search to include newspapers, magazines, blogs, and cycling websites for mentions of sudden deaths among cyclists between 1987 and early 2010, he found 49 cyclist sudden-death stories. In the time frame most often mentioned as ground zero for EPO deaths, 1987 to 1992, López unearthed news reports of 17 sudden deaths in Belgium, Holland, France, and the UK. These numbers are in line with the expected number of deaths from naturally occurring heart failures in athletes and the general population.

According to López's research from 1995 to 2006, 180 athlete sudden deaths were reported in Spain alone—about 15 per year. Of that total, 39 deaths were cyclists and 40 were soccer players. In other words, whether the number of cyclist deaths in Europe in the early 1990s was 15, 17, 18, or 20, those numbers do not reflect a spike, but rather a death rate entirely consistent with normal athlete sudden-death statistics in a single European country and low for all of Europe combined.

Compared to sudden cardiac deaths in both the athletic and larger population, the "explosion" of cyclist deaths that supposedly came at the hand of EPO does not seem like an anomaly; that number of deaths is normal. The anomaly was the arrival of a new, highly effective doping product. Blinded by a rising anti-doping fervor, journalists and medical researchers alike seemed to have superimposed EPO onto normal death rates and created a crisis where there was little, if any, postmortem evidence to suggest a correlation between EPO and fatalities. Yet the ghosts of the mythical 18 cyclists still haunt us today. As recently as 2012, an academic review of scientific studies on the effectiveness and safety of erythropoietin mentions the possible link between EPO and "18 European professional cyclists [who] have died."[24]

The narrative about crime, death, and drugs was believable because—three years after the 1988 approval of EPO use in Europe—the story *sounded* logical. Athletes eager to win plus a potentially dangerous new drug equaled death. When I called López at his home south of Barcelona, he told me he has yet to find a scrap of hard evidence linking EPO with any cyclist's death in the early 1990s. With the weary sigh of a man who had discovered a truth no one wanted to hear, he told me, "Science has not produced so far—at least to my knowledge—any conclusive evidence linking EPO with sudden death." While dozens of papers continue to speculate about a link between EPO and the rash of Belgian and Dutch deaths, "they are just reproducing the myth," López explained.

As López sees it, the role of the EPO deaths in the war on drugs in sport is analogous to the role fictional weapons of mass destruction played in the justification of the United States' invasion of Iraq in 2003. "There was a war to be waged, and the people waging that war needed justification, an excuse, a solid reason," he observed. Turning back to the EPO fiction, he said, "The best reason for waging that war is that doping kills. 'We honest men, we must stop athletes from taking drugs because we are interested in saving their lives.'" By exaggerating and distorting the EPO story, the anti-doping establishment was able to predict a dire future. And a bleak tomorrow creates incentives for stronger, better-funded anti-doping measures while also spinning far more compelling media narratives.[25]

In 1906, Olympic founder Pierre de Coubertin described the Olympic Games as a "program of moral purification."[26] This mission carries on today as an anti-doping errand in a chemically polluted sporting wilderness. For López, there is a link between the foundation of Olympic sports as a morally purifying, soul-cleansing experience and Olympic sports' ongoing efforts to preserve what the WADA code formally labels the "spirit of sport." "Well, actually," López clarified for me, "they are interested in saving their souls, but they pretended that they were interested in saving their lives."

My own search of medical literature finds plenty of warnings about the dangers of too much EPO. And there are many examples of pharmaceutical companies paying physicians kickbacks to overdose patients, a process that inadvertently accelerates the growth of deadly tumors. However, I found no documented instances of EPO killing already healthy humans, athletes or otherwise.

In December 2006, Danish researchers reported that 10 percent of a clinical trial group of 516 head and neck cancer patients on heavy EPO doses experienced accelerating tumor growth, even while undergoing radiation treatment.[27] This confirmed studies going back to 2003, which also showed that EPO could boost cancer growth. And 10 years earlier, a 1996 study of dialysis patients was halted because patients on high EPO dosages suffered more heart attacks than a control group on lower amounts of EPO.[28]

The deaths were not related to something that was inherently destructive about EPO. Instead, they were caused by overdosing. In 2007, Johnson & Johnson's annual EPO sales were $3.5 billion, while Amgen moved $5.6 billion worth of the product.[29] To attain these astronomical numbers, Amgen and Johnson & Johnson built incentive programs that financially rewarded doctors who administered heavy "off-label" doses of EPO to cancer and anemia patients. One West Coast office of six oncologists pocketed $2.7 million in incentives from Amgen in 2006 alone. The nationwide priming of the EPO pump led to a well-documented rash of heart attacks and carcinoma deaths in cancer and renal failure patients—so many that in 2007, the FDA released a report suggesting the dollar-incentivized high doses were neither improving nor extending patient lives.[30]

That said, even massive amounts of EPO don't automatically lead to death. A 2006 paper described two hospitalized South Korean heart-attack patients who accidentally received nearly 10 times their prescribed dose of EPO—318,000 units instead of 33,000. Both patients were smokers, and one had a history of hypertension and diabetes. After discovering the overdose, the hospital closely monitored the patients for symptoms such as elevated blood pressure, nausea, vomiting, shock, and thrombosis (which had already put them in the hospital). Despite the overdose, doctors reported that the two patients experienced none of the negative expected side effects from toxic levels of EPO. While known reactions to EPO overdoses make for a long, serious list—headache, muscle and joint pain, allergic reactions, nausea, itching, seizures, enlarged spleen, elevated blood pressure, and overproduction of blood platelets—the doctors reported that "in the course of close observation, we found none of the specific symptoms we expected as side effects of erythropoietin, and no abnormal objective findings on physical examination." The patients were soon discharged, and their EPO levels returned to normal.[31]

In 1993, a wheezing, clammy-skinned man showed up at a New York emergency room complaining of shortness of breath and a cough. The frail 62-year-old repeatedly told the doctors that he needed a "transfusion to correct anemia" and that he was stricken by "chronically low hematocrit." The ER doctors had a delusional hypochondriac on their hands with a history of self-medicating. The victim, a retired biomedical engineer, had a friend in the pharmaceutical industry who supplied him with Epogen. The arrivee had been injecting himself with EPO every day for several months (EPO is typically administered three times a week). He was also taking daily doses of a stew of other medicines, including penicillin.

When the patient checked into the ER, his hematocrit level was a through-the-roof 70.4 percent, a number that startled doctors used to finding a typical 42 to 54 percent hematocrit in adult males. While the fact that the patient was taking so many other drugs made it difficult to tie his symptoms to EPO alone, a report on the case in the *American Journal of Emergency Medicine* indicated that the months-long overdosing on EPO was causing the patient chest pain and hypertension, and it had worsened symptoms of his existing lung disease. The report pointed out that when a hematocrit level exceeds 70 percent, the amount of oxygen reaching the brain decreases, which in itself can be dangerous. In spite of his spectacular abuse of EPO, the patient recovered and was later released to a psychiatric hospital.

These vignettes are not meant to argue that EPO abuse is safe. It's not. In their write-up of the case, the physicians took the opportunity to warn other doctors to be on the lookout for athletes who self-administer EPO: "It seems likely that an erythropoietin-induced increase in hematocrit, coupled with the dehydration that develops during prolonged exertion, would increase blood viscosity and cause impaired muscle perfusion and possible fatal thrombosis."[32] The point remains, however, that it is extremely difficult to find a case that backs up the press-supported notion that EPO was indiscriminately slaughtering cyclists in the early 1990s.

One reason European athletes may have quickly adopted EPO in Europe in the late 1980s is related to a difference in European and American patent law. Shortly after Amgen successfully cloned EPO in 1982, at least four other biotech firms and the University of Washington separately made the same breakthrough.[33] A court battle handed the U.S. patent to Amgen. European patent law, however, is reluctant to grant patents on naturally occurring substances, and Amgen did not get an EPO monopoly on the other side of the Atlantic. As a result, Europeans had access to EPO from at least three manufacturers.

This pharmaceutical company competition, along with the buying power of Europe's national health care systems, kept EPO prices much lower in Europe. The affordability put the drug within financial reach of struggling European athletes while the drug's distribution from multiple chemical manufacturers may have created more opportunities for gray market product leakage. According to Alessandro Donati, an Italian sports professor and doping investigator, data from the sales of performance-enhancing drugs in Italy show that of 181 million prescriptions studied in 2000, the best-selling ones were erythropoietin and human growth hormone. The €158 million worth of EPO sold in Italy in 2000 did not include amounts brought in from Switzerland, nor the EPO distributed by the Mafia—much of it stolen from pharmacies or obtained from illicit distributors. Donati also cites a 1999 French study that indicated that only one-sixth of global EPO production went to patients with pathologies, with the rest being distributed through underground markets.[34] Because there were more manufacturers of EPO in Europe than in the United States, Europe had more distribution nodes from which the drug could be bought or stolen, he says.[35]

Interestingly, health care system differences ended up saving the lives of cancer victims in Europe compared to the United States. In 2001, Amgen released a new EPO called Aranesp. To spur product sales, the company offered $1,200 kickbacks to doctors for every prescription written. Amgen also ran a TV ad blitz that encouraged patients to ask for Aranesp as an antidote to fatigue. Prescriptions skyrocketed 340 percent in the United States, but increased only 52 percent in Europe. Across the pond, direct-to-consumer marketing is illegal, national health care systems use their buying clout to negotiate lower drug costs, and doctors in those same health care systems are immune to Big Pharma payola.

Five years after the Aranesp release, studies began to indicate that American cancer patients were dying 10 percent more frequently than European cancer sufferers. As it turned out, EPO was accelerating tumor growth; the American sales-and-marketing incentives that got more patients to take more EPO had the unintended effect of killing them off more quickly than in Europe, where patients were shielded from the pharmaceutical company's aggressive sales-and-marketing efforts. While there is no evidence directly linking EPO to any competitive cyclist deaths in Europe, in the United States, there are ample data showing that heavy EPO use incentivized by the oddities of the American health care system was shortening cancer patient lives. This discovery lead to a sterner FDA-mandated "black box" warning on EPO packaging and a decline in American oncologists' enthusiastic EPO prescription writing.[36] The scandal also suggests how EPO's black reputation in sports as a drug of mass destruction got an assist from drug makers' efforts to expand product sales.

DURING A CONVERSATION with López over Skype, I mentioned Michele Ferrari's infamous statement about EPO and orange juice. López said that Ferrari had dared to tell a truth that violated an anti-doping article of faith, one that firmly established itself after the IOC took its more aggressive anti-doping stance in the wake of the 1984 Los Angeles blood-doping episode: If it's a performance-enhancing drug, it must be categorically destructive to health and the spirit of sport. In the severe catechism of anti-doping thought that was hardening after Los Angeles and the 1988 Ben Johnson scandal in Seoul, there was no room for a fact-based argument like Ferrari's. Performance-enhancing drugs must be evil—end of story. For challenging the anti-doping missionaries' creed by suggesting that the *abuse* of drugs is harmful, not drugs in and of themselves, Ferrari was immediately exiled.

"You cannot say Ferrari," López observed. For his orange-juice comment, "he has been condemned. He is in hell and you cannot rehabilitate Ferrari's image or respectability because received wisdom says that Ferrari is the devil."

López was not justifying Ferrari's acts. The Italian doctor repeatedly broke the laws of the land and sports, and he conspired to give certain athletes an illegal performance advantage that others did not share. He was banned for life by the U.S. Anti-Doping Agency for his involvement with Lance Armstrong's doping and for administering and trafficking in performance-enhancing drugs. Even in 1994, he was up to no good. However, what interests López is how journalists who write about doping, and the agencies that create and enforce doping codes, can condemn Ferrari for speaking a truth about EPO when they have used the EPO-kills fabrication as a justification for a steadily growing anti-doping infrastructure.

López is not optimistic that journalists or anti-doping agencies will hold themselves accountable about the true health risks of doping any time soon. Doing so would be to spit in the soup that feeds them. It would also suggest that our responses to drugs are based more on personal bias than on hard data. "People are not interested in listening to other versions" of this colorful, body-strewn doping history, López told me. Excising the "doping kills" fable does no good for the anti-doping evangelists' cause because the falsehood has self-justifying utility. As López put it, the EPO-kills story is useful as an anti-doping foundation myth. Like Knud Enemark Jensen's "death by amphetamines," the tale is factually ignorant but practically useful for the media and anti-doping bureaucracy's "general condemnation and refusal of doping."

As for the inherent ethical contradiction in the twisting of truth by anti-doping activists in order to return athletes to "true sport," López does not think sinister motives are at play. Anti-doping agencies, scientists, and journalists are reluctant to discuss the fictional nature of drug-death stories because these tales serve a moral good that is a descendent of Coubertin's quest for purity. The EPO-kills story "was useful for the anti-doping campaign," López explained. "So it didn't matter if the evidence was good enough or not because it was conducive" to the anti-doping missionaries' goal of imposing a new purity on sports. In fact, López feels that anti-doping campaigners are acting in good faith, rather than willful hypocrisy. "I don't think that they lied on purpose," López told me. "But what they did was create a truth out of circumstantial and scattered evidence. And they believed in their own creation."

CHAPTER 13

FEAR MAKES GOOD COPY

Although a handful of academics like Bernat López have challenged the empirical flimsiness of the death and health danger claims underpinning anti-doping policy, the press generally has not. An honest examination of the true risks of doping would be harmful to both the business of anti-doping and the business of sports media. As López wrote in a 2011 paper on the EPO death fable, "Examining the mythical nature of these stories is bad news for the anti-doping campaign, because athletes, policy-makers, media and public opinion would be less convinced by the health-risk arguments if the history of doping were short of victims."[1]

And victims make good copy. Take track star Florence Griffith Joyner, who died in 1998 after suffering a seizure caused by a blood vessel abnormality called cavernous angioma. The five-time Olympic medalist and two-time world-record holder's autopsy found Tylenol and the antihistamine Benadryl in her system. While the medical report conclusively pointed to suffocation due to a seizure as the cause of death, posthumous media coverage floated the notion that her death was related to doping.

Because doping in sports does not kill many people, at times the media shows its frustration with the lack of bodies. In 1998, the *New York Times* publicly wished that Griffith Joyner's death would be linked to doping. In a September 26, 1998, article, writer Ian Thomsen complained, "For decades now we have been hearing from the medical experts that steroids and other performance-enhancers are destructive. But the warnings have lacked the hardest evidence. The doctors have claimed that these drugs can cause death—but who of any great fame or impact has died as a result?"[2]

Doping stories electrified the headlines in 1998: from the Festina affair to baseball player Mark McGwire's locker-room stash of androstenedione, to the criminal trials of East German sports officials. Events seemed to come so fast and thick that performance-enhancing-drug use was apparently a full-blown public health crisis. And yet, no bodies. Thomsen, whose day job was senior writer at *Sports Illustrated,* mentioned the EPO–cyclist death claim as evidence that doping might be deadly. In the *New York Times*, he wrote, "The willingness to risk everything seems to be borne out by many of the professional cyclists who reportedly use the blood-thickening drug EPO even though the deaths of several colleagues have been linked to that very drug."

To be sure, Thomsen equipped his EPO-kills anecdote with two conditional escape hatches—"seems to be" and "reportedly." While EPO-kills anecdotes might serve a crusader's anti-doping project, at some level, Thomsen knew without the word "EPO" on an autopsy, society's moral outrage was built on a bogus causality between the new blood drug and death. Still in pursuit of proof that might help his cause, Thomsen wrote of Griffith Joyner, "If it could be proved that she used those drugs to win three Olympic gold medals and set two world records in 1988, her name would become a rallying cry for those who believe that the purest of all of mankind's sports has itself been poisoned by the use of those drugs." That is, if only we could prove that Griffith Joyner died from the stuff that everyone says is killing athletes, her death would become the milestone at which sports turned back and returned to a state of sporting Eden.

Two months after the Festina affair showed how little progress anti-doping missionaries had made in reforming the ways of the natives in their pro cycling habitat, the *New York Times* needed a body, an *incarnation,* to show that all the dope-kills fuss amounted to something, that it was not a foolish errand. "If it turned out that Griffith Joyner was in fact poisoned by drugs that she took a decade ago," Thomsen wrote, "then she, a tragic figure at the age of 38, would become the embodiment of the most important, and currently the most futile, cause in her sport."

Once doping can be proven to kill athletes, it becomes a huge story. And yet, lacking hard evidence that any athletes were using drugs to push their bodies into the grave, the story Thomsen was aching to write did not exist.

Following sports gives us a plot-twisting lift from the predictability of daily life. Watching heroes fall is part of that entertainment product. From Barry Bonds to Marion Jones to Lance Armstrong, there is a staring-at-the-car-wreck fascination with watching people far more talented than we fall from grace; they aren't so superior, after all. And when physical harm and death are added to the tragedy, a compellingly sinister element joins sporting gods crashing to earth.

The press also knows that dread captivates. The story of drugs through the 1950s was one of scientific miracles and social panacea. In the 1960s, however, drugs took on a sinister alter ego. With thalidomide and a parade of addicts returning from Vietnam, pharmaceuticals became a source of tragedy, and the media covered this story. Given a choice, readers will choose to learn about the doping transgressions of a superstar over yet another Tour de France race stage report. As sports historian Verner Møller told me, when it comes to keeping the public's interest, "Real news is bad news—bad news about somebody or bad news for somebody."

Møller explained that readers are not interested in a more nuanced understanding of the motives behind doping. "We can't explain to our audience why they are taking this, and justify why they are taking it because that is academic, and that is not interesting for the public. What is interesting is if we can disgrace a star. If we can take a person who has been celebrated and show that he is a culprit, then we have real news."

The media has an incentive to keep the doping story simple, to describe it in elementary terms of good and evil, rather than attempt to explain the complex, interdependent variables of mutual complicity that led to—and continue to support—doping in sports. Both the media and anti-doping agencies like WADA gravitate toward the binary narrative because it fills in the sinister storyline that all pro athletes are guilty until proven innocent. "WADA is an organization which needs to talk about health and protection of athletes and say that we are a success because we have come a long way in testing," Møller said. And as long as the black-and-white doping storyline stays alive, WADA can say, "We need more funding so that we can expand our regime and test the athletes even more."

Running full speed with the EPO-kills story certainly made sense for the press. As sociologist David Altheide explained in his 2002 book *Creating Fear: News and the Construction of Crisis*, we like stories that transport us beyond the ordinariness of our everyday lives. Narratives that take us "outside the boundaries of routine behavior" are fascinating.[3] So much so that, like the EPO-kills-cyclists story, if repeated often enough, we suspend disbelief and begin to accept the story at face value. For instance, when surveyed in the late 1990s, Americans consistently said crime was among the nation's most serious problems. In fact, by 1998, the national murder rate had fallen 20 percent since 1990; the country had never been safer. However, over the same time span, television coverage of murders had risen 600 percent. Americans' spiking fear was not a response to firsthand experience with actual crime but a dread manufactured by exposure to the media's distorted representation of isolated incidents. While dropping crime rates indicated that life in America should have been cause for less anxiety, the projection of a 24-hour murder reel into every living room in the nation made it *feel* like danger lurked outside every suburban front door and in every city park.

Television news turned a shrinking hill of crime into a scary mountain because that was what kept viewers tuned in. Surveys and TV ratings show that people are more likely to tune in to sensational news about humans acting in deviant, criminal ways than stories about people behaving predictably.[4] This phenomenon creates a feedback loop where our fears are continuously fed by a heavily distorted view of life that in itself is powerfully intoxicating.[5] As a result, the daily news does not reflect reality, but instead constructs a version of truth that satisfies readers' interests and curiosities—and keeps them glued to the TV and telling their friends about what they have seen. The news product was crafted to keep viewers around in the increasingly crowded cable and Internet universe, not to reflect the relative mundanity of life in First World America. Call it manipulative or call it business, during the 1990s—the same period when today's anti-doping agencies became established—reporting in the mass media, both in the United States and abroad, shifted from delivering the facts to focusing public interest on deviant or violent happenings.[6]

"Many of these narratives about crime and fear are believable because they 'sound and look right,'" Altheide wrote. "But they are really false, simply incorrect, often created and distorted by news sources . . . and numerous 'reform' and 'social movement' groups."[7]

Anti-doping organizations and their representatives are one such group that has society's moral hygiene and its own self-promotion in mind. Anti-doping agencies and anti-doping researchers distorted the purportedly deadly dangers of EPO to fit their social reform needs. True to Altheide's theory, the media picked up on the "official" EPO-kills version of reality and repeated it so often that soon the public agreed that "everyone knows" EPO is deadly to bike racers.

Anti-doping organizations also used this evangelism of fear in an effort to deliver athletes to a state of drug-free salvation.[8] The alternative to riding clean was death in a bed at the age of 20. Even though there were no certified EPO deaths on hand, by repeating the rumor over and over, the media, anti-doping agents, and even medical scientists manufactured a sense of fear that in turn justified the creation of dramatically more aggressive forms of athlete surveillance, testing, control, and punishment.

Altheide also explains that a fear-driven media story divides society into three categories of actors: predator wolves, virtuous sheep, and crime-fighting sheepdogs; criminals, innocents, and cops, in other words.[9] As EPO stories began to make headlines in the 1990s, the sports world fell into these types. Drug-dealing doctors like Ferrari and the athletes he served were wolves preying on nondoping competitors and young athletes who emulated their chemical ways. Robbed of "fair" racing, the public and some journalists were also victims. "What chance had I against guys riding on amphetamine?" asked Paul Kimmage, a pro rider turned writer, in his 1990 book *A Rough Ride*. "I couldn't understand how they could be happy winning, knowing they had taken a stimulant to do so."[10] The title of Juliet Macur's 2014 book on Lance Armstrong, *Cycle of Lies*, captures the sense of moral aggrievement simmering beneath the *New York Times* journalist's account of a rider who had lied to her face for more than a decade.[11] Other writers were sheepdogs, anti-doping agents trying to keep the doping wolves away from the innocent sheep by doing the investigative work that financially conflicted sports governing bodies would not. The Irish journalist David Walsh made an award-winning career writing investigative books and articles that tore at the protective shield Armstrong built with his cancer-survivor history.

Anti-doping regulators and politicians had long tried to capitalize on this three-actor drama, wheeling themselves up to podiums in the wake of every drug scandal in an effort to pass themselves off as good cops out to maintain peace in the kingdom of fair play. A year after EPO was approved for use in Europe, IOC president Samaranch put a figurative sheriff's hat on his head and a missionary's staff in his hand for the 1988 Seoul Olympics. In his opening remarks, he proselytized, "Doping equals death."[12] When Canadian sprinter Ben Johnson tested positive two weeks later, fellow Canadian and IOC vice president Richard Pound announced that Johnson's expulsion showed that the IOC sheepdogs were not sleeping but doing the hard work to "turn this around to make the slate clean and show the world that we do mean business."[13]

Referring to a fictional tale of death and mayhem caused by EPO, scores of politicians, scientists, journalists, and sports managers promised spiritual and physical salvation while protecting their own power. As López told me, this transition away from reporting straight facts to focusing on stories that sound right or that feed audience entertainment desires was not a matter of the media being wicked or studiously devious. Rather, it was simply the way the media operates in contemporary society. "It's in their DNA," López said. Because the media lives and dies by drawing an audience, they have to tread a line between entertaining and informing. "It's their way of being, they cannot avoid doing that," López explained. "And they will always do that with stories. They will select and give prominence to those stories that tap in to the sensational, the morbid, stories about excess, about death, about drama."

Death by drugs fits the bill. Death by heatstroke or a genetic heart defect does not. The first is a human choice, an indicator of unchecked desire. The latter are mundane circumstances of everyday life. And so in the public's and the media's minds, drugs have become the biggest threat to athlete safety, even though the American College of Sports Medicine (ACSM) shows that heatstroke, heart failure, and head injuries are the most common causes of death among athletes. There are too few deaths related to performance-enhancing drugs—essentially none—for them to make the list of top athlete killers. Death from doping does not warrant a single mention in the ACSM-sponsored publication *Preventing Sudden Death in Sport and Physical Activity.*[14]

Although only one pro cycling death has been conclusively linked to doping—Tom Simpson at the Tour de France in 1967—death by other means is quite common in sports. According to the U.S. National Highway Traffic Safety Administration, in 2013, 743 cyclists were killed on American roads.[15] Playing American football is also a good way to shorten life. Statistics collected by the National Center for Catastrophic Sport Injury Research show that between 1931 and 2015, 1,046 athletes died playing recreational, high school, college, and pro football. Seventeen were killed during the 2015 season; three of those were cardiac failures that took place off the field. ESPN reported that during August and September 2014, more than a dozen football players died from sudden cardiac arrest. Three high school players died during a single week in the fall of 2014, one while warming up and two from injuries related to tackling impacts.[16] In 1968 alone, 36 football players died from head and neck injuries—26 in high school, 5 in college, 4 in recreational play, and 1 in the NFL. Between 1995 and 2015, 59 football players died from heat stroke. Unlike Knud Enemark Jensen, their deaths were not blamed on amphetamines.[17]

While EPO caused only mythical deaths, American football is a killer of record. The sport's overseers have finally become concerned about the long-term effects of repeated head trauma, and high schools now limit the number of hours players can practice in summer heat. However, no global enforcement agency has been established to fight the scourge of football deaths. Compared to its uproar at the fabricated deaths of 18 or so cyclists, the press's relative silence about the very real deaths of hundreds of football players suggests that when drugs are involved, the story taps into a deep wellspring of shared human anxieties that does not exist with real killers like heatstroke, sudden cardiac death, and concussions.

Popular magazines spread the EPO myth to a circle of influence far beyond cycling fans. In some cases, these magazines even used otherwise well-respected scientists who, perhaps blinded by superimposed moral judgments regarding the wrongness of doping in sports, helped spread misinformation and fanned an increase in anti-doping hysteria.

The April 2008 issue of *Scientific American* provides an example. In a thought-provoking article on game theory and doping in sports, science historian and skeptical thinker Michael Shermer retold the story of how French rider Philippe Casado stopped riding with Greg LeMond's GAN team in 1993 because the squad had no organized doping program. Casado moved to an Italian team that ostensibly supported his pharmaceutical needs. Not long after making the move, the Frenchman died of a heart attack while playing rugby. Commenting on Casado's demise, Shermer wrote:

> Whether his death resulted directly from doping is not known, but when HCT reaches around 60 percent and higher, the blood becomes so thick that clots readily form. The danger is particularly high when the heart rate slows during sleep—and the resting heart rates of endurance athletes are renowned for measuring in the low 30s (in beats per minute). Two champion Dutch riders died of heart attacks after experimenting with r-EPO. Some riders reportedly began sleeping with a heart-rate monitor hooked to an alarm that would sound when their pulse dropped too low.[18]

The Casado story was repeated elsewhere in the press. In November 2007, CyclingNews.com reported on a doping panel discussion in Chicago in which LeMond described dropping out of the 1994 Tour de France. LeMond pointed out that seven months later, Casado was dead of a heart attack—implying that the Frenchman's death on a rugby pitch was related to doping on the bike.[19] Sportswriter Bill Gifford retold the same LeMond recollection in a 2008 *Men's Journal* piece.[20]

But while CyclingNews.com and *Men's Journal* simply recounted LeMond's memories of Casado's death (and in so doing further entrenched the speculation that it was related to performance-enhancing drugs), Shermer reported the unproven allegations about Casado's death as fact. It was the case of an esteemed science writer and a self-defined skeptic reinforcing a central myth of the anti-doping movement rather than investigating it.

Shermer, a prolific author, science television host, and veteran cyclist who rode in the Race Across America, is also executive director of the Skeptics Society, a nonprofit dedicated to investigating "fringe science, pseudoscience, and extraordinary claims of all kinds." Yet his *Scientific American* piece reasserted the extraordinary, but empirically groundless claim that EPO killed cyclists. So powerful was the EPO-kills myth that a philosopher of science with Shermer's intellectual chops repeated every one of its sketchy sustaining details without running it through his own filter. And the myth lives on. The notion that EPO is at the root of a glut of cycling deaths got its own performance-enhancing boost when *Scientific American* republished Shermer's story in a 2013 book, *Doing the Right Thing: Ethics in Science*.

When it comes to propping up the EPO-kills shibboleth, both journalists and anti-doping campaigners get an assist from retired pro riders. After removing their last race number, some pros romanticize their own pasts. Whether the rider retired in 1950, 1960, 1970, or 1990, his glory days become representative of a morally and physically pure era before cycling was ruined by drugs. This nostalgia for days before sports had fallen helps feed the erroneous public conception of doping as a relatively new problem and the past as a time of water-fueled fair play.

Bernat López studied this phenomenon. In a 2014 paper he revealed how 1930s and 1940s Italian superstar Gino Bartali argued that after he retired, a new brand of doping changed cycling for the worse. Even though Bartali was quick to adopt the suppository aids popular with his archrival Fausto Coppi when he was racing, in his retirement years, Bartali—a three-time Giro winner and double Tour de France victor—alleged that the new 1950s drugs were destroying the sport. Commenting on a 1959 Tour de France time trial, Bartali muttered, "It is impossible to ride at an average speed of 48 kilometers per hour on a *parcours* of 45 kilometers without having drunk from the 'little bottle.'" He then added that contemporary drugs were turning donkeys into racehorses: "It is impossible to reach this average speed without anti-natural means. If I were still a rider, I would have lost four to five minutes today."[21]

In 1980, 1973 Tour de France winner Luis Ocaña pointed out that during his racing days, amphetamines were not as dangerous as corticosteroids, which riders injected to mask pain and reduce swelling from problems like knee injuries. "Taking amphetamines was ten times better, one thousand times better, it was infinitely less dangerous. Abusing cortisone is serious, very serious," the Spaniard warned. Ocaña's French contemporary Roger Pingeon fretted that the drugs riders were taking in the early 1980s were "far more dangerous" than the drugs used when he was a pro in the 1970s.[22]

Of course, 1980s pros felt *their* era was pristine compared to the 1990s. In his autobiography, *We Were Young and Carefree*, 1983 and 1984 Tour de France winner Laurent Fignon downplayed 1980s doping. "Everyone was behaving in the same way, more or less, and using the same drugs," the French rider recalled. "Until about 1989, drug-taking in cycling was an unsophisticated affair."[23] The doping Fignon participated in was steeped in a freshening nostalgia. Fignon describes pro cycling in 1984 and 1985 as "a high point, a zenith of beauty. It was the pinnacle on a building that was about to crumble; the last great gasp of a golden age that would not return."[24] Some of the golden light dressing those years may emanate from Fignon's successes. When he won the 1983 Tour de France, Fignon was only 23 and it was his first attempt at the race. Fignon explained that his was an unsullied, dignified era because drugs were not transformative. "Back then there was no drug, whatever it might have been, that could turn a donkey into a thoroughbred." After 1993, Fignon claimed, "Nothing was the same again."[25]

The magic donkey. Retired riders are fond of trotting out the metaphor of the burro pharmaceutically transformed into Secretariat. For every retired generation, contemporary drugs are more physiologically effective, technologically advanced, and morally corrupting than the chemicals from their racing days. Nostalgia can sanitize history, and the past is a cudgel riders use to beat down a corrupt present. Recalling his abandonment of the two-day Critérium International race in 1990, Fignon wrote, "I got off my bike. I just quit. I no longer saw any place for me among colleagues with a code of conduct in which honor and sacrifice were old-fashioned eccentricities."[26] In other words, not only had the new drug EPO given the peloton another set of gears, but in Fignon's mind, this drug represented the onset of a new moral decay. "From Coppi to Hinault, passing through the eras of Anquetil and Merckx, there was no magic that could dose up lesser riders to compete on equal terms with the greats," he bemoaned. "Exceptional human beings, like their extraordinary exploits, were authentic."[27]

Greg LeMond beat Fignon by eight seconds in the 1989 Tour. When I spoke to the American about the arrival of EPO, he echoed Fignon's sense of bewilderment and betrayal. "The EPO era just popped up and confused everybody," LeMond recalled. Thanks to speculative press stories, the synthetic hormone also scared him. "I had a teammate that died," LeMond said, referring to Casado's January 1995 death. LeMond was not alone in pointing to EPO as the culprit. Although no hard evidence of a link exists, when Casado passed away at age 30, journalists and riders alike jumped to the conclusion that his heart attack was associated with the blood hormone. "It was a slow growth. You heard rumors about it, but then you had a bunch of deaths," LeMond recollected. "I remember on the French teams, that really got to people—like, 'whoa, this is crazy.'"

Once retired, LeMond and Fignon's former manager Cyrille Guimard also transformed from a pragmatic coach who saw doping as a tool of the trade to an anti-doping campaigner. Guimard raced in the 1960s and 1970s, and in his autobiography, he explained that amphetamines were a "main course" in the pro cyclist's race-day diet. He went on to call the doping of his era "quite trifling," "minimal," "nothing serious," and, prior to the 1980s, "do-it-yourself." In a 2012 interview with French newspaper *L'Humanité*, he argued that 21st-century doping is "light years" ahead of where it was in his day. With doping, "there is an enormous difference between yesterday and today," he claimed. While the drugs of his era mainly had a placebo effect, he said, with EPO "everything is different. It augments performance by 5 percent. We are no longer in the same world."[28]

During his racing and management years, Guimard scorned journalists who tried to hold him accountable for doping, calling them "sanctimonious minds" who made him feel like the subject of a "witch hunt." After his management career ended in the mid-1990s, Guimard's lenience toward doping changed. Suddenly a minister of purity, Guimard advocated adopting a rule that would force pro cyclists to forfeit a year's salary if caught doping. Describing himself as a "partisan of tightening the rules," he also agitated for lifetime suspensions for doping cheats.[29]

When retired Tour de France champions talk, people listen. López suggests that carping from these stars has had a lasting effect on anti-doping policies and enforcement methods. Retired pros often take on roles with national and international sports governing bodies, with the media, with the Olympic movement, or with anti-doping organizations. Louison Bobet became a journalist. Fignon and Guimard worked as commentators. LeMond built a bike company and stayed involved with junior rider development. Anti-doping agencies and national organizing bodies listen to these influential figures when they hold forth on the current state of the sport.

As we have seen, as active racers, riders justified their youthful doping because everyone else did it, and by arguing that dope wasn't that effective anyhow. López argues that such self-justifications ignore the fact that "'new' and 'old' substances never shared the same playing field; taking their careers as a whole, those consuming 'old' substances raced against other people taking more or less the same products, and the same applies to those using 'new' substances."[30] Eliciting a mythic, moral past as an impossible (and fictionalized) ideal that today's world should follow as a model, these nostalgia-infused retired riders demand radical, if not impossible enforcement crackdowns on the modern moral and chemical scourges corrupting cycling. And this wielding of a mythic "better" past reinforces anti-doping propaganda—such as the rumors that LeMond inadvertently built around the supposed deadliness of EPO.*

* Anti-doping inherited Coubertin's sense of religious mission. The idea of pointing to a better, but lost, past as a motivation for moral and physical purity in the present is fundamental to religious ministries: Eden is lost. We should aspire to return. And yet, elite sports are uncompromisingly engaged with the present—the spirit of elite sport is the abandonment of all other concerns in the interest of conquering in this world. The pure greediness of the champion's will to victory is what makes pro and Olympic sports so fascinating; elite sports represent what we all could be if the chocks of social expectation were thrown aside. At the same time, elite sports' essential this-world selfishness is why the anti-doping mission and its quest for spiritual and physical purity have never sat well with world-class sports. Sports' profanity and anti-doping's sacredness are antithetical. Curiously, this tension between the sacred and the profane also made for lively times in Puritan America and may have influenced the United States' historical reluctance to chemically purify its core sports like baseball and football. For an analysis of how the uneasy marriage of the sacred, the profane, and religious mission helped form the American worldview, see Sacvan Bercovitch, *The American Jeremiad* (Madison: University of Wisconsin Press, 1978).

López shows that when they raced, the pro riders criticizing cycling today were eager sports medicine innovators. Once they hang up their racing wheels, though, the same riders attempt to slam the brakes on the current generation of working pros when they repeat the cycle and try to find novel advantages with chemicals. The end result, López explains, is that the retired riders "join the ranks of the claims-makers involved in the construction of the social problem of doping" and push the further radicalization of anti-doping policies and enforcement mechanisms."[31] When journalists profile the retired rider whining about how much cleaner cycling used to be, it reinforces the notion that the sport has fallen into a state of ethical perdition that can only be saved by draconian regulations and punishments.

Scientists working in the anti-doping field are influenced by sensationalistic EPO press coverage as well as the opinions of nostalgic retired stars. These layperson opinions affect academic conclusions in surprising ways. Lacking any corpses surrounded by Epogen cartons or clinically sound autopsies to support a link between EPO use and death, a remarkable number of academic researchers cite articles in the popular press as evidence of the lethality of performance-enhancing drugs. The popular press references are often flat-out wrong. And yet, once a reference to EPO-caused death appears in an academic journal, this "proof" is sanctified by the aura of peer review. It is then repeated over and over in other academic citations. What starts in the popular press as an interesting and lusciously fear-confirming rumor about a drug killing young, elite athletes is run through an alembic of scientific citations. What comes out of the beaker is a nugget of bogus, but apparently empirically validated, "fact."

Take the 2007 book *Blood Sports: The Inside Dope on Drugs in Sport.* Written by respected Australian doping researcher Robin Parisotto, *Blood Sports* claims that EPO "has caused more deaths than all the steroids and stimulants ever used." To support this bold claim, Parisotto writes, "Between 1987 and 1990, 18 cyclists died tragically and suddenly and all from heart attack or stroke. EPO was known to thicken the blood—the common cause of heart attack or stroke. Many victims developed clots that broke off and travelled to their hearts or brains; others died of heart failure, the organ struggling to pump blood the consistency of oil. That EPO was at least in part responsible seemed obvious, but sporting authorities at this stage showed little interest."[32]

Parisotto's phrasing suggests that sporting authorities were not interested in the EPO-death connection because they were not serious about clamping down on doping. While this may be the case, it is also true that the "obvious" connection between EPO and the athletes' sudden deaths was speculation—a jump to conclusions based as much on growing hysteria over doping dangers as the inspection of postmortem studies.

Today Parisotto works as a stem cell scientist in Australia. He also consults on anti-doping protocols and procedures with organizations including the Australian Institute of Sport, WADA, and Russia's anti-doping federation. I called him to ask about the discrepancy between his claims that EPO tops the list of lethal drugs and research showing that EPO hasn't been tied to any athlete deaths.

I had sent López's paper on the myth of EPO as weapon of mass destruction to Parisotto ahead of our call. He complimented the thoroughness of López's research and was not defensive about the challenges it presented to his own conclusions. Parisotto told me that one problem with drawing inferences about the adverse effects of drugs on athletes is that it is difficult to run clinical trials. "In the medical world, you can't conduct an ethical trial on the basis that you might actually kill the patients," Parisotto explained. Clinical trials work the other way; you take a population of afflicted people, give them a drug or placebo, and then monitor which patients get better as a result of the drug. If it turns out that the drug has an unacceptable number of deadly side effects, then it does not get approved. Taking a sample of healthy people and giving them drugs with the intent of making them sick or killing them violates medical ethics. While this sort of testing happened in Nazi Germany and even in the GDR sporting system, contemporary medicine does not allow it today—at least not in democratic nations.

When drawing his conclusions about the link between EPO use and the dying cyclists, Parisotto told me that clinical trial limitations make conjecture inevitable. Doping policy laws are always going to be based on clinically unverifiable assumptions about both harmful *and* performance-enhancing effects of drugs. Speaking of the rider adoption of EPO in the late '80s and early '90s, Parisotto pointed out that "the ethos at the time was that if a little bit works, then more must be better. And I suspect that in those early days, the athletes were using very high dosages of EPO. And because of that, I suspect there was a link between the uncontrolled use of EPO and those deaths." Based on the way weight lifters went crazy with anabolic steroids after John Ziegler introduced Dianabol to sports in the 1950s, Parisotto's inference makes sense.

Parisotto admitted that his conclusions about the deaths of 18 Dutch and Belgian cyclists were deductions made without any observed evidence. Based on what science knew about EPO's capacity to thicken blood, and elite athletes' well-documented habit of taking heavy drug loads for an equally meaty performance enhancement, the doping researcher felt the conjecture was warranted because it would save lives. "You can never actually prove" EPO caused the deaths, Parisotto said. But the apparent correlation seemed too uncanny to ignore. "Jeez, it was pretty strong anecdotal evidence that something is amiss," Parisotto exclaimed.

I proposed to Parisotto that both the press and academic researchers took it at face value that EPO killed cyclists because the connection *sounded* right and because it furthered the anti-doping cause. He confessed that yes, the press reports and books like *Blood Sports* played a propaganda role; they were meant to raise public awareness of doping dangers. "I must admit that the reports of the deaths in the media were an impetus for the public to become informed and for the anti-doping organizations to get off their tails and actually do something about it," he told me.

For some, the hype seemed to work—as LeMond told me, early 1990s media coverage of EPO deaths made him step back and think, "Whoa, this is crazy." And while it's difficult to link an absence of deaths to any media campaign, the fact that no rider has ever conclusively died from EPO might indicate that books like Parisotto's did scare athletes into either not using EPO or into making sure they used it with medical supervision.

As for López's research suggesting the press and the anti-doping community constructed a fearful, fictional narrative about a drug of mass destruction because it furthered a quasi-religious ethical hygiene project, Parisotto thinks it is a reasonable claim. However, he also can't remember "anyone consciously constructing an argument, and I certainly don't recall any of the sporting organizations constructing an argument, that we must do this. If anything, a lot of the sporting organizations were reluctant to do anything about it."

Parisotto wasn't the only scientist from the Southern Hemisphere who let a sense of obligation to the anti-doping cause affect the accuracy of his conclusions. WADA board member and New Zealand University of Otago professor of sports medicine Dr. David Gerrard wrote in a 2008 journal article titled "Playing Foreign Policy Games: States, Drugs and Other Olympian Vices" that EPO caused "formerly fit young athletes" to drop dead "from massive strokes and heart attacks." An ex-Olympic swimmer, Gerrard noted that "post-mortem studies revealed the extent of the damage."[33] And yet, no postmortem study exists that shows a link between EPO and the death of an athlete. The reference Gerrard refers to as the source for his EPO-autopsy claim is a chapter on drugs in sport in a popular Australian sports medicine textbook, *Clinical Sports Medicine*.

Found in the offices of some 20,000 clinicians around the world, a chapter on drugs and sport by Liz Clisby states that EPO use "has allegedly become widespread and may have contributed to the death of a number of European cyclists."[34] Nowhere does Clisby's chapter mention the postmortem studies Gerrard cites as proof for his claim. Following the footnote trail confirms how the EPO-kills notion can start as reported rumor, then quickly ossify into fact through word choice when one clinical or scientific reference cites another. Elsewhere in the same chapter, Clisby takes a more assertive stance, writing, "There have been a number of deaths of endurance cyclists directly related to the use of EPO."[35] The footnoted source for this claim is an August 1989 article in the American medical journal the *Physician and Sportsmedicine*. With this citation, it seems we may be getting closer to the source of this winding tributary of allegations and suppositions.

Titled "Erythropoietin: A Dangerous New Form of Blood Doping," the piece by Virginia S. Cowart explains that EPO was approved by the FDA earlier in 1989 and cites the opinion of former USOC medical director Robert Voy. Warning athletes away from the synthetic hormone, Voy cautions, "If it overshoots what is physiologically tolerable for the cardiovascular and pulmonary system, some athletes will develop heart failure and pulmonary edema. We may even see deaths."[36] Voy's warning was reasonable—taken without doctor's supervision, EPO could kill. Also, the drug was so new that there were little clinical data upon which the doctors could base their recommendations. Advising extreme caution when using this new hormone made physiological and ethical sense. In the *Physician and Sportsmedicine* article, Voy did not state that EPO had killed anyone. However, in his 1991 book, *Drugs, Sport, and Politics*, he describes "an alarming rise in the number of deaths among European cyclists who use erythropoietin." Voy also writes, "I'm sure it won't be long before a high-profile American athlete kills himself or herself using this hormone."[37]

Warning that increased hematocrit levels combined with lower blood volume due to dehydration might cause stroke or heart-attack-inducing "sludging red cells," Cowart's piece also tells readers that the drug's administration method increases its potential for harm.[38] HIV/AIDS had been killing and harming people for years in 1989, so caution with injections was warranted. EPO may be especially dangerous because unlike autologous blood doping, which requires a doctor's assistance, athletes can easily self-administer EPO. Later on in the article, 1984 Los Angeles Olympic drug-testing lab director Don Catlin explains that "erythropoietin can be injected in the privacy of one's home—and nobody else has to know about it."[39] Catlin also mentions EPO's potentially dangerous dose-response curve; because the effects of EPO can cause hematocrit to continue to rise for up to 10 days after the last injection, the dangers can lurk—and even increase—over time. "The danger doesn't end when the race ends," Cowart warns.[40]

Although the *Physician and Sportsmedicine* article toured EPO's dangerous side effects, nowhere did it cite a single death, let alone the "number of deaths" confidently referenced in the Australian sports medicine textbook. In fact, the article cited Michael Downing, Amgen's director of clinical studies, who gave a fairly neutral assessment of EPO risks, saying, "It's difficult to say with certainty what kind of effect erythropoietin would have on persons with healthy kidneys."

If they were not reading the *Physician and Sportsmedicine* piece carefully, however, the *Clinical Sports Medicine* writers might be excused for making their evidence-free leap from plausible harm to dead bodies. The article grabbed readers' attention with an illustration of a giant blood cell crushing a cyclist sprawled on a forbidding forest road. Like a bloody knife in a murder scene, a syringe lies on the ground in front of the rider's shattered wheel. The gargantuan erythrocyte seems to have sprung from the woods in deadly ambush. Behind the cyclist, a single-lane road wends across hills toward a chasing pack of cyclists racing away from a setting moon. A propagandistic film-noir scene, the illustration fused fear, crisis, crime, social disruption, and sports competition into a powerful promotion of the article it illustrated.

"Fear is a social product and not an individual failing," Altheide explains in *Creating Fear*. "Fear is a manufactured response that has been produced by a mass-mediated symbol machine."[41] Here, at the dawn of the EPO era, the medical community painted a picture of doping as a social dynamic between law-abiding victims, doping athletes whose own lawless ambitions ended up murdering them, and a medical community whose good inventions helped enable this dramatic morality tale.

Despite the ease with which academics cited erroneous sources as proof that EPO kills cyclists, some doctors did question why so many were so quick to make such an erroneous leap of faith. In August 1998, the British medical journal the *Lancet* published a study, "Packed-Cell Volume in Elite Athletes," by researchers J. J. M. Marx and P. C. J. Vergouwen. The Dutch scientists tracked the hematocrit levels of 18 male and 28 female Olympic-level athletes over 16 months. To the best of the researchers' knowledge, these athletes were not taking EPO. The scientists found that six of the subjects had naturally occurring hematocrit levels above 50 percent. They also found that some athletes had hematocrit levels as low as 34 percent. Marx and Vergouwen concluded, "Although everything possible should be done to protect athletes against any kind of doping that may be harmful and that may falsify competition, in the case of EPO the IOC and UCI might consider whether taking a nondetectable substance that is able to correct a physiological inequality among competitors should be considered as doping."[42]

In other words, the researchers wondered if athletes handicapped by naturally low hemoglobin counts should be considered dopers for turning to a blood therapy that would create a level physiological playing field. With little evidence that EPO is unsafe when administered under a doctor's supervision, they suggested that EPO could fulfill the fair-play objective central to the anti-doping movement. The authors also pondered whether it was fair to punish athletes with naturally high hemoglobin counts for doping when their red-blood-cell tally was solely a natural phenomenon.

POINTING OUT THAT warnings against the dangers of EPO are founded on a fiction about a glut of cyclist deaths is not an argument for its removal from WADA's list of banned substances. As Michele Ferrari observed, EPO is dangerous when abused. In 2007, the FDA underscored EPO's riskiness when it issued a black box warning for the product, which came about in part because Amgen learned that EPO could accelerate cancer tumor growth. However, this warning was intended for the seriously ill and came 17 years after sports journalists and anti-doping scientists had started screaming that the sky was falling without a single body to prove it.

By focusing on the fear surrounding doping in sports, medical experts channeled significant resources toward a health problem that was almost totally insignificant when compared to other causes of death that are intrinsic to sport such as tackling in football or head injuries in cycling. The sport's administrators at the UCI began the march toward drug prohibition in 1965, yet cyclists died from head injuries for another 38 years until the UCI took steps to slow the carnage by making helmets mandatory for racing in 2003. Emotion, not logic, controlled the sport's response to the risks threatening its athletes.

Writing in the science journal *Nature,* in 2008, researchers Björn Knollmann and Dan Roden reported that sudden cardiac death kills between 500,000 and 1 million Americans and Europeans every year—10 to 20 percent of all deaths in the western world.[43] A study of sudden cardiac deaths in Maastricht, Netherlands, between 1991 and 1994 found that of the 2,030 deaths that occurred outside hospitals during that time period, 375 were sudden. In one Dutch city of nearly 200,000 bike-riding people, sudden death killed 94 residents every year. At exactly the same time, European newspapers were blaming EPO for the sudden death of 18 cyclists worldwide. For 53 percent of the women and 44 percent of the men who died in Maastricht, their sudden cardiac arrest was the first indication of a heart problem. That is, like the pro cyclists who died "from EPO," the 94 sudden deaths in Maastricht came out of the blue. And yet, because the citizens of this Dutch city were not pro cyclists, the apparent glut of sudden deaths was not attributed to EPO, but rather to genetics.

Another study published in the *European Journal of Cardiovascular Prevention and Rehabilitation* in 2006 provided a meta-analysis of 47 scientific papers on sudden death in athletes under 35. The articles covered 1,101 cases of sudden cardiac death in athletes. (Sudden cardiac death is defined as a death within one hour of onset of symptoms, and in a person with no previously identified cardiac condition.) The report concluded that 60 percent of the affected athletes had genetically inherited heart issues or early onset atherosclerotic heart disease. Intense physical workouts triggered the catastrophic heart incidents. With evidence fingering genetics plus extreme exercise as the killer, the researchers exculpated the drug demon: "Doping is often considered to be the main cause of sudden death by the media and lay people," they noted. But this link "seems unlikely, as underlying cardiac diseases account for approximately 90 percent of exercise-related sudden deaths." The popular idea that drugs are the most dangerous risk to athlete health is false, they said, and "contradicted by the large numbers of sudden deaths related to underlying cardiovascular diseases."[44]

Bad genetics and sports themselves seem to be the biggest factors in athlete deaths. Yet these causes did not serve the purposes of anti-doping organizations, so that is not the story that got written in the popular or scientific press.

López does not harbor ill will toward the scientists and journalists whose selective review of events in the 1990s turned EPO into a killer demon. At a time when EPO had just hit the market, it was a no-brainer to make it suspect number one in what seemed like a sudden rash of deaths. It was easy to jump to the conclusion that if cyclists started dropping shortly after the availability of this new blood-thickening potion, the drug had something to do with it.

As for the goals of the anti-doping campaigners who turned speculation into "truth," López writes that at some level, they "had the best intentions at heart." Repeating EPO death tales that had hardened into fact after years of repetition in popular and academic publications was in the interest of saving bodies, souls, and cycling's reputation.[45] In the 1990s, Coubertin's quest for amateur and social purity had been transformed into an expedition for chemical innocence.

These attempts to eliminate a cheating mechanism, however, only served to advertise it further and bestow it with magically transformative powers, quickly making EPO a must-have tool in the modern pro cycling peloton. The good intentions that glossed over the facts in the interest of protecting Coubertinian notions of sports as a builder of character and a shield against moral decline ended up exposing the wonders of EPO to a wider audience of potential customers.

As University of Geneva exercise physiology professor Bengt Kayser discussed in a 2009 research paper, drug hysterias whipped up by the press and the anti-doping community sent a message that doping works. After all, if the drug didn't work, there would not be a fuss over it. And the outcome of this prohibition and demonization "may have the perverse effect of amplifying," rather than eliminating the use of performance-enhancing drugs among pro athletes and the general public alike.[46]

CHAPTER 14

THE WAR ON DRUGS

On October 20, 1970, a group of California state legislators, coaches, athletes, doctors, and journalists gathered around the corner from the Los Angeles Memorial Coliseum at the California Museum of Science and Industry. They had come together to discuss athletes and performance-enhancing drugs. Chaired by Assemblyman Bill Campbell, a 28-year-old L.A. native, the California Assembly Subcommittee on Drug Abuse and Alcoholism hearings began not with a question but with a conclusion: Drugs in sport are bad, and lawmakers need to deal with the problem.

From its opening moments, the meeting proclaimed that the struggle against drug abuse in American society had an analog in sports. As Campbell, an engineer and Harvard MBA, put it in his opening statement, "The fact that we are a drug-oriented society is a well-established cliché; the fact that sports are now included within the context of a 'turned-on society' only confirms the extent to which chemicals are an inseparable aspect of American life."[1]

Drug abuse and an attendant fear of moral decay were on a lot of minds in 1970. After U.S. National Guardsmen opened fire on anti-Vietnam protesters at Kent State University in Ohio on May 4, 1970, a grand jury exonerated the National Guard and blamed the mayhem on the school's "attitude of laxity, over-indulgence and permissiveness."[2] The critique was code for too many laid-back, pot-smoking hippies who disrespected the America their parents had fought for in World War II. Indeed, by the time the grand jury issued its report, one of the protesters was serving a 20- to 40-year jail sentence for possessing marijuana, LSD, hashish, and mescaline. That an American citizen would serve nearly half his life in jail for possessing hallucinogens indicated the severe control measures the country was implementing to return to a more orderly time.[3]

Meanwhile, President Richard Nixon harnessed fears of a hippie-incited value-system breakdown to rally support for Republican candidates in the November 1970 elections. Nixon appealed to what he called the "silent majority" of Americans who were not in the streets protesting Vietnam and who felt threatened by a counterculture rush to discard traditional values. Nixon warned crowds of a "rising tide of terrorism" and "violence, lawlessness, and permissiveness" that threatened to swamp the nation.[4] Highlighting American fears and offering law-and-order solutions were hallmarks of Nixon's administration.

In fact, for the Nixon presidency, drug use equated to domestic terrorism.* In a June 17, 1971, speech asking Congress to fund a new Special Action Office for Drug Abuse Prevention, Nixon argued that the drugs office was necessary to confront substance abuse and addiction, a scourge with "dimensions of a national emergency" that "frightens many Americans."[5]

While Nixon was spotlighting fear and crisis as a means of maintaining his own power, there was some substance to his hyperbole. The *New York Times* reported that more than 1,050 New York City residents had

---

* According to Nixon's domestic policy adviser John Ehrlichman, inventing a war on drugs to scare Americans was a political tool. In 1994, he told writer Dan Baum that African Americans and antiwar hippies were on the White House enemies list. "We knew we couldn't make it illegal to be either against the war or black," Ehrlichman recalled, "but by getting the public to associate the hippies with marijuana and blacks with heroin, and then criminalizing both heavily, we could disrupt those communities. Did we know we were lying about the drugs? Of course we did." Dan Baum, "Legalize It All," *Harper's*, April 2016.

died from narcotics in 1970—up from 199 in 1960, and the most drug deaths in the city's history. Half of the dead were younger than 23, including 215 teenagers.[6] According to estimates from the National Institute of Mental Health, 250,000 heroin addicts walked U.S. streets in 1971, half of them in New York City. In 1971, Nixon told the nation that there were an additional 30,000 heroin-addicted U.S. servicemen in Vietnam and that the financial costs associated with these drugs was $2 billion.[7]

A 1971 congressional report, *The World Heroin Problem,* revealed that 15 percent of Vietnam veterans were addicted to the opioid and that it was killing nearly 20 soldiers a month in Vietnam. Written after an investigative trip to Vietnam by Congressmen Morgan Murphy of Illinois and Robert Steele of Connecticut, the report noted in italicized alarm that "*in the last two years of the war our biggest casualty figures will come from heroin addiction, not from combat.*"[8] Heroin use in Vietnam spiked in 1968 when, reacting to U.S. newspaper articles about pot-smoking G.I.s, the U.S. Army began an assault on marijuana. Drug-sniffing dogs cleaned out barracks, and within weeks, 1,000 soldiers had been arrested for marijuana possession. An in-country media campaign sensationalized the supposed moral and physical collapse that would follow the sparking of a doobie.

While pot use plummeted, fear and hopelessness remained for soldiers fighting a war few believed in. They found a new escape by sprinkling powdered heroin on cigarettes—a powerful high with no telltale odor. As one 20-year-old soldier told a *New York Times* reporter, "You can salute with your right hand, take a hit with your left and blow the smoke in the old man's face, and he'll never know."[9] Street heroin in Vietnam was 94 to 96 percent pure. In the United States, it was cut to 2.5 to 6 percent purity.[10] When addicted soldiers returned home, many turned to mainlining the drug to get the high they got smoking it in Vietnam. Heroin was also affordable in Vietnam, with an eighth of a gram costing about $1.50.[11]

While the military banned marijuana, it liberally distributed amphetamines. A congressional study revealed that between 1966 and 1969, the

U.S. government supplied the average navy, air force, or army soldier with 30 to 40 5-milligram doses of amphetamines per year.[12] Although on par with the average amount of amphetamines American civilians were taking at home for weight loss and mood pick-me-uppers, many soldiers bolstered their government-issued rations with street-distributed speed such as Maxitone Forte, an injectable amphetamine from France that was also popular with European cyclists.

Journalist Michael Herr captured the performance-enhancing, reality-dulling effects of drugs in his Vietnam classic *Dispatches* when he described a long-range reconnaissance patrol soldier. "He took his pills by the fistful, downs from the left pocket of his tiger suit and ups from the right, one to cut the trail for him and the other to send him down," Herr wrote. "He told me that they cooled things out just right for him, that he could see that old jungle at night like he was looking at it through a starlight scope. 'They sure give you range,' he said."[13]

The specter of teenagers too stoned to keep America ahead of the commies and American soldiers gripped by ambition-wrecking addictions raised federal and state alarm bells. *The World Heroin Problem* informed Washington that drugs were curbing national productivity in the form of misspent funds and crime. Heroin addicts would blow an estimated $2.7 billion feeding their habit in 1971. A healthy portion of those dollars came from stealing $8 billion worth of stuff every year and flipping it for a fix—a cost massively compounded when the drug users got ensnared in the penal system. Pointing out that heroin addiction was no longer restricted to "the ghetto areas of our major cities," the report warned that drugs were kneecapping American economic productivity because it was "spreading to the suburbs and is found among the children of the wealthy and well-to-do."[14] Speaking in the era's racial code, the report explained that heroin had spread beyond the inner city and infected the white suburban Americans who populated the country's more exclusive communities.

To address the human and economic costs of these addictions and growing voter unease with hedonistic, antiwar youngsters, Congress passed the Comprehensive Drug Abuse Prevention and Control Act. Signed into law by Nixon on October 27, 1970, this act became the cornerstone of what we now know as the War on Drugs. The legislation also became a monument to a moral panic that in turn helped accelerate the rejection of drugs in sport.

The act created five schedules, or categories, of drugs. While the most dangerous and addictive drugs were supposed to be listed as Schedule I (drugs with no accepted medical use) or Schedule II (drugs with an accepted medical use), they were in fact slotted into categories based on popular fears, rather than on documented dangers. For example, a presidential commission recommended that lawmakers decriminalize marijuana because little evidence indicated the drug was a threat to health or social stability, especially when compared to alcohol. Furthermore, making possession of the popular weed a felony would clog courts and jails. But fearing that a hole in his blanket denunciation of recreational drugs would leave him open to criticism, Nixon ignored the recommendation. Marijuana kept its scientifically irrational but politically logical place as a Schedule I drug.

Declaring a drug use "national emergency," in 1971, Nixon created the national Drug Enforcement Agency (DEA). The DEA was his administration's attempt to bring disparate drug enforcement agencies and treatment methods together under one policing umbrella.

In 1972, Nixon linked the nation's moral health to the War on Drugs. "Any nation that moves down the road to addiction, that nation has something taken out of its character," he observed upon returning from a trip to the world's biggest opium consumer, China. Punishing heroin dealers was now "the highest priority in this administration," Nixon's press secretary added.[15] The drug crisis was everywhere, and the government was ready to respond with preventive and punitive policies. The sheep, wolf, and sheepdog morality tale was set: A crime-fighting Nixon administration would battle evil drug dealers who were taking advantage of innocent young Americans. Linking his antidrug policy to the restoration of America's battered moral character was political theater, one that framed the matter of drugs in the national consciousness as a problem with ethical dimensions that went beyond personal health.

These concerns also underlay Campbell's hearings in California. The meetings were a state-level airing of the drug problem prevalent in society at large as well as the more localized issue of drug abuse in California sports. "Society's mass use of drugs in order to cope with the problems of living is serious indeed," Campbell stated. And the impact of drugs on athletics was "even more alarming," Campbell claimed. "For inappropriate drug use bears the seeds of destroying the notion of competition as we know it and as it has existed since the first Olympic games."[16] Drugs were an assault on the ideal of sports as a place for the realization of our most noble selves—the Olympian-like human whose highest cause is not to win but to fight well.

Campbell went on to praise the original anti-doping regulations put in place to guard the economic stability of thoroughbred racing. "I optimistically believe horse racing policies protect both the nature of the competition and the health of the horse," Campbell explained, before adding that the lawmakers had an obligation to offer human competitors the same protections horses had received long ago.

The hearings collected testimony from physicians for the Los Angeles Lakers, California Angels, and San Francisco Giants, as well as from Gene Donnelly, an Anaheim High School athletic trainer. Asked if the growth of drug problems was mirrored on high school playing fields, Donnelly said the Anaheim police department arrested just two students for drugs in 1961, but hauled off 843 kids for dope in 1969. Since drug use was booming among the high school crowd, Donnelly surmised that drugs were also more popular with athletes, a subset of the larger student body. Donnelly said the athletes who were most vulnerable to the allure of drugs were those about to get cut or who were desperate to compete at a higher level. "It's the third-stringer, the second-stringer that's trying to improve himself," Donnelly explained.[17] When pressed for details on the anti-doping policies at his school or within the California Interscholastic Federation (CIF), the trainer confessed that neither body had any written doping regulations.

Reading the minutes of the California hearings today, you get a picture of lawmakers struggling to reconcile their dark visions of drug abuse with the candid descriptions of how common drug use was among high school, college, and pro players. Retired San Diego Chargers' halfback Paul Lowe frankly recounted how he and his teammates took amphetamine pills for every game—"A couple before the game, an hour and a half; and at the half-time I'll take another one," the player said.[18] Campbell was incredulous when Lowe said the team supplied the drugs. "The coach gives them to you?" he spluttered. Lowe then recounted how the players had saucers of "little pink pills"—anabolic steroids—placed on the lunch tables at training camp. A coach told the players the pills "would help us build strong bodies," Lowe reported. If a player elected not to take the pills, Lowe said, the coach "would suggest there might be a fine."[19]

At one point, Campbell pressed Lowe for his thoughts on whether taking a drug that was "going to supposedly stimulate you to hopefully play better than you would normally play" somehow "jeopardizes the concept of competitive sports." Lowe's response captured the way that unsavory images of unsanctioned drugs in everyday life also influenced attitudes toward the drugs in sport. "I'm a law-abiding citizen—I mean, it's against the law, isn't it?" Lowe said. "So I would figure it should be the same way. It shouldn't be that easy to get for a professional athlete I would think, because it hurts you although you think it might be helping you."[20]

The California discussions on drugs in sports eventually became a national matter. Led by Indiana senator Birch Bayh in June and July 1973, the Senate Subcommittee to Investigate Juvenile Delinquency held a series of hearings on athlete drug use. Bayh stated that the objective was to discover whether there was truth to the rumors and press reports that athletes were being affected by "the drug abuse epidemic confronting the nation."[21]

Donald Cooper, team physician for Oklahoma State University, testified at this federal version of the California hearings Campbell had led three years prior. As a member of the American Medical Association's Committee on Medical Aspects of Sports, Cooper also represented the opinions of America's largest physician's organization, the AMA. Its leaders, Cooper told Bayh, "have for some time been concerned, not only with the general widespread use of drugs by our youth, but also with the special use of drugs by our young athletes."[22]

Cooper took pains to distinguish drug abuse from therapeutic use. Drug abuse was the self-administration of drugs—often in large quantities, he noted—without medical supervision. Therapeutic use, on the other hand, was the administration of a drug under a physician's direction to treat injury, illness, or deficiency. Drugs to restore health were good. Drugs to enhance performance beyond a natural state or to recreate were bad. With that distinction made, Cooper said, "drug abuse in athletics is not an isolated event but mirrors a widespread problem, particularly among the youth of our communities."[23]

Cooper testified that the AMA's concern with doping in sports began in 1957, when a resolution was passed to study potential links between widespread amphetamine abuse among Americans and use of the same drug in college and high school sports. The AMA surveyed 800 college and high school athletes and found that less than 1 percent of the athletes were using amphetamines, "a number that corresponded generally with the relatively low incidence of abuse at the time," Cooper said.[24] Although the AMA did not have studies documenting drug use in college and high school athletes between 1957 and 1973, Cooper explained that more young people in general were taking drugs without a doctor's supervision. Therefore, "it is logical to expect that athletes as members of that subculture have also been influenced to abuse drugs more in recent years. Therefore, our impression is that athletic drug use has increased."[25]

Cooper reinforced his speculative bridge between the larger drug scare and doping in sports when he said, "As members of the youth subculture, athletes are encouraged through sometimes subtle social persuasion from their peers to consume drugs, quite distinct from reasons of taking them for a supposed advantage in sports." However, as Cooper saw it, the prestige associated with winning operated in tandem with social pressures. Referring to a 1967 bike race in Winnipeg, Canada, Cooper said that post-race tests for performance-enhancing drugs did not turn up positives until "after the first six places." The winning riders were not doping; rather, "it was the boys that apparently were looking for some type of supposed outside help or outside support for their benefit because they hadn't put in the training and conditioning necessary."[26]

Historian Ross Coomber has written extensively about how fear of drugs in the world outside sports nurtures and distorts anti-doping measures in sports. Exploring parallels between the marijuana, cocaine, and opium scares in the 19th century and the rise of reactionary responses to modern sports doping, Coomber explains that legends about the dangers of drugs and the supposed power of drugs to destroy the fabric of society are remarkably resistant to evidence that could undermine them. As a result of the durability of myths such as EPO's murderous romp through the pro peloton and racially fueled stories about marijuana turning Mexicans into rampaging killers in the 1930s, these stories continue to "provide a framework of fear on which to justify and substantiate" the expansion of draconian drug controls.[27]

Until the onset of the Great Depression in 1929, there was little public alarm about marijuana in the United States. Although cocaine and opiate abuse generated some earlier national concern, marijuana did not cause a moral panic until the early 1930s, when the drug became a proxy for fear of Mexican immigrants. For U.S. lawmakers and government functionaries, banning marijuana became a way to assuage American fears about immigrants taking American jobs and weakening the country's Anglo-Saxon heritage.

As David Musto reports in his history of U.S. narcotic control, *The American Disease*, cannabis was repeatedly excluded from lists of drugs proposed for regulation by the Harrison Narcotics Tax Act of 1914, a federal law governing the import, production, and sale of opiates and coca derivatives. In his book, Musto explains that the pharmaceutical industry was originally against cannabis regulation because banning the plant would hurt profitability. Drug makers saw all cost and no sense in regulating a plant they primarily used for animal medicines and nonintoxicating ointments. During January 1911 hearings, one pharmaceutical industry representative told House Ways and Means Committee members that cannabis was not habit forming like cocaine and opium. He explained that the source of marijuana's unsavory reputation was "literary fiction," not science—a reputation sullied by prohibition campaigners like the Anti-Saloon League, whose religious objectives found it useful to lump marijuana in with alcohol as a threat to American schoolchildren.[28]

Marijuana's stigma-free ride ended with the Great Depression, when it was associated with apocryphal cannabis-related murder sprees, and, more importantly, job-stealing Mexicans. The drumbeat began in the 1920s and grew in volume throughout the decade. In 1921, for example, a botanist from the U.S. Department of Agriculture described "a very pernicious habit-forming drug used by the lower class of Mexican in certain localities." The drug, marijuana, "has been the cause of several uprisings," he added.[29] On November 26, 1920, Louisiana governor John M. Parker wrote to the U.S. Prohibition Commissioner and described two people "killed a few days ago by the smoking of this drug, which seems to make them go crazy and wild."[30] A story in the South Texas *Cameron Herald* on September 14, 1922, described a Mexican named Clemente Apolinar throwing a rock at an innocent 14-year-old boy who was sailing a toy boat. The child later died from the blow. Another Mexican, Frank Cadena, got high on pot, lost his mind, snuck up on a "beautiful 18-year-old senorita" named Pablita Jiminez as she slept in her bed, and shot her dead.[31]

In both cases, marijuana did not enter the picture until the accused went to trial; the murderers' attorneys filed pleas of insanity by reason of smoking marijuana. According to the *Herald*, 29-year-old Apolinar's "mind was poisoned by the fumes of the marihuana leaf." The article went on to attribute a host of Mexican crimes to cannabis. Seven years earlier, Southern California's *Santa Ana Register* reported that in one Mexican town, marijuana-addled soldiers had murdered 17 people. Further, "90 percent of the murders in Mexico can be laid at the foot of the marihuana bush," the paper informed horrified Southern California readers.[32] Marijuana was a scapegoat whose political utility was far greater than its apparent health risks.

Although these pot reports were fictions written to sell papers, the U.S. government began to heed media-generated dread. A reader's letter in the September 15, 1935, *New York Times* painted a morality tale setting evil Mexicans against innocent Americans: "Marijuana, perhaps now the most insidious of our narcotics, is a direct by-product of unrestricted Mexican immigration." Linking the drug to the exploitation of innocent children, workers, and taxpayers, the letter continued, "Mexican peddlers have been caught distributing sample marihuana cigarettes to school children. . . . Our nation has more than enough laborers. We are supporting millions on the dole."[33] The letter's author, prominent Sacramento eugenicist C. M. Goethe, was also a member of the American Coalition, a racial-purity organization dedicated to keeping "America American."*

Sensitive to these citizen complaints, the government had to do something to halt the arrival of more Mexican drug crime at the Rio

---

* At the time, eugenics was a well-established and respected field of scientific inquiry with supporters including Stanford University president David Starr Jordan, Theodore Roosevelt, Alexander Graham Bell, and W. E. B. DuBois. The Rockefeller Foundation saw so much potential in the discipline that in 1925, it donated $2.5 million toward an American-German eugenics research facility in Munich, Germany. Brown, MIT, Harvard, and Cornell were among many universities teaching eugenics. In an August 8, 1933, article, "Purifying the German Race," the *New York Times* editorialized that Americans should not be concerned about a proposed German sterilization law. Instead, the paper argued, "the measures drafted to weed out physical degenerates who are beyond surgical aid, deaf-mutes and the feeble-minded differ in no important respect from those long advocated in every civilized country. . . . Some 15,000 unfortunates have thus far been harmlessly and humanely operated upon in the United States to prevent them from propagating their own kind." National interest in increasing citizen productivity by culling the gene pool of "low performing" stock motivated medical procedures that seem abhorrent today but that were widely accepted humanitarian policies at the time. By the 1970s, the United States had sterilized 65,000 citizens aged 12 and up—by far the country's most ambitious attempt at increasing national productivity (and one that puts East Germany's doping of 10,000 athletes into perspective).

Grande. Banning pot would allow legislators to appear as if they were addressing wider public fears of job-taking immigrants and a grinding depression. In the same way that responses to EPO in the 1990s were disconnected from any actual athlete deaths but still served the ancillary needs of journalists and officials, the government's response to marijuana had little to do with preserving public safety and everything to do with fulfilling political imperatives.

In 1937, Congress held hearings on regulating marijuana. With the political objectives from the hearings already set, the lawmakers marginalized voices that did not bolster the prevailing narrative that marijuana is a social cancer. While preparing for the hearings, one staffer told the commissioner of the Federal Bureau of Narcotics, Harry Anslinger, that he should arrive prepared with "horror stories—that's what we want."[34] Anslinger, who was also running a radio and newspaper campaign to stigmatize marijuana, had plenty of stories—in fact, he had been feeding them steadily to the press in the form of unsubstantiated police blotter citations. The Marihuana Tax Act became law in 1937.

During the process of drawing up the legislation, lawmakers considered no medical or scientific testimony—primarily because there was no empirical evidence marijuana was addictive, nor any that showed it caused Mexicans (or anyone else) to pick up a knife, gun, or rock and murder innocents. With their conclusions about the immorality of pot already made, they had no use for evidence that challenged these assumptions. Foreshadowing the circumstances that led to the creation of WADA years later, pressure from religious temperance movements, anti-immigrant Anglo-Saxon race purifiers, and a depression-exhausted public hungry to find someone to blame came together as a set of fears that was resistant to evidence. Not unlike the hyperbolic response to a rumor of EPO deaths in cycling, the new U.S. regulations were bureaucratic overkill intended to reassure a media-panicked public.

The War on Drugs that gave birth to today's globe-girdling drug enforcement agencies permanently conditioned Americans to overstate the health risks of performance-enhancing drugs. To illustrate, consider how our perception of drug health risks changes when we are asked to evaluate the danger of the same drug when used for restorative versus additive reasons.

For a patient suffering renal failure or bone cancer, the arrival of a hematologist with doses of EPO is a cause for hope. In this situation, EPO is a managed risk that carries little perceived threat of causing sudden, catastrophic heart failure. It's a lifesaver, not a life ender. Similarly, the 20-year-old college student who is prescribed Adderall to help her manage an attention deficit assumes the best; the risks of taking this amphetamine are not hyped and exaggerated, especially in light of the lifelong positive benefits that come with a college degree.

Prescribe either of these drugs to an athlete preparing for competition, and the relative risk swells to Godzilla-like proportions. Given to a healthy athlete—especially without a doctor's legitimizing prescription scrip—the same drug that gave hope for the best in one circumstance now provokes dread and fear. And yet, this is counterintuitive; the EPO that will not harm a cancer patient will be even less pernicious for an athlete whose body is in top physical condition.

When prescribed as a restorative treatment, a drug is generally regarded as carrying a relatively stable set of potential adverse effects, even though those risks can be dramatically different based on each patient's age, history, and current pathologies. Meanwhile, the risks of performance-enhancing drugs are perceived to be homogeneously terrible, even though the risks are often based on an illogical, sensationalized, and disproportionate response to misrepresented drug tragedies from the past.[35] The war on drugs that built size and momentum throughout the 20th century dramatically affects, and distorts, our approach to doping in sports in the 21st.

CHAPTER 15

AMPHETAMINES FOR ALL

Better than any drug, amphetamines shed light on our conflicted attitudes toward drugs in sports and drugs in everyday life. The story of amphetamines is one of complicity—the enthusiastic adoption by society of chemicals that were simultaneously demonized in the subcontext of sports. Amphetamines' recent history illustrates our ability to stigmatize a substance while also showing extreme reluctance to spit in that same drug's useful chemical soup.

In 1928, a 27-year-old Caltech biochemistry PhD named Gordon Alles was trying to identify a compound that would help asthmatics and allergy sufferers. Alles had done his graduate research on the physiological effects of chemicals, and his new research focused on designing a drug that would relax constricted bronchial passages in people suffering asthma attacks. He was also hoping to find a chemical to ease the symptoms of colds and allergies.

At the time, asthmatics reached for plant-based ephedrine or the hormone adrenaline to alleviate their sometimes fatal condition. Ephedrine was derived from a Chinese herb, ephedra, but demand swamped supply. Adrenaline, meanwhile, had been isolated in 1894, but it had to be extracted from the adrenal glands of slaughterhouse animals.[1] In an effort to create a synthetic molecule that delivered similar, or better, bronchial and congestant relief than these organic solutions, biochemists like Alles tinkered with the atomic makeup of molecules.

Alles began experimenting with a chemical related to adrenaline and ephedrine, beta-phenylisopropylamine, later called amphetamine. Although a German chemist had described the amphetamine compound in 1887, Alles was the first to study its use as a medicine, specifically its stimulating effect on the central nervous system.[2] After first testing amphetamine on dogs and rabbits, in June 1929, Alles injected himself with 50 milligrams of the stuff. He did the same with several allergy patients. (Medical researchers at the time assayed a compound's safety and effect by testing it first on animals, then on themselves, and then on subjects.) While the amphetamine did not do much to relieve the patients' allergy or asthma symptoms, the drug did give Alles and his subjects a sense of exhilaration and well-being. Although Alles did not know it at the time, the effect was caused by the release of dopamine; amphetamine instructs neurotransmitters to travel between brain synapses more rapidly than normal, and this accelerated electrical function creates a sense of alertness. In September 1930, Alles submitted a patent application for amphetamine salt, a form of the drug that could be taken as a pill.*

Meanwhile, the pharmaceutical company Smith, Kline & French (SKF) had learned about amphetamine's biological function when one of its representatives heard Alles discuss his research at a 1929 American Medical Association meeting. Trying to beat the inventor to his own finish line, SKF applied for a patent on the amphetamine molecule, but as a

---

* In his search for an amphetamine variation that would provide asthma relief without the peppy side effects, in 1930 Alles introduced extra oxygen atoms to the amphetamine molecule. When he tried the new compound on himself, he experienced pleasant hallucinations and a hyperkeen awareness of the Los Angeles streetcars passing outside his laboratory. He had invented methylene-dioxyamphetamine (MDA)—a very close molecular brother to methylene-dioxymethamphetamine (MDMA), what we know today as ecstasy. Nicolas Rasmussen, *On Speed: The Many Lives of Amphetamine* (New York: New York University Press, 2009), 18–19.

volatile version patented as the Benzedrine Inhaler. When Alles's patent was approved in 1933, SKF tried to buy it for $250. Alles rejected the pitiful offer. After a year of negotiations, the two parties came to terms; SKF got Alles's patent in exchange for 5 percent royalties on all future sales of a drug SKF branded Benzedrine sulfate.[3]

Alles and his new corporate partner experimented with Benzedrine as a mental-performance enhancer. Separate studies conducted at British and American universities confirmed that the drug increased alertness and seemed to make subjects more effective at simple mental and physical tasks. Reporting in British medical journal the *Lancet* in 1936, the English scientists concluded that while the drug did not actually alter thinking ability, amphetamines boosted subjects' optimism, aggressiveness, and confidence—all of which in turn seemed to enhance their mental performance when taking a test.[4]

In 1936, another group of researchers found that Benzedrine improved the mental performance of children with learning disabilities. Tests at a Rhode Island mental institution led to the counterintuitive discovery that the amphetamines made usually rambunctious kids calmer. These researchers had put their finger on effects that eventfully launched amphetamine-based drugs like Adderall to address attention-deficit/hyperactivity disorder (ADHD). Today we know that attention-deficit disorders and narcolepsy are related to malfunctioning neurotransmitters. For people with these conditions, amphetamines help accelerate the transmission of neurons across synapses at a more normal rate.

Despite evidence that its drug was a cognitive-performance enhancer, SKF did not pursue that sales and marketing avenue, in part because university students were already using Benzedrine—they had discovered that the amphetamine could help them pull all-nighters. Students using a new drug as a study aid was a story with shades of scientific progress and terror that the press could not resist. On April 10, 1937, the *New York Times* reported on "the extraordinary energy-stimulating powers of benzedrine sulphate." The paper explained that the recent British and American studies had revealed that in its normal state, the human brain was running on low octane, its potential "far from being fully realized under ordinary conditions of nutrition or stimulation by what the blood stream has to offer." The *Times* noted that getting Benzedrine into the bloodstream was comparable to putting the brain on high-octane fuel that could "enable it to 'hit on all cylinders.'" Inspired by a drug that could extract latent performance from an underused and underpowered mental machine, the paper enthused over "what we might achieve if only through feeding our cerebral tissues with better harmonic and other activating materials we could realize the full working powers of what we already have."[5] But when *Time* magazine covered the student story the following month, the newsweekly worried about young people misusing a "poisonous brain stimulant." *Time* noted that "cases of over-dosage have been uncovered at the Universities of Minnesota, Wisconsin and Chicago." The stuff was already so popular among the younger set that students had reportedly collapsed, fainted, and developed insomnia.[6]

Leery of launching a drug to satisfy a need the press had already framed as vaguely dissolute, SKF instead marketed Benzedrine as a therapeutic for the relief of depression, low energy, and chronic lack of initiative—a condition then called *anhedonia,* or lacking hedonic feelings.

Benzedrine went to market in 1937. Advertised as a product for patients suffering from "sensations of weakness," "apathy or discouragement," thinking difficulties, and hypochondria, the drug's potential market was as big as the world is wide. The fourth symptom, hypochondria, was particularly fruitful; one-third of all doctor visits are from patients reporting ailments with no identifiable source. As historian Nicolas Rasmussen pointed out in his book *On Speed,* hypochondria was a symptom that "would greatly increase the number of diagnosed depressions to include vast numbers of patients in general practice whose complaints lacked apparent 'organic basis.'"[7] First-year sales hit $95,000 (about $1.5 million in today's dollars). By 1939, sales had tripled to $330,000.[8] In the 1940s, doctors also began to widely prescribe amphetamine as an appetite-suppressing diet aid.

During World War II, amphetamines helped soldiers fight fatigue. In one test from August 1941 to July 1942, air crews on 20 bombing runs from England were given either Benzedrine or a placebo. The results delighted RAF commanders. The crews on Benzedrine had noticeably improved confidence and alertness over those on placebos.[9]

While military researchers in the United Kingdom and the United States were not able to find significant physical performance enhancement from amphetamine, the drug's subjective effect on fighter morale was profound. Especially for British fighters who had been subjected to the demoralizing and relentless Nazi bombing of their home country, amphetamines became an attitude booster that helped them survive in the grim European theater of war.

In the United States, government-sponsored researchers also aggressively investigated how amphetamines could be used to increase soldier performance. Studying methamphetamines, amphetamines, and a new SKF amphetamine variant called Dexedrine (dextroamphetamine), the American researchers were especially keen to understand if the drugs could increase pilot performance at the high altitudes new bomber planes could reach, where lack of oxygen dulled cognition. While amphetamines could not be shown to improve motor control in research studies, the drugs had a noticeable effect on esprit de corps. The study reported that the drug-taking subjects showed "more military appearance" and "devil-take-the-hindmost attitude."[10]

Some 12 million Americans fought overseas, and all were exposed to some of the 500 million Benzedrine tablets the military procured for the war. In 1943 and 1944, SKF reminded Armed Forces physicians of its drug's role in the war by running advertisements in the *Journal of the American Medical Association* that read, "Benzedrine is now an official item of issue in the Army Air Forces."[11] As Rasmussen wrote, the Allies' spirited endorsement of the drug "normalized and fostered amphetamine use on an enormous scale."[12]

When GIs returned from Europe and the Pacific, prescriptions were as easy to come by as a word to the doctor that you were sad or too fat.

By the war's end, Americans at home were popping approximately 1 million amphetamine pills a day for prescribed conditions like depression. Another 1 million pills were being consumed for weight loss. The standard dose was two 10-milligram pills per day.[13] In medicine cabinets across America, a bottle of pep pills soon sat unremarkably next to the aspirin.

The invention and quick mass adoption of tranquilizers like Miltown and Valium in the 1950s and 1960s gradually pushed out amphetamines as a remedy for depression. But even as the first antidepressant was replaced by tranquilizers, amphetamines remained wildly popular into the 1960s. Some protested the drugs' easy distribution. In a letter published in the *New England Journal of Medicine* in 1969, Rochester General Hospital radiologist Charles Lewis challenged the medical community to justify a "gross abuse" of amphetamine prescriptions. "How important are the amphetamines to the practice of medicine?" he fumed. "Would any patients likely have been lost or materially impoverished if these drugs were not available?"[14]

An answer came in short order. Doctor Bernadine Paulshock replied that hospital-based critics like Lewis were technicians "removed from the world of ordinary illness and medical problems." Paulshock argued that while many of the problems she treated with amphetamines were not mortal threats, they were still psychologically and physically impoverishing. She pointed out that depression could be so debilitating for some that it diminished "the possibility for the pleasurable enjoyment of, or even adequate coping with, the everyday routine stresses of their lives." Amphetamines gave Paulshock's patients the push they needed to get by. "I have several patients for whom fatigue or mild despondency is a chronic problem," Paulshock explained. "No organic illness other than 'the tired-housewife' syndrome can be found for their complaints. Small, regular doses of amphetamines, often taken only during the working week when the demands upon their energies and psyches are the highest, keep them functioning, coping, capable of performing and even enjoying their duties."[15]

Along with housewives and businessmen, Hollywood reached to amphetamines for quotidian performance enhancement. As early as 1938, MGM Studios fed a 16-year-old Judy Garland a steady diet of Benzedrine and adrenaline injections to keep her slim. The drugs also allowed the teenager to keep pace with a merciless six-day-a-week film production schedule for *The Wizard of Oz*. Actors had to be on the MGM lot before sunrise for costuming. Filming continued far into the night in a high-pressure project that had actors doing as many as 10 takes per scene. "They'd give us pills to keep us on our feet long after we were exhausted. Then they'd take us to the studio hospital and knock us out with sleeping pills," Garland recalled. "Then after four hours they'd wake us up and give us the pep pills again so we could work 72 hours in a row."[16]

President John F. Kennedy received regular methamphetamine injections together with vitamins and hormones. His doctor was German-trained physician Max Jacobson. Nicknamed Dr. Feelgood, Jacobson also administered pep-me-up treatments to the Rolling Stones, Truman Capote, Tennessee Williams, and an antidrug campaigning congressman from Florida named Claude Pepper. Any patient who came in for a consultation could leave with a prescription. Americans wanted speed to help them not get dropped from the race of life, and doctors and pharmaceutical makers were there to help.

While Benzedrine was still perceived as a relatively harmless medication in the early 1960s, attitudes began to change during the war in Vietnam. American soldiers in Southeast Asia consumed an average of 35 tablets of Dexedrine per year. Congressional testimony and research studies revealed that speed—as the drug was by then commonly called—was handed out "like candy" and soldiers bolstered their military-issued stash with Maxitone Forte, the injectable, French-made dextroamphetamine available just about anywhere in the former French colony. Seven percent of Vietnam soldiers were heavy speed users.[17] Congressional researchers reported that for every soldier who died in Vietnam, 10 returned stateside addicted to heroin or amphetamines.

Vietnam's human carnage was coming home in more than caskets, and the toll of amphetamine addiction began to make Americans reevaluate their positive relationship with the drug.[18]

Amphetamine use peaked in America in 1969, a year before President Nixon's Controlled Substances Act put drugs into distribution-restricting classifications. In 1969, drug makers stamped out between 8 and 10 billion 10-milligram amphetamine doses for a U.S. population of about 200 million. Four billion doses were prescribed by doctors and dispensed by pharmacies. This was enough to supply every person in America—child and adult—with 20 doses for the year. As for the rest, the other 4 to 6 billion pills and inhalers were diverted to gray-market distributors such as diet clinics, self-distributing doctors, and street dealers.[19]

Before the Controlled Substances Act drove nonprescription drug production to underground amphetamine and methamphetamine kitchens, major pharmaceutical firms manufactured 80 to 90 percent of the speed captured in drug busts. Pharmaceutical firms generated enormous profits through gray- and black-market drug-distribution networks such as the distributors who ordered 1.2 million amphetamine pills from Bates Laboratories in Chicago and had them shipped to the 11th hole of the Tijuana golf course.[20] Rasmussen estimates that at that time, 10.6 million Americans consumed the over 110,000 pounds of amphetamines annually manufactured by pharmaceutical companies in the United States. Of those who took amphetamines, roughly a quarter of a million were addicted to it.[21]

Speed was a ragged blade slashing through the 1960s. In San Francisco, the center of the era's counterculture, addiction turned the laid-back Haight-Ashbury district into a no-man's-land of hallucinating speed freaks. Amphetamine-related violent crime became so acute that counterculture celebrities joined forces behind a Speed Kills public service campaign. Radio stations played Frank Zappa's public service announcements: "Hi, wanna die? Start today! Use a little speed." Another Zappa PSA cautioned listeners that speed "will make you just like your mother and father," while rock star John Sebastian of the Lovin' Spoonful warned that the drug will "burn out your brain and your body" and "steal your freedom."[22] Amphetamines were becoming such a bad trip that in 1970, Congress ignored pharmaceutical industry protests and tightened drug distribution by passing the Controlled Substances Act.

In 1969, as all those psychotropic drugs were running through American veins, a young psychiatrist named Arthur Mandell founded the psychiatry department at the newly established University of California, San Diego, medical school. As a Tulane University medical school student in the 1950s, Mandell had a front-row seat for the biological revolution in psychiatry launched by stimulants like amphetamines and tranquilizers like chlorpromazine. When Mandell graduated from medical school in 1958, he entered the field at the peak of Cold War anxieties and at a time when a vanguard of biological psychiatrists saw emerging psychotropic drugs as a cause for hope, a new tool for treatment that operated at the molecular level and replaced, or at least refined, the dull instruments of lobotomy, electroshock, and addictive opiates. Three years after his arrival at the University of California, Mandell was also unexpectedly drawn into the amphetamine-dependent world of American football when San Diego Chargers owner Gene Klein invited the medical professor to work with his spectacularly bad football team.

In the 1970s, sports psychology was not something the macho world of pro football paid attention to. Klein thought bringing on one of the world's leading neuroscientists might help his team crawl up from their position in the bottom half of the league standings. In Mandell's 1976 book about his two and a half years with the Chargers, *The Nightmare Season,* he writes that Chargers head coach Harland Svare "was searching desperately for the answer. Should he use more discipline? Should he be kinder?" Svare hoped Mandell—who Klein called "El Shrinko"—could guide him to those answers.[23]

I met Mandell for lunch among the eucalyptus groves of UCSD—a short walk from the building where the lively-eyed professor emeritus continues his research projects. While steroids helped with long-term strength and power building, Mandell told me amphetamines were football players' game day tools. "Amphetamines were about rage and pain," he said of the players' affinity for speed to get them amped up on game days. "When you are rageful, you don't feel anything. It's a work drug." In *The Nightmare Season,* Mandell explains that for the NFL players he spent two seasons working with, amphetamines were not a party drug, but a once-a-week tool used the same way a truck driver would to finish a long haul or a student would to cram for a test.[24]

Mandell arrived at the Chargers' locker room in 1972. It had been nine years since the team had a winning season. That was also the year the U.S. government made amphetamines, including the popular diet drug Preludin, a Schedule II drug. The classification was applied to the attention-deficit drug Ritalin as well. Doctors now had to maintain records of their prescriptions, and the classification change limited the number of times prescriptions could be refilled. Total U.S. amphetamine production was capped at 400 million 10-milligram doses, severely limiting the drug makers' ability to flood the gray market.[25]

Although the amount of speed being produced in 1972 was one-twentieth of the 1969 production, pharmacies did not report shortages; clearly, a huge quantity of the amphetamines being consumed before 1972 were not being sourced through pharmacies. Still, the massive reduction in production was making speed harder to get. Unable to refill prescriptions over and over again or to purchase pills from diet clinics, Chargers players were buying amphetamines from street dealers and Tijuana pharmacies. Meanwhile, Southern California motorcycle gangs began manufacturing methamphetamine in locations that were decidedly not pharmaceutical clean rooms. Because the players saw amphetamines as a critical part of their game day rituals, Mandell concluded that it would be impossible for him to change the players' behavior. He decided he could protect their health by writing them prescriptions to help ensure they were not taking tainted product from Hells Angels or underground Mexican production facilities.

Along with counseling players about the risk of overdoing their amphetamine consumption, the doctor informed the NFL that it had a drug problem. The NFL responded by attempting to kill the messenger—Mandell told me the football organization attempted to get his California medical license revoked. Having walked out of the medical school ivory tower into the guts of professional sports, Mandell was clueless about the image-management realities of big-time American sports. Thinking back to his naive belief that he could actually change NFL habits by going to the commissioner and telling him what he surely already knew, in retrospect, Mandell came to realize that the move would not be seen as an effort to help football, but instead as a threat to its image. "I provoked it," he told me of the NFL going to the Medical Board of California to get his license yanked. "The error I made was the grandiosity that I felt I was going to change things. It's so silly that I'm almost embarrassed."

While working as volunteer assistant to the Chargers from 1972 and 1974 (to maintain clinical objectivity, he would not accept payment from the team), Mandell also conducted an ongoing survey of drug use in the NFL. He interviewed 86 players from a total of 15 teams. In a 1979 paper published in *Clinical Toxicology,* Mandell reported that two-thirds of the players used amphetamines during games. Half used them regularly. Mandell also had access to another NFL team's bulk drug purchases during the 1968 and 1969 seasons. From those records, he calculated that teams were sourcing enough medicine to provide each player a per-game amphetamine dosage of 60 milligrams in 1968 and 70 milligrams in 1969. (The typical dosage a general practitioner might prescribe to a patient for fatigue or weight loss was 5 to 10 milligrams.) The players also made healthy use of opiate-based painkillers. During the 1969 season, the team distributed enough codeine-based drugs for each player to have 14 pills per game, including the painkiller Darvon (banned by the FDA in 2010 because it caused heart problems), Phenaphen with codeine, Fiorinal (aspirin, barbiturate, and caffeine), Daprisal, and Empirin with codeine. For sleep, per-game consumption total was nine tablets each of Noludar, Seconal, and Butisol.[26]

To put the players' pill use into perspective, Mandell compared their drug quantities to the self-administered dosages of people from other walks of life. The dosages of 5 to 10 milligrams used by quarterbacks and wide receivers aligned with the life role of an author, housewife, or executive. Special team players and linebackers took typical dosages of 15 to 45 milligrams, about the same as a soldier, hyperactive child, or anxious depressive. Defensive ends and defensive tackles took dosages of up to 150 milligrams—an amount comparable to that of an intravenous speed addict.[27]

In *The Nightmare Season,* Mandell writes, "There would be a time, and soon, when a person would have the right to supplement the biochemical in his brain with purchased chemicals. Selective drug use would become a matter of facts, decision and caution rather than a matter of morality."[28] In 1976, Mandell forecast today's selective serotonin reuptake inhibitors (SSRIs), which can selectively enhance mood and alter behavior. And especially with drug companies advertising their lifestyle-enhancing wares on American television, in the 21st century, drug use would become an individual shopping decision. "If the technology is available," people will grab on to it to help them win, Mandell told me. He cited famed Green Bay Packers coach Vince Lombardi's apocryphal quote, "Winning isn't everything, it is the only thing," as the attitude that allows people to easily rationalize using medication to get ahead in sports and life. "Executives I know are premedicating themselves for certain kinds of meetings. For example, if they are not supposed to lose their temper, they use a mild tranquilizer. And if they are going in there to intimidate, they use Adderall."

Today, the United States and New Zealand are the only two countries in the world that allow pharmaceutical companies to advertise directly to consumers. Commenting on the rise of drug company advertising that began in the early 1980s and increased as American lawmakers loosened marketing restrictions throughout the decade, Mandell told me, "That changed everything. In fact, it changed drug design because the marketers are sitting there and helping decide which research path to take." Rather than create drugs for human ailments, it is more cost-effective today for a drug maker to take an existing drug, slightly modify its molecular structure, and then resell it as the solution to a newly invented pathology.[29]

Mandell explained how the structure of medical care in America encourages the increased doping of society. Because health insurance companies limit the number of visits their patients can make to psychotherapists, SSRIs like Prozac became a cheaper, hands-off way to manage depression. "I always did psychotherapy with psychopharmacology," Mandell told me. "I'm going to see you twice a week if I'm going to poison your brain with something and listen to what the hell is happening." By going along with the insurance company rationing of psychotherapy, Mandell said, "Psychiatrists have joined the dealers. They get 15 minutes once a month on the insurance."

And this is where Mandell feels that the pharmaceutical industry's government-blessed power to push drugs directly to the public crosses ethical boundaries graver than those that athletes violate when they dope. Today, when athletes take performance-enhancing drugs, they break the rules of their chosen game, and that is wrong. However, Mandell feels that allowing drug makers to advertise products directly to consumers, along with the fact that American health care incentivizes chemicals as the first line of defense for many physical and mental conditions, is a more severe violation of conscience and moral sense. Allowing pharmaceutical companies to sell us drugs to increase our mental performance and change our brain's chemical structure is a violation of fair play. "There are no policemen left," Mandell said with a shake of his head. "No regulators."

The explosive growth of amphetamine-based ADHD drugs during the 1990s dramatizes Mandell's concern about the ethics of the pharmaceutical industry's unchecked power, especially when it dovetails with society's own quest for enhanced life performance. Before 1980, children who had a hard time focusing, struggled to complete tasks, and made impulsive decisions were called hyperactive, rambunctious, or simply "a handful." In 1980, this set of behavioral characteristics became a medical condition when a new pathology called attention-deficit disorder was added to the American Psychiatric Association's catalog of mental disorders, the *Diagnostic and Statistical Manual of Mental Disorders,* Third Edition (*DSM-III*). In 1987, the revised edition, the *DSM-III-R,* updated the name to attention-deficit/hyperactivity disorder, or ADHD.

Doctors had been aware that amphetamines can calm and focus hyperactive children since the 1930s. And so by 1970, even before ADHD had made its way into the canon of psychiatric disorders, some 150,000 American children were taking amphetamines to treat hyperactivity. By 1995, children were swallowing some 6 million prescriptions for the methylphenidate stimulant Ritalin. U.S. Centers for Disease Control and Prevention surveys revealed that as of 2012, one out of five high-school-aged boys had been diagnosed with ADHD. Overall, about 6.5 million American children aged 4 to 17 have been diagnosed with the condition, and some 4.5 million of those are taking stimulants—sometimes called cognitive-enhancing drugs—to treat their condition. In some states like North Carolina, nearly one-third of boys over the age of nine have been diagnosed with ADHD, making them eligible for drugs like Adderall, an amphetamine-dextroamphetamine mixed salt.[30]

From a few thousand hyperactive kids in the 1960s to 6 percent of the country's youth today, the frequency of ADHD has increased exponentially. As Edward Shorter puts it in his *History of Psychiatry,* this explosion of people now eligible to take amphetamines to normalize their behavior represents "a pathologizing of essentially normal if irksome behavior" that is unparalleled in history. Besides turning personality into a disorder, Shorter notes that these diagnoses "dipped greatly the threshold at which individuals were said to be ill."[31]

Expanding the number of people whose symptoms fell under the ever-expanding definition of ADHD also created a demand for chemical stimulants that is among history's largest episode of performance-enhancing drug use ever. The formal classification of ADHD, along with a push by health insurance companies and drug companies to move patients away from expensive counseling-based care and onto drugs, has been marked by the increase in psychiatric drug sales from $2.5 billion in 1990 to $15.2 billion in 2000. Over the same period, United States prescriptions for ADHD stimulants increased nearly 800 percent, from 225 million doses in 1990 to 1.8 billion in 2000. In terms of base materials, between 1991 and 1999, the number of kilos of raw amphetamine sold in the United States increased 2,000 percent. By 2000, an average of 70 doses of antidepression SSRIs or focus-enhancing amphetamine salts were being sold per American per year—about 7 million doses of neuro-enhancing medicine and far more than the 20 per-person doses annually at the peak of the last speed epidemic in 1969.[32]

Much of this increase in amphetamine sales comes from efforts to improve scholastic performance and, by extension, national output. A significant body of academic research suggests that a better-educated nation is a more economically productive nation. College-educated Americans earn 70 percent more than those who only graduate high school. Unemployment rates are also lower for college graduates—4.1 percent in 2012 compared to 8.8 percent for high school grads and 12 percent for high school dropouts. As UC-Berkeley professors Stephen Hinshaw and Richard Scheffler write in their 2014 book on attention-deficit/hyperactivity disorder, *The ADHD Explosion,* "more learning equals more earning."[33] Data from the Centers for Disease Control and Prevention indicate that kids with ADHD also are injured more frequently than their peers. A child with untreated ADHD costs $1,000 more per year in medical care expenses than a child without ADHD. Research also shows that children with ADHD are 10 to 14 percent more likely to be unemployed as adults, will earn 33 percent less than their peers, and be 15 percent more likely to receive public assistance. By improving the cognitive functions of individuals with ADHD, drugs can, in theory, help eliminate or lessen these lifelong economic and social performance penalties.[34]

At the turn of the 21st century, studies of international academic preparedness showed America slipping further behind other countries. In 2001, President George W. Bush signed the No Child Left Behind Act. The law codified the theory that high scholastic standards combined with the feedback of constant standardized tests would create a better-educated nation and in turn enhance its financial output by creating more productive citizens and reducing social welfare costs. In papers and books going back to the 1960s, Nobel Prize–winning economist Gary Becker had made this notion of students as "human capital" part of the nation's political and educational vernacular.[35] Investments in education, it was said, will generate economic return, making spending in "soft" human needs palatable to right-leaning politicians by turning a social expense into an economic investment with a quantified rate of return. No Child Left Behind took Becker's theories to heart and rewarded schools whose students achieved high test scores by giving them more funding. Low-performing schools were punished with funding cuts and, in some cases, closure.[36]

The No Child Left Behind Act and its 2011 replacement, the Obama administration's Race to the Top, depended on test-centric teaching methodologies. But lots of tests requiring lots of preparation and training are not a good fit for naturally fidgety kids. Nor were these well-intentioned knowledge-measurement exams ideal for kids whose minds tended to work along tangents and diagonals. Educators, doctors, and parents alike turned to amphetamine-based ADHD drugs as a remedy for class-disrupting behaviors and the test-score ruining inability to focus. By facilitating genetically "malfunctioning" brain synapse function, amphetamines can turn restless children into higher-performing test takers. As Hinshaw and Scheffler put it in *The ADHD Explosion,* with school accountability and No Child Left Behind measurements of success, when it comes to children and ADHD, "the push for performance matters."[37] Changing educational policy created a problem; to succeed in 21st-century America, children needed to be ace test-takers. Drug manufacturers had chemicals that would improve performance for children who were not naturally capable of dedicating themselves to this sort of task.

The likelihood of a child being prescribed these contemporary stimulants has much to do with where the child lives and the political needs of the adults who run his or her state and school. *The ADHD Explosion* recounts the story of a 12-year-old boy who moved from Los Angeles to North Carolina's Research Triangle. During the first semester of seventh grade at his North Carolina school, a faculty psychologist called the boy's parents to inform them that their son showed symptoms of ADHD. Although their son had always been a bit scattered, he had done well enough in school in California, and no school representative in Los Angeles ever suggested he had a learning disability.

The child's sudden learning disability was not a matter of changing biology or loss of inhibition on the long haul across the nation, but rather a reflection of the different desires and standards of schools in the American South. Before No Child Left Behind, Texas and North Carolina were the vanguard of states that measured and rewarded school performance using the yardstick of standardized tests. Compared to other states, these schools also have higher ADHD diagnoses and amphetamine prescriptions for 4 to 17 year olds. Pitted against one another for a bigger piece of a finite funding pie, an incentive system emerged in which it made logical sense to get energetic, distracted kids on test-performance-enhancing drugs. Focused, calm kids do better on standardized tests, and they don't screw things up by disrupting the rest of the class who also need to concentrate and stay calm to do well on tests.

The National Survey of Children's Health (NSCH) found that in 2009–2010, 38.1 percent of North Carolina kids had been diagnosed with attention-deficit disorder. In California, 27.3 percent had been diagnosed. Simply by moving to North Carolina, a California middle schooler had a statistically higher chance of being diagnosed with ADHD and having a school administrator or family doctor recommend that the child start taking stimulants not much different than those taken by the San Diego Chargers in the 1970s, and with the same objective: to improve game day performance. After the passage of school accountability laws, nationwide, children aged 8–13 from low-income families saw their ADHD diagnoses rise from 10 to 15.3 percent—a 53-percent increase in performance-enhancing drug use.[38]

Stimulants can work marvels for children with severe learning disabilities—even restoring their cognitive function to the same level as their peers who have no disability. However, kids without learning disabilities are also using ADHD drugs in an additive rather than restorative fashion. They use questionable ADHD diagnoses to gain an unfair competitive advantage over their non-doped fellow students.

Just as schools must build ramps and elevators to grant physically disabled students equal access to public facilities, federal law states that schools must also accommodate learning disabilities. Some of these allowances include extra or unlimited time to take tests and extended time to complete assignments. Given increasing competition for limited college seats, some students and parents saw in these accommodations an opportunity to game the college test admission process, and once in college, artificially enhance their grades. A 2010 study by journalist Melena Zyal Vickers showed that at the University of Chapel Hill in North Carolina, between 1990 and 2009, the number of students applying for attention-deficit disorder and attention-deficit/hyperactivity disorder accommodations increased by 766 percent. Between 1998 and 2008, the number of South Carolina high school students requesting extra time for their SATs grew by 40 percent. Among North Carolina's SAT-taking seniors, 6.6 percent claimed a learning disability, up from 4.7 percent 10 years earlier.[39]

This statewide growth in learning disabilities was not matched by a proportional increase in other disabilities. Of Americans aged 3 to 21, 5.6 percent were diagnosed with attention-deficit syndrome in 2006, up from 3.6 percent in 1981. Over the same time period, the number of Americans with visual, hearing, and other physical disabilities stayed steady at 0.1 percent and the number of those with mental disabilities declined from 2 percent to 1 percent of the population.[40] While the incidence of all other disabilities was declining or remaining stable, the one disability that would gain a student an advantage over his or her peers, and for which drug companies were aggressively advertising amphetamine-based solutions, was increasingly being diagnosed. Students obtain suspect ADHD diagnoses to gain a competitive advantage through two means: legal access to cognitive-performance-enhancing drugs, and access to test-taking accommodations such as more time or a private testing room.

Attention-deficit disabilities are also not evenly distributed across races and classes. Testing advantages and access to prescription cognitive enhancers disproportionately go to wealthy white children—or we should say, ADHD symptoms disproportionately fall on children with the economic resources and family connections required to secure a doctor's ADHD appraisal. An undergraduate diagnosed with attention-deficit disabilities is statistically more likely to be a white male from an affluent family with highly educated parents than nonwhite, female, or from a low-income family. Data suggest that wealthy white males—regardless of whether or not they have a disability—have parents who possess knowledge of their rights, money, and access to the medical levers of power.

A 2012 *Chicago Tribune* investigation of learning disabilities and ACT college entrance exams in Illinois found that 1 in 5 students from affluent Chicago neighborhoods like Highland Park and Lake Forest had learning disabilities and were granted accommodations when taking the ACT. At one high-performing high school, 170 juniors from a single class—1 in 6—had learning disabilities. This compares to a statewide Illinois ratio of 1 in 10 students with learning disabilities. Out of the disabled students from affluent areas, "dozens" scored 30 or higher out of a possible 36 on their ACTs. Scoring 30 or higher is a truly remarkable achievement on the ACT. Before this unusual growth of ADHD diagnoses among affluent high school students, high ACT scores were unheard of among students with learning disabilities. Before these questionable disability diagnoses, students with true attention-deficit problems historically scored *below*, rather than above average on college admission tests.[41]

Especially for Ivy League and elite public schools, competition for admission is intense. A stellar college entrance exam score can mean the difference between going to Stanford or to a community college.

With students granted 50 percent more time—and in some cases extra days—to complete a three-hour ACT, kids who had no actual learning disabilities had a terrific competitive advantage over their peers who were being tested on a shorter playing field. According to an ACT spokesman, nationwide, the number of students applying for learning disability accommodations for the SATs grew to 5 percent of all applicants in 2010–2011, up from 3.5 percent in 2007–2008.[42] A 2011 U.S. Government Accountability Office report revealed that it costs between $500 and $9,000 to secure the disability certifications needed to qualify for SAT or ACT test accommodations.[43] These financial barriers are due in part to the number of students trying to cheat the system—both by taking sanctioned dope and by gaining more time for the chemically focused mind to apply itself to the exam. By demanding proof of legitimate disability, test organizers are attempting to protect honest students and the integrity of their exams. However, efforts to catch cheaters is costly, and those increases are reflected in the cost of the disability certifications—an unintended consequence that may only serve to erect an additional financial barrier for truly disabled students who are not rich, while creating an easily surmountable barrier for students wealthy enough to buy all the needed disability proofs.

Travis Tygart thinks about unfair play in American educational systems. CEO of the U.S. Anti-Doping Agency (USADA), Tygart's dogged work was instrumental in exposing Lance Armstrong's doping past. When I asked Tygart about the number of American kids being treated with stimulants for ADHD, he brought up college entrance exam gaming: "When the parents heard that that was an opportunity for their kids to score better on their SAT because they could take it untimed, whether they had ADHD or not, they were going to their doctors and pushing their doctors to get their kids diagnosed." Tygart observed that increasing test scores in this way is artificial performance enhancement. "The motives are not pure," America's top sports doping cop said.

After law school at Southern Methodist University, Tygart worked in private practice before becoming a full-time USADA general counsel in

2002. He stepped into the leadership role in 2007. Along with leading the investigation that revealed Lance Armstrong's cheating, as USADA counsel, he was deeply involved with the 2003 BALCO steroid manufacturing and distribution scandal. Tygart has an uncompromising belief that rules are rules and athletes are obligated to obey them. However, he also possesses a philosopher's cognizance that the USADA has the preposterous task of trying to create a pure space apart from a world that praises performance-enhancing drugs from cradle to grave, Ritalin to Viagra.

Tygart told me that performance doping in the general population is more prevalent in America than elsewhere in the world. "In the U.S., we are overly sensitized to doing whatever it takes to win," Tygart said. "Whether it's giving kids fraudulently synthetic drugs to help them calm down and do better on an SAT or whatever else it might be, we are more immune to the downsides of that." The USADA has the unenviable, perhaps impossible, task of carving out a chemical-free cloister in the midst of a nation whose citizens and lawmakers have sent strong messages that pharmaceuticals should play an important role in the betterment of everyday life. Indeed, ADHD drug makers are expanding into the adult market by making alarming claims about the personal tragedies that can befall adults who let their ADHD go untreated. One magazine advertisement claims that "adults with ADHD were nearly 2 times more likely to have been divorced" and that 32 percent of depressed people have untreated ADHD. Others feature prominent athletes coming out of the closet about their ADHD. Combining fear with efforts to strip away stigma, the ads work to bring more adults into the amphetamine fold while helping to ensure that children don't graduate away from these drugs after their school years.[44]

A former high school basketball player, Tygart marvels that when you turn on an NBA basketball game on TV, "you'll see how many ads for performance-enhancing drugs, or a drug to wake up, or a drug to go to sleep at night—we are inundated." American lawmakers have made it clear that government will not interfere with drug makers' ability to let the public know about the marvels of their latest chemical creations. The larger contextual issue raised by America's love affair with legal and illegal performance-enhancing drugs animates Tygart—these are issues of morality, transcendence, being, and the marshaling of chemical technology to help people exceed their innate human capacities.

As Tygart sees it, the fact that American 4-year-olds are on speed and wealthy suburban parents are rigging testing systems to increase their offspring's chance of getting into an Ivy League university creates even more reason for sports to carve out a chemical-free space. Tygart understands that the continued and growing popularity of amphetamines 45 years after their usage peak in the late 1960s shows that pharmaceutical manufacturers are doing all they can to get more drugs into more people. "To a certain extent, we are all hanging on for the ride," he told me, referring to the continuing effects of the FDA's 1997 decision to allow drug makers to advertise their products directly to consumers. "And all I am saying is that sport has said, 'We're *not* hanging on for the ride. We're unique. We're a special fair playing field, and we're not just going to go blindly—or without serious consideration—where the U.S. society has gone, the U.S. consumer has gone. We're going to maintain sense and sensibility about what we think is really valuable.'"

Once America's children get into college, many use Adderall and Ritalin like football players—as a workday tool to help them get a job done. A 2005 and 2006 study of 1,811 students at a large southeastern university revealed that 34 percent of the students used illegal (non-prescribed) ADHD stimulants as study aids.[45] This research is in line with other studies showing a 7 to 35 percent stimulant use rate on college campuses.[46] Students said they took the drugs to help them focus, to make up for time lost procrastinating, and to help them manage the stress of finals week. The study found that students perceived drugs like Adderall and Ritalin as true performance enhancers. Female students cited weight loss as another reason for taking ADHD drugs. As Benzedrine was once sold over the counter and through diet clinics for its powerful appetite-suppressing effects, sorority members especially cited using the drug to lose weight before spring break and fraternity formals.

I spoke to one undergraduate at a large California public school to learn about his use of Adderall. The 21-year-old has an Adderall prescription from his doctor. He told me the drug makes him more productive by increasing his focus on the study topic at hand. "It doesn't teach you calculus, but if you are paying attention to the lecture, it keeps your mind out of the weeds," he explained. As for any sense of shame that might come with academic doping, the student said his fellow students fall into two camps. "A lot of people are open about it and are cool with talking about it," he said of using ADHD drugs like Ritalin and Adderall. Others attach "a stigma of being a cheater" to cognitive enhancers. Nearly a century after Gordon Alles discovered the cognitive and physical effects of amphetamines, the drug remains a staple of the American pharmaceutical diet. And unlike drugs in sports, Americans remain torn as to whether their embrace of stimulants for better living is a virtue or a vice.[47]

CHAPTER 16

SUPPLEMENTS: GOVERNMENT-APPROVED DOPE

In 1812, typhoid fever ravaged the rural valleys of New England. In New Hampshire, a fever-stricken 6-year-old boy named Joseph Smith suffered sweats, chills, and diarrhea. Then living with his five siblings and parents, Smith escaped typhoid's grasp after two weeks of delirium. Eighteen years later, Joseph Smith Jr. went on to found the Church of Jesus Christ of Latter Day Saints. His early brush with death and doctors helped make herbal medicine and self-healing integral to Mormon scripture and life. A chain of events was set in motion that led to the birth of Utah's $7 billion nutritional supplement business, unconditional government protection of that industry under the watch of a devout Mormon senator, and the U.S. Olympic Committee's decision to accept funds from an industry that the IOC and the World Anti-Doping Agency had categorically rejected as poisonous to sport.

Although Smith survived typhoid, his childhood medical troubles had only begun. The typhoid infection ended up spreading to his bone marrow—a septic condition we now call osteomyelitis and a common side effect of typhoid in children. Summoned from Dartmouth College, the lead surgeon from a team of doctors confessed, "We can do nothing."

Only leg amputation would save Joseph's life. His mother, Lucy, protested, demanding that the physicians instead attempt to remove the rotten sections of her son's bone.

Lucy's diary recounts what followed: "The surgeons commenced operating by boring into the bone of his leg, first on one side of the bone, where it was affected, then on the other side, after which they broke it off with a pair of forceps or pincers. They then took away the large piece of the bone. When they broke off the first piece, Joseph screamed out so loudly that I could not forbear running to him."[1] Remarkably, the boy survived both the surgery and the removal of 14 more pieces of bone that broke free in the following three months. Three years of recovery in bed and on crutches followed, and the Mormon founder walked with a hitch for the remainder of his life.[2]

Two other family dramas dimmed Smith's view of modern medicine. His sister Sophronia was stricken by typhoid, and after 90 days of illness, doctors said her death was imminent. With the defeated doctors packing their bags, Mormon lore has it that when Lucy clutched her daughter, the girl miraculously recovered.[3] Where modern medicine failed, the parents believed prayer prevailed. Then, in 1825, Joseph's brother Alvin was stricken by "bilious colic" the day's term for what was probably a ruptured appendix. A physician administered a heavy dose of calomel, or mercury chloride, an all-purpose drug of the period. At a time when bloodletting and purging were go-to medical treatments for many human ailments, mercury chloride was thought to purge the body through violent vomiting and diarrhea. It cured you or killed you. After three days of suffering, Alvin died, most likely from calomel poisoning.

These sour experiences with orthodox medicine attracted Smith to the teachings of a New Hampshire herbalist named Samuel Thomson. Known as America's foremost "botanic physician," as one supporter put it in 1839, Thomson knew "the magnificent apparatus of the chemistry of Nature."[4] Capitalizing on the great wave of evangelical revival meetings and camps that swept western New York and New England in the first quarter of the 19th century, Smith formed his church in 1830 and published its founding text, the *Book of Mormon,* the same year. Both Thomson's do-it-yourself healing system and Smith's homegrown church rode the Jacksonian spirit of the times, an anti-elitist world view that squinted suspiciously at monopolies and high priests, whether they be doctor, pope, or king. Where official doctors and monolithic religion so often failed, self-reliance and herbal healing would succeed.

In 1843, Smith told a Mormon congregation that doctors don't know much. "They want to kill or cure you to get your money," he preached. Reject modern medicine with its deadly potions and bloodletting cures, the Mormon prophet urged his flock. Instead of concoctions like calomel that "will kill the patient," Smith admonished his disciples to "take some mild physic [purgative] two or three times and then some bitters [herbs]. If you can't get anything else, take a little salt and cayenne pepper."[5]

Herbal supplements appear in the Mormon church's founding texts, the *Book of Mormon* and *Doctrine and Covenants,* as natural cures essential to divine living. *Doctrine and Covenants* explains that God placed herbs on Earth "for the constitution, nature, and use of man." When followers of the Church of Jesus Christ of Latter Day Saints fall ill, they "shall be nourished with all tenderness, with herbs and mild food, and not by the hand of an enemy," the text commands. Describing early Mormons who survived typhoid, the *Book of Mormon* recalls that "because of the excellent qualities of the many plants and roots which God had prepared to remove the cause of diseases," Mormon ancestors thrived.

For Smith and his followers, using herbal medicine was an exercise in divinity, a component of the path to salvation. By the time Mormon pioneers settled in their promised land in the 1840s, "root medicine" was entwined with their faith in Jesus Christ—so much so that settlers took to using the term "poison doctors" to describe those physicians who practiced bloodletting and dispensed potions like mercury and opiates.[6] Even today, the ephedra shrubs common to the southwestern United States and Mexico are known as Mormon tea for the early settlers who reportedly boiled their leaves and stems to make a beverage.

Joseph Smith also saw economic potential in herbs. In 1813, his homeopathic hero Samuel Thomson patented an herbal doctoring system, "Thomson's Improved System of Botanic Practice of Medicine." For $20 paid to a traveling agent, a family would obtain both Thomson's instructional medicine book and the rights to administer Thomson's botanical recipes. This early multilevel-marketing program offered both economic independence and the appeal of becoming one's own physician. As journalist Dan Hurley puts it in his 2006 book on the supplement industry, *Natural Causes,* "Herbs, free for the picking, were all anyone needed. What could be more in keeping with America's spirit of self-reliance?"[7] These Thomson System agents were the predecessors to today's herbal-supplement multilevel-marketing firms. By 1840, Thomson had sold some 100,000 licenses—an astronomical take worth about $56 million today.

While growing up, Smith also endured economic privations he might not have suffered had his father not been swindled in an herbal-medicine trade deal. In 1784, a retrofitted Revolutionary War merchant ship named the *Empress of China* had opened trade between the United States and China. The boat's payload on that inaugural 15-month voyage included 40 tons of ginseng, a root the Chinese treasured for its supposed sex- and vitality-enhancing powers. Chinese importers paid top dollar for New World ginseng. In 1801, four years before Joseph Jr.'s birth, Smith's father had smelled opportunity. He collected masses of ginseng root from neighboring Vermont farmers and arranged for it to be shipped on the *Empress of China* for sale in Chinese markets. The deal was projected to yield a $4,500 windfall. Considering that Vermont farmland sold for about $2 an acre in the early 1800s, this was an extraordinary amount of money—enough to expand the family's modest landholdings with plenty of cash left over for farm equipment and buildings. Smith Sr.'s ginseng made it to Canton and sold for a small fortune, but the shipping agent disappeared to Canada with the money, and Smith never saw a dime. The family had to sell the farm to pay debts related to the sour deal. Nevertheless, the financial and medical potential of herbal remedies remained a family presence for the boy.

Although Smith met his end in 1844 in Carthage, Illinois, at the hands of a mob, his followers made their way west and eventually parked their wagons for good overlooking Utah's Great Salt Lake. By the 1960s, the herbal medicine that steeped into Smith's Mormon faith was being sold the world over by herbal and vitamin supplement outfits, many based in Utah like Weider, Nature's Way, and Nutraceutical. The latter firm is a Park City–based supplement conglomerate formed by Mitt Romney's investment firm Bain Capital in 1993. Also a Mormon, Romney would later organize the scandal-shaken 2002 Salt Lake City Winter Olympics and run for U.S. president in 2012. Many of the supplement firms that sprang up, such as Nu Skin of Provo, Utah, were multilevel-marketing companies that built their success on global networks of families and friends who sold products and the prospect of wealth to one another. These Utah pyramid sales enterprises were a Thomson System for the 20th century. Today, a quarter of the $36 billion U.S. nutritional supplement industry sales are funneled through Utah.[8]

By the 1990s, the salubrious sheen that had enhanced the dietary supplement industry was wearing off. In 1989, contaminated batches of the amino acid L-tryptophan sent at least 36 Americans to the grave.[9] Touted as a cure for sleeplessness and anxiety, L-tryptophan supplements caused the crippling connective tissue disease eosinophilia-myalgia syndrome (EMS) in some 5,000 people. Tests of other dietary-supplement products in the 1990s turned up arsenic, sheep placenta, and more surprises. When the California Department of Health Services tested 260 samples of herbal products from Asia, it found that 83 contained lead, arsenic, mercury, or drugs not on the label. When police pulled over an apparently drunk driver in Scottsdale, Arizona, it turned out that he had been poisoned by a nutritional supplement containing paint remover.

Six reports in the *New England Journal of Medicine* in 1997 depicted the behavior of an industry largely indifferent to the health of its customers. From a 15-year-old boy who was treated with herbs for the lymphatic cancer Hodgkin's disease to a woman whose white blood cells were wiped out by a product that claimed it would clean her intestines, the *Journal*'s executive editor, Dr. Marcia Angell, stated that if the dietary supplement makers were held to prevailing safety and efficacy standards, "most of them would be shut down.[10] In the process of conducting a tax evasion investigation on supplement maker Metabolife, the IRS discovered documentation showing that 5 deaths, 26 strokes, 18 heart attacks and 43 seizures had been attributed to its products.[11]

These were the sort of tragedies that had led to the creation of the FDA 90 years earlier. In 1905, journalist Samuel Hopkins Adams penned a series of articles for *Collier's* magazine titled "The Great American Fraud." "Gullible America will spend this year some seventy-five millions of dollars in the purchase of patent medicines," he wrote on October 7, 1905. This sum would buy Americans "huge quantities" of opiates, narcotics, "liver stimulants," and above all, "undiluted fraud," he added.[12] In the series of articles, later published as a book, Adams documented how patent medicines and tonics made unverifiable claims about their health-restoring powers, even though many of the "medicines" were in fact toxic. For example, headache medicines often contained acetanilide, a painkiller that, while powerful enough to temporarily alleviate pain, also caused heart attacks. "Fraud, exploited by the skillfulest of advertising bunco men, is the basis of their trade," Adams fulminated.[13]

The potion makers took steps to deflect Adams's criticism. They enlisted a crafty bit of economic blackmail to force newspapers to take their side in the brewing war against drug safety legislation. The curative makers added a "red clause" to their advertising contracts stipulating that the agreement would become void if a law passed restricting the sale of their patent medicines. At the turn of the 20th century, newspapers were packed with advertisements for life-enhancing nostrums; the elixir makers provided a reliable stream of advertising revenue. The red clause helped ensure that the newspapers were financially motivated to agitate against government food and medicine regulation. Newspapers met legislative rumblings about clamping down on patent medicine fraud with stern editorials defending consumers' rights to self-medication, manufacturers' liberty to pursue unfettered free enterprise, and the evils of an overbearing government.

Despite these maneuverings, Adams's "Great American Fraud" eventually helped push Congress to pass the Federal Food and Drugs Act of 1906. Signed into law by President Theodore Roosevelt, the legislation made it a crime to transport across borders or sell an "adulterated or misbranded" food or drug. The law also gave the government the power to test foods and drugs to ensure the contents matched the ingredients on the label. In 1916, the act ended sales of Clark Stanley's Snake Oil Liniment, an elixir supposedly made with oil from snakes and bursting with the capacity to "oil dry joints" and remedy sprains, bunions, sore throats, and dog bites. Americans had been snapping up this wonder salve since 1897. When government scientists tested Stanley's product, they learned that it held little more than mineral oil and a bit of beef fat. The product was shut down and the supplement industry had a new nickname.[14]

For the first time, the U.S. government was committed to protecting consumers from unscrupulous food makers and drug manufacturers. In 1927, the execution of the act was centralized under a new federal enforcement body, the Food and Drug Administration.

According to the original Food and Drugs Act, nutritional supplements fell within the scope of the FDA's responsibility. According to the law, drugs "shall include all medicines and preparations recognized in the United States Pharmacopeia or National Formulary for internal or external use." The clause that followed seemed to put herbal medicines under the FDA umbrella as well, since it governed "any substance or mixture of substances intended to be used for the cure, mitigation, or prevention of disease of either man or other animals." However, the potion makers found an ingenious rhetorical out by claiming that their products were not designed to directly target illness in the manner of chemical-based pharmaceuticals but rather were meant to supplement diet. Drugs target disease. Food and food supplements just provide energy. The difference was critical, and it opened a back door to the supplement industry we know today.

This dodge goes way back. For example, in the early 1900s, edible potions and pills infused with radiation became all the rage. Popularized after Marie and Pierre Curie's discovery of radioactivity in 1898, the idea was that minute doses of radiation would trigger the endocrine system and fire up the production of bone- and muscle-building hormones. One advertisement encouraged Americans to get plenty of sleep, exercise, eat unprocessed foods, and "drink plenty of fresh, invigorating, natural radioactive water from the Radium-Spa." In 1927, a champion golfer and horse-racing aficionado named Eben Byers died at 51. A big believer in what was then called "mild radium therapy," Byers had consumed 1,400 bottles of a patented and widely available radiation-laced energy water called Radithor. Byers also watered his racehorses with the drink to boost their performance. By the time of Byers's death, gaping abcesses yawned where his jaws and teeth used to be, and cavities bored through his skull. Because Byers was a prominent eastern businessman and socialite, his gruesome death by radiation poisoning attracted the FDA's attention. The agency eventually shut down the Radithor business. Byers's obituary in the *New York Times* mentioned an FDA warning "against 'radioactive' drugs because of serious injuries to users."[15]

Despite harming consumers, the supplement industry thrived throughout the 20th century by sticking to the message that its products were either food or a food additive—a mere spice, so to speak. Supplement maker and retailer GNC was a notorious offender. In 1984, the U.S. Postal Service brought charges against GNC for falsely representing the healing powers of 13 products including "Risk Modifier," "Life Expander," and "Mental Acuity Formula." That same year, the FDA prosecuted GNC for selling an evening primrose oil supplement as a cure for high blood pressure, multiple sclerosis, and arthritis. When reminded of these cases in a 1992 deposition, GNC CEO and chairman of the board Jerry Horn argued that while his company did sell pills, they were really "a food—it's a food product."[16]

Horn went on to describe an L-tryptophan pill as a form of sustenance: "You know, like broccoli, you might buy broccoli in a pill form." The deposing attorney poked at the CEO's claim with a taunting query: "When people are thinking about taking an L-tryptophan pill, they're not going to sit down and try to figure out which wine goes with it or anything like that?" The deposition was over a lawsuit regarding the contaminated batches of L-tryptophan that had made their way into supplements. The tryptophan caused a rash of hospitalizations for the incurable EMS. By July 1990, 27 of what would become 36 people had died and 1,531 EMS cases had been reported in the United States.[17]

With store-bought supplements killing or disabling alarming numbers of Americans, in 1990, Congress finally took a harder look at the industry and its propensity to make drug-like claims outside the reach of the FDA. After two years of investigations, an FDA task force recommended that many supplements with supposed therapeutic powers should be placed under the agency's control and that the FDA should test the products' health and curative claims before they could go to market. The 1991 proposal would hold vitamins, minerals, and herbs to the same standards as other FDA-regulated medicines.

Threatened by accountability, the supplement industry had a fit. When you traffic in snake oil, the last thing you want is a federal chemist testing the purity and efficacy of your potion. With the dietary supplement industry and the lawmakers on its payroll spinning the FDA proposal as an example of jackbooted federal forces trampling sacred constitutional rights, retailers urged customers to tell Congress to halt the looming clampdown on American freedoms. Health food store handouts warned customers, "Write to Congress today or kiss your supplements goodbye!" Stores kept notepads on display for customers to jot angry missives to their representatives.[18]

Longtime Utah senator Orrin Hatch managed to put a moratorium on the proposed FDA regulations until March 1993. A Mormon raised on Joseph Smith's scriptures, Hatch had sold vitamins as a boy and claimed he used them every day. Utah's supplement industry leaders were reliable contributors to Hatch's election coffers, and the stalling tactic bought time for Hatch to introduce a law that protected the supplement industry from FDA busybodies. The law was called the Dietary Supplement Health and Education Act (DSHEA). Hatch pressed his case for this supplement-industry protection act in a series of congressional hearings in July and October 1993. In July, he told a House of Representatives subcommittee that just as the FDA does not prohibit people from eating foods that are high in fat, cholesterol, or sugar, "so it should not attempt to impose unreasonable and unnecessary regulations on dietary supplements that many consumers want."[19]

Aligning himself with the 100 million Americans he claimed also used supplements, at an October 21, 1993, hearing Hatch testified that he had personal skin in the game. "I really believe in them," he said. "They make me feel better, as they make millions of Americans feel better. And I hope they give me that little added edge as we work around here."[20]

Reaching to herbs and vitamins framed Hatch as a traditionalist, a regular family-values guy following in the footsteps of his Mormon ancestors. "For 4,000 years, nutritional supplements have complemented the daily diet," he stated. And that was a heritage worth saving, a legacy of benefits "passed down from generation to generation."[21] Even though the 36 people killed by contaminated L-tryptophan supplements had tombstones testifying otherwise, Hatch argued that supplement makers should be trusted with the "primary responsibility to self-regulate and to assure the public of the integrity of their products."[22] Further, allowing the industry to keep its own nose clean would keep the economy pumping in Utah. "The State of Utah has an important nutritional supplement industry that contributes over $700 million to the national economy," Hatch reminded his fellow lawmakers. "We must consider the adverse economic impact that burdensome regulations could have on Utah and other states."[23]

In Hatch's view, Americans did not need protection from supplement sellers; they needed safe harbor from a freedom-, health-, and industry-killing FDA. Without the DSHEA, Hatch said the FDA would "continue its life and death grip on products which have been proven to enhance public health."[24] In addition, Hatch argued at the same hearing, when it came to self-medicating with supplements, Americans were grown-ups. "I think it is time to quit treating the American consumers like we are a bunch of idiots," Hatch protested. "We are not a bunch of idiots. We can make consumer choices and we do know what we are doing."[25]

In an October 5, 1993, editorial, "The 1993 Snake Oil Protection Act," the *New York Times* blasted Hatch's ploy. The fight the supplement industry billed as a matter of protecting consumer choice was really "about the right of unscrupulous companies and individuals to maximize profits by making fraudulent claims," the paper wrote.[26] But the supplement industry was too powerful to be halted by worries over consumer protection. On October 25, 1994, President Bill Clinton signed the DSHEA into law; the industry was given a federal blessing to carry on its traditional ways.

Reflecting on the legacy of the DSHEA, in 2002, U.S. Anti-Doping Agency chief Frank Shorter said it was like building a freeway across a state, but with only "one patrolman for the entire state." With supplement manufacturers racing for market share, and with a federal law protecting them from the consequences of their claims, Shorter pointed out that plenty of supplement pushers were speeding, and a lot of athletes were getting caught for illegal substances found in the supplements, including the anabolic steroid nandrolone.[27]

From the time of Joseph Smith's medical tribulations to today, the appeal of herbal supplements lies in their so-called naturalness. Herbal medicine is attractive because the synthetic chemical pharmacopeia has such a rotten reputation. Taking supposedly "natural" supplements to heal ailments gives people a sense of agency over their health while also giving a satisfying finger to the nefarious Big Pharma forces who pay doctors to prescribe their products. Whether in 1830, 1930, or today, there is an oft-justified perception that orthodox pharmacology is rigged and does not have patients' best interests in mind; as a result, the public is drawn to self-diagnosis and the benign appeal of natural medicines.

The DSHEA became law the year that the Netscape Navigator web browser made the Internet accessible to everyone. And with the expansion of the World Wide Web in the mid-1990s, the public suddenly had at its fingertips a resource that made everyone feel like a medical expert. As Oklahoma State pharmacology professor Steven Pray wrote in the *Journal of Child Neurology* in 2012, with the web, a seeker could instantly conjure up a multithousand hit throng of homegrown solutions to any human condition, ailment, or disease.[28] The DSHEA gave supplement sellers the legal freedom they needed to supply this new world of Internet doctors.

The DSHEA locked out the FDA by formally classifying supplements as foods rather than food additives or drugs. In the United States, foods are presumed safe until they cause harm. Drugs and food additives are presumed unsafe until the manufacturer proves them harmless. It's a difference in assumed wholesomeness that allows supplement manufacturers to push products with none of the mandatory testing costs borne by the pharmaceutical industry. Because the FDA could only act against a supplement manufacturer *after* its product harmed or killed, the DSHEA effectively turned the public into the supplement makers' lab animals. As Pray put it in 2012, the "DSHEA provides that manufacturers can sell dietary supplements for virtually any medical condition without pretesting for safety on humans or animals. Patients who purchase dietary supplements take the place of the laboratory rats used in legitimate safety research."[29]

The DSHEA was in fact so artfully designed to protect Utah's "Cellulose Valley" of herbal supplement makers that they have no legal obligation to turn over adverse findings to the FDA. Unlike the pharmaceutical industry, if a supplement maker knows its products are making people sick or killing them, the manufacturer can keep that knowledge under its hat. By effectively shielding the supplement industry from lawsuits and pushing the cost of supplement quality control onto taxpayers, the burden for testing supplement safety was shifted to the FDA, an organization Hatch and other conservative lawmakers repeatedly criticized for being slow, ineffective, and clogging up America's right to healthy business and life-improving potions. Another supplement industry supporter, New Mexico congressman Bill Richardson linked this personal right to federal savings. At an October 21 hearing, Richardson stated that "the safe use of dietary supplements could save this country billions of dollars in health care costs each year if adequate information could be given to the public on labels and pamphlets and the public was allowed to make choices."[30] DSHEA supporters saved the supplement industry from oversight by assigning responsibility to a government agency, cursed that same bureaucracy as an example of overreaching big government, and then boasted about how much money the government would save when Americans supplemented themselves into good health.

As for the notion that supplementation saves health care dollars, a 2015 study of the nation's emergency rooms published in the *New England Journal of Medicine* suggests that might not be the case. The study authors tracked ER visits in 63 hospitals between 2004 and 2013 and discovered that 23,005 of the visits during that time were for complications related to dietary supplements. A common cause for the emergency room visits was cardiovascular events related to weight-loss and energy products. Hospitalization was required for 2,154 of the supplement emergencies—a significant financial burden for taxpayers and supplement takers alike.[31]

Every year, Utah companies do over $7 billion worth of business selling vitamins, testosterone boosters, and herbal remedies. In the six-year election cycling leading up to 2012, some of those billions sloshed back to Hatch as $1.1 million in campaign contributions from the pharmaceutical and nutritional products industry. The senator is well compensated for protecting the industry that walks in the footsteps of Joseph Smith's advocacy for self-prescribed herbal medicine.

And because the supplement industry has served up a mislabeled or unlabeled consumer buffet of ingredients that include arsenic, radiation, pesticides, cow brains, sawdust, and the anabolic steroid nandrolone, it has a chair right next to Big Pharma in the pantheon of business sleaze. In February 2015, the New York State attorney general sent cease and desist letters to Walmart, Target, Walgreens, and GNC when analysis of supplements bought at the four retailers revealed that as many as five out of six products did not contain the herbs on their labels or contained unidentifiable substances. For instance, analysis of GNC ginkgo biloba supplements turned up asparagus, rice, and spruce, but no ginkgo biloba.[32]

THE 2002 WINTER OLYMPICS took place in Utah, and in advance of the Games, IOC medical commissioner Prince Alexandre de Mérode accused supplement makers of compromising athletes with impure root medicines. Concerned about the Olympic brand becoming tainted by the seedy supplement industry, Mérode committed the unpardonable sin of publicly accusing Senator Hatch and his home state industry of poisoning the world's finest athletes.

At a December 12, 2000, IOC athlete and Medical Commission meeting, IOC members and athletes discussed the risks inherent to supplements, both for athlete health and in terms of violating anti-doping regulations. With supplement manufacturers under little financial or legal incentive to accurately label their products, Olympic athletes could easily test positive for a substance they had no way of knowing was in a supplement. And they did. In advance of the 2002 Olympics, American bobsled team member Pavle Jovanovic was disqualified when he tested positive for traces of the steroid norandrostenedione. He blamed it on a contaminated supplement, and IOC and USOC tester Don Catlin agreed that the metabolites found in the rider's system were probably from a tainted nutrition booster.[33] Contaminated supplements were a risk not just to athlete health and eligibility but also, more importantly for the IOC, to the scandal-free shine of the Olympic brand.

At a December 2000 IOC session in Lausanne, Switzerland, Mérode singled out Hatch and American supplement manufacturers for endangering athlete health. "He is directly implicated in this affair," Mérode said of the Utah lawmaker's efforts to protect supplement manufacturers. Mérode also suggested that the United States was the biggest user and misuser of supplements.[34] WADA chairman Richard Pound also chimed in from Lausanne, criticizing the American supplement industry's "not at all reliable" product labeling. "There are tons of prohibited drugs in the middle of all that," Pound warned of the contaminated products.[35]

For Hatch, Mérode's charge was insufferable. "I am tired of this childish finger pointing," the senator grumbled from his office in Washington, D.C. "The last time I checked, neither the prince nor the athletes were experts in food and drug law."[36] Speaking to Salt Lake City's *Deseret News,* Hatch spat, "I'm offended by these jerks. The IOC does not have the privilege of making U.S. food and drug law." The senator found the European sporting administrators' paternalism and concern for public well-being particularly offensive. All the IOC should be concerned with, Hatch said, "is the impact of supplements on athletes in competition." Outside of a sporting event, the IOC had no business forwarding its opinions about "whether supplements should be sold to others," Hatch told his local newspaper. "Those jerks don't know what they are talking about."[37]

While it is best to regard the IOC's expressions of concern for athlete purity with a degree of suspicion, the constant parade of athletes testing positive for polluted supplements was a public relations nightmare, especially in the run-up to the events. Long before the commencement of the 2002 Games, elite athletes had on more than one occasion tested positive for nandrolone and other steroids and claimed that the illegal drug came from contaminated supplements. The IOC's concern was such that it funded a study to find out just how often supplements are contaminated. In 2000 and 2001, University of Cologne researchers tested 634 supplements purchased randomly in shops, online, and by phone in North America, Europe, and Australia. Of these, 14.8 percent contained steroid prohormones. The researchers found that supplements from companies that also sell prohormones are more likely to be contaminated with those same subtances.[38] Although blaming contaminated supplements is often a cheater's first line of defense, thanks in part to the regulation-free zone the DSHEA had built around supplements, many really were dirty, and the IOC and WADA were justified in taking a devoted supplement champion and protector to task, especially as his state would be hosting the Olympics in two years.

With hard proof on hand that supplements were often laced with performance-enhancing drugs, in advance of the Salt Lake City Games, the IOC sent two letters to the FDA imploring it to take steps to clean up America's dietary supplement industry. At the December Lausanne meeting, however, Mérode said that the FDA never replied.[39] The IOC also urged Olympic teams and national organizing committees not to strike sponsorship deals with American supplement companies.

I asked WADA science director Olivier Rabin how the organization deals with a country like the United States where federal law bans oversight of the production and sale of supplements. "For us, it is very simple," Rabin told me. "We list the doping agents based on three usual criteria. One, performance enhancement; two, risk to the health of the athlete; and three, potential violation of the spirit of sport. So we don't really care where the drug is going to end up." In other words, WADA's banned substance list indicates what is legal and what is not, but WADA stays out of the business of telling countries how to police their own drug and potion makers. In the United States, with the government banned from taking an aggressive approach to policing supplement makers, that puts the burden of keeping illegal stuff out of their bodies on athletes.

"We've got a high number of examples of so-called dietary supplements that are contaminated with synthetic drugs," Rabin told me. A pharmacologist and toxicologist who worked in drug development and marketing before joining WADA, Rabin believes that the high contamination rate stems from the fact that many supplements are useless. "Most of the time, natural products that are sold by these companies don't have an effect, and if they want their product to have an effect, and for people to buy these products again, they put something into it that has an effect."

Knowing they are selling a high percentage of snake oil, some supplement manufacturers add drugs to their remedies so consumers will feel the kick promised on the product label. Mixing in unlabeled steroid precursors, for example, ups the chance that customers see an improvement in their musculature and form and come back for more. According to Rabin, what makes this reality scary is that the purity of the drugs used to spike supplements is often dodgy. "Sometimes the quality of the drugs we find is very, very poor," he said. Additionally, Rabin noted that drug concentrations in laced supplements vary wildly. Sometimes "we find cases of dietary supplements that are adulterated with supra-pharmacological concentrations of drugs," he said. "The drugs that are contained in those products are even higher than pharmaceutical grade. This can only create very serious side effects." Confusing labeling is another problem. Rabin told me that if the drugs are on the label, "they are presented in such a way that it would be very, very difficult for most people to be able to identify that this is a drug of risk."

While the IOC medical commission was worried about supplements ruining athletes' careers and Olympic sponsor reputations, the USOC did not mind. In advance of the 2002 Salt Lake City Winter Olympics, the Salt Lake City Organizing Committee and its fellow benefactor, the U.S. Olympic Committee, cashed $20 million in sponsorship checks from Utah-based anti-aging-elixir sales company Nu Skin. The deal also provided for a Nu Skin subsidiary, Pharmanex, to become the exclusive Olympic licensee for supplements. That is, the deal allowed a supplement company to bless itself with Olympic symbols.[40] It was a mutual-back-scratching arrangement. American athletes got money to help with their training, and Nu Skin got to bask in the cleansing glow of Coubertin's chivalric spirit of sport.

Nu Skin's acquisition of Pharmanex had followed Hatch's deregulation of the supplement industry in 1994. The purchase added

Pharmanex's cash cow of nutritional supplements to what was then Nu Skin's portfolio of age-defying skin creams and hair-restoration tonics. Today, a 1-ounce bottle of Nu Skin's ageLOC Future Serum lotion costs more than $200. To move its expensive products, Nu Skin relies on a multilevel-marketing scheme. An important part of the Nu Skin business involves recruiting new sales agents who pony up cash to start their own Nu Skin microdistribution businesses. It's a pyramid structure in which salespeople are measured as much by their ability to bring in more salespeople (who have to purchase $1,200 starter kits) as by their ability to sell to end consumers. *Fortune* magazine reported in 2012 that these distributors are the source of much of Nu Skin's income. "To qualify for multilevel commissions, they must purchase or sell at least $100 of its merchandise every month; they and their recruits must collectively generate at least $2,000 in monthly sales," the magazine reported.[41]

In exchange for its $20 million donation to the USOC, the supplement maker became an official Olympic sponsor with the right to associate its name and products with Olympic athletic endeavor. Nu Skin even splashed Olympic symbolism—rings, torches, inspirational sporting videos—into its sales force recruiting meetings. The Nu Skin donation was part of an $840 million sponsorship program called Olympic Properties of the United States (OPUS). The advertising deals bankrolled both the Salt Lake City Games and U.S. Olympic team preparations for the 2004 Athens Summer Games. Nu Skin founder Steve Lund and his wife also personally donated $506,000 to the Salt Lake City Organizing Committee.

Salt Lake City's *Deseret News* reported on October 16, 1999, that at the previous day's 10th annual Nu Skin convention, then–Olympic organizer candidate Mitt Romney told 10,000 Nu Skin distributors that the Olympics and Nu Skin sales were both "about taking control of your life and managing your own destiny."[42] Nu Skin's $20 million donation was more than a philanthropic gesture to help Salt Lake City dig out of the financial shortfall it faced in preparing for the Games. At the sales meeting that rallied sales associates with a flame-lighting show and

Olympic sports video, Lund explained how Nu Skin now had the right to print the Olympic rings on its business cards. Although a small detail, the Olympic symbol granted legitimacy in a world wary of multilevel-marketing supplement dealers and fly-by-night supplement hustlers. "We have aligned ourselves with the Olympics because this alignment helps you do your jobs better," Lund proclaimed. Connecting Nu Skin with the Olympics would "further mainstream our brands in the business community."[43]

Speaking to a *Deseret News* reporter about the deal in 2000, one marketing expert said, "People are going to assume Nu Skin products are of Olympic caliber." Another industry observer told the paper that Nu Skin would make its $20 million investment back "in spades." With the Olympic endorsement as a counter to public relations scandals then dogging the company and the dietary supplement industry, he said, "They have just given every single one of their salespeople ammunition to make sales."[44]

Mainstreaming Nu Skin—"Olympi-cize our entire operation," in the words of a Nu Skin spokesman[45]—also meant pushing it out from under a cloud of product sales and marketing lawsuits, nearly $3 million in Federal Trade Commission fines, and a devastating 1991 exposé on the ABC news show *Nightline*. In that news program, reporter Barbara Walters asked her American audience, "Is Nu Skin nothing but a scheme promising the American dream while for many delivering only the nightmare?"[46]

When Lund's friend Mitt Romney decided to run for president a decade later, Lund used two shell companies to channel more than $2 million in donations into Romney's presidential political action committee. Nu Skin is also a longtime contributor to supplement hero Orrin Hatch. Hatch's son Scott is a supplement industry lobbyist.[47] When IOC medical commissioner Mérode warned athletes to stay away from supplements, Romney joined Hatch in defending the Utah industry from the meddlesome Belgian, arguing that Pharmanex was a model company when it came to product testing and labeling.

Today, Nu Skin promises that its products like ageLOC Future Serum and the $60-per-month ageLOC Vitality nutritional supplement will turn back time. In the words of the company's chief scientific officer Joseph Chang, the company's research has "given us a key to the preservation of youth."[48] Harkening back to French testosterone pioneer Charles-Édouard Brown-Séquard telling his audience at the Société de biologie in Paris in 1899 how injections of dog testicle juice gave him energy to bound up stairs like a man half his age, an ageLOC promotional video shows two mice aged "the equivalent of 96 years old." One mouse's diet has been supplemented with an "ageLOC Vitality Ingredient." The other rodent gets its regular diet, but no ageLOC boost. The video shows the mice in side-by-side cages. Save for the occasional twitch of an ear, the elderly mouse on the left looks one paw this side of mouse heaven. Meanwhile, the 96-year-old mouse with ageLOC coursing through its veins roots around in his bed of straw like an Olympic decathlete.[49]

Scientists raise eyebrows when they hear about such dodgy anti-aging claims. "If someone tells you they know what the mechanism of aging is, they are trying to kid you," National Institute on Aging research scientist Richard Millar told *Fortune* magazine, dismissing the ageLOC gene-transformation claims as marketing hype.[50] Both Nu Skin and Pharmanex have spent significant time in court defending themselves against, and settling fines over, charges that their products don't do what their advertising and sales agents claim. As *New York Times* reporter T. W. Farnam detailed in 2011, among Nu Skin's fines is a $1.2 million settlement with the Federal Trade Commission over bogus advertising that was later upped by another $1.5 million when Nu Skin was found violating the terms of the original settlement.[51] In 2014, the Chinese government accused Nu Skin of running a pyramid scheme and fined the company $540,000 and six employees $241,000.[52] In early 2016, the company paid $47 million to settle a class-action lawsuit related to the Chinese pyramid scheme claims.[53]

When America's Olympic athletes promoted the Nu Skin brand by wearing its logo on their clothing, they helped scrub off a little of this bad PR grime. The sponsorship granted a noble Olympic aura to a company and industry that has steadfastly resisted efforts to regulate the purity and efficacy of its products. In the interest of paying the bills and offering athletes financial support, the USOC had to pay lip service to notions of pure sports and link up with an industry with an abhorrent record of failing to go the extra mile to protect its customers. As doping historian John Hoberman explains in *Testosterone Dreams,* with the supplement industry, doping is "a matter as much of semantics as of pharmacology. From a marketing standpoint, the ideal product would combine the power of a doping drug with the comfortable familiarity of a home remedy."[54] Sponsoring Olympic athletes helped push along this semantic shift by aligning supplement products with Coubertin's enduring spirit of youthful restoration through sports. Indeed, Coubertin's vision of the Olympics as a revitalizer of body and spirit, as something that delivers "a delicate balance of mind and body, the joy of a fresher and more intense life, the harmony of the faculties, calm and happy strength," could well stand in as a Nu Skin marketing promise.[55]

When the USOC accepted $20 million from Nu Skin, it was a work of legerdemain showing that, as Hoberman put it, "some sports officials are perfectly willing to encourage athletes to stuff themselves with chemicals if this practice can be presented as an alternative to what is officially defined as doping."[56] Enlisting American athletes as TV pitchmen for Nu Skin demonstrated the U.S. Olympic movement's reluctance to spit in the financially nourishing but ethically curdled soup of supplement industry support.

In 2011, a team of British medical researchers found that athletes who consume nutritional supplements are three and a half times more likely to also use performance-enhancing drugs than athletes who avoid supplements. Additionally, the researchers found that supplement-using athletes have a more positive attitude toward performance-enhancing pharmaceuticals and are more willing to believe that those substances will improve their performance. According to the research, supplements seem to smooth the transition from legal herbal aids to illegal performance-enhancing drugs while also priming young athletes to experiment with doping drugs.[57]

Other research shows that amateur athletes take doping behavior cues from professionals and Olympians who make supplements part of their performance-enhancement regime. In 2012, a team of George Washington University social scientists found that when athletes make the decision to take potentially harmful drugs like anabolic steroids, the choice is not the studied result of careful deliberation about doping's health risks. Instead, the researchers found that athletes use intellectual short cuts—a *heuristic,* in academic jargon—when deciding to dope. A heuristic is a rule of thumb drawn from previous experiences that helps us make quick decisions in the face of ambiguity. In the case of doping, in their study published in the *Journal of Health Psychology,* the researchers found that when athletes debated whether legal or illegal drugs were more powerful, the athletes' rule of thumb was if it's illegal, it must be better.

This study did not assess whether illegal drugs *actually* made an athlete perform better than when on legal nutritional supplements. It evaluated what athletes *think* is more effective and how that conclusion might affect their willingness to dope. The study surveyed 132 randomly identified male NCAA and summer competitive league collegiate players from sports including tennis, basketball, swimming, soccer, golf, diving and lacrosse. Of these, 75 percent reported having used legal performance-enhancing substances during their lives—for example, protein powders or creatine. None admitted to having used illegal performance-enhancing drugs.

Results showed that a belief that illegal drugs are more effective than legal drugs was a strong predictor of an athlete's personal willingness to dope. In other words, news reports of pro athletes being busted for doping convinced collegiate athletes that illegal drugs must be better than the stuff available at the local GNC. Why? Athletes concluded that even if the IOC and WADA had strongly warned athletes away from dietary supplements, if pros were willing to risk their careers to use these and stronger products, then the stuff must make a big difference. "We call this the illegal-is-effective heuristic," the researchers concluded.[58]

And so, with the U.S. Olympic athletes proudly displaying the Nu Skin logo, youngsters and oldsters around the world got the message that in spite of the constant barrage of stories regarding the danger of taking supplements, they must be worth it. After all, if the best in the world were using them, shouldn't everyone?

CHAPTER 17

CHARLIE FRANCIS: TAKE IT TO MAKE IT

With a nutritional supplement company underwriting the 2002 and 2004 U.S. Olympic teams, the United States Olympic Committee signaled that supplements were not only ethically acceptable in elite sports but essential to Olympic performance. In the track and field events, the requirement for supplemental assistance went beyond herbs and botanicals. There—especially in the sprint disciplines—doping was mandatory to be competitive. Just saying no to drugs was saying no to your career.

In the 1980s, track coach Charlie Francis built a Canadian national track program whose success far exceeded its nominal budget. Francis died in 2010, but his 1990 book, *Speed Trap*, recounts his years coaching Olympic stars Ben Johnson and Angella Issajenko. The book is a nonjudgmental account of how drugs were essential not only to Olympic-level track and field sports medicine, but an expression of the true spirit of sport—pushing human performance where it had never gone before.

Francis attended Stanford on a track scholarship and competed for the Canadian Olympic team at the 1972 Munich Olympics. He first mixed drugs with sports while a Stanford junior in 1970. Having heard that amphetamines could help delay fatigue—something Francis dreaded in an upcoming 440-yard event—the 22-year-old from Toronto decided to try amphetamines. This was in the San Francisco Bay Area in 1970, during the height of an American love affair with amphetamines that would not be surpassed until today's ADHD explosion. Francis recalled that "the drugs weren't exactly scarce at Stanford, where every dorm light would be blazing at 5:00 a.m. during exam week." His experiments with Dexedrine did not lead to athletic success. "If you're not prepared by your training," he concluded, "*nothing* will help you."[1] Francis's initial experience with speed taught him that the notion of drugs turning a donkey into a thoroughbred was a myth.

In Munich, Francis was impressed by the level of support backing the European track teams from both sides of the Iron Curtain. He recalls seeing Soviet 100-meter star Valeriy Borzov, an eventual double gold medalist, come to the track with an entourage. Five people busied themselves adjusting Borzov's blocks and attending "to his every need." Watching the communist teams go about their business in Munich showed Francis that peak performance enhancement was the product of a systematic support system with many interrelated people, parts, and sciences.

Munich also taught Francis that the Eastern Bloc athletes did not have a monopoly on pharmaceutical Olympic-performance enhancement. He recalls American discus thrower Jay Silvester passing a Munich dorm room and asking New Zealand discus thrower Robin Tait, "Hey, Robin, you got any spare Dianabol? I'm out." Silvester went on to take silver in Munich. Steroids were legal at the time, so there was nothing untoward in the exchange. Francis was impressed by both the apparent effectiveness of the drugs for track athletes and the casualness with which international athletes used them. "During my two weeks in Munich, I heard story after story about names and cases—many of them big names, including Olympic champions. I learned that steroids were especially helpful for sprinters in major competitions, to surmount the physical stress of multiple rounds of heats."[2]

Canada's Olympic organizing body was frugal. Unlike other countries, the Canadian authorities stuck to their guns about enforcing athletes' amateur status. This commitment to Pierre de Coubertin's values hamstrung the Canadian athletes by forcing them to hold on to jobs while training for international competitions. Looking for every possible way to stay on par with the world's best athletes, in 1973, Francis read up on the effect of steroids on athletic performance. He decided to make the synthetic hormone part of his personal training regime for the upcoming Canadian national games. Francis's family doctor prescribed Dianabol. Francis recounted that, when combined with increased training loads under the then-novel periodization training methods introduced by Canada's recently hired Polish coach, Gerard Mach, the steroids made a difference. Francis felt stronger, less fatigued, and able to push himself further. He also saw his mood lift. "Subjectively I felt cheerful and positive," he recalled.[3] Although he was only a part-time athlete, Francis won at nationals.

As Francis recalls, doping was an accepted part of a far more professional, data-attentive, and detail-oriented European approach to training than that followed by the North Americans. As Francis recounts, Canadian track and field athletes labored "in a chronic state of nervous system exhaustion."[4] While Canadian coaches would run athletes into the ground, Mach understood that to expand an athlete's performance load, he had to stress him by alternately increasing and reducing workloads and shifting stresses between muscular and aerobic systems. Although periodization is a training norm today, in the early 1970s, it was novel, mainly because it was being perfected in secret by the East German and Soviet sports programs. Canadians and Americans picked up information on periodization and interval training in dribs and drabs, usually at international meets. Impressed by the effectiveness of the communist training methods, when Francis became a coach, he demanded that his own athletes combine high-intensity efforts with lower-intensity recovery workouts.

In 1973, the year the San Diego Chargers hired psychiatrist Arnold Mandell to help team players with their mental game, Francis recalled that many Canadian coaches were smitten with sports psychology and even hypnosis. Coach Mach was not among them. "Preparation is number one, number two, number three, number four, number five, number six," the old-school coach was fond of saying. "When you get to number 97, we'll talk about psychology."[5] Francis saw Eastern Bloc training infrastructure firsthand when Mach took his Canadian charges to the Polish national training center in Warsaw. Francis was impressed that the stadium designers had built the athlete dorms underneath the stadium so they were convenient for access to the field; it exemplified how a holistic, systematic approach to performance enhancement should control as many variables as possible, letting the athletes focus entirely on their events.

Attention to competitor needs carried on through day-to-day life as well. Francis recalled that at one point, the Canadians grew tired of drinking mineral water at all their meals. Mach made a phone call and 80 cases of Coca-Cola showed up to diversify the training table. Whether it be organizing travel visas, designing periodized training plans, or delivering soft drinks, "In Poland, bureaucrats had been assigned to fulfill his wishes, rather than impede them," Francis marveled. The Polish athletes Francis met on this trip joked about their steroid use, yet, Francis writes, they all understood that "drugs were an essential part of the game."[6]

In 1976, Francis began coaching the Scarborough Optimists track club in Toronto. It was also the year Canada embarrassed itself by not winning a single gold medal at its own outrageously costly Summer Games in Montreal. The following year, a 15-year-old Jamaican immigrant began showing up at Francis's workouts, shod in high-top basketball shoes. The neophyte's name was Ben Johnson.

By 1979, Francis was coaching Johnson and another talented sprinter, Angella Issajenko, on the Canadian national team. Doping, while nominally illegal since 1975, was still considered essential for any athlete who wanted to take a step onto the podium. While Issajenko was making steady progress in her training, Francis concluded that she would need to incorporate steroids into her program if she was going to be competitive at the 1980 Moscow Olympics. "Angella wasn't losing ground because of a talent gap," Francis recalls. "She was losing because of a drug gap, and it was widening by the day. . . . I arrived at a central premise which would guide my counsel for Angella, as well as for Ben and my other top male sprinters when they reached a similar crossroads: An athlete could not expect to win in top international competitions without using anabolic steroids."[7]

Francis approached the high-performance problem pragmatically. Rather than putting his "head in the sand while his athletes fell behind," he reached for drugs, which had become "an essential supplement at the world-class level, an indispensable ingredient within a complex recipe."[8] In terms of the safety of his athletes, Francis, like the Chargers' Mandell, argued that without coach and doctor oversight, athletes would put themselves into greater danger by self-medicating and by obtaining drugs from street dealers. At a national coaches meeting in July 1979, Doug Clement, the head doctor for Canadian track and field's governing body, stated the prevailing opinion that the side effects of small doses of anabolic steroids were no more dangerous than birth control pills. While Clement was against drugs because he felt they imbalanced the playing field, Francis recalled Clement also admitting that some of his colleagues in other countries attended anti-doping conferences to learn how to help their athletes avoid drug positives.[9]

Issajenko's personal physician prescribed Dianabol, in part to treat anemia. Francis's athletes were taking far lower doses than weight lifters. He cited a male power lifter who was taking 135,000 milligrams of steroids per year. In comparison, Issajenko took 700 milligrams for her combined indoor and outdoor seasons. Her yearlong dose was equal to what a weight lifter stacking multiple steroids and testosterone might take in two days. Despite the modest dosages, the addition of steroids to Issajenko's interval training worked; her times progressed steadily. However, Canada decided to go along with the U.S. boycott of the Moscow Olympics, and Issajenko could not compete for gold in 1980. Nonetheless, in February of that year, she broke the 200-meter world record.

Four years later, the size and power of the East German athletes preparing for the Los Angeles Olympics astonished Francis. He recalls 6-foot 6-inch, 330-pound, 1976 gold medal shot-putter Udo Beyer squatting 855 pounds without effort, and a 130-pound javelin thrower doing 205-pound snatch lifts. The East German doping regime had put the German athletes far outside the boundaries of normal human performance; Francis described one of their javelin throwers tossing a spear so far it sailed outside the javelin field and into the high jump pit, where athletes scrambled to avoid being impaled. "Out of respect for the drug-linked progress in this event, and to protect athletes and spectators alike, the IAAF later modified the javelin so that it would nose-dive, shaving about 50 feet off the throwers' range," he recalled.[10]

The year before the 1984 Los Angeles Games, Francis noted that drug regimes were becoming more complicated. He took Issajenko to Dr. George "Jamie" Astaphan, a doctor trained at the University of Toronto, who, while inexperienced with sports pharmacy, promised to help the coach and athlete sort out the use of a new generation of drugs athletes were turning to in part to stay ahead of dope tests. Another doctor who worked with the U.S. Olympic team, Los Angeles–based Dr. Robert Kerr, suggested Issajenko take the steroid Anavar rather than Dianabol because it was more effective for women.[11] In 1982, Kerr published a book whose title captured his attitude toward doping in sport: *The Practical Use of Anabolic Steroids with Athletes*. Kerr believed that since he could not stop the use of nonprescription drugs, it was better for athletes to take steroids under close medical supervision than to freelance on their own. Along with steroids, Kerr prescribed a relatively new discovery, human growth hormone—an injected drug originally developed to treat dwarfism. The Los Angeles doctor also recommended the synthetic amino acid levodopa, also know as L-dopa, for Issajenko's training cocktail.

Astaphan went along with Kerr's suggestions but later made a few tweaks, replacing the L-dopa with another drug used to treat high blood pressure. He also suggested vitamin B13 injections and injections of aqueous testosterone. "He obtained all of these for us and never billed us in full, as he knew that our means were limited," Francis wrote.[12] In sum, the doctors worked together with coach and athlete to create a doping program that floated in a gray area of technical legality, but within the bounds of what was normal and expected for an athlete to be competitive at the world-record level.

After learning that a group of American female track athletes were using three times the level of Issajenko's steroid and growth hormone dosages, Francis explained that the Canadian team was "conservative by U.S. standards." Indeed, the United States Olympic Committee had created its drug-testing lab at UCLA to help American athletes dope to the last possible minute, then ensure that the drugs were out of their systems before any event-day tests. "In Los Angeles," Francis wrote, "American athletes would come into the Olympic Games at their drug-supported best."[13] The preemptive drug screening worked; no U.S. athletes tested positive at the 1984 Games, and the Americans thumped the medal count, taking 83 gold medals to Romania's runner-up total of 20.

Commenting on the difference between athletes who used drugs to enhance performance and those who didn't, Francis wrote that his track athletes chose to dope because they understood the truth in the motto "If you don't take it, you won't make it." In cultures like track and field and pro cycling, where drugs were part of the overall training equation, not taking them compromised the very performance-enhancing values that put athletes at the top of their game. The pro cyclist who didn't take drugs in 1998 was also the cyclist who didn't give up the comforts of home in the United States or Australia and who didn't sacrifice the security of a college career to chase a dream.

Francis came to understand that to enter the rarified ranks of the world's elite required a refusal to compromise—this was the true spirit of sport. Those who chose not to dope, Francis argued, "tend to be the same people who are unwilling to leave a school or a job for full-time training, or move away from friends and family to find the best possible coach, or make the myriad other sacrifices that go into becoming a world-class athlete. They may be healthier, more well-rounded individuals for their concessions, but they will not reach the top. The best athletes, for better or worse, are the most single-minded ones."[14]

Francis's belief in the necessity of uncompromising dedication at the Olympic gold medal level also applies in pro cycling. From the time a rider gets up in the morning and weighs himself on a scale to the moment he flops down on a massage table after six hours on a bike, the pro cyclist's life is stripped bare of the accoutrements of civilization most of us consider normal. And that is by design. The job is singular; when not preparing to race, the riders are racing. Everything else is a distraction. Their obsession with their sport is total, uncompromising. And it has to be that way because their competitors are just as obsessed. In a culture where doping was considered a key component of the winning lifestyle, taking it out of the picture would be, for many, an unacceptable compromise of the very values that put them on the road to a professional sports career.

Reflecting on his own path to doping, British pro cyclist David Millar writes in his autobiography that it would have been illogical not to dope. "In the context of my development, I had acted normally," Millar says in *Racing Through the Dark*. "I relied heavily on other people guiding me and had been let down by the people around me, particularly my team. It would have been out of the ordinary, unusual for me to have not made the mistakes I'd made. So, in conclusion, I was normal . . . and I had always thought I was different."[15]

Similarly, Tyler Hamilton writes that after doping became part of his professional norm, he didn't worry about it. Unlike his U.S. Postal Service teammate Jonathan Vaughters, who constantly fretted over why riders had to dope, why the UCI didn't enforce the rules, and whether the police would show up, guilt for Hamilton became an emotion "most of us had given up long ago."[16]

Hamilton goes on to note that his decision to start doping about 1,000 days into his pro cycling career was not about "honor or character." He had seen good people dope and bad people ride clean. Instead, the decision to dope was the cumulative effect of "a thousand days of getting signals that doping is okay, signals from powerful people you trust and admire, signals that say *It'll be fine* and *Everybody's doing it.* And beneath all that, the fear that if you don't find some way to ride faster, then your career is over."[17]

Hamilton expresses the paradox of pro sports as it shudders through the shock of being subjected to a new moral absolutism about the corruptive influence of nonprescribed drugs. The reality Hamilton describes facing in 1997 is no different than the one the president of the American College of Sports Medicine described in a September 12, 1960, letter to the *New York Times.* Dr. Albert Salisbury Hyman explained to *Times* readers that for professional athletes, taking drugs was an economic decision, not one of ethics.

"The professional athlete has a job to do which may be his sole livelihood," Hyman wrote. "Under such conditions it is an accepted fact that he may employ any means which will permit him to achieve his best possible physical performance. The calculated risks of these means are a recognized part of the inherent occupational hazard of any given professional sport."[18]

That neither Hamilton nor Francis suffered any particular doping guilt isn't evidence of a perverted moral character. Instead, it points to the fact that pro cyclists, like track and field athletes Johnson and Issajenko, had long inhabited a moral space where work drugs were not just overlooked, but expected as a component of professional behavior.

CHAPTER 18

DSHEA, STEROIDS, AND BASEBALL'S SALVATION

Nineteen ninety-three was a terrific year for Major League Baseball (MLB). The National League added teams in Denver and Miami. The World Series stretched to six games, with the Toronto Blue Jays dramatically repeating as World Series champions when Joe Carter stroked a three-run walk-off dinger in the ninth to seal the victory over the Philadelphia Phillies. Ballpark attendance swelled to record levels, with 70 million fans in the seats, up from 55 million the year before. New stadiums were in development in Texas, Colorado, and Cleveland. Things in baseball were good.

And then in 1994, it all came crashing down. A money spat between players and team owners saw the players walk out in August. The 1994 World Series was canceled. America's major league stadiums gathered dust and lost money for 232 days. When the strike ended in April 1995, the players returned, but America did not. Feeling betrayed by the walkout, fans avoided the nation's ballparks. Attendance sagged, TV ratings dropped, and merchandise sales lagged. Major League Baseball was dying. To get butts in the seats, baseball needed spectacle. It needed excitement. It needed home runs, and lots of them.

Blasting a baseball over an outfield wall requires finesse and form, of course, but most of what puts a ball into the seats comes from muscle power. And yet tradition-bound baseball had mostly shunned the sort of brawn building that it takes to swat a white pill 400 feet. Like football players in the 1950s and 1960s, MLB players and coaches thought weight lifting would bind athletes with bulging musculature and impede batting and running speed. Hustle and flexibility were a hitter's cherished assets. Barbell-shunning sluggers like Hank Aaron and the willowy Ted Williams believed powerful hitting began and ended with quick wrists. Aaron, the first to break Babe Ruth's home run record, weighed about 185 pounds. The 1970s star said in 2002 that "I didn't have much power in my upper body, but my forearms were big and that allowed me to use a big bat." Aaron's weight training consisted of squeezing a grip machine to build forearm strength. But teams fined players who were caught lifting.[1]

Thanks in no small part to the success of an Oakland Athletics slugger named Jose Canseco, that gym phobia began to melt in the mid-1980s. As a 19-year-old in 1983, Canseco bucked tradition and dedicated himself to weight-room workouts. Then playing for the A's farm team, the scrawny 6-foot 3-inch, 185-pound Cuban believed putting more power into his swing would help him make the big leagues. By 1985, twice-daily lifting sessions and steroid-assisted recovery saw Canseco bulk up to 230 pounds. His performances swelled, too. Seeing Canseco's success, other A's players soon hit the weight room as well.

The A's called up Canseco to the Show in 1985. The following year, he won the AL Rookie of the Year award. In 1988, Canseco's .307 batting average, 124 RBIs, and 42 home runs won him the league's MVP award and helped the A's win the division title and go to the World Series. Committed weight training, anabolic steroids, and DSHEA-blessed testosterone-precursor supplements like androstenedione helped transform Canseco into an enhanced performer whose $4.7 million contract made him the highest-paid player in the game.[2] As journalist Howard Bryant wrote in his 2006 book, *Juicing the Game*, Canseco understood how drugs could augment an already talented player's natural performances. "He knew that anabolic steroids helped him burst better toward second," Bryant wrote of Canseco, who stole 40 bases in 1988. "He knew they gave him the kind of power a hitter needed to be a 40-homer player."[3]

Canseco's 40 bases and 40 home runs that year provided vivid proof that steroids enhanced performance in quantifiable ways. The A's won four division titles between 1988 and 1992 and made three World Series. *Baseball Weekly* scribe Pete Williams described the 1989 World Series champion Athletics as "a forearm-bashing, swaggering advertisement for weightlifting."[4] By the time the strike was over in 1995, players like Canseco and bulked-up teams like the A's had established themselves as proof that drug-powered players could bring spectacle to baseball at the very time the sport was scrambling to reclaim its fans.

In 1996, Baltimore Orioles slugger Brady Anderson combined the supplement creatine with lots of power lifting. Creatine, along with the steroid precursor androstenedione, was a cornerstone of the multibillion-dollar supplement industry. A naturally produced organic amino acid that increases the body's creation of adenosine triphosphate (ATP), creatine helps the body recover from workouts and reportedly can also increase quickness. For baseball players grinding through grueling schedules that had them playing consecutive games on the road for weeks at a time, it was a godsend. To obtain a typical daily dose of 20 grams of creatine naturally, you would have to eat 15 to 20 pounds of meat. Supplements allowed players to get that amount by mixing bubble-gum-flavored creatine powder into a glass of water. Along with androstenedione, creatine was only as far away as the nearest Walmart. Fueled by dedicated weight lifting and creatine to help with recovery, in 1996, Anderson swatted 12 lead-off home runs in 12 consecutive games. Thrilled fans elected him to the All-Star team.

Five years earlier, scouts would not have seen this potential in Anderson. A lackluster performer, the graduate of Southern California's Carlsbad High School had just been demoted from the Baltimore Orioles to the minor leagues. Stunned by his fall from the bigs, Anderson rejected the conventional bulk-is-bad wisdom and started a hard-core weight program. Anderson's physique transformed. Called back to the Orioles in 1992, his newfound power delivered performances that fans—and by extension, team owners—adored. Anderson smacked 21 home runs for the year—double the 10 home runs he hit in the previous four years.

Anderson's transformation helped change baseball and the American public's collective opinion about weight lifting, muscle-bound players, and supplements like creatine and androstenedione. Other players also took notice of the financial windfall that came with Anderson's hard work and chiseled look: his salary increased from $35,000 in 1992 to $1.8 million in 1993 and grew to $7.2 million in 2001, his last full year in the sport.

Although Anderson claimed he never took anabolic steroids, his open use of creatine emphasized a vivid causal relationship between chemicals and marvelous sporting returns. The success of speedy sluggers like Anderson also influenced older players who entered the game in an era when players could be fined for lifting. "I'm going to take all the natural, legal supplements that I can to get this 36-year-old body around the bases," Phillies veteran Rex Hudler told *Baseball Weekly*'s Williams in 1997.[5] First drafted by the New York Yankees in 1978, Hudler added, "I'm not going to take something illegal that might hurt or kill me. But technology has come a long way with what can be done naturally. That's why guys are a little stronger and a little faster." Stronger indeed. The cover of the May 7, 1997, *Baseball Weekly* featured Popeye-muscled San Diego Padre third baseman and 1996 National League MVP Ken Caminiti breaking a bat in half under the headline "PUMPED!"

Weight rooms became standard issue in the smaller, home run–friendly stadiums being built at the time. And their clubhouses played the role of supplement distribution centers. Williams describes Saint Louis Cardinals coach Dave McKay stocking locker rooms with supplements with names like Met Max, Lean Gainer, and Power Creatine. "The old thinking was that there was no place for weights in baseball,"

McKay recalled. But by the mid-1990s, "At least half the team's position players consume the products as routinely as sunflower seeds and chewing gum," Williams wrote. Players were walking endorsements for the supplements. "It's the best product on the market today," A's slugger Mark McGwire gushed about Power Creatine, the product from supplement maker Champion Nutrition. *Baseball Weekly* subscribers might have been excused for thinking they were reading an advertisement, not a reporting piece, when McGwire told Williams, "It helps with strength and endurance and not just with weightlifting. The results have just been outstanding. I wish I had started taking it sooner."

So how did players like McGwire, Canseco, and Anderson get away with openly taking and promoting supplements that were, in the case of androstenedione, steroid precursor compounds that Penn State steroid expert Dr. Charles Yesalis identified as belonging to the anabolic-androgenic steroid class of drugs?[6] After all, by 1988, androstenedione, or andro, had been banned by WADA, the NFL, and the IOC. However, it was not banned by MLB, nor was it federally classified as an anabolic steroid. To understand this loophole, we have to go back to the passage of the Anabolic Steroids Control Act in 1990 and two key events that immediately preceded it.

In December 1988, Yesalis and a team of co-researchers published the results of a survey of performance-enhancing drug use among 3,406 12th graders at 46 public and private high schools across the United States. The findings, published in *JAMA: The Journal of the American Medical Association,* reported that 6.6 percent of surveyed students said they had used anabolic steroids. Two-thirds started using at age 16 or younger, and 21 percent reported that they got their drugs through a perfectly legal channel—the family doctor.[7]

At about the same time, anabolic-androgenic steroids hit the headlines big time when Canadian sprinter Ben Johnson was busted for using the drug at the 1988 Seoul Olympics. The Canadian government commissioned an inquiry into doping in Canadian sports, and the 600-page result, the Dubin Inquiry report, massed testimony from 122 witnesses and 48 steroid users that showed that anabolic-androgenic steroid use was chronic in Olympic sports.

News of the bust of the fastest man on Earth, coupled with publication of data on high school performance-enhancing drug use in one of the world's most prestigious medical journals, created what Yesalis called "a perfect storm." From his Penn State office, Yesalis told me that in the days following Johnson's positive test, reporters could not get enough of the steroid scandal. "I gave 200 major interviews in a month," Yesalis marveled. "I was on the front page of every newspaper in the country." Yesalis said the public and legislators didn't like hearing that their kids were using the same drugs that took down an Olympic hero. The situation was too awkward for U.S. lawmakers to ignore, and that prevailing emotion spurred political action.

Until this point, anabolic-androgenic steroids were nominally illegal; their use was not explicitly prohibited by the Controlled Substances Act, but technically they could only be taken with a doctor's prescription. In preparation for a new bill that would add steroids to the schedules of DEA-controlled substances that had been created with 1970's Controlled Substances Act, Congress held two years of hearings on what was being presented as a silent threat to America's youth. Testifying before Delaware senator Joseph Biden on April 3, 1989, Olympian and U.S. track and field coach Pat Connolly described the rise in steroid use during her three decades in the sport. Connolly told Biden that 30 to 40 percent of the women on the 1984 and 1988 U.S. Olympic track teams used steroids in training. She also informed the senator that the problem was not just a matter of morally weak individual athletes, reminding him that his own government's sanctioning body, the U.S. Olympic Committee, had established a drug-testing program in advance of the 1984 Los Angeles Games to help American athletes "find better ways to keep from being detected by official testing." Another athlete, 28-year-old sprinter Diane Williams, told Biden that years of steroid use had left her with debilitating side effects such as depression, facial hair, and a deeper voice.[8]

In testimony on the pending legislation, California congressman Mel Levine gave the hormone drug the weight of a moral panic when he described steroid use as an American "plague." Citing Yesalis's finding that 20 percent of high school steroid users got the drugs from their doctors, Levine argued that the "quiet drug epidemic raging among our young people" needed to be addressed by sending a message that "steroids are dangerous drugs and that it is unacceptable to prescribe them for non-therapeutic purposes." Using steroids in sports was cheating, Levine said. And when it came at the hands of high school and junior high coaches, "it is a betrayal of the trust that the athletes have placed in their coaches."[9]

In a separate statement at the same hearings, Leslie Southwick, deputy assistant to the U.S. attorney general, explained that steroids had not been regulated like other drugs because they did not fit the mold of recreational drugs that drag down national productivity or threaten moral order. Although the Department of Justice had been investigating illegal steroid trafficking since 1985, Southwick testified that there was little momentum to get the drugs on the controlled substances list because "anabolic steroids are not taken to get 'high' or to 'escape from reality,' but to enhance physical performance and to improve physical appearance."

Until 1988, apart from the 1938 law stating that prescription drugs could not be handed out without a doctor's order for the treatment of a disease, there were no federal guidelines specifying which steroids were prohibited and under what circumstances. In 1988, two years before Southwick testified, as part of a larger bill targeting the crack cocaine epidemic, an amendment to the Federal Food, Drug, and Cosmetic Act made it a federal crime to distribute steroids without a physician's order to treat a disease, but the emphasis was on busting drug traffickers, not users.[10] Lacking evidence that steroids had the psychoactive effects of other banned drugs like cocaine and heroin, Southwick pointed out that the government had little data to justify or motivate the singling out of steroids as a moral and social threat like other banned recreational drugs.* She explained that since 1985, the Department of Justice had dedicated over 22,000 attorney hours prosecuting some 150 steroid cases, but under statutes such as mail fraud, international smuggling, wire fraud, and criminal conspiracy—not for violations involving the use of a controlled substance. The Anabolic Steroids Control Act of 1990 would change all that, criminalizing steroids on both the supply and demand sides.

Perhaps knowing that emotion and fear are a more powerful law-making locomotive than logic, Southwick said steroids were a moral threat. "Setting aside the question of whether the scheduling of anabolic steroids is appropriate," she stated—deftly deferring to scientists the assessment of health risks—the attorney general's office supported jailing steroid-pushing coaches and trainers because there was ethical cause. "The desire and hope to excel in sport" is a basic American value, she said. And those who "pervert" that American way "with the promise of instant athletic prowess to be obtained from an injection, deserve criminal punishment." Elsewhere, Southwick doubled down on the theme of steroids as a moral travesty, stating that the drugs threatened children and led to a "perversion of a valued tradition in our country whereby excellence in sports is determined by personal effort and achievement, not chemical enhancement."[11]

After two years of hearings and more research revealing alarming steroid use in high schools and colleges, Yesalis said, "Virtually every state in the union passed a law about the non-prescription use of anabolic steroids." The 1990 law reclassified steroids and human growth hormones as Schedule III controlled substances, lumping them in with the same "hard drugs" Nixon declared war against in the 1970s. Join-

---

* In its eagerness to make a show of concern, Congress ruled steroids controlled substances without going through a required vetting process involving the attorney general and the U.S. Department of Health and Human Services. Because lawmakers skipped the formal evaluation of the steroids' safety and potential for abuse, in 1988 the American Medical Association protested the intrusion of political points-making into the controlled substances list. See Carol Cole Kleinman and C. E. Petit, "Legal Aspects of Anabolic Steroid Use and Abuse," in *Anabolic Steroids in Sport and Exercise,* 2nd ed., ed. Charles E. Yesalis (Champaign, IL: Human Kinetics, 2000), 344–345.

ing the Schedule III drug club as number 15 on the list of 25 substances was methandrostenolone. Some 32 years after Ciba Pharmaceuticals had marketed that chemical under the name Dianabol and U.S. weight lifting coach John Ziegler had encouraged his young American athletes to take it to prepare for battle against the Soviets, the steroid was officially unwelcome at the sporting training table.

The Anabolic Steroids Control Act of 1990 also criminalized the distribution of steroids by coaches, imposing sentences of up to five years in jail for individuals who "endeavor to persuade or induce" others to use the substances.[12] President George H. W. Bush made it clear that cracking down on steroid pushers was meant to appeal to the same sort of social anxieties that Nixon cited in the 1960s. The steroids law was part of the larger Comprehensive Crime Control Act of 1990 that also created drug- and gun-free school zones.

Upon signing the bill into law on November 29, 1990, Bush said, "The American people deserve tough new laws to help us prevail in the fight against drugs and crime." Criminalizing the use and distribution of drugs like steroids would grant Americans their "right to be free from fear in their homes, in their streets, and in their neighborhoods," he said.[13] In the 1950s, society's collective dread over evil communist infiltrators finding their way across U.S. borders fueled the promotion of steroids. Three decades later, social anxieties about crack-using deviants already inside the nation were used to ban those same drugs.

As for the drug companies manufacturing the time-tested steroids, Yesalis said, "It was very obvious to myself and the people I was working with and the feds that anabolic steroids were being diverted from the legitimate distribution cycle." But, he added, "The drug companies didn't really care." The amount of steroids being made by drug companies far exceeded the therapeutic medical demand. "They were making way more than you could ever need for medical conditions," Yesalis explained. It was the story of amphetamines all over again. Although researchers found no evidence that drug companies were selling directly into the black market, pharmaceutical companies were averting their gaze as the medical community wrote unneeded prescriptions to meet amateur athlete demand. "Things were going out the back door in a black market way," Yesalis told me.

The genesis of 1990's Anabolic Steroids Control Act is important to the story of bulked-up baseball players in the late 1980s and the 1990s for two reasons. For players incorporating steroids into their weight training regime in the 1980s, there was little criminal risk in using steroids—none if they had a team doctor's order for them. As for baseball's internal regulations, MLB drug policy simply demanded player compliance with federal drug law. The MLB would not specifically prohibit steroids until 1991—and since the Major League Baseball Players Association did not agree to the ban, that directive only applied to minor league players. It was not until 2002 that the union accepted the steroid prohibition and made it part of the formal collective bargaining agreement.[14]

An exhaustive 2007 investigation into doping in baseball led by former U.S. senator George Mitchell, the *Mitchell Report*, revealed that before 2002, few players were aware that baseball even had a policy regulating the use or possession of steroids.[15] And so during the years when weight lifting caught fire in baseball, there were few explicitly legal prohibitions against a sports medicine that perfectly suited the game's new style of explosive power play.

During Canseco's 1985 rookie year and through the 1988, 1989, and 1990 seasons when the Oakland Athletics were destroying old weight lifting shibboleths by winning three league titles and a World Series, steroids were not explicitly prohibited inside or outside baseball. Until 1990, it was inevitable that they would become an accompaniment to the hours that players were spending in the weight room—especially when they led to financial reward for players and team owners alike. In 2007, Cincinnati Reds All-Star pitcher Jack Armstrong told the *New York Daily News* that during his era, 1988 to 1994, 20 to 30 percent of players were "juicing in a big way." In Armstrong's opinion, 60 to 80 percent of his colleagues were using steroids in lower doses to maintain "enough of an edge to keep the oversized paychecks coming."[16] Of course, that does not mean the doping players got a free ride. When Canseco came to bat against the Red Sox in the 1998 American League championships, Fenway Park fans jeered "Steroids! Steroids!" The next night the Bostonians chanted, "Just say no! Just say no!" In response, Canseco tipped his hat to the crowd, later saying he took the taunts as a compliment: "They were having fun and so was I."[17]

As for creatine and steroid precursors like androstenedione, the 1990 Anabolic Steroids Control Act did not include these substances, so they were not prohibited at all. Creatine is the drug East German molecular scientists created as a performance-enhancing and drug-test-evading bridge between precompetition anabolic steroid doping and the day of an event. Androstenedione is a synthetic male hormone that when taken as a nasal spray converts into testosterone. It is one metabolic step away from being a steroid, and the patent application for androstenedione suggests that it could raise testosterone levels over 200 percent in 15 minutes. John Hoberman described androstenedione and its cousins as hormonal products positioned "inside the legally protected gray zone between testosterone (a controlled substance) and genuine supplements" like vitamins.[18]

Passage of the 1990 act forced steroid use underground for ballplayers. However, because the steroid precursors creatine and andro were not added to the controlled substances list, these steroid precursors (also known as prohormones) grew popular as a legal alternative to illegal steroids. They provided the testosterone-boosting effect of steroids, but were one Controlled Substances Act–skipping step further down the metabolic chain of physiological reactions. As Baltimore Orioles shortstop Mike Bordick put it in 1997, "Everyone, it seems, is looking for the non-anabolic alternative to steroids."[19]

The supplement industry grew fat on baseball-inspired sales of androstenedione and creatine. One andro seller promoted its wares as "The Product Behind Mark McGwire's 70 Home Runs." Advertisements explained that you will "take your testosterone levels to new heights with this botanically derived extract and see why professional baseball player Mark McGwire is continually pounding home runs into the stratosphere."[20]

All was well until 1998, when Associated Press reporter Steve Wilstein spotted a bottle of andro in Saint Louis Cardinals slugger Mark McGwire's locker. Wilstein's August 23, 1998, story began, "Sitting on the top shelf of Mark McGwire's locker, next to a can of Popeye spinach and packs of sugarless gum, is a brown bottle labeled androstenedione." With that, what had been normal and acceptable was about to undergo a strange and dramatic transformation.

A month earlier, the Tour de France's Festina affair had set the sports world alight with talk of doping scandal. On August 21, two days before Wilstein's andro story broke, the *New York Times* reported on a German court's conviction of three doctors and coaches for doping teenage swimmers with steroids in the former East Germany. "This is the first time that sports officials have been convicted of injuring athletes by systematically giving them hormones," a German attorney stated, emphasizing to American readers, "It is important to note that all of the swimmers in this case were minors."[21]

The depth of the physical and psychological damage that East German steroid doping visited upon children hit the public consciousness just weeks after bike racers in France were being tossed in jail. American lawmakers could not easily wave away the miasma of social deviance and ethical toxicity gathering around doping in general and steroids in particular. And in the midst of it all, Mark McGwire was nine home runs away from tying Roger Maris's 1961 record of 61 homers in a single season. The race to best Maris was especially compelling because McGwire was not in it alone; he was hitting runs neck-and-neck with Sammy Sosa, a likeable Chicago Cubs slugger from the Dominican Republic.

Given the sinister context of sports doping in August 1998, when Wilstein's roving eye landed on McGwire's perfectly legal bottle of andro, the pills seemed to represent all that was wrong with the world, placed in plain view for every American man, woman, and child to see. The only difference between the nutritional stuff you could pick up from McGwire's locker or the local CVS and the chemicals that sent German teenagers clawing at the walls with depression and agonizing menstrual complications seemed to be semantics. One man's toxic drug was another country's food supplement.

Although the difference between a steroid and a steroid precursor wasn't really clear to most Americans, there was a general conviction that they both made a teenage body do things to itself that news from France and Germany was suggesting was not good at all. Because of the times, the "brown bottle labeled androstenedione" leading Wilstein's story contained a moral and social weight far beyond a few ounces of supplement pills.

Rather than recoiling at the discovery, Major League Baseball pointed to the law that followed the passage of the anabolic steroid act, the Dietary Supplement Health and Education Act (DSHEA) of 1994. Written as it was to protect the nutritional supplement industry from FDA oversight, the DSHEA expressly made andro and creatine legal and available to anyone who strolled into a health food store. After Wilstein's story broke, Commissioner of Baseball Bud Selig told Senator Mitchell he had never heard of andro. He visited a Milwaukee drugstore and the pharmacist on duty pointed him to the shining bottles of the product on the store shelves.[22]

Andro was a controlled substance in Canada, however, and in 1999, Don Catlin of UCLA's drug testing lab told the *New York Times* he regularly fielded puzzled inquiries from around the world as to why the drug-warrior United States allowed a doping product to be sold without a prescription. "They can't understand how something like andro, which their countries all banned a long time ago, is prevalent in America," Catlin said. "We're generally seen as the protectors internationally, with a government committed to fighting drug abuse around the world." Catlin added, "This is very embarrassing. Androstenedione is a steroid, there's no question about it. It shouldn't be available."[23]

"This is a snake-oil exemption," fumed Dr. Sidney M. Wolfe, director of Public Citizen's Health Research Group. Barry McCaffrey, the retired general who would throw a hand grenade into Juan Antonio Samaranch's efforts in 1999 to keep Olympic anti-doping under the IOC roof, was appalled by the DSHEA protection of steroid precursors. Noting that the IOC, the NFL, and the NCAA had all banned andro, he pointed to the hypocrisy of a law that put the burden of proving a product's safety on the FDA, not the manufacturer: "And we have in place this huge apparatus to keep drugs away from youth in America. But since McGwire's revelation, andro sales have gone up five- to tenfold. You can get it everywhere, classified as a food supplement, which sounds so benign."[24] As John Hoberman describes the effect of the DSHEA, "Populist pharmacology was now the law of the land."[25] After the law went into effect, the supplement market exploded, growing 50 percent to $12 billion in annual sales.[26]

"Obviously, baseball has a great responsibility," baseball commissioner Bud Selig said of the reported dangers of androstenedione. The league assigned two Harvard scientists the task of researching andro safety—a job that would take at least two years, plenty of time to end the homer-filled 1998 season on a flush of long-ball bonhomie. "I want to be very careful that we are proceeding with all of the empirical data that one should have," Selig said. "And it doesn't exist at this point," he added, spritzing an aroma of responsibility over his dismissal of Catlin's concerns.[27]

Major League Baseball players' union boss Donald Fehr pointed out that baseball was operating inside the legal and ethical lines Congress had drawn. Picked on by anti-doping critics, Fehr responded, "No one can be faulted for staying entirely within the rules. We look forward to hearing from our medical representatives." Fehr's statement was at once evasive and truthful. Baseball players were following Congress's lead in turning to supplements for performance enhancement. The DSHEA made clear that the medicine cabinet held the answers to life's problems. And in 1998, baseball, like the tech-fueled stock market, was on a tear; it was in no one's interest to derail a government-sanctioned train that many thought would never build momentum again after the 1994 strike.

The press did not want to spoil the American supplement soup, either. The week after the AP broke the McGwire andro story, perpetually grumpy *Boston Globe* columnist Dan Shaughnessy defended the slugger:

> In McGwire's case, it is misleading to write that he's using a "performance-enhancing drug." He's a baseball player, not an Olympic sprinter. There's nothing sold at drugstores that would help any of us hit a home run in the big leagues. . . . Meanwhile, how many other baseball players are taking the same stuff? McGwire probably doesn't go more than a couple of days without hitting against a pitcher who uses andro. While we're at it, what about creatine, another dietary supplement sold over the counter, also used by McGwire? What about MET-Rx (endorsed on radio and in print by Mo Vaughn)?
>
> McGwire's been a good citizen, never one to disgrace the uniform. Most recently he's dedicated his charity efforts to awareness and funding for abused children. And now he's got to read that he's a bad example to young athletes? Please.[28]

Both the Cardinals and other baseball scribes ostracized Wilstein for breaching the unwritten confidentiality contract that allows journalists admittance into MLB locker rooms. By turning a legal substance into a scandal, Wilstein turned writers into the enemy. Androstenedione was legal and blessed by Congress. Even though McGwire's andro use might have broadcast the hypocrisy inherent in the DSHEA's shielding of performance-enhancing drugs, no one stood to make money or friends by turning a beloved player into an object lesson in the complicity of American substance-control policies and the posturing of legislators who preached inner-city law and order out of one side of their mouths and pushed drugs onto suburban ball fields from the other. The teams. The commissioner of baseball. The supplement industry and its benefactors in Congress. The home-run-thrilled fans. The salary-rich players and money-making TV networks. In 1998, it was difficult to find a voice willing to spit in baseball's DSHEA-enriched soup.

McGwire was not defensive about androstenedione, either. "It's legal," he explained. "There's absolutely nothing wrong with it." McGwire, a member of the 1984 Olympic baseball team, told Wilstein he had been using the testosterone-producing supplement for over a year. "Everything I've done is natural," McGwire explained. "Everybody that I know in the game of baseball uses the same stuff I use."[29] The Cardinals backed him up with a statement from its medical staff: "Due to current research that lacks documentary evidence of any adverse side effects, the Cardinals' medical staff cannot object to Mark's choice to use this legal and over the counter supplement."[30] The number of players that could fit through the DSHEA loophole was limitless. Wilstein's piece also cited Sosa, who claimed not to use andro but eagerly embraced creatine because he believed the supplement helped him maintain his home-run-hitting mass and strength.

In the same piece, Boston Red Sox slugger Mo Vaughn told Wilstein, "Anything illegal is definitely wrong. But if you get something over the counter and legal, guys in that power-hitter position are going to use them." Vaughn was a paid spokesman for MET-Rx, manufacturer of testosterone precursors and a major campaign contributor to supplement-industry champion Senator Orrin Hatch. Androstenedione was sold in Great Earth vitamin stores, a chain of 138 outlets in 23 states that sold the product by mail order and over the counter in a bundle deal called an "Andro-Flav Stack."

The DSHEA gave baseball a government-blessed doping loophole the MLB could use to explain away the performances that had fans filling baseball stadiums once again. Enhanced by government-blessed drugs like andro and creatine, and using anabolic steroids in the shadows, players delivered a new era of power-hitting baseball, and fans loved it. As sportswriter Bob Herbert put it in 1998, "Each new home run gives the nation a thrill." By the end of the season, four players would hit more than 50 home runs—a first in baseball history. McGwire's outsized arms delivered pure entertainment. "Kids idolize him. Fans have been filling ballparks from coast to coast to watch him swing his mighty bat," Herbert marveled before cautioning, "A lot of young people will be looking on, admiring their hero, trying to follow his example, trying their best to be like Mark."[31] Hall-of-famer Ted Williams told the *Nightline* TV news show that in all his years watching baseball, he had never seen anyone "that absolutely crushed the ball as much" as McGwire. "I think people go to the ballpark to see if he's going to hit one over the moon," Williams marveled.[32]

By 1998, the bigger-player, longer-ball revolution was in full froth, and so too was the economy. The season kicked off with McGwire smashing a grand slam against the Los Angeles Dodgers. Two weeks after McGwire's March 31 homer, a one-year-old Internet search site called Yahoo issued its initial public offering, which soared 154 percent its first day and left its Stanford graduate student owners with an $848 million company on their hands. One analyst told the *Wall Street Journal* that even though few of the new Internet companies generated income, "The market is somehow justifying these ridiculous capitalizations."[33] Neither baseball nor Wall Street was interested in asking hard questions about the performance miracles at hand.

In September of that season, McGwire hit his 62nd home run of the year while playing against Sosa's Cubs. After the hit, Sosa ran in from his position in right field, and McGwire met him in an enormous bear hug. They exchanged high fives and embraced again. It was a heartwarming moment between competitors whose mutual admiration seemed to express Coubertin's ideal of sports as builder of human character and goodwill. With memories of the 1992 Los Angeles race riots still present in American minds, the sincere and highly public show of affection between the white and black players was especially poignant. A September 4 *New York Times* headline trumpeted, "A Sport Is Reborn—the Home Run, America's Signature Feat, Invigorates Baseball; September's Aura Restored to Fans."[34] Like post-Festina pro cycling invigorated by a young cancer survivor named Lance Armstrong in 1999, baseball stood up from the muck of its greed-sullied recent past and was suddenly vital, immediate.

The summer of 1998 was a success both for baseball and the supplement industries. McGwire ended the season with 70 home runs, Sosa with 66; both shattered Roger Maris's record. Baseball had its mojo back, and the supplement industry was benefitting from the public's eager emulation of its heroes' drug habits. According to a 2006 *ESPN* magazine report on drugs in baseball, androstenedione sales rose 1000 percent, up to $55 million, after McGwire's success in 1998.[35] Nike also milked the chemically fueled home run race, running a cheeky TV advertisement in 1999 in which blonde actress Heather Locklear and an attractive brunette pass on Cy Young Award winners Tom Glavine and Greg Maddux for the more muscular—and harder hitting—Mark McGwire. The tagline? "Chicks dig the long ball."*

Allowing the free flow of many potentially harmful steroids was, as doping historian John Hoberman put it, "curious behavior on the part of a society whose official response to casual drug use was supposed to be the slogan 'Just Say No.'" And even though giving steroid prohormones like andro a pass "confronted American society with its own conflicted attitude toward performance-enhancing substances," the political will to address this hypocrisy did not exist.[36] That is, until the BALCO scandal hit the headlines in 2003.

---

* Nineteen ninety-eight was also the year that the FDA approved the male impotence drug Viagra and the first television ads for the product hit the airwaves. The ad featured former Senate majority leader Bob Dole promoting the drug's sexual-performance-enhancing powers. The senator was permitted to push drugs on TV because of a change in federal law in 1997, when Congress allowed drug companies to include a telephone number or web site in advertising where consumers could go to learn about a drug's contraindications. Eliminating the old requirement that all potential drug complications had to be advertised along with the therapeutic qualities gave drug companies free rein to advertise more aggressively. U.S. drug marketing on television increased from $220 million in 1996 to $664 million in 1998. By 2000, drug ad spending on TV more than doubled again, to $1.574 billion. Sports fans felt the results of that messaging gusher. In 1999 alone, Viagra spent $90 million informing TV watchers of its ability to enhance sexual performance. The same year, drug maker GlaxoSmithKline dedicated $92 million to advertising the antidepressant Paxil. M. B. Rosenthal, E. R. Berndt, J. M. Donohue, R. G. Frank, and A. M. Epstein, "Promotion of Prescription Drugs to Consumers," *New England Journal of Medicine* 346, no. 7 (2002): 498–505.

A U.S. Anti-Doping Agency investigation that year revealed that a California supplement manufacturer and distributor, the Bay Area Laboratory Co-operative, was distributing illegal performance-enhancing drugs to hundreds of athletes in track, football, and baseball. The scandal got mountains of media coverage, so much so that the U.S. government found it necessary to react, even if doing so conflicted with the spirit of its 1994 DSHEA deregulation of supplement makers. In February 2004, U.S. attorney general John Ashcroft handed down a 42-count indictment against BALCO operatives.

Two weeks earlier, President George W. Bush let the public know that the executive office didn't like cheaters, either. In his 2004 State of the Union address, Bush warned the nation that "the use of performance-enhancing drugs like steroids in baseball, football, and other sports is dangerous and it sends the wrong message: that there are shortcuts to accomplishment and that performance is more important than character. So tonight I call on team owners, union representatives, coaches, and players to take the lead, to send the right signal, to get tough, and to get rid of steroids now."[37]

When Bush dropped steroids into his address to Congress, he elevated performance-enhancing drugs to a high level of national moral concern. Included within a speech that focused on the War on Terror and the threat to "families, schools, and religious congregations," doping practices that had long resided at the heart of elite sports, and were even sanctioned by U.S. Olympic coaches, were now officially frowned upon in the United States. President Bush's call to stop steroid use signaled that, in spite of the DSHEA, the administration was determined to arrest a moral decline the public had come to associate with BALCO. As was the case when Nixon launched his war against recreational drugs in the 1960s, Bush's call to purge the nation of drugs that had long been part of elite sports was at once about capitalizing on social anxieties to protect his own political power and about shielding America's performance-minded youth from pharmaceutical substances—many of which Congress had successfully argued Americans should be able to buy whenever they liked.*

"I know of no instance where any society has successfully controlled the explosion of technology," Charles Yesalis told me. "You just can't stop this stuff." In spite of his cynicism, he still testified repeatedly for lawmakers even though he knew they were using him as a prop in their power-maintenance charade. "It bothered me a hundred times more that kids were using these [drugs]," Yesalis said.

Yesalis testified before Congress on six occasions. Those experiences taught him that congressional hearings about drugs in sports are about presenting a façade. "Politicians can all get face time on TV with these hearings," he told me. "It's one thing the Republicans and Democrats can agree on. . . . It's good theater."

Looking back at his efforts to work with lawmakers to curb steroid use, Yesalis said, "I just didn't realize that we were trying to deal with the ocean coming on shore and trying to throw it back at the oncoming tide." Along with Internet distribution channels and offshore pharmaceutical suppliers, Yesalis said it is just about impossible to stop suppliers, let alone change the behaviors that create demand. "Whether it's in war, whether it's in business—it's part of human nature to gain an edge. It's how we are wired," he said.

Not wanting to miss out on an opportunity to look like it, too, was on the job stopping crime and social deviance, in 2005, Congress held more hearings on drugs in sports. It called in MLB executives and players like McGwire and Sosa and attempted to get them to confess to the error of their steroid-enabled ways. Some baseball union representatives were furious that the same congressmen who had turned the nation's supermarkets and drugstores into walk-in distribution centers for drug-laced

* In the same speech, the president underscored his commitment to policies that were inadvertently pushing ADHD drugs on American schoolchildren. Rebuffing criticism of the No Child Left Behind Act, Bush assured the nation, "Testing is the only way to identify and help students who are falling back." While Bush's educational goals were admirable, Americans turned to reliable performance-enhancing drugs to execute his vision.

supplements were now concerned with kids taking what baseball players did. After all, these were the same legislators who had long agitated for the unregulated sale and distribution of a cornucopia of supplements, including androstenedione and L-tryptophan, the amino acid sold as a food supplement that killed at least 37 people before the FDA had enough evidence to pull it from health food store shelves in 1990. Congress had opened a $7 billion door to doping, and now it was scolding baseball for stepping through it. When California Angels pitcher Derrick Turnbow tested positive for androstenedione in 2003, he was slapped with a two-year ban. Player association general counsel Gene Orza was outraged. "Derrick Turnbow did not test positive for a steroid," Orza complained. "He tested positive for what the IOC and others regard as a steroid, but the U.S. government does not."[38]

Not long after Bush's 2004 State of the Union speech, the U.S. House of Representatives passed the Anabolic Steroid Control Act of 2004. Sponsored by Senator Joe Biden and co-sponsored by Orrin Hatch, the act tightened the earlier 1990 Anabolic Steroids Control Act by reclassifying some steroid precursors like androstenedione as Schedule III controlled substances. Biden said the change would help stop drug use by athletes, "especially by youngsters and teenagers." Due largely to the public attention brought on by the BALCO scandal, "supplements" like andro that the U.S government had previously classified as harmless food enhancements and aggressively shielded from any FDA safety testing were suddenly deadly controlled substances with significant criminal penalties for nonprescribed distribution. The drugs had not changed, but BALCO had created political capital in coming out against the social disorder they represented.

What led staunch supplement defender Orrin Hatch to ban a best seller like andro? Two things. First, the 2004 act excluded dehydroepiandrosterone (DHEA), an androgenic hormone precursor present in many muscle-building and anti-aging supplements. An all-purpose dietary supplement also advertised for cancer and cardiovascular disease prevention, as well as weight loss, DHEA had been regulated by the FDA until the DSHEA reopened the sales gates in 1994.[39] Asked why this special exemption was carved into an act designed to end use of these gray-area precursors, State University of New York pharmacology professor Arthur Grollman explained it was because DHEA constituted "60 percent of the supplement market out in Utah." An adviser to Illinois senator Richard Durbin while he was drafting the 2004 bill, Grollman stated that "the only reason Utah would agree to go along with the bill is because he [Hatch] thinks steroids are very bad for our young people, but he would just like DHEA kept out of it."[40] When asked why the 2004 act did not regulate dehydroepiandrosterone along with androstenedione, Hatch told the *New York Times*, "There is a big argument that DHEA is very beneficial for health and well being."[41]

So while banning andro would probably hurt sales of some supplements produced by Hatch's constituents, another popular steroid precursor was artfully exempted from the 2004 Anabolic Steroid Control Act. In addition, the supplement industry was not losing sleep over the loss of andro because it had crafted new steroid precursors that promised to be even more effective than the now off-limits drug. Knowing that androstenedione was about to become a stale drug, Hatch saw a win for everyone in the 2004 act. Backing it made him look like he was against performance-enhancing drugs, all the while knowing that new and better substances in the pipeline would keep his supplement industry benefactors busy.[42]

President George W. Bush signed the updated act into law on October 22, 2005. Androstenedione, that East German invention turned favorite of baseball superstars and their high school and college aspirants, was no longer available over the counter at your local health food store. In fact, getting caught with andro could get you thrown in jail for a year; selling it could send you away for five.

That a small-government, low-tax Republican like Bush saw steroid-eating football and baseball players as a problem worth more intrusive government policy and new taxpayer expenditures was a remarkable compromise for a businessman and politician who had been enriched by the fan-pleasing effects of steroids. As an owner of the Texas Rangers from 1989 to 1998, Bush cashed in when performance-enhancing drugs helped resurrect baseball after the 1994 strike. Following the strike, Rangers fan attendance dropped so precipitously that in 1996, the franchise's value fell to $138 million from $157 million.[43] Ranger fans were so turned off that they initially avoided the seats of a brand-new taxpayer-funded, home run–friendly stadium that Bush and his fellow Rangers owners had pushed through.

In 1996, spectacular slugging, base stealing, and fielding from Rangers Iván Rodríguez and MVP Juan González helped the team win the American League West title. Fans swarmed back in to see Rodríguez set a record for the most doubles hit by a catcher—swatting past a record set in 1930. Rodríguez filled seats by leading the Rangers in hits, at bats, and runs scored. He would later test positive for steroids. In his book about his life in baseball, *Juiced*, Jose Canseco claims he regularly injected Rodríguez with steroids. Canseco also said he educated González—a player who some call the greatest hitter in Rangers' history—on how to use the muscle-building drugs.[44] In October 2001, Canadian customs officers seized a bag containing steroids, syringes, and clenbuterol that had been unloaded from a Cleveland Indians flight. When González's assistant came to pick up the bag, González denied ownership.[45]

Enhanced with legal and illegal drugs, González and Rodríguez resurrected Bush's team in its hour of need. Season revenue of $25.5 million in 1996 suddenly made the Rangers' stadium the best-performing ballpark in the MLB. In 1998, the Rangers franchise sold for $250 million. Juiced players made a better entertainment product, and that helped grow Bush's original $606,302 investment into a $14.9 million payout.

Bush was not alone in benefiting from the windfall generated by performance-enhancing drugs. Even after the BALCO scandal implicated scores of professionals in baseball, football, and athletics, baseball and football marched to higher profitability and fan interest. In 2001, Major League Baseball generated $3.5 billion in revenue. The 10 years that BALCO spent manufacturing and distributing steroids and human growth hormones coincided with the best decade of ticket sales in MLB history.[46]

While fans might say that doping in sports turns them off, their rush to fill stadiums in the years following the 1994 strike suggests otherwise. Outside sports, Americans see performance-enhancing drugs and procedures as a basic human right. From Viagra to Prozac to Adderall to the mystery supplements filling health food store shelves, society is eager for pharmaceuticals that can improve performance in the game of life.

Mike Plant has feet in the worlds of baseball and cycling. His day job is executive vice president of business operations for the Atlanta Braves, and he is also a member of the UCI Management Committee. From 1988 to 1995, he ran Medalist Sports, a race promotion company that presented the Tour du Pont bicycle race in those years. When I asked Plant about the intersection between performance enhancement in everyday life and in sports, he said, "People are looking for more of an edge in everything they do. Sexual performance, competitive athletic performance, diet." For all these things and more, there is a "substance or some type of medical assistance to help you achieve those things." Plant was USA Cycling president from 1995 to 2002, and his long experience in sports management and promotion tell him that Americans like watching the effects of performance-enhancing drugs from afar. "I look back at baseball and the home-run chase of Bonds and Sosa—there was a lot of chatter about what was going on there when those guys were spanking that ball over the wall. But people liked it," Plant told me. "People, they got engaged in it and they paid attention to it."

An earlier scandal over fixed game shows on television offers insights as to why Americans don't seem to care about cheating in sports like baseball, or even about the sometimes-deadly illogic of mass drug deregulations like the DSHEA. In 1957, America's collective attention turned to a new form of entertainment making its way into millions of postwar homes—the television quiz show. Over a 14-week period, a Columbia University English instructor named Charles Van Doren knocked off contestant after contestant in a show called *Twenty One*.

Van Doren kept America in thrall with his encyclopedic command of cultural, historical, and scientific facts. Then, in 1958, news broke that the show had supplied Van Doren with answers ahead of time. The contest was a fraud. *Twenty One* ratings plummeted, and several other similarly rigged shows were canceled.

Sensing an opportunity to harvest political capital through a show of defending the public good, Congress convened for hearings on the quiz-show scandals. Called to testify on November 2, 1959, Van Doren revealed that the show was designed to build drama week by week with a series of scripted ties and wins between contestants who were chosen for their qualities as everyday people. Then-president Dwight Eisenhower held a press conference in which he expressed his dismay that a TV quiz show had defrauded him and his nation. At about the same time, it came out that Mutual Broadcasting System had accepted $750,000 from Dominican Republic dictator Rafael Trujillo in exchange for seven hours of monthly positive spin about his rule of the Caribbean nation. In 1960, Congress passed laws banning quiz-show fixing. *Congressional Quarterly* reported that the hearings leading up to the passing of the laws were the most publicized ever.[47]

Although rigged quiz shows faded away, the television networks continued to produce content of little substance. By 1961, Federal Communications Commission (FCC) chairman Newton N. Minow told a gathering of the National Association of Broadcasters that they were generating slag, "a vast wasteland" of content.[48] Minow's colorful characterization stuck even as the television business entered a glory era of profitability. Even after public and political outrage over the quiz-show scandals died down, thirst for TV dissipation was insatiable. Before long, CBS was making so much money that the network had enough cash on hand to buy the New York Yankees, a toy company, and a large publishing house.

When the 1990s baseball supplement and steroid use came to light, fans responded in much the same way as they did when they learned that Charles Van Doren's knowledge was artificially enhanced; they expressed outrage and then flocked to stadiums and TV sets for more of the same. Although the public might say it hates being entertained by fabulists, our actions suggest that we do not mind at all, as long as the spectacle from the prevarication is good.

Echoing the "don't spit in the soup" ethos that informed pro cycling throughout the EPO years, Van Doren explained that the rigging of the quiz shows was common knowledge in the television industry, but people did not speak out. "Why would they?" he asked in a 2008 *New Yorker* story about the scandal. "At the height of the boom, there were as many as twenty-four prime-time shows, each giving away significant sums, attracting large audiences, and producing large profits for the sponsors."[49]

Call them fraud or well-crafted drama, baseball and quiz shows were money generators. In October 24, 1959, the *Nation* magazine published an article titled "Hail, Blithe Spirit!" by the screenwriter and novelist Dalton Trumbo. In this scathing essay about the quiz-show scandals, Trumbo dismantled the low ethical standards of the television networks and of the federal government, which had given the networks priceless public airwaves with few obligations. Trumbo, a writer who was blacklisted during the 1950s Red Scare in Hollywood, explained that fraud lies at the heart of American entertainment.[50] He forecast the type of truth-in-performance scandals that would descend upon sports entertainment during the late 20th and early 21st centuries. "Some contended they appeared on the show, not as legitimate contestants, but as paid entertainers: 'If the truth were known, there wouldn't be any entertainers,'" Trumbo wryly observed of the game-show fraud. Unknowingly foreshadowing the drug cheating that would come to be the foundation of many sports entertainment enterprises, Trumbo captured the public's indifference to amorality in entertainment when he wrote, "When your expectations are fulfilled—when the fraud is finally revealed—we are never surprised, and rarely angry. Publicly and before the children, we deplore it. Privately, we admire its audacity, and marvel that it went undetected for so long. We sharpen our wits on the details (but never its cause) and are wiser citizens for what it has taught us."[51] A half-century before Jose Canseco, Mark McGwire, Lance Armstrong, the DSHEA, and Orrin Hatch, Trumbo captured the paradox of America's simultaneous desire for the sacred and profane, for purity and excess, in sports entertainment.

CHAPTER 19

IF IT'S INHERITED, IS IT CHEATING?

In 1972, the journal *Science* published a quizzically titled piece, "Gene Therapy for Human Genetic Disease?" Written by UC San Diego researcher Theodore Friedmann and Massachusetts General Hospital's Richard Roblin, the paper set forth a thrilling proposition: "In our view, gene therapy may ameliorate some human genetic diseases in the future."[1] That is, at some point, science might give doctors the tools to genetically disarm genes that cause diseases such as cystic fibrosis and cancer. Replace the defective gene with a normal gene and the disease and its symptoms are gone. While it took technology a few decades to catch up with the writers' visionary thinking, in 1991, Friedmann was able to claim that labs like his were no longer simply managing the tragic human consequences of genetic defects. Instead, he said, "we're looking at therapy for the defect itself."[2]

Today, DNA manipulation is routinely used on plants and animals, and research continues on humans. "The field has moved greatly in the past decade," Friedmann noted in 2015.[3]

As is the case with any therapy used to restore the sick, sports began to consider how that same technology might make athletes better than well. One form of this emerging genetic therapy uses genes to instigate the production of insulin-growth factor 1 (IGF-1), a process that could help repair tissues damaged by trauma or genetic defects. Since 2004, Friedmann has served as head of a WADA genetic doping panel that advises the anti-doping agency on gene therapy advances and ways to detect sports gene doping. He has pointed to IGF-1 as the type of gene therapy that could be used to strengthen muscles or joints, whether injured or normal. Other forms of gene modification could trigger production of EPO.[4] "The science is not all that difficult and can be reproduced by well-trained people in many thousands of laboratories all over the world," Friedmann observed. However, the technology is still immature, and Friedmann clarified that using gene therapy on athletes would be exceptionally risky. It would "be frivolous, dangerous, and in my mind, would constitute medical malpractice," he said in 2005.

Nonetheless, the will to win is strong, and the appeal of having access to a performance-enhancing tool before it has been embraced by others makes this new form of doping highly appealing to some. "As technology advances, there will be those with the means and motivation who will be willing to try," Friedmann said.[5] As far back as 1972, he acknowledged that gene therapy had an irresistible draw for abuse when he wrote, "We are aware that physicians have not always waited for a complete evaluation of new and potentially dangerous therapeutic procedures before using them on human beings."[6]

Gene modification presents a science fiction future in which a cyclist could raise his natural hematocrit, a discus thrower could increase his muscle mass, or parents could create an embryo that would produce a child with the tennis physique of the Williams sisters. And this technology could deliver a future where enhancement does not come from an athlete's personal decisions, but rather from choices made by the athlete's parents or their modified antecedents. If and when this day comes, sports will have to fit athletes who had no hand in their own genetic enhancement into a 20th-century crime-and-punishment infrastructure that places blame on the shoulders of self-doping individuals.

To learn more about how close we might be to gene therapy for performance enhancement, I called Henry Greely, director of Stanford University's Center for Law and the Biosciences and a prolific writer and commentator on bioengineering. Greely studies the ethical and social implications of biotechnologies. He has also written on human performance enhancement through drugs and genetic engineering—also known as bioengineering.

Greely outlined several ways scientists could theoretically genetically engineer a human with the physical characteristics of a champion athlete. One is to identify the genetic traits you want the future human to have, generate thousands of embryos, genetically profile every one of them, and then isolate the embryo that most closely matches this ideal genetic makeup. "If you took two great cyclists, a male and a female, and you made a thousand embryos from them, you could choose the one that, based on what we know, looked like it would be the best—assuming that we can correlate some of these genetic variations with performance," Greely explained.

This method of genetic selection for performance enhancement is a way of accelerating the otherwise grindingly slow process of evolution. As journalist Michael Specter reported in the *New Yorker* in 2014, natural selection shortcutting is already being practiced in China, where the gene therapy company Beijing Genomics Institute (BGI) helps parents screen out female embryos (boys are preferred in China) or locate embryos with genetic traits statistically more likely to be found in highly intelligent people. Stephen Hsu, a Michigan State theoretical physicist working on the project, said infinitesimal genetic differences could determine "whether you are Albert Einstein or not getting into college." At least in theory, with small tweaks to an embryo in utero, Hsu explained, "you could rev up human intelligence quite a bit. Or you can explain the difference between Stephen Hawking and the average person."[7] Evolutionary processes and mere chance already make genetic selections every minute of every day; sophisticated genetic engineering could give humans the same power to bend nature to fit our social and economic preferences.

It took 10 years and $3 billion to map the first human genome.[8] Specter reported that today, for about $1,000, Chinese genetic engineering companies can map a person's DNA in a few days. BGI can analyze the DNA of a 10-week-old fetus and identify whether that baby has Down syndrome. Human fate is written in genes, and today's technology is rapidly moving to a point where a parent can decide not just whether to abort a fetus with defects, but also to adjust a child's characteristics in the womb. Isolate the genetic profile of a Serena Williams or a Greg LeMond, and it is not a stretch to imagine either parents or the state modifying embryos in an effort to secure future athletic success.

Greely explained that another way we might someday enhance performance is through somatic gene therapy, where DNA is changed in millions of cells en masse. For example—and Greely cautioned that this is still hypothetical and rife with unknown complications—an athlete with a low natural hematocrit would be inoculated with a virus that would in turn "infect" the entire organism's cells with new genetic material that would transform the person's oxygen-carrying capacity. With this sort of genetic performance enhancement, the genes you inherit from your parents would not matter as much as they do today. The genetic supermarket would replace the genetic lottery; rather than chance, money and access to medical facilities would become the defining factor in the physiological-endurance sweepstakes. "Whatever genes you are born with, we are going to overcome either by giving you the protein those genes make in ways we like, or by swapping out your genes as an adult or as a child," Greely explained.

To be sure, the long-term health consequences of this process are unknown, and, like Friedmann, Greely feels this sort of genetic engineering is "pretty reckless." Danger lies in the fact that we do not know how various genetic and environmental factors work in concert. Greely gave the example of a cyclist engineered to have a hematocrit of 54, but then "maybe he strokes out at age 12." Speaking of such unknown complications, Greely emphasized, "We don't know, and it will be a long time before we do." Genes often do more than one thing, so editing a gene to improve one performance trait could have catastrophic side effects. Indeed, in 2015, the journal *Nature* reported that when Chinese scientists modified 86 human embryos with the intent of editing out a defect that causes a deadly blood disorder, the researchers found that of the embryos that survived, only a small subset reproduced with the gene modification intact. More alarmingly, the researchers observed a number of off-target mutations in unexpected parts of the gene.

Genetically solving one problem can create unintended others. And while lab testing on a rat can show us the lifetime consequences of genetic manipulations in that animal, scientists have no idea how genetic feedback loops plus the influence of environment and age might influence a patient's health over an 80-year human lifespan. Furthermore, the benefits and penalties of passing on these mutations to all future generations are likewise unknown.[9] As Friedmann wrote in 1972, "The irreversible and heritable nature of gene therapy means that the tolerable margin of risk" is even narrower than when testing medical therapies whose consequences are limited to the patient and not shared with generations of offspring.[10]

Greely told me that another way we might someday engineer a better athlete is through germ-line engineering, in which one part of the DNA strand is edited to remove or modify a trait. This technique is already widely used in agriculture and livestock to breed seeds and animals with specific characteristics. For example, many crops in the United States have been genetically modified to resist the effects of certain weed killers. Genetically modified salmon are now available to U.S. shoppers. Pigs are bred using gene therapy to grow bigger muscles, and milk cows are bred without horns to eliminate the cruel process of physically burning off horn buds.

Germ-line engineering is less complicated than somatic gene therapy because it only has to operate on a single gene. Once the DNA molecules in a single fertilized egg are modified, that egg multiplies, passing on its modified genetic characteristics to every cell in the resulting organism. That organism's offspring also inherit the changes. This type of genetic tinkering has obvious attraction for those born with inherited diseases—it gets humanity to the "defect-free" future that the 1900s eugenics movement wanted to pursue, but ideally in a more humane fashion.

In his 2002 book on the consequences of the biotech revolution, *Our Posthuman Future,* Francis Fukuyama points out that if the day arrives when editing can selectively fix human genetic defects, the technology will trigger a debate on what role government should take to improve society's overall performance. For example, if biotechnology eventually delivers the ability to engineer more intelligent children, a new form of paternalistic eugenics could take root. Fukuyama writes, "It is entirely plausible that an advanced, democratic welfare state would reenter the game, intervening this time not to prevent low-IQ people from breeding, but to help genetically disadvantaged people raise their IQs and the IQs of their offspring."[11] Though East Germany's steroid program proves that a concern for safety does not always curb state-run medical practices, presuming that the genetic tinkering required to create smarter kids could be proven safe and effective, such an advancement would present governments with a tool for addressing stubborn socioeconomic inequalities and injustices—and in so doing, relieve a country from some of the economic and social burdens of poverty and dependence. Genetic engineering could level (or tilt) the playing field of life. Similarly, athletes on a soccer squad who did not have the genetic makeup of the top players could use gene therapy to put themselves at an equal physiological baseline with their colleagues.

Sports fascinate because unfairness is their essence. Irish law lecturer Eoin Carolan writes, "Elite athletes represent inequality at its most refined, revered by the public not for their normalcy but rather for their ability to achieve that which the ordinary athlete, let alone the average citizen, cannot." Possessing inherited genetic qualities that are forever beyond the reach of the rest, the world's best athletes are manifestations of pure inequality. However, Carolan observes, "it is rarely, if ever, suggested that these athletes be handicapped so as to compensate others for the comparative disadvantages of their birth."[12]

As with any medical discovery meant to restore sick people to health, athletes and their sports medicine experts will inevitably look for ways to turn a restorative therapy into an additive one. As Harvard University genetic researcher George Church put it, once gene editing is successfully used to treat diseases like Alzheimer's or muscular dystrophy, "I think enhancement will creep in the door." Whether it is the executive who wants to improve his cognitive skills or the athlete who wants to bulk up, the appeal of restorative gene therapies will be too strong to resist.[13]

Another form of performance enhancement could combine the sort of top-down athlete selection process developed in East Germany with modern gene therapy technologies. Sports education and talent-identification programs single out potential athletic talent in grade school and filter those promising youngsters into sports schools where they focus intensely on perfecting their athletic craft. These schools existed in East Germany and are fundamental to China's Olympic team selection process today. They also exist in Australia and European countries influenced by the post–Cold War diaspora of Eastern Bloc coaches. Programs like Australia's Institute of Sport identify promising young athletes and train and educate them in sports-specific schools.

With gene-selection therapy, a country could take the talent-winnowing process a step further by genotyping an already select group of athletes, and then checking their genetic profiles to identify those with the most potential. As part of their talent-identification efforts, pro cycling teams could require neo-pros to supply their personal genotype. Along with past race results and other physiological data like maximum oxygen-carrying capacity, a manager could use this genetic profile to better assess a rider's future potential. And, of course, should the genetic map indicate huge latent talent, the athlete could use this quantified promise of future performance to command a better salary. With DNA mapping becoming so affordable, national or professional teams could invest in genetic-code databases that capture the characteristics of their most talented athletes. Part of the qualification process could involve comparing the neo-pro's genetic makeup to that of the proven elites—giving coaches an additional statistical data point to use when evaluating the probability that an athlete might go far in delivering results. While these futuristic visions of performance-enhancement technology and policy oversimplify the enormous medical and ethical complexity of genetics, social conditioning, and of course individual psychology, demand is there, and science naturally gravitates toward what is possible and what is funded.

Sports are a theater of war, nationalist striving, commercial enterprise, and personal ambition. It is no stretch to imagine that should bioengineering ultimately deliver the ability to create or select an embryo genetically coded with Sir Bradley Wiggins's dominant cycling capacity or Kelly Slater's preternatural surfing talents, individuals and governments alike would seize it. After all, looking back at how the Cold War affected the behavior of sports governing bodies on both sides of the Iron Curtain, there is little reason to assume humans have learned much from this lesson. As recently as 2015, it was revealed that Russia had run a state-sponsored Olympic doping program with the knowledge and cooperation of the IAAF.[14] As an exhaustive WADA report summarized in November 2015, in the interest of producing winners, "Russian athletes, coaches, national and international sports federations, the Russian Anti-Doping Agency (RUSADA) and the Moscow WADA-accredited laboratory" were all complicit in enabling Russian athlete doping.[15]

In quasi-democratic states like Russia and dictatorships like China, the will of the government supersedes personal rights. In China, the government has shown great desire to be considered something more than an industrial backwater (as evidenced by the $42 billion China spent on the 2008 Summer Olympics). It seems naïve to assume that government functionaries would not seize on genetic opportunities to project a larger sporting image on the wall of public opinion. Likewise, democracies like the United States have a solid track record of putting geopolitical ambitions above narrower anti-doping initiatives; given the right combination of diplomatic tensions and personal politician ambitions, democracies might also fund aggressive, sports-focused genetic engineering in a quest to deliver Olympic results. Indeed, the continued existence of the DSHEA indicates that for many American leaders and citizens, anti-doping is more an act of political theater than an expression of a rejection of chemical enhancement.

Whether it is possible to engineer a better athlete depends first of all, says Greely, on "figuring out whether there are some genetic sequences that correlate with being Lance Armstrong, or Michael Phelps, or Michael Jordan, or anybody else who has way-beyond-normal skills." Setting aside the intellectual and physiological elements necessary to make a champion, Greely cautioned that we currently are far from understanding if there is a genetic connection at all, let alone whether we could clone those genetic traits, should they exist as a reproducible package. "It's not clear that we'll ever get there," Greely said. He emphasized that future performance-enhancing gene therapies are not likely to turn a donkey into a Secretariat because sports abilities come from "a complex set of traits, both physical and mental, that have lots and lots of genes involved in them, as well as lots of environment and chance."

The law of unintended consequences casts a large and threatening shadow here. And if the technology proves viable, Greely thinks the changes would be more in the nature of pushing a back-of-the-pack athlete into becoming a middle-of-the-pack athlete, not into one who is dropping the field like an Eddy Merckx. The opportunity to counter the degrading effects of age or bad luck in parental choice would create a tremendous market opportunity for gene therapy companies, and one that performance-enhancement-loving Americans might embrace with the same gusto they show for DHEA, testosterone, Botox, and Viagra.

When it comes to more limited physiological characteristics such as blood-oxygen-carrying capacity, genetic engineering holds more promise. "It probably is the case that you could figure out genetic variations that give people an unusually high level of hemoglobin," Greely informed me. "Which would be presumably doing the same sort of thing that EPO does." In short, re-creating the swimming, basketball playing, or cycling package that is a Phelps, Jordan, or Armstrong is a Gordian knot; pull one performance-enhancing gene thread here, and a thousand others could be tightened and modified in unknown, potentially fatal ways. But once you narrow down what you want to modify, things enter the realm of possibility of today's genetic technology. "The narrower the trait you are looking at," Greely said, "the better your chances of finding a manageable number of genes that are involved."

The work of a company like BGI potentially has big implications for performance enhancement in sports and society. A 2010 study the company did with researchers at the University of California–Berkeley found that Tibetans who lived above 14,000 feet had some 30 genes with mutations different from the lowland ancestral group they split from 3,000 years earlier. Half of these mutations were related to how the highlanders metabolize oxygen. Rasmus Nielsen, a professor who worked on the study, said it was among the fastest genetic mutations ever seen in humans; for a group to adapt as quickly as the high-altitude Tibetans had, "a lot of people would have had to die simply due to the fact that they had the wrong version of a gene."[16]

While most genetic adaptations take place over millions of years, BGI's ability to pinpoint the exact gene mutations that allowed a subset of humans to survive and thrive living two and a half miles high in the atmosphere may have potential for athletes. Rather than letting chance deliver athletes who have this rare Tibetan genetic structure, gene therapy could be used to either manufacture or select an embryo with the same oxygen-metabolizing characteristics as the mountain people who gained their qualities through 3,000 years of genetic evolution. Alternatively, somatic gene therapy might someday allow a cyclist or mountain climber to introduce a gene virus into his body that would give him the same qualities as those inherited by Tibetans. Gene doping opens the possibility of accelerating the tedious evolutionary process that only occasionally delivers genetic freaks like a Greg LeMond or an Eddy Merckx.

For a decade, EPO was undetectable because there was no test for it. In the future, genetically engineered athletes might be similarly invisible. WADA-affiliated researchers suggest that genetically modified genes would produce different amounts of proteins or enzymes than unmodified genes, and these differences could be used to flag gene dopers.[17] However, like the East German swimmers unknowingly fed steroids from the age of 9, genetically modified athletes may also be completely innocent of their own doping. A child who is genetically modified from birth to be a superior athlete has no control over his or her artificial design. As Fukuyama puts it, genetic modification is "like giving your child a tattoo that she can never subsequently remove and will have to hand down not just to her own children but to all subsequent descendants."[18] How will governing bodies deal with athletes who want to compete, have the genetically enhanced makeup to do so, yet had no personal agency over the manipulation they received from their parents?

Anti-doping agencies like WADA know that genetically enhanced athletes will eventually take to Olympic and professional playing fields. WADA held its first workshop on the issue in 2002, and Friedmann helped organize the task group to study genetic performance enhancement. WADA wants to be ahead of this new form of performance enhancement in a way that governing agencies were not with EPO.

So far, WADA seems to be taking a law-and-order approach. A statement issued at the conclusion of a 2008 gene-doping symposium stated WADA's intent to work with international police forces to put laws in place that would punish the possession and trafficking of gene-doping technologies, "including reagents for genetic manipulation." That the 2008 conference was cosponsored by Russian sports authorities and held in Saint Petersburg suggests that the hosts, who we now know were running their own state-funded doping program, might have been excited to take part in the conference so that they could obtain the inside dope on WADA's developing anti-genetic-doping tactics. By helping devise WADA's anti-genetic-doping policy, the host country's state doping program would be well prepared to avoid the anti-doping organization's future snares.[19]

How national and sports governments manage genetic enhancement is a future surveillance-and-punishment battlefield. Some countries may loosely regulate gene therapies (with animals, crops, and even humans, China and the United States seem to be following this laissez-faire path), while other nations may take a more draconian approach to banning the procedures. Many European countries have outlawed the genetic manipulation of plants and livestock. Either way, if the past is a model, the rich will be able to access genetic manipulation or genetic predictive tests no matter where they are. It's likely that in sports, the same sort of socioeconomic stratification will happen. While WADA outlaws the practice, those with the assets will seek out the procedures, especially since they are undetectable.

On the flip side, Fukuyama points out that genetic engineering may eventually be seen not as a creator of inequality and unfairness, but as a leveler. "If people get upset enough about genetic inequality," he writes, there will be two alternative courses of action. One is to ban it. Like attempting to bar EPO in sports during the years when it was undetectable, this option may prove untenable if genetic engineering proves too attractive to halt. At that point, Fukuyama suggests, "a second possibility opens up, which is to use that same technology to raise up the bottom."[20] On one hand, the fair play of the naturally uneven playing field is preserved through a ban on genetic doping. On the other, the natural unfairness of sports could potentially be leveled with those same genetic-engineering practices. Either way, our anxieties about genetic engineering may stem from deep-rooted fears about letting technology run so far that it unhitches humanity from the comfort of an unchanging essential identity.

Genetic engineering, anti-aging drugs, and surgical procedures confront us with the possibility that we will someday separate ourselves from what it means to be a human who is born, lives, ages, and dies. In a future of invisible, innocently inherited physical enhancements, today's anti-doping dramas and the demonization of athletes who dope will seem hopelessly quaint—early shudders of protest at the prospect of technology forever altering what it means to be human. Our anxieties over genetic and pharmacological athletic-performance enhancements are not so much over the athletic consequences, but rather how allowing these procedures to proceed could shake the foundations of human identity.

As Mary Shelley explored in 1818 with *Frankenstein,* humans harbor long-held anxieties about using science to alter the human essence and potentially unleashing destructive unintended consequences. Whether society embraces or attempts to barricade these fruits of modernity will test our resolve to not become complicit with technologies that can make us better than well.

CHAPTER 20

MORAL DRIFT AND THE AMERICAN WAY

The morality parable of dope-free sheep and drug-fiend wolves satisfies our innate need for order. Sorting the world into good and bad reassures us that chaos can be held at bay. Like religion, a war for pure sports offers a reassuring hope in the unseen. We fix our eyes on the possibility of a comforting state that in fact never existed in elite sports. "To me, sport was a religion with its church, dogmas, service," Olympic founder Pierre de Coubertin wrote.[1] Anti-doping is a contemporary manifestation of Coubertin's view of athletics as a pedagogic project, "a practical school of chivalry" where youth learn that success and soul-saving chastity are "affirmed only through uprightness and loyalty."[2]

Contemporary clean-sports efforts carry on this religious mission: based on fears of a fall into a moral and physical hell, anti-doping campaigns attempt to save athletes from the irrepressible will to win that makes them great competitors in the first place. Allowing an alternative version of events in which the hand-wringing public, media, and anti-doping puritans would be complicit alongside doping athletes is upsetting. It suggests the fair play "everyone says" is so important is in fact a cheap illusion that's been used to manipulate us—all while we've been thinking it has been inspiring us. To admit the illogic of anti-doping religion overturns the reassuring moral order, makes us one with the scary wolf we despise, and does not satisfy our need for stability.

Especially in the United States, we celebrate the science of changing self and performance as an American virtue. Untrammeled by tradition, scorning aristocratic ways, and unburdened by Old World religious orders, Americans built a name for themselves as a people who are always willing to reboot to realize the unthinkable—what Mark Twain described in 1873 as a pioneer ability to rush through "astounding enterprises" with "a magnificent dash and daring and a recklessness of cost or consequences."[3] Public and press hysteria about the doping of athletes may be a way for us to deflect deeper social and personal complicities over our simultaneous desire for constant progress—faster, higher, stronger—and our need for social stability.

It's hard to confront our own collusion in the government sanction of wholesale direct-to-consumer drug and supplement pushing and our willing cooperation as consumers of lifestyle-enhancing drugs. So we don't. Maintaining the useful illusions of chemical purity and the inherent evil in drug-using athletes allows us to blame individuals like Lance Armstrong and Ben Johnson and saves us from dealing with the more difficult reality that doping is a social and political problem, not just a matter of weeding out dishonest individuals. As John Hoberman puts it, "The failure of national and international sports federations to control doping is primarily a political phenomenon, though it is conventionally misrepresented as being caused by the moral degeneracy of individual athletes."[4] Confronting our own complicity with performance-enhancing drugs demands a level of intellectual humility that is hard to conjure up when the easier option of blaming others is so close at hand.

There is an instructive parallel between the incentives fertilizing doping in sports and the motives that encourage Big Pharma to spend $42 billion a year creating demand for its products—far more than it spends on research. In a 2013 essay on the corruption of pharmaceutical markets, Carlton University professor Marc-André Gagnon writes that the pharmaceutical industry's financial emphasis on sales and marketing over developing life-saving drugs is not the product "of rogue corporations, but rather of systemic market incentives. Individual companies are left with little choice but to use these objectionable practices in order to survive in the corrupt market structure."[5]

Every year the pharmaceutical industry spends an average of $61,000 per American doctor marketing its wares to physicians. Drug companies conduct and ghostwrite research as much to create sales arguments for existing drugs as to invent new ones. Even as the industry stimulates demand by manufacturing new pathologies through savvy marketing, it rewards its shareholders without technically committing an ethical trespass.[6] Although the hardworking scientists inside these pharmaceutical companies may have the best of intentions to end disease and suffering, a mesh of economic and political incentives has moved an entire industry's moral compass in a direction that is at odds with those noble goals.

Writing of corruption in the pharmaceutical industry in 2013, Harvard University ethicist Lawrence Lessig defined institutional corruption as the systemic, legal, and even ethical influences that corrode an institution's ability to execute by sidetracking it from its original purpose.[7] In the same way that a magnet can draw a compass needle away from true north, institutional corruption can pull an organization and its collective members away from their ethical North Star. This is not a sudden eruption from the norms binding civil society—a shooting death, a bank robbery. Instead, it is a gradual drift that takes place in plain sight and often within the boundaries of existing laws and moral standards.

When it comes to performance-enhancing drugs, both professional sports and the fans of those sports have been pulled away from a pole star that is itself a useful illusion, an idealized state of fair play unsullied by pharmaceutical cheating. This "corruption" of a pure state that never existed has come around not because bad people took advantage of good people. To borrow Lessig's term, that kind of interpretation of institutional corruption is "kindergarten ethics," a simplistic filtering of life's complexities that sees the world as black and white, good and bad. "Sometimes perfectly decent souls intending the very best for all nonetheless produce harm," Lessig writes.[8] The task of understanding this institutional compass drift is difficult because it is so complex; in the case of pro sports, it is doubly so because the hope in an unseen standard of chemical-free, pure-sports perfection is a recent fabrication forced upon sports that, like society at large until the 1960s, had previously accommodated drug taking as a necessary and even moral act.

The rise and fall of Lance Armstrong exemplify how institutional moral drift affected cycling's enforcement of anti-doping moral strictures. "Lance Armstrong was the most bankable cover subject *Outside* has ever had this side of Mount Everest," wrote the magazine's editor Christopher Keyes in 2014.[9] *Outside* featured Armstrong on the cover 10 times. The Texan also made the cover of *Sports Illustrated* 11 times, and like the stardom that led to Muhammad Ali's 38 *SI* covers and Michael Jordan's 57, Armstrong was a cultural phenomenon whose influence radiated far beyond his own sport and whose draw was critical to justifying the $600,000 fee *Sports Illustrated* charged for an advertisement on its back cover. The Lance Armstrong story was not just about his wins; it was also about how he made the sport of cycling a much bigger American story than it was before his first Tour de France victory in 1999.

Knowing Armstrong represented a financial jackpot for the sport and that he inspired millions of Americans to get off their butts and exercise, cycling governing bodies focused on the good he brought to the sport. Steve Johnson was the president of USA Cycling during the Armstrong era. When I met with Johnson at USA Cycling headquarters in Colorado Springs, he told me, "I can tell you categorically that I've never had a conversation with anybody that I've known in the Olympic movement that's talked about institutionalized doping programs as a solution to the problem of international success." Johnson's careful wording allows him to avoid complicity with *institutionalized* doping while sidestepping any claim about the individualized doping that was rampant among Euro-level American pro cyclists during his tenure. The small-government design of the Amateur Sports Act of 1978 ensured that doping would never be a state-funded effort in the United States as it was in East Germany. However, USA Cycling's passivity in the face of common American doping was a lingering effect of the Amateur Sports Act's presidential demand that Olympic sports deliver victories on international stages. Armstrong's story of a return from near-certain death to world champion was a magnet that pulled USA Cycling and the UCI away from their commitment to clean sports. Not a force that caused a sudden change in direction, Armstrong's success instead precipitated gradual institutional drift at USA Cycling that led it to allow doping through omission rather than feed or halt it through commission.

Johnson was a University of Utah sports science professor when he began consulting with USA Cycling. Over time, his relationship deepened, and in 2000, Johnson became the organization's CEO. How he came into that position helps illustrate why a single-minded focus on ridding the sport of doped cyclists could clash with the gravitational pull of a larger set of incentives motivating the Olympic organizing body's actions. It also shows how anti-doping ethics is not a black-and-white issue, but rather a matter of interpreting varying shades of gray.

In 1987, a 47-year-old banker and ex-American speed skating champion named Thomas Weisel hired Eddie Borysewicz to coach him in cycling. When Weisel started a pro team in 1989, Borysewicz led the squad, which eventually became the Subaru-Montgomery pro cycling team in the early 1990s. By 1997, as Weisel worked on the IPO of a new company called Yahoo, he combined forces with Mark Gorski, a retired Olympian, Wells Fargo banker, and USA Cycling coach, to create the U.S. Postal Service team. That squad hired talented young Americans, including Lance Armstrong, George Hincapie, Tyler Hamilton, and Marty Jemison. Spanish doctor Pedro Celaya was brought on to manage the team's use of EPO and other performance enhancers.

When Celaya proved too cautious, the team managers replaced him with another Spanish doctor, Luis García del Moral, who prescribed more aggressively than Celaya. In 1999, Armstrong won his first Tour de France. The post-race celebratory dinner saw Armstrong's manager Bill Stapleton and coach Chris Carmichael toasting the team's success with its new manager, Belgian Johan Bruyneel. Upon his return to the United States, Armstrong met President Bill Clinton and Vice President Al Gore at the White House. Sponsorships flooded in. Gorski drew upon the sales talents honed during his five-year stint as a Wells Fargo executive and inked some 20 new deals that made the team flush with cash. In the months following his July 1999 win, Armstrong personally closed $7.5 million in sponsorship deals, including one that made him spokesman for pharmaceutical company Bristol-Myers Squibb.[10]

Riding on this public interest and flush with money from his investment business, Weisel started a new sports marketing company, Tailwind Sports. With Gorski as Tailwind CEO, in 2000, Weisel capitalized on cycling's growing cachet as "the new golf" among affluent business people and created the Champion's Club, a group of wealthy executives who donated upward of $100,000 a year to the USA Cycling Development Foundation, a charitable organization that benefited young American riders. In exchange for their philanthropy, these highly driven businessmen (most were men) got behind-the-scenes access to the U.S. Postal Service team and VIP treatment at the Tour de France. The foundation gave Weisel insight on how USA Cycling was run. He did not like what he saw.

Weisel knew Steve Johnson because they were teammates on a masters cycling team. At the time, Johnson was still working as a professor and consulting with USA Cycling. Johnson told me that the organization was a financial and organizational mess. It "had a lot of divisiveness," Johnson said. "It was chaos." Over time, Weisel's foundation gained a voting position on the USA Cycling board of directors, and that gave Weisel the foothold he needed to clean house. Johnson stepped into the CEO position, and later Weisel selected former Motorola director Jim Ochowicz as USA Cycling's president. Ochowicz also took a job as a broker with Weisel's investment company and began managing money for UCI president Hein Verbruggen—a personal relationship with the

UCI chief that Ochowicz had enjoyed since 1999, when Ochowicz had managed the Dutchman's investments at another brokerage firm in Milwaukee. The world of elite cycling management was as small and interrelated as the characters in a Jane Austen novel.[11]

The meshed connections created a system of small incentives and personal allegiances that worked to pull the sport's moral compass needle away from the still very aspirational direction of clean racing. While anti-doping missionaries were trying to impose post-Festina purity on the cycling natives, other factors, including the UCI and USA Cycling's mission to grow the sport in the United States, did not always align with this clean-sport project.

When the French newspaper *Le Monde* broke the news that Armstrong's urine sample from the first day of the 1999 Tour had come up positive for illegal corticosteroids, the UCI, under Verbruggen's leadership, knowingly or unknowingly helped get Armstrong off the hook. Dr. García del Moral wrote a prescription for a saddle-sore ointment containing the steroid and backdated it. The UCI accepted the scrip and Armstrong was free to continue down the path to winning his first of seven Tours. The following year, a French TV crew filmed U.S. Postal Service team doctors dumping medical debris at a highway rest stop. The waste included a blood-doping product called Actovegin. Though it was not listed as a banned substance, Actovegin violated the spirit of anti-doping rules. When news of the discovery broke in the fall of 2000, Gorski deflected it with a story that the team carried Actovegin to treat road rash and for a diabetic team mechanic. The UCI did not take action.

While Weisel has long denied any knowledge of doping on Armstrong's teams, in 2008, he expressed a pragmatic point of view, telling the *Wall Street Journal* that when it came to performance-enhancing drugs in pro cycling, the sport should follow the model of U.S. sports like baseball and football: "Handle the problem below the surface and keep the image of the sport clean. . . . Most fans couldn't care less."[12]

When I asked Johnson how he could not have known that U.S. cyclists were doping, he told me that he never had any hard evidence to run with. The network of connections between Armstrong's long-time financial backers and USA Cycling's leadership and board of directors made it likely that if anyone came to Johnson with news of Armstrong doping, Johnson would tell the Texan before alerting anti-doping agencies. Personal allegiances, financial obligations, and even love of cycling pulled USA Cycling's ethical compass needle toward growth and asset protection, rather than antidrug campaigning—which was the job of WADA and USADA, anyhow. In 2010, when Floyd Landis sent a 1,080-word e-mail to Johnson detailing the U.S. Postal Service team's drug use, Johnson responded by having a USA Cycling attorney contact Armstrong's agent Bill Stapleton. Armstrong quickly contacted the domestic team Landis was riding for and told it to fire Landis. With proof in his hand that USA Cycling leadership would put protecting its golden goose ahead of staying on board the anti-doping morality bandwagon, Landis set up a meeting with USADA's Travis Tygart—and in so doing, pulled the first thread that led to the eventual unraveling of Armstrong's claims that he never doped.[13]

To understand the forces that would lead governing bodies like USA Cycling and the UCI to selectively enforce their anti-doping rules for Armstrong, it helps to look back at Lessig's definition of institutional corruption as a "strategic influence" that is legal and even ethical. It diverts an institution from its primary purpose and also undermines that institution's inherent trustworthiness. There was nothing illegal about the nest of relationships built around Weisel, Johnson, Verbruggen, and Armstrong. And in terms of growing the sport of cycling by getting more Americans riding and racing and watching European racing on television, the relationships made a lot of strategic sense. Even letting Armstrong off the hook when his team was discovered with a blood booster in 2000 is also within the bounds of legality, since Actovegin was not specifically banned. Keep in mind, too, that in 2000, WADA was in its infancy and did not have today's moral and scientific authority.

Seen at the policy level, Weisel's efforts were doing a lot of good for American cycling by funneling funds into development programs that gave kids vital experience—hard times racing on mud-slicked Belgian roads while lashed by wind, rain, and Europe's best young riders. The program helped set the character- and muscle-building foundation for the American riders, who could now consistently challenge the Europeans on their own turf. Nonetheless, the subtle network of incentives, the small "economies of influence," would seem to make it more likely for Verbruggen to accept a ginned-up steroid prescription, knowing that the man who started Armstrong's team also could get him invested in Silicon Valley's hottest IPOs and help cycling recover from the devastating crisis that was 1998's Festina affair.

In a sense, the quiet institutional deviances that allowed Lance Armstrong to thrive on the roads of Europe, and in turn helped cycling bloom in America, can be seen as an ethical drift that served a legitimate moral end. After all, if the price of getting thousands of Americans off their couches and out spinning their legs and revving their hearts while pretending they are Lance on the Col du Galibier is overlooking a few doping positives, is that such a bad trade off—especially when anti-doping enforcement was so new and widely disregarded?

An argument can be made (and Johnson and Verbruggen seemed to have made it to themselves in 2000) that the act of letting the cancer survivor Armstrong slide after his Actovegin positive was outweighed by the cost of kicking an already staggering Tour de France and its fresh American cancer hero less than two years after the Festina affair. Hypocrisy? Sure, but seen in the light of the larger troubles caused by another ruined Tour de France and further bedraggled sport, they had good reason to deviate from still coagulating anti-doping norms in the interest of serving the larger good of cycling growth. In the interest of protecting sponsors and building the sport's feel-good image, the UCI and USA Cycling applied what doping researcher Verner Møller calls "linguistic sugar-coating" on "the bitter pill of sport."[14]

When I proposed to Johnson that Verbruggen and his successor Pat McQuaid might have had pragmatic reasons for not taking Armstrong down while he was raising the collective image of cycling, he admitted there may be some truth to that proposition. Knowing that Johnson rebuffed riders Floyd Landis and Dave Zabriskie when they brought U.S. Postal Service team doping programs to his attention, his response is telling. "I understand why Pat and Hein might have done what they apparently did," Johnson told me. "But you don't condone it, necessarily."

In 2013, two criminology professors compared the ethical and regulatory frameworks of pro cycling during the Armstrong era to the mortgage industry abuses and exotic derivatives trading that led to 2008's global financial collapse. The researchers, Nancy Reichman from the University of Denver and Ophir Sefiha from Western Carolina University, point out that both pro cycling and the financial markets are under enormous pressure to enhance performance. "How does one create a regulatory environment that encourages actors to push their limits, maximize their potential, and create new frontiers of performance while maintaining individuals' health and the integrity of a level playing field?" they ask.[15]

We know how EPO pumped up cyclist performances. On Wall Street, traders began inflating their portfolio performances by packaging and reselling derivative financial products like collateralized debt obligations (CDO) and asset-backed securities (ABS). In the simplest terms, these products shifted risk from one party to another. Like the clinical-trial EPO used by early adopting endurance athletes in the 1980s, the financial instruments "were unconventional, complex, and poorly understood," Reichman and Sefiha write. But they also created new profit centers for banks. Like EPO when it first hit the scene in the late 1980s, CDOs were designed for short-term performance enhancement. Few worried about the long-term health of the products' users. Of course, now we know what happens when global bankers pump up returns by trading instruments that no one understands—the market collapsed and the global economy crumpled.

Pro cycling responded to the widespread adoption of EPO and other bioengineered drugs by criminalizing the behavior with minimal input from the athletes themselves. Especially after the Festina affair, drugs in cycling were presented as an immediate, pressing danger to riders' moral and physical health. The ethics of the matter were assumed and were not up for discussion: EPO is bad; it should be prohibited and its users punished. Sports regulators banned the products, set up a 24-hour police surveillance system (in- and out-of-competition testing and daily whereabouts reporting), and created strict punishments for transgressions.

While cycling acted with quick, paternalistic sanctimony, the world of finance's response was a thing of drowsy indifference. Wall Street regulators assumed that natural risk management would ensure that traders supervised their own behavior and would shy away from super-hazardous bets. That is, the financial industry treated its workers the same way pro cycling did until the 1960s, when there were no quasi-religious morality police imposing value judgments on the wheelmen of the road. In the new, highly regulated environment, cyclists were no longer adults, working in a laissez-faire marketplace regulated by the desire to become rich and stay alive and healthy, but were transformed into children, assumed to be guilty, who must be watched to preserve sporting purity. This was not the case on Wall Street.

Reichman and Sefiha propose what might have happened in cycling had it been treated like the financial markets, and vice versa for Wall Street under cycling's crime-and-control model. If pro cyclists had the power of bankers to dictate how they were governed, the criminologists speculate that EPO blood doping, like derivatives, "would be understood not as cheating, but as innovation."[16] Further, what minimal regulation existed would only be verified through periodic rider "stress tests" meant to ensure that they were not going to physically collapse and bring others down with them—both in terms of crashing out riders and harming the sport's overall brand value. Rather than monitoring athletes' morality, the tests would watch their health and physical soundness. These stress tests would also monitor the overall financial stability of the pro cycling business.

Were the markets for financial derivatives treated like cycling, innovations like CDOs would be seen as dirty and morally insidious. "An independent party would evaluate new instruments and either allow or disallow their use based on their impact on the spirit of the market," Reichman and Sefiha explain.[17] Rules would dictate that the use of certain return-boosting financial instruments would lead to a banker's ejection from the financial playing fields for two years or more. All market participants would be presumed guilty of fiscal malfeasance and would be under constant surveillance to curb immoral behavior. Associating with experienced CDO consultants could lead to ejection from the financial community. They would also have to register their whereabouts with a policing authority so that they could be located and examined 365 days a year. Not showing up for checkup would be the same as being caught using speculative trading instruments. Banker trading activity would be stored and could be reexamined for transgressions for 10 years. The overarching objective of this system would be to protect the moral purity of the bankers and the organizations they represented.

This thought experiment reveals the shortcomings in both a police state and a self-regulating approach to curbing performance enhancement. Reichman and Sefiha point out that because pushing the boundaries of performance is natural and celebrated in elite sports and finance, "regulation that draws bright line rules around performance enhancement and then seeks to deter rule-breaking by sanctions is problematic given that pushing limits is routine, valued, and highly rewarded."[18] The spirit of elite sports, like that of high finance, is about breaking limits in the interest of attaining unprecedented output. And the demonization of the cheater as a morally decrepit aberration ignores the larger truth that there are enormous organizational and social pressures making this "outrageous" behavior perfectly rational—forces complicated by the fact that performance-enhancing drugs and procedures are acceptable *everywhere in society* save under certain circumstances on a playing field.

The researchers conclude that neither the hands-off (Wall Street) nor the police state (cycling) model takes the necessary time and energy to understand what motivates sports and financial cultures and the individual players' will to push themselves to the limits of human potential.

Nor do these systems appreciate the financial and psychological rewards that motivate the actors' actions. By grasping the intrinsic and external rewards that inspire performance enhancement, they propose we might come up with better solutions for stopping the behaviors that can both harm athlete health and tilt the playing field against those who choose not to dope to win.

In 2004, a trio of British and Australian professors argued in the *British Journal of Sports Medicine* that if sports organizing bodies were serious about protecting athlete health, they would legalize doping that is not harmful to athlete health and focus their efforts on banning injurious drugs like anabolic steroids. The article points out that classical musicians take performance-enhancing beta-blocker drugs. These pharmaceuticals help performers manage stage fright and lower the physical effects of stress. And although elite classical music is easily as competitive as professional sports, the writers point out that "there is no stigma attached to the use of these drugs. We do not think less of the violinist or pianist who uses them." The authors contend that if certain nonharmful drugs were legalized, fans would be able to enjoy athletic performances with the same nonjudgmental attitude we bring to a concert hall today.[19]

The authors note that sports today are rigged to reward those athletes who win the genetic lottery. The athlete with the naturally occurring 52 percent hematocrit is a born winner, and the slob with the 42 percent just has to suck it up. Yet because EPO is outlawed, athletes now take the drug with an eye toward not getting caught, rather than taking safe amounts. Today, the two legal methods of increasing hematocrit are relatively expensive. Hypoxic air machines cost upward of $7,000, while training at altitude requires significant travel funds—an economic barrier and playing-field-tilter, especially for athletes who live in Third World sea-level countries. On the other hand, when the article was published in 2006, the authors wrote that EPO treatment cost about $122 a month. "Even if the Epogen treatment begins four years before an event, it is still cheaper than the hypoxic air machine," they explain. In 2000, the cost of an EPO test was about $130 per sample. Rather than spending mountains of money on testing athletes for doing something that merely attempts to level a genetically uneven playing field, the authors suggest sports governing bodies spend those testing funds "on grants to provide EPO to poorer athletes" as well as tests to ensure that their hematocrit stays within a healthy range. Doing so would kill two birds with one expenditure; it would preserve the fair play that sports organizations have dedicated themselves to saving while also helping to protect athlete health.[20]

The writers argue that while prohibitions might appear to preserve health, they can instead have unintended harmful consequences. During the 1920s, the U.S. prohibition on alcohol increased the dangers of alcohol use. Without bars to go to, people drank in private, drinking more than they had before and downing noxious concoctions of homemade moonshine. Alcoholism and deaths went up, not down. Similarly, under today's performance-enhancing-drug ban, athletes look for drugs that are still in clinical trials and so new they do not show up in drug tests; this creates a demand for drugs whose effects on the human body are relatively unknown. They also point out what Dianabol-populizer Ziegler saw right away in the 1950s: Athletes take drugs in amounts proportional to the performance gain they want, not according to a doctor's safe-dosage guidelines. The *British Journal of Sports Medicine* writers concluded that the prohibition of doping in sports—and the default moral outrage that meets any suggestion of a rethinking of the current dope-equals-evil schoolyard approach to the problem—paradoxically encourages athletes to push the limits of both dosages and new pharmaceuticals.[21]

When I phoned 1984 Olympic gold medalist Alexi Grewal to talk about this book, our conversation turned to Lance Armstrong's downfall and what his rejection by the American public says about us. Grewal pointed out that Armstrong started in cycling as a brash Texas outsider. He was a punk whose impatience with European cycling protocol raised hackles on both sides of the Atlantic. And then he became the ultimate insider whose role as cycling's most valuable asset gave him the leverage needed to control governors all the way from the U.S. Congress to USA Cycling to the UCI's McQuaid and Verbruggen. "At first Lance was a little bit outside of the boundaries, the protocol that requires respect for other riders," Grewal recalled. "And then he became the boundary. And he enforced the boundaries. And he protected many, many people in high positions who are still there because Lance never gave them up."

Armstrong was a Texas bull in the European china shop—and after smashing around, he ended up becoming the boss of that very shop. It was a parable of American power and irreverent colonialism that appealed to a swath of fans in the United States far wider than the country's then-limited population of leg-shaving, Colnago-fetishizing bike racers. Indeed, beginning with his 1993 world championship win, where a 22-year-old Armstrong soloed to victory in a pissing Norwegian rain, Armstrong's impudence and his seven Tour wins moved cycling off the bike geek pages of *VeloNews* and onto the mainstream cover of *Sports Illustrated.* Reflecting on Armstrong's brashness, Grewal observed that unlike the quiet dignity of Miguel Indurain, who had won five Tours in a row before Armstrong's arrival, "That's why we loved him, because he was us. Lance Armstrong is us. Lance Armstrong is the United States. And that's why we hate him so much—because in Lance we see ourselves. Lance represented everything that is America."

America's most accomplished cyclist represents his nation's conflicted attitudes about using performance-enhancing drugs and medical procedures to get ahead in life. What we do, sports people should not. Armstrong's success, and his spectacular downfall, put the spotlight on our own inability to confront the reality that we Americans are loath to spit in the soup that keeps us mentally sharp, muscled, and ready to get ahead. And yet, maybe it is the case that our silence regarding athletes and politicians pitching Viagra, and our seeming indifference to the pharmaceutical industry's eager willingness to turn the United States—and its rambunctious kids—into a nation of people just one pill away from realizing their full human-performance potential, is a form of American pragmatism.

Call it victory or call it moral collapse, American society's embrace of the very drugs we love to hate can be seen as a collective shrug of the shoulders—a sloughing off of the quaint impossibility of a doped society's attempts to impose religious purity on elite sports and a rejection of the notion that authoritative paternalism should replace rationalism as a free human's guiding light.

EPILOGUE

THE SPIRIT OF SPORT

The foundations of anti-doping don't withstand close historical scrutiny. Health risks, unfair advantage, and the spirit of sport are all compromised artifices rolled out at various times to fulfill the financial, nationalistic, or social needs of the constellation of interests surrounding Olympic and professional sports. Smoke and mirrors. The driving rationale of elite sports is high performance—sheer ambition indifferent to everything save victory. Doping follows the logic of continually expanding the limits of human output. If elite sports have a transcendent essence or animating spirit, it lies in the marshaling of available technologies to gain a competitive advantage. As historian Paul Dimeo has argued, Olympic-level sports are not about rediscovering a lost era when everyone was equal and took to the field to build personal character. Instead, Dimeo writes, "The point of training and preparation is to make the playing field uneven."[1]

Around the world, but especially in the United States, our natural habitat is an ocean of pharmaceuticals. Given this cultural reality, the odds seem remote that pro sports could carve out its own fantasy island of chemical purity.

John Hoberman writes that we "crusade against those drugs that symbolize diminished productivity and personal degeneration" while we celebrate on national TV "lifestyle drugs that are intended to enhance the various performances of an aging population."[2] We criminalize drugs that represent moral deviance and crippled national performance and build protective legislative moats around those that enhance and extend life for an aging population. We allow drugs to be pushed on society with unregulated vigor, and we elect legislators who consistently place the financial health of drug and supplement makers over the physical well-being of the public. And yet by clinging to the notion that doping in sports is an act of individual degeneracy rather than collective complicity, we avoid confronting the discomfiting fact that performance-enhancing drug use is a group achievement, not a solitary delinquency.

To borrow the thoughts of doping researcher and philosopher Verner Møller, our schizophrenic, reality-denying attitudes and policies toward drugs in sports suggest that when we wag our fingers at sports dopers, we are really just expressing "a matter of taste," not some sort of bedrock morality. Given that society at large consumes massive quantities of performance-enhancing drugs, but without the horrifying consequences that anti-doping missionaries assure us will befall athletes if they do not turn from their traditional ways, Møller suggests, "The only real justification the opponent of doping can offer is that he just doesn't like it."[3]

Given that the history of anti-doping is, as Dimeo describes it, a story "waist high in hypocrisy,"[4] is the anti-doping movement worth it? Knowing that our attitudes of whether a drug is good or evil seem to be informed as much by emotion and payola as logic, should we throw up our hands, call home the pure sports missionaries from their global outposts, and admit that anti-doping is a hopelessly compromised holy war, a historically blind exercise in futility and evasion?

I don't think so, if only for one reason: elite athletes are role models whose actions affect consumer behavior. They did not ask for this role, and they have no legal or inherent social obligation to accept it. But it has been handed to them nonetheless. And the success of doped athletes moves billions of dollars worth of nutritional supplements every year and inspires one-tenth of our nation's high schoolers to use steroids and growth hormones. While the history of anti-doping is hip deep in ethical mire, the past need not condemn the project's future. The quest for a state of pure sports can still serve as a useful and inspirational model for society at large.

To grasp this aspirational notion, consider influential neurologist George Miller Beard's 1881 comments on America's thirst for drugs. "Nowhere else shall we find such extensive, gorgeous, and richly supplied chemical establishments as here," Beard wrote in his book *American Nervousness, Its Causes and Consequences.* A Yale graduate and a field doctor in the American Civil War, Beard marveled at his country's hyperactive drive to succeed through technical invention. "Not only in proprietary medicines, but in physicians' prescriptions, as well as in self-doctoring, this continent leads the world," Beard wrote. "A physician can live here on half the number of families that would be needed to support him in Europe, on the same terms."[5]

The story is hardly different today. American patronage of drug establishments is still a thing of manic awe. According to a 2016 *Wall Street Journal* story, in 2015, Americans spent $425 billion on drugs.[6] A 2014 study of anabolic steroid use found that 2.9 to 4 million Americans aged 13 to 15 have used the hormone.[7] According to the U.S. Centers for Disease Control and Prevention (CDC), the primary gateway to heroin addiction, which kills nearly 10,000 Americans every year, is prescription opioid painkillers like oxycodone. According to the CDC, prescription-painkiller users are 40 times more likely to become addicted to heroin than marijuana smokers.[8]

CDC researchers also report that 11 percent of all Americans 12 and older take antidepressant medications. Among 18- to 44-year-olds, these mood enhancers are the most-used drugs in America. Eight percent of antidepression drug users do not have symptoms of the disease, suggesting that many use the drugs in an additive fashion, rather than a restorative one. That is, instead of using drug therapies to get back to normal, they are doping to be better than normal.[9]

Of course, the public's appetite for prescription drugs is matched by its hunger for illegal ones. Analyzing drug residues excreted into municipal wastewater systems, epidemiologists can quantify illegal drug use without relying on questionably accurate surveys. A 2013 study of two Canadian cities, one large and one small, found doses of cocaine in the wastewater of 38 out of 1,000 citizens. For every 1,000 people, there were 28 doses of ephedrine. The researchers observed a significant spike in the party drug Ecstasy (MDMA) on Sundays, when sewers carried the remainders from Saturday night's festivities.[10] In 2015, the European Monitoring Center for Drugs and Drug Addiction reported that a three-year study of wastewater in 50 European cities from 2011 to 2015 saw similar drug-use trends in Europe.[11]

During the first decade of the 21st century, WADA consistently found that about 2 percent of all tested athletes were positive. But to assume that 98 percent of elite and amateur athletes are not doping is incorrect. In a meta-analysis of multiple studies of athlete-reported drug use in North America, Europe, and Australia, Paul Dimeo and fellow researcher John Taylor found that actual drug use is much higher than what WADA was turning up. The WADA results are "not representative of the wider usage of doping drugs within international sport," Dimeo and Taylor concluded. Their research suggests doping rates are more in line with data from a study that revealed that 43 percent of a large sample of elite Australian athletes showed probability of doping.[12]

In 2003, WADA examined 151,210 athlete dope test samples. In 2010, the agency tested 258,267. Although the intrusiveness of the anti-doping regime increased along with the number of banned drugs, there was no corresponding increase in the number of athletes being caught. As WADA pointed out in a 2013 self-review, "Despite the significant increase in testing and the ability to detect more sophisticated substances, there has been no apparent statistical improvement in the number of positive results." The WADA working group that wrote the analysis noted that if positive tests for marijuana and asthma medications were taken out, the number of positives would be less than 1 percent. "The real problems are the human and political factors," the group concluded, pointing to the social and economic forces working against the drive to eliminate drugs from sports.[13]

Surveys of performance-enhancing drug use among elite German athletes in 2005 and 2007 confirm the conclusion that most doping athletes get away with it. As with the world outside sports, doping is common—as high as 48 percent among aspiring German Olympians. Using a survey technique designed to elicit honest responses from athletes who might be threatened by questions about drug use, researchers Werner Pitsch and Eike Emrich found that 20 to 39 percent of the athletes on the German Olympic A, B, and C teams reported taking performance-enhancing drugs in 2005, and 26 to 48 percent reported doping at least once in their sporting careers.[14] When the German researchers repeated the survey in 2007, 10 to 35 percent of German Olympic hopefuls reported using performance-enhancing drugs. The study also found that younger, lower-tier athletes competing at the national level were more likely to dope than established international stars.* The German studies showed that WADA is right—the level of doping in elite sports is much higher than the 1 to 2 percent that the agency is snaring. From the Tour de France to the race of life, turning to chemicals is the norm.

Of the 20 Tour de France races between 1990 and 2010, only three winners have not been caught or implicated in doping scandals. And

---

* Pitsch and Emrich theorized that the higher reported usage in 2005 did not come from a decline in overall doping but was due to a higher number of cyclists and weight lifters in the 2005 study than in 2007. The researchers proposed that the different attitudes toward doping among national and international athletes was the result of a cost-benefit analysis. For athletes trying to get to the top, there is little financial loss in getting caught but lots of reward for winning. Meanwhile, for established international pros, there are high prestige and financial costs for doping—they have made it to the top, and they don't want to lose the financial security that comes with success on the global stage. Furthermore, for international top-tier athletes, the risk of doping is higher because, relative to aspiring national-level athletes, pros undergo more testing and surveillance. Werner Pitsch and Eike Emrich, "The Frequency of Doping in Elite Sport: Results of a Replication Study," *International Review for the Sociology of Sport* 47, no. 5 (2012): 571.

doping is not limited to pros. Between 2001 and mid-2015, the U.S. Anti-Doping Agency sanctioned 88 American cyclists for various performance-enhancing drug violations. Along with erstwhile Tour champs Lance Armstrong and Floyd Landis, the USADA handed punishments to amateur and masters riders that included a 45-year-old and a 49-year-old at the 2012 New York Gran Fondo; a 41-year-old category 3 racer; a 62-year-old masters rider who received a two-year ban for using EPO, amphetamines, and steroids; and a rider who got popped for EPO at age 49 and then again for drugs at age 51. Eleven other riders tested positive for recreational drugs like marijuana. In a 2015 study of these cases, researchers April Henning and Paul Dimeo noted that these cycling-obsessed amateurs were ambitiously asserting their relevance in local cycling tribes. To strut their age-defying fitness, the amateurs took "the next step towards the pseudo-professionalization of their hobby by using doping drugs.[15]

From amateur masters races to Tour de France pros, in our world of "extensive, gorgeous, and richly supplied chemical establishments," drugs are seen as an empowering human right and a tool to bend the forces of time. The WADA code cites three justifications for its anti-doping project: (1) performance-enhancing drugs give unfair advantage; (2) doping is unhealthy; and (3) doping violates the spirit of sport. Athletes caught taking substances that violate two out of three of these principles are busted.

Emotionally, these are noble foundations, but we've seen how the "preservation of athlete health" argument is full of holes—dangers intrinsic to sports are far greater than extrinsic risks of medically supervised performance-enhancing drug use. And even with drugs being as common in sports as in the world at large, elite athletes are still healthier than the rest of us. When a team of French medical researchers studied the 786 French riders who raced the Tour de France in the years 1947 to 2012, they found that the Tour riders had a 41 percent lower mortality rate than the overall French population.[16] As for unfair advantage, logic can make a strong case that doping should be *encouraged* to allow less genetically blessed athletes a fair shake against competitors who won the DNA lottery.

Which leaves us with the spirit of sport, described in the 2015 WADA code as "the essence of Olympism," "what is intrinsically valuable about sport," and "the celebration of the human spirit, body, and mind." Historically speaking, the values intrinsic to the earliest versions of professional sports were to entertain and advertise. Commerce and diversion were pro sports' raison d'être, not the resurrection of aristocratic fantasies about restored feudal social orders and character-building fair play.

WADA code writers constructed a version of the spirit of sport that is a modern echo of Coubertin's desire to create, in his words, "an aristocracy, an elite"[17] of sparring athlete knights who would revitalize European moral fiber. Turning from the crass capitalistic values of an ascendent merchant bourgeoisie and tamping down proletarian agitations for economic and social opportunity, the Olympics served economic and social masters. "The hour of proletarian revenge has sounded," Coubertin warned the king of Belgium at Antwerp City Hall in 1920. "Let him turn instead to intense exercise."[18] For Coubertin, the spirit of sport was the preservation of social order by means of an appeal to an illusion of fair play. This was Coubertin's "glittering dream of ancient Olympism."[19] However, when a five-member team spent more than two years drafting the original WADA code between 2000 and 2003, using sports to restore feudal order was not at the top of their minds. As historian Ian Ritchie documented in a 2013 history of the origins of WADA's "spirit of sport" clause, the drafters added the phrase because anti-doping regulations needed a mechanism to snare cheaters who used drugs that were safe and not unfair, but which revealed an *intent* to cheat.

As Ritchie explains, "Some substances and methods may not in fact be performance enhancing, but users believe they are."[20] And the *will* toward subterfuge represented a moral depravity that the code needed to be equipped to eliminate. The "spirit of sport" clause did just that. Also, some substances did not in themselves warrant inclusion on

WADA's banned list because they were neither dangerous to athletes nor performance enhancing. Marijuana does not make fast bike racers faster or motor skills sharper. Nor does the drug slaughter nearly 90,000 Americans a year, unlike alcohol. Although it does not meet the unfair advantage threshold nor have a record of harming athlete health, pot is nonetheless on the WADA banned list because its outlaw presence is contrary to the positive image of sports as a character-building redeemer of body and spirit.

But just because the spirit of sport is an ideal rather than an intrinsic sporting essence does not mean it can't serve a purpose. Indeed, Coubertin's vision of "the glittering dream of ancient Olympism" is, like most religious myths, a fiction at the service of calling forth our better selves. Fair play is a made-up contrivance for those who want to impose their fundamentalist values on athletes. However, just because the spirit of sport is a social construct does not mean we should discard it, especially when society could benefit from dope-free role models to counter the enormous commercial and government forces promoting the medicalization of every aspect of our lives.

As I hope this book has shown, anti-doping rules and regulators have caused governments, sports governing bodies, athletes, fans, and sponsors to twist themselves into contortions that condemn doping in public while embracing it in private. That is, to not spit in their own drug-enriched soup. But the fact that humans and their systems are flawed is why crusaders exist—to attempt to push us closer to a state of ethical purity.

Rationally, emotionally, and physiologically, we know that the amount of drugs Americans take is not good for us. Exercise, fresh air, and better diet are cures far more powerful than any smorgasbord of ailment-targeting pharmaceuticals. Should anti-doping missionaries gain a foothold in elite sports and gradually turn athletes into knights who perform for us without chemical aid, sports could become a worthy role model for our overdosed society at large.

Anti-doping's spirit of sport foundation is not a return to a fallen state, but rather a push toward something new and unprecedented in modern sports' 150-year history. The spirit of sport is a rhetoric of hope—an argument that athletes and their supporters can find promise in the unseen. Today's pure sports acolytes may have risen from an ignoble crucible, but their banging on about a lost state of athletic purity may be anti-doping's most redemptive element. Pure sports is a construct—a glittering dream. To propose, with Coubertin, that "the essential is not to conquer, but to fight well" may be quaint and out of touch with the commercial, victory-seeking essence of Olympic and professional sports, but just because it is made up does not mean it can't tack sports away from a world mediated by chemicals and manipulated by the mercantile obligations of pharmaceutical companies.[21]

While fraught with complicity and built on a foundation of exaggerated health fears and trumped-up moral panic, the anti-doping mission can still serve a high moral purpose. The risks of our massively drugged society are real, not fictitious. And the social harm caused by doping sportspeople is tiny compared to that done by cynical legislators and drug makers who enrich themselves on the backs of an addicted, manipulated, and aging populace. Just ask the thousands of Americans being harmed by opiates, the 6 percent of American children on performance-enhancing amphetamines, and half the nation that is being fleeced by an unregulated supplement industry. In this sense, sports' conflicted attempt to step away from the chemistry bar and stagger outside into the bright sunlight of some ideal of pure play is admirable because it is an effort to confirm our basic humanity.

ACKNOWLEDGMENTS

This book leans on a community of sports and cultural historians. By burrowing in dusty archives and tracking the winding tributaries of the historical record, these researchers have revealed a great deal about the story of doping in sports. Because university professors tend to write for one another, however, their revelations often stay trapped in academic journals and university press publications—titles limited to those with access to a college library and a tolerance for dense academic prose. The obscurity of their work is compounded because these historians often reveal facts that undermine the received wisdom that doping in sports is both inherently evil and corrosive to fair play.

As a matter of self-defense and self-righteousness, popular media and the anti-doping establishment are naturally more interested in stories that support a good-versus-evil morality tale than they are in histories that question the logic of their cause. However, historians are obligated to document the full course of events, even if doing so reveals themes that challenge the foundation of the anti-doping crusade.

When an academic like Spanish historian Bernat López reports that, based on available historical facts, EPO is not a drug of sporting mass destruction and that anti-doping organizations are more interested in preserving social order than athlete health, one response is to dismiss his work without a hearing because it sounds like an argument for legalizing drugs in sports. In this playground version of good-guy-versus-bad-guy doping, using the historical record to point out weaknesses in anti-doping logic is tantamount to supporting drugs in sports. If you are not with the war on drugs, then you must be against it. But this binarily dismissive argument—pulled as it is from the prohibitionist garage—does not serve transparency, athletes, or fans.

With his books *Mortal Engines* and *Testosterone Dreams*, University of Texas professor John Hoberman has established himself as a towering historian of doping in sports. Both in his generous personal conversations with me and through his writing, Hoberman contributed mightily to my understanding of the complicities that make the history of performance-enhancing drugs in sports so fascinating.

In Scotland, the University of Stirling's Paul Dimeo was a terrific help in one-on-one discussions, at doping conferences I attended with him, and with his outstanding 2007 book, *A History of Drug Use in Sport, 1876–1976: Beyond Good and Evil.*

Danish historians Verner Møller and Ask Vest Christiansen have done years of eye-opening work on the social, economic, and political inconsistencies that throw the purity of the anti-doping mission into question. Møller's 2008 book, *The Doping Devil*, is a spirited analysis of the moral hysteria that blurs a sober understanding of the roots of doping in sports.

If there is one book everyone should read to understand France's greatest bike race, it is Ball State University historian Christopher Thompson's astonishing *The Tour de France: A Cultural History.* This book, along with many stimulating telephone and e-mail conversations with Thompson, greatly informed my understanding of how attitudes toward doping in cycling have changed since the 1800s.

California State University–Fullerton professor John Gleaves's writings on the history of horse racing, amateurism, and the 1984 Olympic

Games were invaluable for shedding light on how once acceptable sports doping became stigmatized and how anti-doping replaced antiprofessionalism as the Olympics' defining bête noire.

Bernat López's research on EPO and the media and sports science community's ability to capitalize on drug fears was radically eye-opening.

Thomas Hunt's 2011 book, *Drug Games*, was an invaluable resource for understanding the history of Olympic doping, as were my personal conversations with the University of Texas professor on how his conclusions have been modified since he published that work.

Likewise, Rob Beamish and Ian Ritchie's 2006 book, *Fastest, Highest, Strongest: A Critique of High-Performance Sport*, provided a critical historical and sociological framework for understanding that doping is not contrary to high-performance sports but rather is a symptom of their boundary-pushing essence.

Along with this raft of academics, I'm obliged to the athletes, coaches, doping scientists, enforcement agents, and sports administrators who generously gave me their time to talk about how drugs in sports have evolved from a sign of moral progress to a problem of social decay. While the historical record provides an unsparing vantage on the hypocrisies and compromises that punctuate the history of doping in sports, the people who are directly affected by society's deep fondness for chemical enhancement give this same history emotional and human weight.

Thanks are also due to my editor at VeloPress, Ted Costantino, and to Connie Oehring and Nicholle Carrière, who helped shape this account of the sprawling story of doping in sports.

Finally, this book would not exist without the support of my wife, Melinda, and our two sons, Sammy and Nico. For years they listened to me rattle on about society's dual love affair with pharmaceuticals and sports, and for that they deserve a medal.

NOTES

CHAPTER 1. THE ORIGINS OF DOPING

1 Jeré Longman, "The Marathon's Random Route to Its Length," *New York Times*, April 20, 2012.
2 "Cambridge Lad Wins Marathon Road Race," *Brooklyn Daily Eagle*, August 31, 1904.
3 Charles Lucas, *The Olympic Games: 1904* (St. Louis, MO: Woodward and Tiernan, 1905).
4 Mark Dyreson, *Making the American Team: Sport, Culture, and the Olympic Experience* (Urbana: University of Illinois Press, 1998), 78.
5 See Eric Dunning and Kenneth Sheard, *Barbarians, Gentlemen, and Players: A Sociological Study of the Development of Rugby Football* (New York: New York University Press, 1979).
6 Christopher S. Thompson, *The Tour de France: A Cultural History* (Berkeley: University of California Press, 2008), 12–13.
7 "Half a Million Cyclists," *New York Times*, May 3, 1912.
8 Peter Nye, *Hearts of Lions: The History of American Bicycle Racing* (New York: W. W. Norton, 1988), 34.
9 Ibid., 62.
10 For a history of the birth of professional cycling in Europe, see Thompson, *Tour de France*, chapter 1, "La Grande Boucle: Cycling, Progress, and Modernity."
11 Ibid., 15.
12 For an analysis of the early lack of alarm at doping, see Verner Møller, *The Doping Devil* (Copenhagen: Books on Demand, 2008), chap. 1 and 2; and Paul Dimeo, *A History of Drug Use in Sport* (London: Routledge, 2007): 17–50.
13 "Six Days' Race Ended," *New York Times*, December 16, 1900.
14 "Doping a Racer," *Morning Call* (San Francisco), November 26, 1894.
15 "'Dope' an American Term," *New York Times*, April 7, 1901.
16 See John Gleaves, "Enhancing the Odds: Horse Racing, Gambling and the First Anti-Doping Movement in Sport, 1889–1911," *Sport in History* 32, no. 1 (2012): 26–52; and

John Hoberman, *Mortal Engines: The Science of Performance and the Dehumanization of Sport* (New York: Free Press, 1992), 269–280.

17 "Winner of Cycle Race Protested," *New York Times*, October 19, 1903.

18 "Miller Far Ahead of All," *New York Times*, December 10, 1897.

19 "Cyclists in Slow Race," *New York Times*, December 12, 1903.

20 "Cyclists Behind Record," *New York Times*, December 9, 1903.

21 Robert Christison, "Observations on the Effects of Cuca, or Coca, the Leaves of the Erythroxylon Coca," *British Medical Journal* (1876): 528.

22 Ibid., 529.

23 Ibid.

24 Ibid.

25 Ibid., 530.

26 Ibid., 531.

27 Peter Karpovich, "Ergogenic Aids in Work and Sport," *Supplement to The Research Quarterly of the American Association for Health, Physical Education, and Recreation* 12, no. 2 (1941): 433.

28 Ibid. (emphasis in original).

29 Ibid.

30 Ibid., 445.

CHAPTER 2. PIERRE DE COUBERTIN AND THE FAIR PLAY MYTH

1 Pierre de Coubertin, *L'éducation en Angleterre: Colléges et Universités* (Paris: Hachette, 1888).

2 Ernest K. Ensor, "The Football Madness," *Contemporary Review*, November 1898, 751–760.

3 See Eric Dunning and Kenneth Sheard, *Barbarians, Gentlemen, and Players: A Sociological Study of the Development of Rugby Football* (New York: New York University Press, 1979).

4 Andrew Jennings, *The New Lords of the Rings: Olympic Corruption and How to Buy Gold Medals* (London: Pocket Books, 1996), 34.

5 Pierre de Coubertin, *Olympism: Selected Writings*, ed. Norbert Müller (Lausanne, Switzerland: International Olympic Committee, 2000), 535.

6 Ibid., 537.

7 Pierre de Coubertin, "The Olympic Games of 1896," *Century Illustrated Monthly Magazine* (November 1896): 39–53.

8 Coubertin, *Olympism*, 482.

9 Ibid., 598–599.

10 Ibid., 654.

11 Ibid.

12 World Anti-Doping Agency, *World Anti-Doping Code, 2015* (Montréal, Québec: World Anti-Doping Agency, 2015), 14.

13 Verner Møller, *The Doping Devil* (Copenhagen: Books on Demand, 2008), 177.

14 Ibid.

CHAPTER 3. THE FALL OF COUBERTIN'S IDEAL

1 Rob Beamish and Ian Ritchie, *Fastest, Highest, Strongest: A Critique of High-Performance Sport* (New York: Routledge, 2006), 16.

2 For a detailed account of Avery Brundage's bread war, see Robert K. Barney, Stephen R. Wenn, and Scott G. Martyn, "Avery Brundage and the Great Bread War," in *Selling the Five Rings: The International Olympic Committee and the Rise of Olympic Commercialism* (Salt Lake City: University of Utah Press, 2002).

3 Lewis Mumford, *Technics and Civilization* (Chicago: The University of Chicago Press, 1934), 303, 305.
4 Ibid., 305.
5 Ibid., 306
6 Beamish and Ritchie, *Fastest, Highest, Strongest,* 35.
7 For Glickman's account of this day, see Marty Glickman and Stan Isaacs, *The Fastest Kid on the Block: The Marty Glickman Story* (Syracuse, NY: Syracuse University Press, 1996), 17–24.
8 Bud Greenspan, "Why Jesse Owens Won 4 Gold Medals," *New York Times*, August 9, 1981.
9 Barbara Smit, *Sneaker Wars: The Enemy Brothers Who Founded Adidas and Puma and the Family Feud That Forever Changed the Business of Sport* (New York: Ecco, 2008), 11.
10 Ibid., 52.
11 Ibid., 69. See also Richard Hoffer, *Something in the Air: American Passion and Defiance in the 1968 Mexico City Olympics* (New York: Free Press, 2009), 128–129.
12 Jack Ellis, "'Games Must Go On,' Says Brundage," *Stars and Stripes*, September 7, 1972.
13 Jerry Kirshenbaum, "The Golden Days of Mark the Shark," *Sports Illustrated*, September 11, 1972; Smit, *Sneaker Wars*, 105.
14 International Olympic Committee, *Olympic Marketing Fact File: 2016 Edition* (Lausanne, Switzerland: International Olympic Committee, 2016); Tripp Mickle, "IOC Reprices TOP Deals at $200M," *Sports Business Journal*, February 17, 2014.
15 Mumford, *Technics and Civilization*, 306–307.
16 Council of Europe, Committee of Out-of-School Education, *Doping of Athletes: Reports of the Special Working Parties* (Strasbourg: Council of Europe, 1964), 48.

CHAPTER 4. THE HOT ROMAN DAY WHEN DOPING WENT BAD

1 Cited in John Gleaves and Matthew Llewellyn, "Sport, Drugs and Amateurism: Tracing the Real Cultural Origins of Anti-Doping Rules in International Sport," *International Journal of the History of Sport* 31, no. 8 (2013): 8.
2 Wythe Williams, "Parade of Athletes Will Mark Opening of Olympics Today," *New York Times*, July 28, 1928.
3 Gleaves and Llewellyn, "Sport, Drugs and Amateurism," 2. See also John Gleaves and Matthew P. Llewellyn, "Charley Paddock and the Changing State of Olympic Amateurism," *Olympika* (2012): 1–32.
4 Gleaves and Llewellyn, "Sport, Drugs and Amateurism," 6–7.
5 Ibid., 9–10.
6 Société Medicale Belge d'Education Physique et de Sports, "Rapport sur le doping," undated, IOC Archives.
7 Pierre de Coubertin, *Olympism: Selected Writings*, ed. Norbert Müller (Lausanne, Switzerland: International Olympic Committee, 2000), 652 (emphasis in original).
8 International Olympic Committee, *Olympic Rules, 1946* (Lausanne, Switzerland: International Olympic Committee, 1946), 28.
9 Council of Europe, Committee of Out-of-School Education, *Doping of Athletes: Reports of the Special Working Parties* (Strasbourg: Council of Europe, 1964), 51–52.
10 For a detailed reconstruction of the circumstances of Jensen's death, see Verner Møller, "Knud Enemark Jensen's Death During the 1960 Rome Olympics: A Search for Truth?," *Sport in History* 25, no. 3 (2005): 452–471. See also Paul Dimeo's discussion in *A History of Drug Use in Sport, 1876–1976: Beyond Good and Evil* (New York: Routledge, 2007), 55–56.
11 Møller, "Knud Enemark Jensen's Death," 470.
12 Timothy Noakes, "Exercise in the Heat," in *Clinical Sports Medicine*, ed. Peter Bruker and Karim Khan (Sydney, Australia: McGraw-Hill, 2007), 800.

13 Les Woodland, *The Crooked Path to Victory: Drugs and Cheating in Professional Bicycle Racing* (San Francisco, CA: Cycle Publishing/Van der Plas, 2003), 108.
14 *Proper and Improper Use of Drugs by Athletes: Hearings Pursuant to S. Res. 56, Section 12,* 93rd Cong. 1 (Washington, DC: U.S. Government Printing Office, 1973), 25.
15 Dimeo, *History of Drug Use*, 55.
16 Møller, "Knud Enemark Jensen's Death," 462.
17 Council of Europe, *Doping of Athletes*, 3.
18 Dimeo, *History of Drug Use*, 88.
19 Council of Europe, *Doping of Athletes*, 5.
20 Peter Karpovich, "Ergogenic Aids in Work and Sport," *Supplement to The Research Quarterly of the American Association for Health, Physical Education, and Recreation* 12, no. 2 (1941): 433.
21 Dimeo, *History of Drug Use*, 121.
22 Council of Europe, *Doping of Athletes*, 6.
23 Dimeo, *History of Drug Use*, 103.
24 Barrie Houlihan, *Dying to Win: Doping in Sport and the Development of Anti-Doping Policy* (Strasbourg, France: Council of Europe, 2002), 35–36.
25 Robert O. Voy and Kirk D. Deeter, *Drugs, Sport, and Politics* (Champaign, IL: Leisure Press, 1991), 6.
26 Ludwig Prokop, "The Problem of Doping," in *Proceedings of International Congress of Sport Sciences, 1964*, ed. Kitsuo Kato (Tokyo: Japanese Union of Sport Sciences, 1966), 267–268.
27 Møller, "Knud Enemark Jensen's Death," 467.
28 Ibid., 468.
29 Ibid., 466.
30 Ibid.
31 Ibid., 467.
32 Ibid., 465.

CHAPTER 5. DOPING BECOMES A CRIME

1 Christopher S. Thompson, *The Tour de France: A Cultural History* (Berkeley: University of California Press, 2008), 22.
2 Ibid., 228–229.
3 Ibid.
4 Jack Olsen, "A Race Not Always to the Swift," *Sports Illustrated*, August 22, 1966.
5 Bil Gilbert, "Problems in a Turned-on World," *Sports Illustrated*, June 23, 1969.
6 Thompson, *Tour de France*, 235.
7 Ibid., 234.
8 Ibid., 232–236.
9 Ibid., 242.
10 Council of Europe, Committee of Out-of-School Education, *Doping of Athletes: Reports of the Special Working Parties* (Strasbourg: Council of Europe, 1964), 50.
11 Thompson, *Tour de France*, 234.
12 Ibid., 238.
13 Ibid., 234.
14 David Millar, *Racing Through the Dark: The Fall and Rise of David Millar* (London: Orion, 2011), 94.
15 Thompson, *Tour de France*, 112.
16 Ibid., 197.
17 Christophe Bassons, Peter Cossins, and Benoit Hopquin, *A Clean Break: My Story* (London: Bloomsbury Sport, 2014), 156.
18 Millar, *Racing Through the Dark*, 95.

CHAPTER 6. THE BIRTH OF THE WORLD ANTI-DOPING AGENCY

1 World Anti-Doping Agency, *World Anti-Doping Code, 2015* (Montréal, Québec: World Anti-Doping Agency, 2015), 11.
2 Andrew Jennings, *The New Lords of the Rings: Olympic Corruption and How to Buy Gold Medals* (London: Pocket Books, 1996), 30.
3 John Hoberman, "How Drug Testing Fails: The Politics of Doping Control," in *Doping in Elite Sport: The Politics of Drugs in the Olympic Movement*, ed. Wayne Wilson and Edward Derse (Champaign, IL: Human Kinetics, 2001), 242.
4 Ibid., 266.
5 For two detailed accounts of the IOC's attempts to control the first World Conference on Doping in Sport, see Dag Vidar Hanstad, Ivan Waddington, and Andy Smith, "The Establishment of the World Anti-Doping Agency: A Study of the Management of Organizational Change and Unplanned Outcomes," *International Review for the Sociology of Sport* 43, no. 3 (2008): 227–249; and Jim Ferstle, "World Conference on Doping in Sport," in *Doping in Elite Sport: The Politics of Drugs in the Olympic Movement*, ed. Wayne Wilson and Edward Derse (Champaign, IL: Human Kinetics, 2001), 275–286. One IOC member who did think WADA needed to be independent was WADA's founding president, Richard Pound. For his perspective on WADA's birth, see Richard W. Pound, *Inside the Olympics: A Behind-the-Scenes Look at the Politics, the Scandals, and the Glory of the Games* (Etobicoke, Ontario: John Wiley & Sons Canada, 2004), 67–81.
6 John Hoberman, "Offering the Illusion of Reform on Drugs," *New York Times*, January 10, 1999.
7 Ferstle, "World Conference," 279.
8 Duncan Mackay, "Tony Banks Criticizes IOC at the World Conference on Doping in Sport," *Guardian*, February 3, 1999.
9 Thomas M. Hunt, *Drug Games: The International Olympic Committee and the Politics of Doping, 1960–2008* (Austin: University of Texas Press: 2011), chapter 8.
10 Paul Montgomery, "IOC Credibility Questioned as Drug Meeting Starts," *New York Times*, February 3, 1999.
11 Hein Verbruggen, "Reflections for the World Conference on Doping in Sport," 1999, http://oldsite.uci.ch/english/news/news_pre2000/hv_990127_1.htm.
12 Carlos Toro, "Samaranch: 'Debe reducirse drásticamente la lista de productos que son doping,'" *El Mundo*, July 26, 1998.
13 "The Olympics' Drug Problem," *New York Times*, August 9, 1998.

CHAPTER 7. DOPING AND THE COLD WAR

1 Harry S. Truman, "Recommendation for Assistance to Greece and Turkey: Address of the President of the United States," 80th Cong. 1 (1947).
2 Frederick Taylor, *Dresden: Tuesday, February 13, 1945* (New York: Perennial, 2004), 315.
3 Steven Ungerleider, *Faust's Gold: Inside the East German Doping Machine* (New York: St. Martin's, 2013), 28.
4 Rob Beamish and Ian Ritchie, *Fastest, Highest, Strongest: A Critique of High-Performance Sport* (New York: Routledge, 2006), 77.
5 For a summary of the role of sports clubs in the development of East and West German sports systems after World War II, see ibid., 77–84.
6 Ibid., 86.
7 Ibid., 87.
8 Ibid., 90.

9 Ungerleider, *Faust's Gold*, 180.
10 Mike Dennis and Jonathan Grix, *Sport Under Communism: Behind the East German "Miracle"* (New York: Palgrave Macmillan, 2012), 89.
11 Beamish and Ritchie, *Fastest, Highest, Strongest*, 104.
12 John M. Hoberman, *Mortal Engines: The Science of Performance and the Dehumanization of Sport* (New York: Free Press, 1992), 217.
13 Ungerleider, *Faust's Gold*, 181.
14 Beamish and Ritchie, *Fastest, Highest, Strongest*, 93; Ungerleider, *Faust's Gold*, 67.
15 Ungerleider, *Faust's Gold*, 72–73.
16 Pierre de Coubertin, *Olympism: Selected Writings*, ed. Norbert Müller (Lausanne, Switzerland: International Olympic Committee, 2000), 583.
17 Beamish and Ritchie, *Fastest, Highest, Strongest*, 27.
18 Kathrine Switzer, "The Girl Who Started It All," *Runner's World*, May 2007.
19 Beamish and Ritchie, *Fastest, Highest, Strongest*, 90, 92–93.
20 Hoberman, *Mortal Engines*, 222.
21 Ungerleider, *Faust's Gold*, 26–28.
22 John Hoberman, "How Drug Testing Fails: The Politics of Doping Control," in *Doping in Elite Sport: The Politics of Drugs in the Olympic Movement*, ed. Wayne Wilson and Edward Derse (Champaign, IL: Human Kinetics, 2001), 262.
23 Charlie Francis, *Speed Trap: Inside the Biggest Scandal in Olympic History* (New York: St. Martin's, 1990), 105.
24 Ibid., 107–108.
25 Ibid., 108.
26 Beamish and Ritchie, *Fastest, Highest, Strongest*, 62, 64, 91.
27 James Riordan, *Soviet Sport Background to the Olympics* (New York: Washington Mews Books, 1980), 15.
28 Yevgeny Rubin, "The Soviet System: A Better Life for Better Athletes," *New York Times*, November 12, 1978.
29 James Riordan, *Sport in Soviet Society: Development of Sport and Physical Education in Russia and the USSR* (Cambridge: Cambridge University Press, 1977), 162.
30 Nikolai Ozolin, "The Soviet System of Athletic Training," in *International Research in Sport and Physical Education*, ed. Ernst Jokl and Emanuel Simon (Springfield, IL: Charles C. Thomas, 1964), 468.
31 Lynne Luciano, *Looking Good: Male Body Image in Modern America* (New York: Hill and Wang, 2001), 55.
32 Avery Brundage, "I Must Admit—Russian Athletes Are Great!," *Saturday Evening Post*, April 30, 1955.
33 "Soviet Satellite Sends U.S. into a Tizzy," *Life*, October 14, 1957.
34 John F. Kennedy, "The Soft American," *Sports Illustrated*, December 26, 1960.
35 *Proper and Improper Use of Drugs by Athletes: Hearings Pursuant to S. Res. 56, Section 12,* 93rd Cong. 1 (Washington: U.S. Government Printing Office, 1973), 151.
36 Thomas M. Hunt, "Sport, Drugs, and the Cold War: The Conundrum of Olympic Doping Policy, 1970–1979," *Olympika* 16 (2007): 22.
37 *Proper and Improper Use of Drugs by Athletes*, 139–140.
38 Bil Gilbert, "Problems in a Turned-on World," *Sports Illustrated,* June 23, 1969.
39 "Effect of Drugs to Aid Athletes Studied by U.S.," *New York Times*, August 22, 1976.
40 Craig R. Whitney, "Sports Medicine Shares in East German Success," *New York Times*, December 22, 1976.
41 Neil. E. Amdur, "German Women's Success Stirs U.S. Anger," *New York Times*, August 1, 1976.

CHAPTER 8. ANABOLIC STEROIDS: SPORTS AS *SPUTNIK*

1 John D. Fair, "Isometrics or Steroids? Exploring New Frontiers of Strength in the Early 1960s," *Journal of Sport History* 20, no. 1 (1993): 3.
2 For Ziegler's biography, see ibid., 1–24.
3 Ibid., 4.
4 Juan De Onis, "Russians Rout U.S. Team, but Face Loss of Title if They Don't Play Chinese," *New York Times*, January 30, 1959.
5 Damion Thomas, *Globetrotting: African American Athletes and Cold War Politics* (Urbana: University of Illinois Press, 2012), 76.
6 Ibid., 77–78.
7 Robert Daley, "Seeing Red," *New York Times*, February 3, 1959.
8 Fair, "Isometrics or Steroids?," 6.
9 For a discussion of the historical inaccuracy of transposing today's performance-enhancing drug standards onto Ziegler's 1950s acts, see Rob Beamish and Ian Ritchie, *Fastest, Highest, Strongest: A Critique of High-Performance Sport* (New York: Routledge, 2006), 109.
10 Bob Goldman, Patricia J. Bush, and Ronald Klatz, *Death in the Locker Room: Steroids and Sports* (South Bend, IN: Icarus Press, 1984), 73.
11 Charles Brown-Séquard, "Note on the Effects Produced on Man by Subcutaneous Injections of a Liquid Obtained from the Testicles of Animals," *Lancet* 134, no. 3438 (1889): 105–107.
12 John M. Hoberman, *Mortal Engines: The Science of Performance and the Dehumanization of Sport* (New York: Free Press, 1992), 75.
13 Ibid., 147–148.
14 Francis Hackett, "Books of the Times," *New York Times*, May 24, 1945.
15 Paul De Kruif, *The Male Hormone* (New York: Harcourt, Brace, 1945), 221.
16 Ibid., 223.
17 Steven Ungerleider, *Faust's Gold: Inside the East German Doping Machine* (New York: St. Martin's Press, 2013), 58, 59.
18 Ibid., 130.
19 Fair, "Isometrics or Steroids?," 22.
20 Ibid., 7.
21 Ibid., 23.
22 Jan Todd and Terry Todd, "Significant Events in the History of Drug Testing and the Olympic Movement," in *Doping in Elite Sport: The Politics of Drugs in the Olympic Movement*, ed. Wayne Wilson and Edward Derse (Champaign, IL: Human Kinetics, 2001), 71.
23 "Team Physiologist Claims Nearly All U.S. Weightlifters on Steroids," *Los Angeles Times*, July 16, 1972.

CHAPTER 9. THE REDS ARE WINNING

1 Kevin Sullivan and Mary Jordan, "In Central America, Reagan Remains a Polarizing Figure," *Washington Post*, June 10, 2004.
2 Ronald Reagan, "Remarks at a Luncheon Meeting of the United States Olympic Committee in Los Angeles, California," March 3, 1983, in John T. Woolley and Gerhard Peters, The American Presidency Project, Santa Barbara, CA, http://www.presidency.ucsb.edu/ws/?pid=40995.
3 Ronald Reagan, "Remarks at the Annual Convention of the National Association of Evangelicals in Orlando, Florida," March 8, 1983, in John T. Woolley and Gerhard Peters, The American Presidency Project. Santa Barbara, CA, http://www.presidency.ucsb.edu/ws/?pid=41023.

4 Thomas M. Hunt, *Drug Games: The International Olympic Committee and the Politics of Doping, 1960/2008* (Austin: University of Texas Press, 2011), chap. 5.
5 Bjarne Rostaing and Robert Sullivan, "Triumphs Tainted with Blood," *Sports Illustrated*, January 21, 1985.
6 Gerald M. Boyd, "Reagan Terms Nicaraguan Rebels 'Moral Equal of Founding Fathers,'" *New York Times*, March 2, 1985.
7 Joseph Durso, "Study Stirs Divided Reactions," *New York Times*, January 13, 1977.
8 President's Commission on Olympic Sports, *The Final Report of the President's Commission On Olympic Sports* (Washington, DC: U.S. Government Printing Office, 1977), 12.
9 Craig R. Whitney, "Sports Medicine Shares in East German Success," *New York Times*, December 22, 1976.
10 Ibid.
11 President's Commission, *Final Report*, 1.
12 Ibid.
13 Ibid., 45.
14 Ibid., 48.
15 Ibid., 45.
16 Ibid., 45–46.
17 Ibid., 124.
18 Gerald R. Ford, "In Defense of the Competitive Urge," *Sports Illustrated*, July 8, 1974.
19 Richard M. Nixon, *RN: The Memoirs of Richard Nixon* (New York: Grosset & Dunlap, 1978), 20.
20 Michael Beschloss, "The President Who Never Earned His Varsity Letters," *New York Times*, November 14, 2014.
21 Ibid.
22 Ford, "In Defense of the Competitive Urge."
23 Thomas M. Hunt, "Countering the Soviet Threat in the Olympic Medals Race: The Amateur Sports Act of 1978 and American Athletics Policy Reform," *International Journal of the History of Sport* 24, no. 6 (2007): 809.
24 Transcript of interview with Vice President Hubert H. Humphrey, "The Russian Sports Revolution," NBC-TV, May 22, 1966.
25 Neil Amdur, "As '84 Games Grow Near, Pressure Builds on U.S.O.C.," *New York Times*, November 13, 1983.
26 Cited in Hunt, "Countering the Soviet Threat," 807.
27 Amateur Sports Act of 1978, Pub. L. No. 95-606, 92 Stat. 3045 (1978).

CHAPTER 10. SPINNING OLYMPIC GOLD: L.A. 1984

1 Gerald R. Ford, "In Defense of the Competitive Urge," *Sports Illustrated*, July 8, 1974.
2 Pierre de Coubertin, *Olympism: Selected Writings*, ed. Norbert Müller (Lausanne, Switzerland: International Olympic Committee, 2000), 648, 650.
3 *Montréal 1976: Official Report*, vol. 1, *Organization* (Ottawa, Ontario: IOC, 1978), 15.
4 Ibid., 18.
5 Thomas C. Hayes, "The Olympics Balance Sheet," *New York Times*, July 28, 1984.
6 "Quebec's Big Owe Stadium Debt Is Over," CBC News, December 19, 2006; Robert Colvile, "From 'Big Owe' to Pure Profit," *Guardian*, August 14, 2004.
7 Joel Kotkin, "Ballot Drives Threaten '84 Los Angeles Games," *Washington Post*, December 13, 1977.
8 Ibid.
9 Associated Press, "LA Plans to Sign Olympic Games Contract," May 17, 1978.
10 Peter Ueberroth, Rich Levin, and Amy Quinn, *Made in America: His Own Story* (New York: W. Morrow, 1985), 61. For accounts of Ueberroth's Los Angeles negotiating tactics, see also Robert K. Barney, Stephen R. Wenn, and Scott G. Martyn, *Selling*

the Five Rings: The International Olympic Committee and the Rise of Olympic Commercialism* (Salt Lake City: University of Utah Press, 2002), 193–202; Stephen R. Wenn, "Peter Ueberroth's Legacy: How the 1984 Los Angeles Olympics Changed the Trajectory of the Olympic Movement," *International Journal of the History of Sport* 32, no. 1 (2015): 1–15; and Kenneth Reich, *Making It Happen: Peter Ueberroth and the 1984 Olympics* (Santa Barbara, CA: Capra Press, 1986).

11 Rob Beamish and Ian Ritchie, *Fastest, Highest, Strongest: A Critique of High-Performance Sport* (New York: Routledge, 2006), 25.

12 See Barney, Wenn, and Martyn, *Selling the Five Rings*, 193–202.

13 Wenn, "Peter Ueberroth's Legacy," 4.

14 Ray Kennedy, "Miser with a Midas Touch," *Sports Illustrated*, November 22, 1982. In *Making it Happen*, Reich reports that the 1984 Games earned $76 million from interest alone (87).

15 Barney, Wenn, and Martyn, *Selling the Five Rings*, 194–195.

16 Ibid., 195–196.

17 Ibid., 197–198; and Wenn, "Peter Ueberroth's Legacy," 4–5.

18 Barney, Wenn, and Martyn, *Selling the Five Rings*, 200.

19 Wenn, "Peter Ueberroth's Legacy," 5.

20 Ibid., 4.

21 Thomas M. Hunt, *Drug Games: The International Olympic Committee and the Politics of Doping, 1960–2008* (Austin: University of Texas Press, 2011).

22 John Hoberman, "How Drug Testing Fails: The Politics of Doping Control," in *Doping in Elite Sport: The Politics of Drugs in the Olympic Movement*, ed. Wayne Wilson and Edward Derse (Champaign, IL: Human Kinetics, 2001), 245.

23 Coubertin, *Olympism*, 583.

24 Robert O. Voy and Kirk D. Deeter, *Drugs, Sport, and Politics* (Champaign, IL: Leisure Press, 1991), 101.

25 Richard W. Pound, *Inside the Olympics: A Behind-the-Scenes Look at the Politics, the Scandals, and the Glory of the Games* (Etobicoke, Ontario: John Wiley & Sons Canada, 2004). 235. For Pound's perspective on how 1984 opened IOC eyes to the Games' enormous TV revenue potential, see 169–172.

26 Hunt, *Drug Games*, 71.

27 Hoberman, "How Drug Testing Fails," 242.

28 Jan Todd and Terry Todd, "Significant Events in the History of Drug Testing and the Olympic Movement," in *Doping in Elite Sport: The Politics of Drugs in the Olympic Movement*, ed. Wayne Wilson and Edward Derse (Champaign, IL: Human Kinetics, 2001), 79. Some reports put the total positive tests at 30, with 15 athletes being disqualified. See Randy Harvey, "Pan Am Games: 1983 Drug Battle Continues in '87," *Los Angeles Times*, August 5, 1987; Craig Neff, "Caracas: A Scandal and a Warning," *Sports Illustrated*, September 5, 1983; Frank Litsky, "Tully Returns and Wins Gold," *New York Times*, August 27, 1983.

29 Frank Litsky, "Some U.S. Athletes Leave Games at Caracas Amid Stiff Drug Tests," *New York Times*, August 24, 1983.

30 Todd and Todd, "Significant Events in the History of Drug Testing," 79.

31 Voy and Deeter, *Drugs, Sport, and Politics*, 102, 104.

32 Thomas M. Hunt, "Sport, Drugs, and the Cold War: The Conundrum of Olympic Doping Policy, 1970–1979," *Olympika* 16 (2007): 20–21. IOC member and WADA president Richard Pound noted that until the creation of WADA, the IOC's anti-doping code was "more accurately, the written musings of a succession of medical commissions and sub-commissions that would have been impossible for anyone to enforce properly." *Inside the Olympics*, 69.

33 Hunt, *Drug Games*, 73.

34 Ibid., 72.

35 Todd and Todd, "Significant Events in the History of Drug Testing," 79.
36 "Drug Testing at Issue," *New York Times*, April 29, 1983.
37 Elliott Almond, Julie Cart, and Randy Harvey, "The Olympic Dope Sheet Is Redefined," *Los Angeles Times*, November 13, 1983.
38 "Report on the Seminar of the Medical Commission of the IOC," September 25–October 2, 1983, IOC Medical Commission Records, Folder IOC, SD1: Comm. Méd.: Rapp. Sessions, CE 1968–1984, IOCL, quoted in Hunt, *Drug Games*, 73.
39 Richard Moore, *The Dirtiest Race in History: Ben Johnson, Carl Lewis and the 1988 Olympic 100M Final* (London: Bloomsbury, 2012), 112.
40 For accounts of the 20 positive tests in Los Angeles, see chapter 7, "The Prince and the Missing Paperwork," in Moore, *The Dirtiest Race in History*; Andrew Jennings, *The New Lords of the Rings: Olympic Corruption and How to Buy Gold Medals* (London: Pocket Books, 1996), 237–249; and Jim Ferstle, "Evolution and Politics of Drug Testing," in *Anabolic Steroids in Sport and Exercise*, ed. Charles E. Yesalis (Champaign, IL: Human Kinetics, 2000), 386–387.
41 Pound, *Inside the Olympics*, 68.
42 Moore, *The Dirtiest Race in History*, 113.
43 Randy Harvey, "'84 Olympics Documents Shredded," *Los Angeles Times*, August 30, 1994.
44 Jo Williams, "Drug Abuse Widespread, Says GB Doctor," *Scotsman*, July 16, 1996. See also Hoberman, "How Drug Testing Fails," 244.
45 Transcript of "Olympics," *Panorama*, BBC One, London, March 15, 1999.
46 Barney, *Selling the Five Rings*, 270–271.

CHAPTER 11. THE SPORTS ACT DELIVERS: GOLD IN '84

1 U.S. President's Commission on Olympic Sports, *The Final Report of the President's Commission on Olympic Sports* (Washington, DC: U.S. Government Printing Office, 1977), 48.
2 Venlo Wolfsohn, "Lack of Facilities Hurts U.S. Olympic Cyclists," *Washington Post*, June 23, 1979.
3 Swedish Olympic Committee, *The Official Report of the Olympic Games of Stockholm, 1912* (Stockholm, Sweden: Wahlström & Widstrand, 1913), 454.
4 Christopher S. Thompson, *The Tour de France: A Cultural History* (Berkeley: University of California Press, 2008), 238.
5 Ed Burke to coaching staff, Dave Prouty, Mike Fraysee, Dot Saling, Hannah North, Tom Schuler, and Pete Van Handle, September 30, 1983 (in the author's possession).
6 John Gleaves, "Manufactured Dope: How the 1984 US Olympic Cycling Team Rewrote the Rules on Drugs in Sports," *International Journal of the History of Sport* 32, no. 1 (2015): 6.
7 For a discussion of how the IOC's anti-doping regulations became more specific and broader over time, see ibid., 4–6.
8 Gary R. Blockus, "Blood in Their Veins, Medals in Their Closet," *Morning Call* (Allentown, PA), June 2, 1996.
9 Bjarne Rostaing and Robert Sullivan, "Triumphs Tainted with Blood," *Sports Illustrated*, January 21, 1985.
10 Ibid.
11 Ibid.
12 Blockus, "Blood in Their Veins, Medals in Their Closet."
13 Kenneth Reich, "Doctor and Cyclist Defend Practice of Blood Doping," *Los Angeles Times*, January 12, 1985. See also Harvey Klein, "Blood Transfusions and Athletics: Games People Play," *New England Journal of Medicine* 312 (March 1985): 854–856.

14 For a history of the Soviet sports machine's development for the Los Angeles Olympics, see Philip A. D'Agati, *The Cold War and the 1984 Olympic Games: A Soviet-American Surrogate War* (New York: Palgrave Macmillan, 2013), 57–78.
15 Blockus, "Blood in Their Veins, Medals in Their Closet."
16 Peter N. Sperryn, *Sport and Medicine* (London: Butterworths, 1983), 27.
17 For the evolution of clinical moral attitudes on blood doping in sports, see Ivan Waddington, *Sport, Health and Drugs: A Critical Sociological Perspective* (London: E & FN Spon, 2000), 146–151.
18 Norman Gledhill, "The Ergogenic Effect of Blood Doping," *Physician and Sportsmedicine* 11, no. 9 (September 1983): 87–90.
19 Gleaves, "Manufactured Dope," 9.
20 Richard Ben Cramer, "Olympic Cheating: The Inside Story of Illicit Doping and the US Cycling Team," *Rolling Stone*, February 14, 1985.
21 Tim Foskey, "19th Hole," *Sports Illustrated*, February 4, 1985.
22 Mike F. Huntington and Scott A. Strecker, "19th Hole," *Sports Illustrated*, February 4, 1985.
23 Lynne Richter, "19th Hole," *Sports Illustrated*, February 4, 1985.
24 Reich, "Doctor and Cyclist Defend Practice of Blood Doping."
25 Morley Myers, "U.S. Sweeps Two Cycling Gold Medals," United Press International, July 30, 1984.
26 Kenneth Reich, "Blood-Doping Dilemma," *Los Angeles Times*, January 26, 1985.
27 Michael Goodwin, "Blood-Doping Unethical, U.S. Olympic Official Says," *New York Times*, January 13, 1985.
28 Klein, "Blood Transfusions and Athletics," 856.
29 Ibid.
30 Waddington, *Sport, Health and Drugs*, 151.
31 For a discussion of the IOC's rule modifications, see Gleaves, "Manufactured Dope," 12–14.
32 See Alessandro Donati, "The Silent Drama of the Diffusion of Doping Among Amateurs and Professionals," in *Doping and Public Policy*, ed. John Hoberman and Verner Møller (Odense: University Press of Southern Denmark, 2004), 45–75.

CHAPTER 12. DR. FERRARI WAS RIGHT

1 Jean-Michel Rouet, interview with Michele Ferrari, cited in Cyclisme-Dopage.com, www.cyclisme-dopage.com/actualite/1994-04-22-lequipe.htm.
2 Paul Dimeo, *A History of Drug Use in Sport, 1876–1976: Beyond Good and Evil* (New York: Routledge, 2007), 118.
3 For an assessment of the risks and benefits of erythropoietin in cycling as well as its performance-enhancing efficacy, see Jules Heuberger, Joost Tervaert, Femke Schepers, Adriaan Vliegenthart, Joris Rotmans, Johannes Daniels, Jacobus Burggraaf, and Adam Cohen, "Erythropoietin Doping in Cycling: Lack of Evidence for Efficacy and a Negative Risk-Benefit," *British Journal of Clinical Pharmacology* 75, no. 6 (2013): 1406–1421.
4 Lawrence M. Fisher, "Stamina-Building Drug Linked to Athletes' Deaths," *New York Times*, May 19, 1991.
5 For a technical description of the physiology of erythropoietin, see Heuberger et al., "Erythropoietin Doping in Cycling," 1407–1408.
6 Tyler Hamilton and Daniel Coyle, *The Secret Race: Inside the Hidden World of the Tour de France: Doping, Cover-ups, and Winning at All Costs* (New York: Bantam Books, 2012), 58.
7 Eugene Goldwasser, *A Bloody Long Journey: Erythropoietin (EPO) and the Person Who Isolated It* (Princeton, NJ: Xlibris, 2011).

8 Ibid., 119.

9 Richard L. Brandt and Thomas Weisel, *Capital Instincts: Life as an Entrepreneur, Financier, and Athlete* (Hoboken: Wiley, 2003), 117.

10 Nicolas Rasmussen, "On Slicing an Obvious Salami Thinly: Science, Patent Case Law, and the Fate of the Early Biotech Sector in the Making of EPO," *Perspectives in Biology and Medicine* 56, no. 2 (Spring 2013): 208, 218.

11 Fisher, "Stamina-Building Drug Linked to Athletes' Deaths."

12 Ibid.

13 Allan J. Erslev, "Erythropoietin," *New England Journal of Medicine* 324, no. 19. (May 9, 1991): 1343.

14 Ibid., 1342.

15 Ibid.

16 Ibid., 1341.

17 William Leith, "Cyclists Don't Die Like This," *Independent*, July 14, 1991.

18 Dave Kindredo, "Cycling's Deadly Downward Spiral," *Sporting News*, July 19, 2004.

19 Steven Downes, "Fear on the Marathon Starting Line," *Sunday Herald*, April 22, 2001.

20 Hamilton and Coyle, *The Secret Race*, 57.

21 Bernat López, "The Invention of a 'Drug of Mass Destruction': Deconstructing the EPO Myth," *Sport in History* 31, no. 1 (2011): 84–109.

22 Ibid., 89.

23 Ibid., 101.

24 H. B. Truong and E. J. Ip, "A Review of Erythropoietin Abuse: An Analysis of Effectiveness and Safety in Exercise," *Journal of Sports Medicine and Doping Studies* 2, no. 2 (2002).

25 For a study of how moral panics lead to regulations in sport, see Chas Critcher, "New Perspectives on Anti-Doping Policy: From Moral Panic to Moral Regulation," *International Journal of Sport Policy and Politics* 6, no. 2 (2014): 153–169.

26 Pierre de Coubertin, *Olympism: Selected Writings*, ed. Norbert Müller (Lausanne, Switzerland: International Olympic Committee, 2000), 599.

27 Kathleen Sharp, *Blood Medicine: Blowing the Whistle on One of the Deadliest Prescription Drugs Ever* (New York: Plume, 2012).

28 Alex Berenson and Andrew Pollack, "Doctors Reap Millions for Anemia Drugs," *New York Times*, May 9, 2007.

29 Sharp, *Blood Medicine*, 343.

30 Berenson and Pollack, "Doctors Reap Millions for Anemia Drugs." For a summary of the "calamitous catalog of clinical evidence" leading to the EPO black-box warning, see "Sacrificing the Cash Cow," *Nature Biotechnology* 25, no. 4 (April 2007): 363. In an effort to fight back against the black-box warning and a cap that the federal Center for Medicare and Medicaid Services (CMS) put on EPO dosing, Amgen spent $9.1 million on lobbying in the first half of 2007—nearly what the company had spent in all of 2006. Some of those funds added to the nearly $400,000 in health care industry contributions to two pharma-friendly members of Congress who attempted to claw back Amgen's EPO revenue by overturning the patient and taxpayer-protecting CMS rulings. See "Lack of Data Mires Aranesp in Controversy," *Nature Biotechnology* 25, no. 11 (November 2007): 1193

31 Dae-Hee Shin, Young-Il Kwon, Sung-Il Choi, Ui-Soon Park, Je Lee, Jin-Ho Shin, Jae-Ung Lee, Soon-Gil Kim, Jeong-Hyun Kim, Heon-Kil Lim, Bang-Hun Lee, and Kyung-Soo Kim, "Accidental Ten Times Overdose Administration of Recombinant Human Erythropoietin (rh-EPO) up to 318,000 Units a Day in Acute Myocardial Infarction: Report of Two Cases," *Basic and Clinical Pharmacology and Toxicology* 98 (2006): 222–224.

32 K. R. Brown, W. J. Carter, and G. E. Lombardi, "Recombinant Erythropoietin Overdose," *American Journal of Emergency Medicine* 11, no. 6 (1993): 619–621.

33 Rasmussen, "On Slicing an Obvious Salami Thinly," 209.

34 Alessandro Donati, "The Silent Drama of the Diffusion of Doping Among Amateurs and Professionals," in *Doping and Public Policy*, ed. John Hoberman and Verner Møller (Odense: University Press of Southern Denmark, 2004), 59–61.

35 For an analysis of illicit performance-enhancing drug distribution channels (and the complicity of anti-doping agencies with these middlemen), see Letizia Paoli and Alessandro Donati, *The Sports Doping Market: Understanding Supply and Demand, and the Challenges of Their Control* (New York: Springer, 2014).

36 Rasmussen, "On Slicing an Obvious Salami Thinly," 209. Kathleen Sharp's 2012 book, *Blood Medicine,* explores this EPO pay-for-overdose scandal in depth.

CHAPTER 13. FEAR MAKES GOOD COPY

1 Bernat López, "The Invention of a 'Drug of Mass Destruction': Deconstructing the EPO Myth," *Sport in History* 31, no. 1 (2011): 86.

2 Ian Thomsen, "Flo-Jo Case Leaves Risk of Drugs Sill in Question," *New York Times,* September 26, 1998.

3 David L. Altheide, *Creating Fear: News and the Construction of Crisis* (New York: Walter de Gruyter, 2002), 9.

4 Ibid., 20.

5 Ibid., 21–22.

6 Ibid., 11–12.

7 Ibid., 11.

8 See ibid., 175–183, for discussion of how traditional religions use fear of death to maintain authority and modify their followers' beliefs and behaviors.

9 Ibid., 22.

10 Paul Kimmage, *A Rough Ride: An Insight into Pro Cycling* (London: Stanley Paul, 1990), chapter 8.

11 Juliet Macur, *Cycle of Lies: The Fall of Lance Armstrong* (New York: HarperCollins, 2014).

12 Michael Janofsky, "Samaranch Calls Drug Users 'The Thieves of Performance,'" *New York Times,* September 13, 1988.

13 Michael Janofsky, "Johnson Loses Gold to Lewis After Drug Test," *New York Times,* September 27, 1988.

14 Douglas J. Casa and Rebecca L. Stearns, eds., *Preventing Sudden Death in Sport and Physical Activity* (Sudbury, MA: Jones & Bartlett Learning, 2016).

15 "Traffic Safety Facts," National Highway Traffic Safety Administration, May 2015.

16 "Football Death Is 3rd in Recent Days," ESPN.com, October 2, 2014, http://espn.go.com/espn/story/_/id/11626686/high-school-football-player-dies-suffering-head-injury-third-recent-death.

17 *Annual Survey of Football Injury Research*, National Center for Catastrophic Injury Research, University of North Carolina, March 11, 2016.

18 Michael Shermer, "The Doping Dilemma," *Scientific American* 298, no. 4 (2008).

19 Mark Zalewski, "Experts Discuss the Legal Side of Doping in Sport," CyclingNews.com, November 9, 2007.

20 Bill Gifford, "Greg LeMond vs. the World," *Men's Journal*, July 2008.

21 Bernat López, "'The Good, Pure Old Days': Cyclist's Switching Appraisals of Doping Before and After Retirement as Claims Making in the Construction of Doping as a Social Problem," *International Journal of the History of Sport* 31, no. 17 (2014): 2146.

22 Quoted in ibid., 2145.

23 Laurent Fignon, *We Were Young and Carefree* (London: Yellow Jersey Press, 2009), Kindle ed., chapter 33.

24 Ibid., chapter 19.

25 Ibid., chapter 33.

26 Ibid., chapter 29.
27 Ibid., chapter 33.
28 Eric Serres, "Cyrille Guimard: 'Le sport peut-il encore être preserve face au business?,'" *L'Humanité*, June 15, 2012.
29 López, "The Good, Pure Old Days," 2148.
30 Ibid., 2151.
31 Ibid., 2153
32 Robin Parisotto, *Blood Sports: The Inside Dope on Drugs in Sport* (Melbourne, Australia: Hardie Grant, 2006), 36.
33 David F. Gerrard, "Playing Foreign Policy Games: States, Drugs and Other Olympian Vices," *Sport in Society: Cultures, Commerce, Media, Politics* 11, no. 4 (2008): 461–462.
34 Liz Clisby, "Drugs and the Athlete," in *Clinical Sports Medicine*, ed. Peter Bruker and Karim Khan (Sydney, Australia: McGraw-Hill, 2007), 873.
35 Ibid., 888.
36 Virginia S. Cowart, "Erythropoietin: A Dangerous New Form of Blood Doping?," *Physician and Sportsmedicine* 17, no. 8 (August 1989): 116.
37 Robert O. Voy and Kirk D. Deeter, *Drugs, Sport, and Politics* (Champaign, IL: Leisure Press, 1991), 69.
38 Cowart, "Erythropoietin," 116.
39 Ibid., 116–117.
40 Ibid., 116.
41 Altheide, *Creating Fear*, 23.
42 J. J. M. Marx and P. C. J. Vergouwen, "Packed-Cell Volume in Elite Athletes," *Lancet* 352, no. 9126 (1998): 451.
43 Björn C. Knollmann and Dan M. Roden, "A Genetic Framework for Improving Arrhythmia Therapy," *Nature* 451, no. 7181 (2008): 929–936.
44 Karin Bille, David Figueiras, Patrick Schamasch, Lukas Kappenberger, Joel I. Brenner, Folkert J. Meijboom, and Erik J. Meijboom, "Sudden Cardiac Death in Athletes: The Lausanne Recommendations," *European Journal of Cardiovascular Prevention and Rehabilitation* 13, no. 6 (2006): 14.
45 López, "The Invention of a 'Drug of Mass Destruction,'" 102.
46 Bengt Kayser, "Current Anti-doping Policy: Harm Reduction or Harm Induction?," in *Elite Sport, Doping and Public Health*, ed. Verner Møller, Mike McNamee, and Paul Dimeo (Odense: University Press of Southern Denmark, 2009), 157.

CHAPTER 14. THE WAR ON DRUGS

1 California Assembly Interim Subcommittee on Drug Abuse and Alcoholism, *Drug Abuse in Athletics, Transcript of Proceedings*, October 20, 1970, opening statement of Assemblyman William Campbell, 1 (hereafter cited as *Drug Abuse in Athletics*).
2 John Kifner, "Student Head and Teacher Are Seized at Kent State," *New York Times*, October 20, 1970.
3 Ibid.
4 Warren Weaver, "President Scores Tide of Terrorism," *New York Times*, October 20, 1970.
5 Dana Adams Schmidt, "President Orders Wider Drug Fight; Asks $155 Million," *New York Times*, June 18, 1971; "Excerpts from President's Message on Drug Abuse Control," *New York Times*, June 18, 1971.
6 Martin Arnold, "Narcotics Deaths Put at over 1,050," *New York Times*, December 30, 1970.
7 Schmidt, "President Orders Wider Drug Fight."

8 *The World Heroin Problem; Report of Special Study Mission: Composed of Morgan F. Murphy, Illinois, Chairman [and] Robert H. Steele, Connecticut, Pursuant to H. Res. 109 Authorizing the Committee on Foreign Affairs to Conduct Thorough Studies and Investigations of All Matters Coming Within the Jurisdiction of the Committee,* May 27, 1971, 92nd Cong. 1 (1971), 18.
9 Norman E. Zinberg, "G.I.'s and O.J.'s in Vietnam," *New York Times*, December 5, 1971.
10 Ibid.
11 *World Heroin Problem*, 18–19.
12 Nicolas Rasmussen, *On Speed: The Many Lives of Amphetamine* (New York: New York University Press, 2009), 190
13 Michael Herr, *Dispatches* (New York: Knopf, 1977), 5.
14 *World Heroin Problem*, 4.
15 James M. Markham, "President Calls for 'Total War' on U.S. Addiction," *New York Times*, March 21, 1972.
16 *Drug Abuse in Athletics*, 1.
17 Ibid., 38.
18 Ibid., 43.
19 Ibid., 44.
20 Ibid., 48.
21 Hearings Before the Subcommittee to Investigate Juvenile Delinquency in the United States, Committee on the Judiciary, *Proper and Improper Use of Drugs by Athletes*, June 18, July 12, and July 13, 1973, 93rd Cong. 1 (1973) (call to order by U.S. Senator Birch Bayh), 2.
22 Ibid., statement of Oklahoma State team physician Donald Cooper, 5.
23 Ibid., 6.
24 Ibid.
25 Ibid., 7.
26 Ibid.
27 Ross Coomber, "How Social Fear of Drugs in the Non-sporting World Creates a Framework for Doping Policy in the Sporting World," *International Journal of Sport Policy and Politics* 6, no. 2 (2014): 175.
28 David F. Musto, *The American Disease: Origins of Narcotic Control* (New Haven, CT: Yale University Press, 1973), 217.
29 Ibid., 330.
30 Ibid., 218–219.
31 "The Gallows Plant," *Cameron Herald*, September 14, 1922.
32 "Jackson Wants County Law So He Can Land on Marihuana Garden," *Santa Ana Register*, July 28, 1915.
33 C. M. Goethe, letter to the editor, *New York Times*, September 15, 1935.
34 Musto, *American Disease*, 227.
35 For discussion of this phenomenon, see Coomber, "How Social Fear of Drugs in the Non-sporting World Creates a Framework," 184–185.

CHAPTER 15. AMPHETAMINES FOR ALL

1 Nicolas Rasmussen, "Making the First Anti-Depressant: Amphetamine in American Medicine, 1929–1950," *Journal of the History of Medicine and Allied Sciences* 61 (2006): 293.
2 Nicolas Rasmussen, *On Speed: The Many Lives of Amphetamine* (New York: New York University Press, 2009), 22.
3 Ibid., 22–24.
4 William Sargant and J. M. Blackburn, "The Effect of Benzedrine on Intelligence Scores," *Lancet* 228, no. 5911 (1936): 1385–1387.

5 "Efficiency of Brain Held Due to Its 'Fuel'; Cells Found Speeded Up by Synthetic Drug," *New York Times*, April 10, 1937.
6 "Pep-Pill Poisoning," *Time*, May 10, 1937.
7 Rasmussen, "Making the First Anti-Depressant," 315–316.
8 Rasmussen, *On Speed*, 41.
9 Ibid., 64–65.
10 E. L. Corey and A. P. Webster, "Field Study of the Effects of Benzedrine on Small Arms Firing Under Conditions of Acute Fatigue," June 2, 1943, USNA, RG 341, Series 44, box 123, folder "Benzedrine: NAVY Reports," quoted in Rasmussen, *On Speed*, 80.
11 Benzedrine advertisement, *Journal of the American Medical Association* 123, no. 10 (1943).
12 Rasmussen, *On Speed*, 84.
13 Rasmussen, "Making the First Anti-Depressant," 318–319.
14 Charles Lewis, letter to the editor, *New England Journal of Medicine*, December 11, 1969.
15 Bernadine Paulshock, letter to the editor, *New England Journal of Medicine*, February 5, 1970.
16 Neil Norman, "Dark Side of Oz: The Exploitation of Judy Garland," *Express*, April 5, 2010.
17 Rhonda Cornum, John Caldwell, and Kory Cornum, "Stimulant Use in Extended Flight Operations," *Airpower Journal* (Spring 1997): 11.
18 Rasmussen, *On Speed*, 190.
19 Ibid., 220.
20 Juan De Onis, "U.S.-Mexican Effort Turns Pot to Alfalfa," *New York Times*, January 17, 1970.
21 Rasmussen, *On Speed*, 177.
22 Frank Zappa, John Sebastian, Do It Now public service announcement audio files, www.doitnow.org/pages/psatable.html.
23 Arnold J. Mandell, *The Nightmare Season* (New York: Random House, 1976), 24.
24 Ibid., 175.
25 Rasmussen, *On Speed*, 220.
26 Arnold J. Mandell, "The Sunday Syndrome: A Unique Pattern of Amphetamine Abuse Indigenous to American Professional Football," *Clinical Toxicology* 15, no. 2 (1979): 228.
27 In 1978, *Sports Illustrated* detailed injuries that came about when players took the field in an amphetamine-induced "paranoid rage state." The article covered the NFL's attempt to pull Mandell's license, the medical community's rise to the doctor's defense, and players like defensive lineman Houston Ridge, who collected $302,000 after suing the Chargers when amphetamines kept him playing even after he had broken his hip. John Underwood, "Speed Is All the Rage," *Sports Illustrated*, August 28, 1978. For an attorney's account of Mandell's medical license hearings, see Robert C. Baxley, "The Mandell Case and Proceedings for Revocation or Suspension of a Physician's and an Attorney's licence," in *Amphetamine Use, Misuse, and Abuse*, ed. David E. Smith, Donald R. Wesson, Millicent E. Buxton, Richard B. Seymour, J. Thomas Ungerleider, John P. Morgan, Arnold J. Mandell, and Gail Jara (Boston: G. K. Hall & Co., 1979), 303–317. According to Baxley, the Houston Ridge case was settled for $265,000, not the $302,000 cited in *Sports Illustrated*.
28 Mandell, *Nightmare Season*, 180.
29 For more on the invention of pathologies to fit existing drugs, see Marcia Angell, *The Truth About the Drug Companies: How They Deceive Us and What to Do About It* (New York: Random House, 2004); Nikolas Rose, "Becoming Neurochemical Selves," in *Biotechnology: Between Commerce and Civil Society*, ed. Nico Stehr (New Brunswick, NJ: Transaction Press, 2004); and Andrea Tone, "Tranquilizers on Trial," in *The Age of Anxiety: A History of America's Turbulent Affair with Tranquilizers* (New York: Basic Books, 2008).

30 Stephen P. Hinshaw and Richard M. Scheffler, *The ADHD Explosion: Myths, Medication, Money, and Today's Push for Performance* (New York: Oxford University Press, 2014), xxvi.

31 Edward Shorter, *A History of Psychiatry: From the Era of the Asylum to the Age of Prozac* (New York: Wiley, 1997), 291.

32 Nikolas Rose, "Becoming Neurochemical Selves," in *Biotechnology: Between Commerce and Civil Society*, ed. Nico Stehr (New Brunswick, NJ: Transaction Press, 2004), xxvii, 104. According to U.S. Drug Enforcement Agency drug production quotas, 151,455 kg of the stimulants amphetamine and methylphenidate were produced in the United States in 2016, compared to 80,000 to 100,000 kg of stimulants produced in 1969. Reflecting skyrocketing popular demand, from 2006 and 2016, production of the Ritalin drug methylphenidate more than doubled, from 36,000 kg to 96,750 kg. For analysis of increasing stimulant use, see Daniel J. Safer, "Recent Trends in Stimulant Usage," *Journal of Attention Disorders* 20, no. 6 (2016): 471–477. Safer points out that U.S. stimulant prescriptions increased to 58 million in 2014 from 10 million in 1993. Of the 46 million stimulant prescriptions written in 2010, 23 million were for youth.

33 Hinshaw and Scheffler, *The ADHD Explosion*, 92.

34 Ibid., 93.

35 See Gary S. Becker, *Human Capital: A Theoretical and Empirical Analysis, with Special Reference to Education* (New York: National Bureau of Economic Research, 1975).

36 Hinshaw and Scheffler, *The ADHD Explosion*, 90–91.

37 Ibid., 80.

38 Ibid., 70, 79.

39 Melana Zyla Vickers, "Accommodating College Students with Learning Disabilities: ADD, ADHD, and Dyslexia," John W. Pope Center for Higher Education Policy (March 2010), 7.

40 Ibid., 4

41 Diane Rado, "Many Illinois High School Students Get Special Testing Accommodations for ACT," *Chicago Tribune*, August 29, 2012.

42 Nirvi Shaw, "More Students Receiving Accommodations During ACT, SAT," *Education Week*, May 14, 2012.

43 U.S. Government Accountability Office, *Higher Education and Disability: Improved Federal Enforcement Needed to Better Protect Students' Rights to Testing Accommodations*, November 2011, Report to Congressional Requesters, GAO-12-40, 19.

44 Hinshaw and Scheffler, *The ADHD Explosion*, 110–115.

45 A. D. DeSantis, E. M. Webb, and S. M. Noar, "Illicit Use of Prescription ADHD Medications on a College Campus: A Multimethodological Approach," *Journal of American College Health* 57, no. 3 (2008): 315–324.

46 Sean E. McCabe, John R. Knight, Christian J. Teter, and Henry Wechsler, "Non-Medical Use of Prescription Stimulants Among US College Students: Prevalence and Correlates from a National Survey," *Addiction* 100, no. 1 (2005): 96–106; D. L. Rabiner, A. D. Anastopoulos, E. J. Costello, R. H. Hoyle, S. E. McCabe, and H. S. Swartzwelder, "The Misuse and Diversion of Prescribed ADHD Medications by College Students," *Journal of Attention Disorders* 13, no. 2 (2009): 144–153.

47 For further analysis of American university students' attitudes toward cognitive enhancers, see Tanya Dodge, Michelle Stock, and Dana Litt, "Judgments About Illegal Performance-Enhancing Substances: Reasoned, Reactive, or Both?," *Journal of Health Psychology* 18 (2013): 962–971; and Kelline R. Linton, "Scholastic Steroids: Is Generation Rx Cognitively Cheating?" *Pepperdine Law Review* 39, no. 4 (2012): 989–1050.

CHAPTER 16. SUPPLEMENTS: GOVERNMENT-APPROVED DOPE

1 John Heinerman, *Joseph Smith and Herbal Medicine* (Springville, UT: Bonneville Books, 2009), 5.
2 Richard L. Bushman and Jed Woodworth, *Joseph Smith: Rough Stone Rolling* (New York: Alfred A. Knopf, 2005), 21.
3 Heinerman, *Joseph Smith and Herbal Medicine*, 9.
4 Samuel Thomson, *Report of the Trial of Dr. Samuel Thomson, the Founder of the Thomsonian Practice, for an Alleged Libel in Warning the Public Against the Impositions of Paine D. Badger, as a Thomsonian Physician Sailing Under False Colors* (Boston: Henry P. Lewis, 1839), 28.
5 Heinerman, *Joseph Smith and Herbal Medicine*, 1.
6 Ibid., 28.
7 Dan Hurley, *Natural Causes: Death, Lies, and Politics in America's Vitamin and Herbal Supplement Industry* (New York: Broadway Books, 2006), 30.
8 Timothy Egan, "Stupid Pills," *New York Times*, February 6, 2015; Statista.com, "Retail Sales of Vitamins and Nutritional Supplements in the United States from 2000 to 2017," report generated May 7, 2016.
9 L. A. Swygert, E. E. Back, S. B. Auerbach, L. E. Sewell, and H. Falk, "Eosinophilia-Myalgia Syndrome: Mortality Data from the U.S. National Surveillance System," *Journal of Rheumatology* 20, no. 10 (1993): 1711–1717.
10 Denise Grady, "Articles Question Safety of Dietary Supplements," *New York Times*, September 17, 1998.
11 Hurley, *Natural Causes*, 117.
12 Samuel Hopkins Adams, *The Great American Fraud* (New York: P. F. Collier & Son, 1905), 3.
13 Ibid.
14 Hurley, *Natural Causes*, 33.
15 "Eben M. Byers Dies of Radium Poisoning," *New York Times*, April 1, 1932; Ron Winslow, "The Radium Water Worked Fine Until His Jaw Came Off," *Wall Street Journal*, August 1, 1990.
16 Deposition of Jerry D. Horn, L-Tryptophan Litigation, U.S. District Court, District of South Carolina Columbia Division, August 11, 1992.
17 Leslie A. Swygert, E. F. Maes, L. E. Sewell, L. Miller, H. Falk, and E. M. Kilbourne, "Eosinophilia-Myalgia Syndrome: Results of National Surveillance," *Journal of the American Medical Association* 264, no. 13 (1990): 1698–1703.
18 Steven W. Pray, *A History of Nonprescription Product Regulation* (Binghamton, NY: Pharmaceutical Products Press, 2003), 213.
19 *Regulation of Dietary Supplements, Hearing Before the Subcommittee on Health and the Environment of the Committee on Energy and Commerce, H.R. 509, H.R. 1709, and S. 784*, July 29, 1993, 103rd Cong. 1, statement of Senator Orrin Hatch, 9.
20 *Legislative Issues Related to the Regulation of Dietary Supplements: Hearing of the Committee on Labor and Human Resources United States Senate*, October 21, 1993, 103rd Cong. 1, statement of Senator Orrin Hatch, 5.
21 *Regulation of Dietary Supplements*, statement of Senator Orrin Hatch, 6.
22 Ibid., 7.
23 Ibid., 6.
24 *Legislative Issues Related to the Regulation of Dietary Supplements*, statement of Senator Orrin Hatch, 5.
25 *Agriculture, Rural Development, Food and Drug Administration, and Related Agencies Appropriations for 1994, Hearings Before a Subcommittee of the Committee on Appropriations, House of Representatives*, October 18, 1993, 103rd Cong. 1, statement of U.S. Senator Orrin Hatch, 28.

26 "The 1993 Snake Oil Protection Act," *New York Times*, October 5, 1993.
27 Selena Roberts, "Athletes Guess on Supplements," *New York Times*, January 30, 2002.
28 Steven W. Pray, "Orrin Hatch and the Dietary Supplement Health and Education Act: Pandora's Box Revisited," *Journal of Child Neurology* 27, no. 5 (2012): 562.
29 Pray, "Orrin Hatch and the Dietary Supplement Health and Education Act," 562.
30 *Legislative Issues Related to the Regulation of Dietary Supplements*, statement of Congressman Bill Richardson, 3
31 A. I. Geller, N. Shehab, N. J. Weidle, M. C. Lovegrove, B. J. Wolpert, B. B. Timbo, R. P. Mozersky, and D. S. Budnitz, "Emergency Department Visits for Adverse Events Related to Dietary Supplements," *New England Journal of Medicine* 373, no. 16 (2015): 1531–1540.
32 Anahad O'Connor, "New York Attorney General Targets Supplements at Major Retailers," *New York Times*, February 3, 2015.
33 Roberts, "Athletes Guess on Supplements."
34 Scott Taylor, "IOC Decries Use of 'Supplements,'" *Deseret News*, December 12, 2000.
35 Stephen Wilson, "IOC Says U.S. Part of the Problem When It Comes to Banned Steroids," *Reno Gazette-Journal*, December 13, 2000.
36 Ibid.
37 Taylor, "IOC Decries Use of 'Supplements.'"
38 H. Geyer, M. K. Parr, Y. Schrader, and W. Schäzer, "Analysis of Non-Hormonal Nutritional Supplements for Anabolic-Androgenic Steroids—Results of an International Study," *International Journal of Sports Medicine* 25, no. 2 (2004): 124–129.
39 Taylor, "IOC Decries Use of 'Supplements.'"
40 Lisa Riley Roche, "$20 Million Nu Skin Sponsorship Will Help Supplement the Games," *Deseret News*, October 6, 1999.
41 Peter Elkind and Doris Burke, "Nu Skin and the Short-Sellers," *Fortune*, October 26, 2012.
42 Lisa Riley Roche, "Nu Skin Takes Pragmatic Approach," *Deseret News*, October 16, 1999.
43 Ibid.
44 Edward L. Carter, "Games Big Step for Nu Skin," *Deseret News*, May 9, 2000.
45 Ibid.
46 Quoted in Elkind and Burke, "Nu Skin and the Short-Sellers."
47 Eric Lipton, "Support Is Mutual for Senator and Utah Industry," *New York Times*, June 20, 2011.
48 Joseph Chang, "Understanding Our Anti-Aging Science," Nu Skin Anti-Aging Science video, https://www.millionsofmeals.com/content/science/en/anti-aging-science/science_video.html.
49 Nu Skin, "Two Genetically Identical Mice," promotional video, https://www.youtube.com/watch?v=F0xztxncsLU.
50 Elkind and Burke, "Nu Skin and the Short-Sellers."
51 T. W. Farnam, "Donation Helps Romney Get Some Skin in the Presidential Game," *New York Times*, September 12, 2011.
52 Bloomberg News, "Nu Skin Shares Gain on Speculation That Chinese Probe Is Easing," March 24, 2014; Nu Skin press release, "Nu Skin Provides Update on China Regulatory Reviews," March 24, 2014.
53 Reuters, "Skincare Product Maker Nu Skin Settles Class Action Suit," February 26, 2016.
54 John M. Hoberman, *Testosterone Dreams: Rejuvenation, Aphrodisia, Doping* (Berkeley: University of California Press, 2005), 33.
55 Pierre de Coubertin, *Olympism: Selected Writings*, ed. Norbert Müller (Lausanne, Switzerland: International Olympic Committee, 2000) 534.
56 Hoberman, *Testosterone Dreams*, 33.
57 S. H. Backhouse, L. Whitaker, and A. Petróczi, "Gateway to Doping? Supplement Use in the Context of Preferred Competitive Situations, Doping Attitude, Beliefs, and Norms," *Scandinavian Journal of Medicine and Science in Sports* 23 (2013): 244–252.

58 Tonya Dodge, Michelle Stock, and Dana Litt, "Judgments About Illegal Performance-Enhancing Substances: Reasoned, Reactive, or Both?," *Journal of Health Psychology* 18, no. 7 (2013): 962–971.

CHAPTER 17. CHARLIE FRANCIS: TAKE IT TO MAKE IT

1 Charlie Francis, *Speed Trap: Inside the Biggest Scandal in Olympic History* (New York: St. Martin's Press, 1990), 25.
2 Ibid., 37.
3 Ibid., 48.
4 Ibid., 50.
5 Ibid., 52.
6 Ibid., 53.
7 Ibid., 83.
8 Ibid.
9 Ibid., 84.
10 Ibid., 133.
11 Ibid., 140.
12 Ibid.
13 Ibid., 141.
14 Ibid., 292.
15 David Millar, *Racing Through The Dark: The Fall and Rise of David Millar* (London: Orion, 2011), 209.
16 Tyler Hamilton and Daniel Coyle,*The Secret Race: Inside the Hidden World of the Tour de France—Doping, Cover-ups, and Winning at All Costs* (New York: Bantam Books, 2012), 114.
17 Ibid., 46.
18 Albert Salisbury Hyman, letter to the editor, *New York Times*, September 12, 1960.

CHAPTER 18. DSHEA, STEROIDS, AND BASEBALL'S SALVATION

1 Mike Freeman, "Lean and Mean," *New York Times*, September 30, 2002.
2 Tom Maloney, "Blue Jays Divided on Use of Androstenedione: Canseco, Others Sold on Performance Enhancing Drug," *Ottawa Citizen*, August 23, 1998.
3 Howard Bryant, *Juicing the Game: Drugs, Power, and the Fight for the Soul of Major League Baseball* (New York: Viking, 2005), 106.
4 Pete Williams, "Lifting the Game," *Baseball Weekly*, May 7, 1997.
5 Ibid.
6 John M. Hoberman, *Testosterone Dreams: Rejuvenation, Aphrodisia, Doping* (Berkeley: University of California Press, 2005), 48.
7 William E. Buckley, Charles E. Yesalis III, Karl E. Friedl, William A. Anderson, Andrea L. Streit, and James E. Wright, "Estimated Prevalence of Anabolic Steroid Use Among Male High School Seniors," *Journal of the American Medical Association* 260, no. 23 (1988): 3441–3445.
8 Michael Janofsky, "Testimony on Steroid Use by Olympians," *New York Times*, April 4, 1989.
9 *Anabolic Steroids Control Act of 1990: Hearing Before the Subcommittee on Crime of the Committee on the Judiciary on H.R. 4658*, 101st Cong. (1990), statement of Congressman Mel Levine.
10 Anti-Drug Abuse Act of 1988, Pub. L. No. 100-660, 102 Stat. 4181 (1988). This law also instructed the government to conduct a two-year study of steroid and human growth hormone use by high school and college students. See also George J. Mitchell, *Report to the Commissioner of Baseball of an Independent Investigation into the Illegal Use*

of Steroids and Other Performance Enhancing Substances by Players in Major League Baseball (Commissioner of Baseball, 2007), 19 (hereafter cited as *Mitchell Report*).

11 *Anabolic Steroids Control Act of 1990*, prepared statement of Deputy Assistant Attorney General Leslie Southwick.

12 Anabolic Steroids Control Act of 1990, H.R. 4658, 101st Cong. (1989–1990).

13 George H. W. Bush, "Statement on Signing the Crime Control Act of 1990," November 29, 1990, www.presidency.ucsb.edu/ws/?pid=19114.

14 *Mitchell Report*, 25.

15 Ibid., 25.

16 Wayne Coffey, "Former All-Star Jack Armstrong Hoping to Set Record Straight on Steroid Era," *New York Daily News*, December 8, 2007.

17 Peter Gammons, "Socking It to the Red Sox," *Sports Illustrated*, October 17, 1988.

18 Hoberman, *Testosterone Dreams*, 49.

19 Williams, "Lifting the Game."

20 Andrew L. T. Green, "Spreading the Blame: Examining the Relationship Between DSHEA and the Baseball Steroid Scandal," *Boston University Law Review* 90, no. 1 (2010): 417–418.

21 Edmund L. Andrews, "3 Guilty of Giving Drugs to East German Athletes," *New York Times*, August 21, 1998.

22 *Mitchell Report*, 79.

23 Bill Pennington and Jack Curry, "Andro Hangs in a Quiet Limbo," *New York Times*, July 11, 1999.

24 Ibid.

25 Hoberman, *Testosterone Dreams*, 46.

26 Ibid., 46.

27 Pennington and Curry, "Andro Hangs in a Quiet Limbo."

28 Dan Shaughnessy, "The Persecution of McGwire a Crime," *Boston Globe*, August 26, 1998.

29 Steve Wilstein, "'Andro' OK? Testosterone-Producer Legal in Baseball, Banned by Others," *Indiana Gazette*, August 23, 1998.

30 "Cardinals, McGwire Agree on 'Androstenedione' Issue," *Capital* (Annapolis, MD), August 24, 1998.

31 Bob Herbert, "In America; a Hero and His Shadow," *New York Times*, August 27, 1998.

32 Philip M. Boffey, "Editorial Observer; Post-Season Thoughts on McGwire's Pills," *New York Times*, September 30, 1998.

33 Joan Rigdon, "Yahoo! IPO Soars in First Day, but Honeymoon May Not Last," *Wall Street Journal*, April 15, 1998.

34 George Vecsey, "Sport of the Times: A Sport Is Reborn—the Home Run, America's Signature Feat, Invigorates Baseball; September's Aura Restored to Fans," *New York Times*, September 4, 1998.

35 Shawn Assael and Peter Keating, "Who Knew? Part III, 1998–2001 Cause and Effect, The Writer," *ESPN* magazine, November 9, 2005, espn.go.com/espn/eticket/story?page =steroids&num=8.

36 Hoberman, *Testosterone Dreams*, 45.

37 George W. Bush, "Address Before a Joint Session of the Congress on the State of the Union," January 20, 2004, http://www.presidency.ucsb.edu/ws/?pid=29646.

38 Associated Press, "Pitcher Receives Two-Year International Ban," January 6, 2004, http://espn.go.com/mlb/news/story?id=1701535.

39 Carol Cole Kleinman and C. E. Petit, "Legal Aspects of Anabolic Steroid Use and Abuse," in *Anabolic Steroids in Sport and Exercise*, 2nd ed., ed. Charles E. Yesalis (Champaign, IL: Human Kinetics, 2000), 343–344.

40 Hurley, *Natural Causes*, 191–192.

41 Anne E. Kornblut and Duff Wilson, "How One Pill Escaped the List of Controlled Steroids," *New York Times*, April 17, 2005.

42 Hoberman, *Testosterone Dreams*, 45.
43 Tom Ferrey, "A Series of Beneficial Moves," ESPN.com, November 1, 2000, http://static.espn.go.com/mlb/bush/timeline.html.
44 Jose Canseco, *Juiced* (New York: HarperCollins, 2005), 133–136.
45 *Mitchell Report*, 95–96.
46 Bryant, *Juicing*, 325.
47 William Boddy, *Fifties Television: The Industry and Its Critics* (Urbana: University of Illinois Press, 1990), 218.
48 Newton N. Minow, "Television and the Public Interest," *Federal Communications Law Journal* 55, no. 3 (2003), www.fclj.org/wp-content/uploads/2013/01/Speech.pdf. For Minow's 50-years-after reflection on his 1961 "Vast Wasteland" speech, see Newton N. Minow, "A Vaster Wasteland," *Atlantic Monthly*, April 20, 2011.
49 Charles Van Doren, "All the Answers," *New Yorker*, July 28, 2008.
50 The 2001 motion picture *Trumbo* explores the story of the writer's blacklisting.
51 Dalton Trumbo, "Hail, Blithe Spirit!," *Nation*, October 24, 1959.

CHAPTER 19. IF IT'S INHERITED, IS IT CHEATING?

1 Theodore Friedmann and Richard Roblin, "Gene Therapy for Human Genetic Disease?," *Science* 175, no. 4025 (March 3, 1972): 954.
2 "Meet the Mr. Greengenes of Biotech Gene Therap: UCSD's Theodore Friedmann Makes No Apologies for Scientists Tinkering with What He Calls Nature's 'Mistakes,'" *Los Angeles Times*, May 29, 1991.
3 Scott LaFee, "Friedmann Recognized for Pioneering Gene Therapy Research," *thisweek@ucsandiego*, January 29, 2015.
4 World Anti-Doping Agency, "Gene Doping," *playtrue*, no. 1 (2005).
5 "Interview: Dr. Theodore Friedmann," *playtrue*, no. 1 (2005).
6 Friedman and Roblin, "Gene Therapy for Human Genetic Disease?," 952.
7 Michael Specter, "The Gene Factory," *New Yorker*, January 1, 2014.
8 Ibid.
9 David Cyranoski and Sara Reardon, "Chinese Scientists Genetically Modify Human Embryos," *Nature*, April 22, 2015.
10 Friedmann and Roblin, "Gene Therapy for Human Genetic Disease?," 953.
11 Francis Fukuyama, *Our Posthuman Future: Consequences of the Biotechnology Revolution* (New York: Farrar, Straus and Giroux, 2002), 81.
12 Eoin Carolan, "The New WADA Code and the Search for a Policy Justification for Anti-Doping Rules," *Seton Hall Journal of Sports and Entertainment Law* 16, no. 1 (2006): 7–8.
13 Ed Yong, "What Can You Actually Do with Your Fancy Gene-Editing Technology?" *Atlantic*, December 2, 2015.
14 Dave Sheinin and Will Hobson, "Top Russian Athletes Participated in Systemic, State-Sanctioned Doping, Report Says," *Washington Post*, November 9, 2015.
15 World Anti-Doping Agency, "The Independent Commission Report #1: Final Report," November 9, 2015.
16 Specter, "The Gene Factory."
17 "Can It Be Detected?," *playtrue*, no. 1 (2005): 5.
18 Fukuyama, *Our Posthuman Future*, 94.
19 World Anti-Doping Agency, "WADA Gene Doping Symposium Calls for Greater Awareness, Strengthened Action Against Potential Gene Transfer Misuse in Sport," June 11, 2008.
20 Fukuyama, *Our Posthuman Future*, 158–159.

CHAPTER 20. MORAL DRIFT AND THE AMERICAN WAY

1 Pierre de Coubertin, *Olympism: Selected Writings*, ed. Norbert Müller (Lausanne, Switzerland: International Olympic Committee, 2000), 654.
2 Ibid., 223.
3 Mark Twain, *Roughing It* (New York: Oxford University Press, 1996), 415.
4 John M. Hoberman, *Testosterone Dreams: Rejuvenation, Aphrodisia, Doping* (Berkeley: University of California Press, 2005), 240.
5 Marc-André Gagnon, "Corruption of Pharmaceutical Markets: Addressing the Misalignment of Financial Incentives and Public Health," *Journal of Law, Medicine, and Ethics* 41, no. 3 (2013): 573.
6 Ibid., 572–573.
7 Lawrence Lessig, "'Institutional Corruption' Defined," *Journal of Law, Medicine, and Ethics* 41, no. 3 (2013): 553.
8 Ibid., 553.
9 Christopher Keyes, "Are We Ready for Lance Armstrong's Return?," *Outside*, April 22, 2014.
10 Reed Albergotti and Vanessa O'Connell, *Wheelmen: Lance Armstrong, the Tour de France, and the Greatest Sports Conspiracy Ever* (New York: Dutton, 2013), 126–127; Richard L. Brandt and Thomas Weisel, *Capital Instincts: Life as an Entrepreneur, Financier, and Athlete* (Hoboken, NJ: Wiley, 2003), 169.
11 Reed Albergotti and Vanessa O'Connell, "New Twist in Armstrong Saga," *Wall Street Journal*, January 17, 2013; Albergotti and O'Connell, *Wheelmen*, 131–134.
12 Albergotti and O'Connell, "New Twist in Armstrong Saga."
13 Albergotti and O'Connell, *Wheelmen*, 248–249.
14 Verner Møller, "The Anti-Doping Campaign—Farewell to the Ideals of Modernity?," in *Doping and Public Policy*, ed. Verner Møller and John Hoberman (Odense: University Press of Southern Denmark, 2004), 153.
15 Nancy Reichman and Ophir Sefiha, "Regulating Performance Enhancing Technologies: A Comparison of Professional Cycling and Derivatives Trading," *Annals of the American Academy of Political and Social Science* 649 (September 2013): 99.
16 Ibid., 114.
17 Ibid.
18 Ibid., 115.
19 J. Savulescu, B. Foddy, and M. Clayton, "Why We Should Allow Performance Enhancing Drugs in Sport," *British Journal of Sports Medicine* 38, no. 6 (2004): 667.
20 Ibid., 668.
21 Ibid.

EPILOGUE: THE SPIRIT OF SPORT

1 Paul Dimeo, *A History of Drug Use in Sport, 1876–1976: Beyond Good and Evil* (New York: Routledge, 2007), 129.
2 John M. Hoberman, *Testosterone Dreams: Rejuvenation, Aphrodisia, Doping* (Berkeley: University of California Press, 2005), 182.
3 Verner Møller, "The Anti-Doping Campaign—Farewell to the Ideals of Modernity?," in *Doping and Public Policy*, ed. Verner Møller and John Hoberman (Odense: University Press of Southern Denmark, 2004), 150.
4 Dimeo, *A History of Drug Use in Sport*, 135.
5 George M. Beard, *American Nervousness: Its Causes and Consequences: A Supplement to Nervous Exhaustion (Neurasthenia)* (New York: G. P. Putnam's Sons, 1881), 64.
6 Peter Loftus, "U.S. Drug Spending Climbs," *Wall Street Journal*, April 14, 2016.

7 Harrison G. Pope Jr., Gen Kanayama, Alison Athey, Erin Ryan, James I. Hudson, and Aaron Baggish, "The Lifetime Prevalence of Anabolic-Androgenic Steroid Use and Dependence in Americans: Current Best Estimates," *American Journal on Addictions* 23, no. 4 (2014): 371–377.

8 Centers for Disease Control and Prevention, "Today's Heroin Epidemic," July 2015, www.cdc.gov/vitalsigns/pdf/2015-07-vitalsigns.pdf.

9 L. A. Pratt, D. J. Brody, and Q. Gu, *Antidepressant Use in Persons Aged 12 and Over: United States, 2005–2008*, NCHS data brief no. 76 (Hyattsville, MD: National Center for Health Statistics, 2011).

10 Viviane Yargeau, Bryanne Taylor, Hongxia Li, Anglea Rodayan, and Chris D. Metcalfe, "Analysis of Drugs of Abuse in Wastewater from Two Canadian Cities," *Science of the Total Environment* 487, no. 1 (2014): 722–730.

11 European Monitoring Centre for Drugs and Drug Addiction, *Wastewater Analysis and Drugs: A European Multi-city Study* (Luxembourg: European Monitoring Centre for Drugs and Drug Addiction, 2015), www.emcdda.europa.eu/topics/pods/waste-water-analysis.

12 Paul Dimeo and John Taylor, "Monitoring Drug Use in Sport: The Contrast Between Official Statistics and Other Evidence," *Drugs: Education, Prevention and Policy* 20, no.1 (2013): 45.

13 World Anti-Doping Agency, *Report to WADA Executive Committee on Lack of Effectiveness of Testing Programs* (Montréal, Québec: World Anti-Doping Agency, 2013).

14 Werner Pitsch and Eike Emrich, "The Frequency of Doping in Elite Sport: Results of a Replication Study," *International Review for the Sociology of Sport* 47, no. 5 (2012): 563.

15 April D. Henning and Paul Dimeo, "Questions of Fairness and Anti-doping in US Cycling: The Contrasting Experiences of Professionals and Amateurs," *Drugs: Education, Prevention and Policy* 22, no. 5 (2015): 405.

16 Eloi Marijon, Muriel Tafflet, Juliana Antero-Jacquemin, Nour El Helou, Geoffroy Berthelot, David S. Celermajer, Wulfran Bougouin, Nicolas Combes, Olivier Hermine, Jean-Philippe Empana, Grégoire Rey, Jean-François Toussaint, and Xavier Jouven, "Mortality of French Participants in the Tour de France (1947–2012)," *European Heart Journal* 34, no. 40 (2013): 3145–3150.

17 Pierre de Coubertin, *Olympism: Selected Writings*, ed. Norbert Müller (Lausanne, Switzerland: International Olympic Committee, 2000), 581.

18 Ibid., 225.

19 Ibid., 552.

20 Ian Ritchie, "The Construction of a Policy: The World Anti-Doping Code's 'Spirit of Sport' Clause," *Performance Enhancement & Health* 2, no. 4 (2013): 198.

21 Coubertin, *Olympism*, 587.

INDEX

ABOUT THE AUTHOR

Mark Johnson's previous book for VeloPress, *Argyle Armada: Behind the Scenes of the Pro Cycling Life*, recounts a year in the life of the Garmin pro cycling team. Having covered cycling as a writer and photographer since the late 1980s, Mark often focuses on the business of pro cycling—a topic that frequently intersects with the sport's long history of doping. Along with U.S. publications *VeloNews*, *Velo*, and *Road*, his work is published in *Cycling Weekly* in the United Kingdom, *Vélo* in France, and *Ride Cycling Review* and *CyclingNews* in Australia as well as general-interest publications including the *Wall Street Journal*. A category II road cyclist, Mark has bicycled across the United States twice and completed an Ironman triathlon. A graduate of the University of California, San Diego, he also has an MA and a PhD in English literature from Boston University. His other passion is surfing, which he does frequently from the home he shares with his wife and two sons in Del Mar, California.